Modernization in a Chinese Style

Cai Fang • Li Daokui • Yao Yang
Huang Qunhui • Jiang Xiaojuan

Modernization in a Chinese Style

palgrave
macmillan

Cai Fang
China Top Think Tanks at the Chinese Academy of Social Sciences
Beijing, China

Yao Yang
National School of Development
Peking University
Beijing, China

Jiang Xiaojuan
Chinese Public Administration Society
Beijing, China

Li Daokui
Academic Center for Chinese Economic Practice and Thinking
Tsinghua University
Beijing, China

Huang Qunhui
School of Economics
Chinese Academy of Social Sciences
Beijing, China

This translation is supported by the **B&R Book Program**.

ISBN 978-981-95-6918-2 ISBN 978-981-95-6919-9 (eBook)
https://doi.org/10.1007/978-981-95-6919-9
Translation from the Chinese language edition: "中国式现代化" by Cai Fang et al., © Beijing Guoyanhuazhang Culture and Media Ltd. 2022. Published by CITIC Press Corporation. All Rights Reserved.

Jointly published with CITIC Press Corporation, B&R Book Program

This Palgrave Macmillan imprint is published by the registered company Springer Nature Singapore Pte Ltd.
The registered company address is: 152 Beach Road, #21-01/04 Gateway East, Singapore 189721, Singapore

Preface

Advancing Chinese Modernization Through High-Quality Development

How should we set the course for the next three decades? The answer lies in the Report to the 20th National Congress of the Communist Party of China (hereinafter referred to as "the Report"). The Report systematically elaborates on the mission and tasks of the new journey in the new era, sets forth the Party's central task going forward, and details the defining features, essential requirements, strategic arrangements, and guiding principles of Chinese modernization.[1]

So, how was the concept of Chinese modernization proposed and developed? What are its essential features and requirements? How can we comprehend its strategic roadmaps and primary objectives?

The Emergence and Essential Features of Chinese Modernization

Chinese modernization, a new path explored on a new journey in a new era, marks a major new judgment, generalization, and proposition proposed after profound reflection on the overarching themes and main threads of the Party's century-long history.

[1] Hold High the Great Banner of Socialism with Chinese Characteristics and Strive in Unity to Build a Modern Socialist Country in All Respects—Report to the 20th National Congress of the Communist Party of China (Chin. ed.) (October 16, 2022) [N/OL]. People's Daily, [2022-10-26]. http://paper.people.com.cn/rmrb/html/2022-10/26/nw.D110000renmrb_20221026_3-01.htm

In his speech delivered at a Ceremony Marking the Centenary of the CPC on July 1, 2021, General Secretary Xi Jinping pointed out, "As we have upheld and developed socialism with Chinese characteristics and driven coordinated progress in material, political, cultural-ethical, social, and ecological terms, we have pioneered a new and uniquely Chinese path to modernization, and created a new model for human advancement."[2]

In November of the same year, at the Sixth Plenary Session of the 19th Central Committee of the CPC, General Secretary Xi Jinping further emphasized, "The Party has led the people in pioneering a uniquely Chinese path to modernization, creating a new model for human advancement, and expanding the channels for developing countries to achieve modernization." The resolution adopted at the session explicitly proposed to "promote national rejuvenation through a Chinese path to modernization."[3]

In July 2022, at a seminar on studying the spirit of important speeches made by General Secretary Xi Jinping and preparing for the 20th CPC National Congress, attended by leading officials at the provincial and ministerial levels, General Secretary Xi Jinping emphasized, "We have succeeded in promoting and expanding Chinese modernization," and further stated, "We must insist on pushing forward the great rejuvenation of the Chinese nation through a Chinese path to modernization. We must neither retrace our steps to the rigidity and isolation of the past, nor take the wrong turn by changing our nature and abandoning our system. We must base the development of the country and the nation on our own strength, and firmly keep the destiny of China's development and progress in our own hands."[4]

The new journey to build China into a modern socialist country in all respects is, in *essence, progressing steadily* along the path of Chinese

[2] Xi Jinping, Speech at A Ceremony Marking the Centenary of the Communist Party of China (Chin. ed.) [OL]. [2021-07-01]. http://www.gov.cn/xinwen/2021-07/01/content_5621847.htm

[3] Resolution on the Major Achievements and Historical Experience of the Party over the Past Century (Chin. ed.) [OL]. [2021-11-16]. http://www.gov.cn/zhengce/2021-11/16/content_5651269.htm

[4] On the seminar of "Learning the Instructions of General Secretary Xi Jinping in His Important Speeches and Welcoming the 20th National Congress of the Party" for provincial- and ministerial-level officials, Xi Jinping emphasized: hold high the great banner of socialism with Chinese characteristics and write a new chapter in building a modern socialist country in all respects (Chin. ed.) [OL]. [2021-07-27]. http://www.gov.cn/xinwen/2022-07/27/content_5703131.htm

modernization. This path has been systematically elaborated in the Report, which calls for a comprehensive grasp of its intrinsic characteristics.

First of all, Chinese modernization represents the path to achieving the great rejuvenation of the Chinese nation. It is highlighted in the Report that from this day forward, the central task of the CPC will be to lead the Chinese people of all ethnic groups in a concerted effort to realize the Second Centenary Goal of building China into a great modern socialist country in all respects and to advance the rejuvenation of the Chinese nation on all fronts through a Chinese path to modernization.

Secondly, Chinese modernization embodies the combination of universality and individuality. The Report stresses that Chinese modernization is the socialist modernization pursued under the leadership of the CPC. It contains elements that are common to the modernization processes of all countries, but it is also characterized by features that are unique to the Chinese context.

Finally, five features of Chinese modernization were clarified in the same report: modernization of a huge population, common prosperity for all, material and cultural-ethical advancement, harmony between humanity and nature, and peaceful development.

Chinese Modernization and a New Form of Human Civilization

Fundamentally, Chinese modernization represents the concrete pursuit of socialist modernization. It is a manifestation of the development path of socialism with Chinese characteristics and constitutes an inevitable choice and essential pathway toward realizing the rejuvenation of the Chinese nation.

Looking ahead, Chinese modernization is defined by nine essential requirements. The Report proposes the following essential requirements of Chinese modernization: upholding the leadership of the CPC and socialism with Chinese characteristics, pursuing high-quality development, developing whole-process people's democracy, enriching the people's cultural lives, achieving common prosperity for all, promoting harmony between humanity and nature, building a human community with a shared future, and creating a new form of human advancement.

Notably, this marks the first occasion that the essential requirements of Chinese modernization are systematically synthesized and formally articulated.

Creating a new form of human advancement is the ultimate objective of the above-mentioned requirements. The foundational logic suggests that the relationship between Chinese modernization and a new form of human advancement can be understood as follows: Chinese modernization is the pathway toward a new form of human advancement, while the new form of human advancement fully embodies the civilizational aspirations inherent in Chinese modernization.

From Two-Step Strategic Plan to a Systematic, Synergistic Path

Building a modern socialist country in all respects and advancing national rejuvenation through Chinese modernization cannot be achieved overnight or in a single stroke. It must be advanced with firm steps and in an orderly manner while maintaining both steadiness and progress.

The importance of strategic planning is evident. According to the Report, the overall strategic arrangement for building China into a great modern socialist country in all respects follows a two-step strategic plan: first, to basically achieve socialist modernization from 2020 to 2035, and then, to develop China into a great modern socialist country that is prosperous, strong, democratic, culturally advanced, harmonious, and beautiful from 2035 through the mid-twenty-first century. The next 5 years will be a critical period for getting construction of a modern socialist country off to a good start.

At the same time, it is essential to make adequate preparations for potential risks. The Report emphasized that building a modern socialist country in all respects is a great and arduous undertaking. The future is bright, yet the road ahead is long and challenging. Thus, it is necessary to be more mindful of potential dangers, prepare for worst-case scenarios, and be ready to withstand high winds, choppy waters, and even dangerous storms.

In the process of advancing Chinese modernization, China must stay committed to five major principles and apply a broader array of strategies and methods. The Report states that on the journey ahead, China must firmly adhere to the five major principles: upholding and strengthening the Party's overall leadership, following the path of socialism with Chinese characteristics, pursuing a people-centered development philosophy, remaining committed to deepening reform and opening up, and carrying forward the fighting spirit. The whole Party and the Chinese people must strengthen their sense of purpose, determination, and self-confidence, refusing to be intimidated by fallacies or pressure and pressing forward fearlessly despite difficulties. It is essential to coordinate development and security, strive to overcome various challenges on the road ahead, and open up new horizons for our cause through tenacious struggle.

Chinese modernization is undoubtedly a comprehensive endeavor that requires the coordinated efforts of multiple parties. To this end, the Report notes that building a modern socialist country in all respects requires giving priority to high-quality development; that education, science and technology, and human resources provide fundamental and strategic support; that people's democracy is an essential element; and that respecting, adapting to, and protecting nature are inherent imperatives. The Report also emphasizes the importance of building a modern socialist country under the rule of law.

High-Quality Development Is Priority of Chinese Modernization

In the top-level design of Chinese modernization, the Report proposes, "To build a modern socialist country in all respects, we must, first and foremost, pursue high-quality development." The dual circulation strategy has thus become an inevitable requirement as well as a key pathway in advancing Chinese modernization. Domestic circulation, as the mainstay of this new development pattern, urgently needs to be strengthened in terms of its internal momentum and reliability. Specifically, efforts should be made to unswervingly prioritize economic development, further deepen reform and opening up, stay focused on the goal of high-quality development, coordinate development and security, and align demand-side management with the strategy of expanding domestic demand and supply-side structural reform. Moreover, it is necessary to accelerate the development of a unified national market, tap into the potential of the domestic market, and continuously stimulate growth momentum through market-oriented and law-based mechanisms, thereby laying solid material and technological foundations for Chinese modernization.

With the increasing emphasis on domestic circulation, accelerating the establishment of a new development pattern—where domestic circulation serves as the mainstay supported by international circulation, with both reinforcing each other smoothly and efficiently—has become a strategic move in response to profound changes unseen in a century. This also implies that China's domestic and external demand structures will undergo certain adjustments. On the one hand, in the context of shifting global economic dynamics, external demand will face long-term structural adjustments; on the other hand, such adjustments present significant challenges to expanding aggregate demand, making the role of domestic demand all the more critical. These structural adjustments will have far-reaching implications. Coupled with the rapid advance of digitalization, the contribution of foreign trade, especially merchandise trade, to China's economic growth is expected to decline over the next 5–10 years following the 20th CPC National Congress, while the share of service trade will gradually increase. Global trade patterns will exhibit a trend of fragmentation, and emerging markets are expected to become China's key trading partners.

Only by addressing the bottlenecks and challenges that constrain domestic demand can China ensure the smooth and efficient operation of domestic circulation even under extreme conditions. Unlocking the potential of domestic demand depends on further reform and opening up, strengthening internal capabilities, and achieving comprehensive circulation across consumption, manufacturing, technology, investment, services, and finance. Particular focus should be placed on the synergistic effects of technological innovation and consumption upgrading.

To enhance the resilience and safety of industrial and supply chains, the role of "chain-leading" enterprises should be fully leveraged, advancing supply chain security, agility and flexibility, value creation, and ecosystem coordination in multiple dimensions. This will systematically drive independent innovation throughout the industrial chain and enhance the stability and competitiveness of the supply chain. The deeper integration of a strong, controllable, and resilient supply chain with the industrial chain will help Chinese enterprises boost their comprehensive international competitiveness, support the high-quality development of related industries, and ensure that core segments of industrial chains remain within China while also leveraging the advantages of the global division of labor. Ultimately, this will promote positive interplay between domestic circulation and international circulation, enabling transformative improvements in the quality, efficiency, and dynamism of economic development.

Chinese enterprises should seize the opportunities offered by high-quality development. By leveraging digital transformation and green development, they can clarify their strategic roles and build data-driven enterprises, enhance strategic source industries, and accelerate the development of world-class enterprises renowned for superior product quality, brand reputation, innovation leadership, and modern management. Particularly for enterprises with large-scale investments, broad influence across sectors, and strong leadership in driving industrial growth, it is essential to leverage their strengths to facilitate efficient coordination and integration across upstream and downstream supply chains, as well as production, supply, and sales. This will provide strong support for ensuring smooth national economic flows and for building the new development pattern.

As a forward-looking top-level design and strategic roadmap, Chinese modernization sets the course for the next three decades. Looking ahead, China must remain committed to deepening reform and opening up, continue to drive high-quality development through market-oriented and law-based means, steadily advance common prosperity, and accelerate the development of a unified national market and the modernization of China's governance system.

Beijing, China Cai Fang

Prologue

Top-Level Design and Key Pathways of Chinese Modernization

The Report to the 20th National Congress of the CPC systematically elaborated on the key characteristics and rich connotations of Chinese modernization and presented the top-level design and strategic roadmap for building a modern socialist country in all respects. According to the Report, Chinese modernization is the modernization of a huge population aiming for common prosperity for all, integrating material and cultural-ethical advancement, based on harmony between humanity and nature, and pursued through peaceful development.

Five years ago, the 19th CPC National Congress set the goal of basically realizing socialist modernization by 2035. The fifth Plenary Session of the 19th CPC Central Committee further specified this goal by defining it as transforming China into a moderately developed country by that time. These two goals are consistent in substance. Quantitatively, this means raising China's GDP per capita to $23,000 (calculated at constant 2020 prices and fixed exchange rates), approximating the current economic standing of countries such as Portugal. Using GDP per capita as a benchmark is a straightforward and concise method for gauging a country's level of economic and social development or modernization. Meanwhile, its correlation with other key development indicators helps reveal both the scope and essence of what it means to "basically realize modernization."

Therefore, examining the journey from the current stage—when GDP per capita stands at around $10,000—to the target of $23,000 offers valuable insight. Identifying the key development indicators that require improvement and clarifying the essential pathway from China's current position to its intended destination will help define the major tasks and necessary measures for achieving basic modernization.

Challenges to Be Addressed on the Path to Basically Realizing Modernization

Basically realizing modernization by 2035 represents a long-term vision, a strategic imperative, and top-level design for China. However, reaching this milestone requires bridging multiple developmental gaps across critical dimensions. At the same time, China must be prepared to withstand potential shocks and respond to emerging short-term challenges as they arise. Therefore, efforts should be directed toward tackling pressing challenges while advancing the long-term vision, identifying the challenges that must be remedied to achieve basic modernization and proposing concrete policy recommendations. First, it is necessary to establish a mechanism of creative destruction to significantly narrow the labor productivity gap between China and its reference countries. Second, efforts to reallocate resources should be continued in order to accelerate the narrowing of the urban–rural dual economic structure. Third, the development of mutual social support, social protection, and public welfare should be strengthened to accelerate the improvement of the social security system with Chinese characteristics.

A Window of Opportunity to Address Modernization Challenges

To meet the goals of becoming a high-income country by the end of the 14th Five-Year Plan and reaching the status of a moderately developed country by 2035, China must maintain an average annual growth rate of around 5% in GDP per capita over the next 15 years. This entails crossing the threshold for high-income countries, as defined by the World Bank, before 2025 and reaching the middle range of high-income economies by 2035. According to the World Bank's 2022 fiscal year classifications, the threshold for high-income countries is a Gross National Income (GNI) per capita of $13,205. Given that China's GNI and GDP per capita are very close, GDP per capita is used here as the basis for analysis. It is predicted that China's potential growth rate over the next 15 years will be sufficient to achieve these goals. However, some key economic and social indicators, which are representative of modernization, do not automatically improve in lockstep with rising per capita income. Accordingly, narrowing the gaps between these critical indicators and the targets should become a focal point for policy-making and implementation during this period.

The path to basic modernization by 2035 will see China transition from an upper-middle-income economy to a high-income one—essentially crossing the threshold from a developing to a developed status. This critical window can be divided into two stages, each presenting different challenges. The first challenge is ensuring a stable transition through the middle-income stage while avoiding the middle-income trap that has plagued many countries—a task that is now largely within reach. The second challenge is consolidating and elevating China's status as a high-income economy while narrowing, and ultimately closing, the gap in key development indicators relative to developed countries. Successfully overcoming both challenges is far from easy; they will fundamentally shape China's long-term development outcomes and define the essence of basic modernization.

Based on current prices and the annual average exchange rate, China's GDP per capita reached $12,551 in 2021, approaching the World Bank's threshold for high-income economies. Countries with GDP per capita between $12,000 and $23,000 make up the lower tier of high-income nations. China's long-term goal for 2035 is to move beyond this tier and enter the ranks of moderately developed countries. Therefore, this development stage can be aptly described as the journey "from threshold to midway point" of modernization. By benchmarking against 21 countries that have consistently remained within this income range in recent years, we can better identify which modernization-related indicators—beyond income per capita—should be prioritized for accelerated progress (World Bank, 2022a).

Given the vast number of possible indicators, this analysis highlights a few core metrics that can serve both as goals for achieving basic modernization and as essential means to that end. These indicators reflect the quality of economic growth, the balanced development between urban and rural progress, and the degree of common prosperity already achieved or still to be pursued in China. Drawing on the latest World Bank data, Table 1 presents the following indicators: labor productivity (the GDP per

Table 1 "From threshold to midway": Selected indicators of high-income countries (USD, %)

	Labor productivity	*Agricultural labor productivity*	*Proportion of agricultural employment*	*Urbanization rate*	*Proportion of government expenditure*
China	31,234	5609	25	61	–
Benchmark countries	65,578	19,134	7	71	35
China's gap	48	29	368	87	–

Data Source: World Bank Database, https://data.worldbank.org

worker), agricultural labor productivity (value added per agricultural worker), the proportion of agricultural employment (percentage of total labor force), urbanization rate (urban permanent population as a percentage of total population), and the proportion of government expenditure (public spending on goods and services as a percentage of GDP). It then compares China's figures with the simple average level of countries in the "from threshold to midway" category and calculates the gap between China and the average level (expressed as a percentage of the average value).

This comparison of key indicators illustrates both China's current level of modernization and its aspirational targets, helping to define the measures necessary to close the gap with advanced countries. Specifically, improving these indicators will not only help maintain and enhance potential growth on the supply side, but also foster conditions to realize growth potential on the demand side, ensuring the full utilization of growth potential. Based on the gaps shown in Table 1, the following conclusions can be drawn: China's overall labor productivity urgently needs to catch up. Key approaches include improving agricultural labor productivity, accelerating the transfer of surplus agricultural labor, and further raising the urbanization level. Higher urbanization and more balanced urban–rural development will require significant improvements in social welfare.

Tapping New Sources of Productivity Growth

From a quantitative perspective, labor productivity not only reflects the current level of economic development or modernization but also reveals a country's capacity to meet future development goals. Therefore, from the perspective of aligning objectives with means, labor productivity serves as a core indicator of modernization. Considering the constraints China faces in sustaining economic growth, productivity improvement has become an indispensable source of new momentum. In terms of medium-term to long-term development goals, underdeveloped labor productivity remains the biggest weakness in China's pursuit of basic modernization. At present, the GDP generated per employee in China has yet to reach even half the average of countries classified as lower-middle to high-income countries—a stark gap. Furthermore, as China's economic growth slows, the barriers to productivity gains have grown more pronounced, and the pace of productivity improvement has declined, making the goal of catching up even more challenging.

Broadly speaking, there are three main pathways to improving productivity. The first is frontier innovation—independent innovation at the cutting edge of science and technology, which is then translated into productivity gains. The second is leveraging the latecomer advantage, namely improving productivity by learning from, imitating, and adapting the advanced technologies of developed countries to meet local application needs. These two pathways represent the sources of productivity, with research institutions, R&D departments, and businesses acting as the primary vehicles of innovation. The third is resource reallocation, which relies on the self-driven dynamics of market entities such as enterprises. Through spontaneous competition and the principle of survival of the fittest, this process narrows productivity gaps across industries, regions, and enterprises, thereby raising overall productivity. Resource reallocation serves as the key mechanism by which innovation is transformed into real productivity gains.

Given the overall increase in China's level of economic development, the latecomer advantage in technology has diminished due to narrowing gaps with developed countries. Meanwhile, the transfer of production factors, such as labor force, from agriculture to non-agricultural sectors has slowed down, leading to a shrinking scope for resource reallocation. As a result, productivity improvements now depend increasingly on independent innovation at the cutting edge of science and technology. This shift helps explain why China's productivity growth is decelerating. The average annual growth rate of real GDP per worker fell from 9. 1% in 1991–2001 to 10.2% in 2001–2011 and then dropped to 6.6% during 2001–2020. Similar trends have been observed in total factor productivity (Research Group of the *Jingshan Report*, 2019). At the same time, China's labor productivity remains only 48% of the average level in comparable lower-middle to mid-income countries.

Nonetheless, the potential for rapid productivity growth in China is far from exhausted, and opportunities still exist. As the country approaches high-income status, independent innovation is expected to play an increasingly important role in boosting productivity—a process characterized by increasing returns and a virtuous circle effect. In the meantime, China still enjoys considerable room to absorb existing global technological achievements and continue leveraging its latecomer advantages for a substantial period. Most importantly, the potential for resource reallocation within the Chinese economy remains vast.

At the stage of rapid economic growth in China, the transfer of labor force from agriculture to non-agricultural sectors, particularly manufacturing, has created efficiencies in resource reallocation and was a key driver of productivity gains. Amid the waning of the productivity growth drivers, two crucial dimensions remain for further productivity improvements through reform. The first is extending resource reallocation along industrial chains. According to China's national industrial classification standards, the manufacturing sector alone includes 31 major categories, 191 intermediate categories, and 525 subcategories. This indicates that even within manufacturing, the chain for resource reallocation is sufficiently long, offering ample room for further productivity gains (Cai Fang, 2022). The second direction is to deepen resource reallocation among enterprises within industries and sectors. At more advanced stages of development, productivity growth increasingly relies on competition among firms, by allowing more efficient enterprises to survive and expand while less productive ones exit or cease operations. As reforms continue to foster this environment of creative destruction, significant productivity gains can be expected.

Eliminating the Urban–Rural Dual Economic Structure

The transfer of surplus agricultural labor began with China's reform and opening up in the late 1970s. By providing low-cost labor on a large scale to non-agricultural industries, this process facilitated the reallocation of resources across urban and rural areas, regions, and industries, driving China's rapid economic growth. This process, known in development economics as dual economy, ultimately led to the diminishing of surplus agricultural labor, a significant narrowing of the productivity gap between agriculture and non-agriculture, and greater equality in income and basic public service levels between urban and rural areas—in short, a weakening of the urban–rural dual structure. Since 2010, however, as the working-age population has peaked and began to decline, the pace of labor transfer has slowed. As a result, China's economic growth has entered a phase of deceleration as it returns to a more normalized trajectory. According to development economics, this marks the arrival of the Lewis turning point. Yet given China's specific conditions, the characteristics of an unlimited labor supply have not entirely disappeared. Therefore, the arrival of the Lewis turning point does not mean the fundamental elimination of the dual economic structure.

Fully tapping the potential of the dual economy and eliminating its structural remnants is essential—not only for promoting common prosperity through high-quality development, but also for addressing the challenges of a new stage of development. On the one hand, the potential for resource reallocation between agriculture and non-agriculture, and between urban and rural areas, has yet to be exhausted. This is evident in the excessively high proportion of agricultural labor force in China—currently 3.7 times the average of peer countries, while the urbanization rate is only 87% of the same benchmark. This explains China's low agricultural productivity relative to international levels and underperformance in non-agricultural sectors. On the other hand, the urban–rural divide in income and basic public services remains stubbornly persistent, resulting in unequal access to overall household income and essential services. Moreover, since most migrant workers lack urban household registration (*hukou*), a gap of around 18 percentage points exists between the urbanization rates of the permanent population and the registered population—meaning that the dual structure has been transplanted into the cities themselves.

The persistence of the urban–rural dual economic structure not only indicates untapped economic growth potential, but also underscores the significant gap between the current pattern of urban–rural development and the goal of basic modernization. The period from now to 2035 presents a window of opportunity to dismantle this structure—critical for both basically realizing modernization and maintaining economic growth within a reasonable range. The key breakthrough lies in a new model of urbanization centered on people. "People-centered" means that the ultimate goal of urbanization is to enable migrant workers to settle permanently in urban areas, which in turn requires accelerating household registration reform.

This reform is a prime example of an institutional innovation with high dividends and increasing returns. First, raising the urbanization rate of the permanent population means more people will live and work in urban areas, reducing the share of agricultural employment, expanding non-agricultural employment, and improving productivity through resource reallocation—thus significantly boosting potential growth. Next, raising the urbanization rate of registered population and narrowing—and ultimately eliminating—the gap between the urbanization rate of the permanent population and the registered population can not only help stabilize the supply of labor for non-agricultural industries, but also, by reducing income disparities and gaps in basic public services among residents, enhance both consumption capacity and propensity to consume, thereby significantly boosting overall social demand. Lastly, fostering balanced development between urban and rural areas will promote the growth of both agriculture and non-agricultural industries, improve rural living standards, and expand access to basic public services for rural residents, ultimately achieving the goal of eliminating the urban–rural dual economic structure.

Accelerating the Development of China's Social Welfare System

Whether it is to protect workers during the process of creative destruction that enhances productivity, to eliminate the urban–rural dual economic structure by narrowing gaps in urban–rural income and basic public services, or to address weakening consumption demand resulting from accelerated population aging, all these require a significant enhancement of China's social mutual support, social protection, and public welfare. This coincides with a characteristic observation summarized by the German economist Adolf Wagner, known as Wagner's Law. Wagner noted that as the level of development rises, so does the demand for social protection, anti-monopoly and regulatory measures, contract enforcement, and law enforcement, as well as cultural, educational, and public welfare services. As these are predominantly public goods that require government provision and funding, the share of government expenditure in GDP correspondingly rises (Henrikson, 1993).

Although the official data for China on the ratio of government expenditure to GDP are not yet available—making direct comparison with reference countries in Table 1 impossible—a meaningful pattern emerges when this ratio is examined alongside per capita GDP. Specifically, during the developmental phase when GDP per capita rises from \$10,000 to \$23,000—a range that broadly corresponds to the transition "from threshold to midway" of modernization (Fig. 1)—this ratio grows from 22.2% in the lowest-income country to 34.3% in the highest-income one, or from an average of 23.9% among the first five countries to 34.3% among the last five. This surge can be regarded as a critical leap forward in the formation of the social security system—a stage termed the Wagner Acceleration Phase.

The argument that China should follow Wagner's Law and proactively increase government expenditure in social welfare during the Wagner Acceleration Phase is based not only on the fact that China is currently at the stage of transition "from threshold to midway," but more importantly, on the challenges the country must confront during this period. In 2021, China's natural population growth rate was only 0.34‰—the lowest level since 1960—signaling the beginning of an era of negative population growth. With 14.2% of its population aged 65 and above, China has formally entered the ranks of aging societies by international standards. This demographic turning point is historically unprecedented for China and will inevitably bring entirely new challenges.

In recent years, the decline in China's potential growth rate due to deepening population aging, along with rising demands for elderly care and pension security, has drawn considerable attention from both economists and policymakers. However, the anticipated impact of negative population growth and further aging on consumer demand has yet to receive sufficient policy attention. Population-related pressures on consumption manifest through three effects: population size effect, age structure effect, and income distribution effect. That is, when population growth stagnates or reverses, the proportion of elderly population rises, and disparities in income and basic public services widen, consumption is significantly constrained. While the first two effects are driven by long-term demographic trends and are difficult to reverse, improving income distribution and promoting more equitable access to basic public services constitute the most feasible and effective policy tools to mitigate such shocks.

Adhering to general development principles does not mean mechanically reproducing the statistical trajectory associated with the Wagner Acceleration Phase—for instance, by narrowly focusing on raising the proportion of government expenditure in GDP. Rather, the priority should

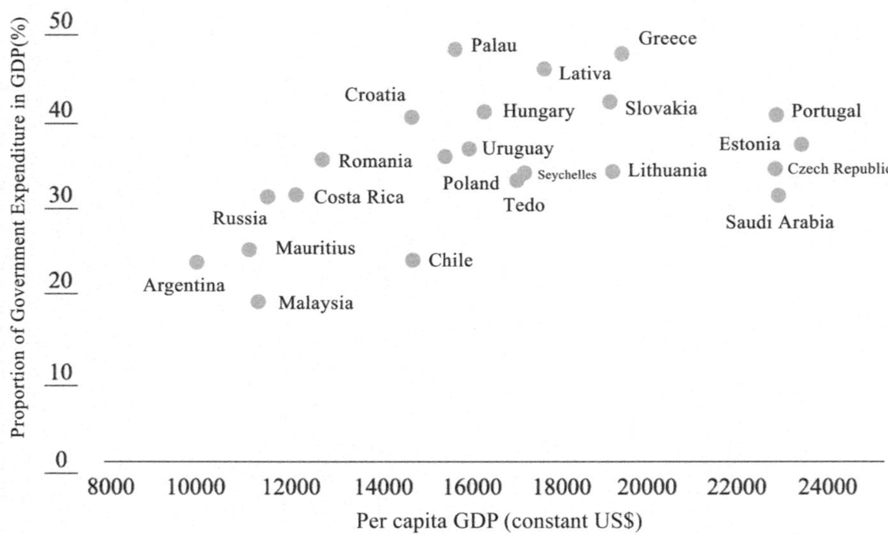

Fig. 1 Proportion of government expenditure in GDP increases with income level. Data Source: World Bank Database, http://data.worldbank.org/

be to enhance people's well-being and address their concrete needs. These include universal access to childcare, education, employment, healthcare, elderly care, housing, and social assistance. Accordingly, China must establish and improve a comprehensive social welfare system and its corresponding institutional frameworks to ensure lifespan-wide basic public services that cover all residents. Guided by the overarching goal of common prosperity, and following the principle of doing what is feasible, this institutional framework—that focuses on providing higher-quality and more equitable basic public services—represents China's pathway toward the development of a social security system.

The Focus of Efforts to Expand the Middle-Income Group

A key indicator of achieving common prosperity is the transition to an olive-shaped social structure. With a population of more than 1.4 billion, China has a middle-income group of more than 400 million. To fully leverage the country's vast market and ensure consumer demand for sustained economic growth, it is essential to expand the size of the middle-income group and establish an olive-shaped social structure. Achieving this requires enhancing social mobility.

Olive-Shaped Social Structure Yet to Be Formed

Since reform and opening up, especially after the 18th CPC National Congress, the horizontal movement of the Chinese population has significantly increased. This includes large-scale cross-regional and cross-sector movements, such as migration between urban and rural areas, across provinces, among the eastern, central, and western regions, and across industries, professions, and businesses. In this sense, China has developed into a society characterized by high mobility of both population and labor force. Over the past few decades, labor migration between urban and rural areas has played a significant role in boosting workers' incomes, contributing greatly to macroeconomic growth and productivity.

At present, incomes in both urban and rural areas have been growing rapidly. However, disparities still remain, and the Gini coefficient for household income in China remains above 0.4. A key factor behind this income disparity lies in the fact that while horizontal mobility is relatively fluid, vertical mobility remains insufficient. In other words, China has yet to establish a typical olive-shaped social structure. The channels for upward mobility—in terms of educational attainment, occupational status, and income groups—are not yet smooth enough. Vertical movement has not advanced in tandem with horizontal movement.

According to the latest data from the National Bureau of Statistics, China's middle-income group exceeds 400 million people. However, given the country's total population of over 1.4 billion people, this still represents a relatively small proportion. According to the current criteria for defining the middle-income group—a typical three-member household would have an annual income ranging from RMB 100,000 to RMB 500,000. According to this standard and the income quintile data for urban and rural residents, the data indicate that most middle-income earners are concentrated in the high- and upper-middle-income urban groups. Therefore, the middle-income group, as it currently stands, is still too small to form a truly large and representative segment of the population. In conclusion, the olive-shaped social structure has yet to be fully realized.

Constraints on Social Mobility

The incomplete formation of the olive-shaped social structure is fundamentally due to insufficient social mobility. What are the primary factors restricting social mobility in China?

During the initial phase of China's reform and opening up, horizontal social mobility was relatively smooth for an extended period. However, with the slowdown of economic growth, social mobility—particularly horizontal movement—has begun to decelerate. In the past, rapid economic growth, educational expansion, and industrial restructuring generated a wealth of opportunities, allowing individuals to achieve Pareto improvement—that is, people could enhance their prospects without depriving others of similar opportunities. As these opportunities have diminished, social mobility has increasingly taken on a "zero-sum game" nature: that is, improved chances for some may come at the expense of reduced opportunities for others. Consequently, economic growth deceleration generally exerts a negative impact on social mobility.

Meanwhile, China's aging population is on the rise. In 2021, the country's population growth rate—considering both birth rate and mortality—was just 0.34‰ and was expected to reach 0‰ by 2022. According to international standards, China has officially entered an aging society, with 14.2% of the population aged 65 and above.

An aging society also undermines social mobility. Firstly, at the individual level, as people age, they tend to seek fewer changes in occupation, residence, and lifestyle, leading to a deceleration in horizontal mobility. Secondly, at the aggregate level, the reluctance of individuals to embrace change contributes to a broader societal trend of reduced horizontal mobility in an aging society. This deceleration inevitably impacts vertical mobility. Thirdly, in social terms, an aging society requires the development of an age-friendly environment that adapts to changes, including aspects such as employment, entrepreneurship, and living conditions, although this process takes considerable time. Before such an environment is fully established, all these factors will continue to slow down social mobility.

It should be noted that while the slowdown of economic growth aligns with the natural progression of development stages, and population aging is an irreversible trend that inevitably dampens social mobility to some extent, there remains substantial potential for enhancing social mobility by removing various institutional and systemic barriers.

China tracks two key indicators of urbanization: the urbanization rate of the permanent population, which has now reached 64.72%, and that of the registered population, which is currently only 46.7%. This means that the proportion of people with urban household registration (*hukou*) is significantly lower than the proportion of permanent urban residents by about 18 percentage points. This discrepancy highlights the large number of migrant workers who have achieved horizontal mobility but not corresponding vertical mobility. It indicates that the current household registration system remains a significant institutional barrier to expanding the middle-income group.

The Focus of Efforts to Promote Social Mobility

After analyzing the institutional factors, it is natural to explore the policy focus areas and initiatives needed to promote social mobility. In other words, where should public policies be directed?

First of all, promoting social mobility relies on reform and institutional development. At the current stage of development, advancing reform can generate increasing returns and tangible dividends, helping to eliminate institutional and systemic barriers that hinder economic growth, income increases, narrowing of income disparities, and social mobility.

In line with the CPC Central Committee's goal of basically realizing socialist modernization by 2035, China is entering a critical 13-year window during which economic reforms, adjustments to social policies, and institutional improvements will play a pivotal role in securing the benefits of reform. During this period, China's GDP per capita is projected to rise from $12,000 to $23,000. The level of social mobility the country aspires to achieve can be benchmarked against countries at a similar stage of development—that is, using the average level of countries with a per capita GDP between $12,000 and $23,000 as a reference. In terms of primary distribution, secondary distribution, and tertiary distribution, while each has its unique function, policy coordination is essential to drive social mobility forward.

Secondly, in the area of primary distribution, the focus should be on the allocation of production factors and their reasonable distribution among owners. The most pressing reform task here is to dismantle the urban–rural dual economic structure. The next 13 years represent a critical window period for addressing this duality. Generally speaking, as income levels, modernization, and urbanization advance, the proportion of agricultural employment declines. Compared to reference countries, China's urbanization rate still lags by about 10 percentage points, and the reduction in agricultural labor force is behind by approximately 18 percentage points.

Therefore, efforts should be made on two fronts. On the one hand, it is necessary to continue advancing new urbanization and facilitate the transfer of the agricultural labor force to narrow the gap with reference countries. On the other hand, it is essential to close the gap between the urbanization rate of the permanent population and that of the registered population, enabling migrant workers to become urban residents and thereby transforming horizontal mobility into vertical mobility. This will yield solid reform dividends from both supply and demand sides. On the supply side, increasing the non-agricultural labor force, improving labor participation rates, and redistributing resources can boost productivity and economic growth. On the demand side, increasing residents' income, narrowing income gaps, and alleviating future concerns can significantly expand consumption, ensuring sustained growth in aggregate domestic demand and ultimately fostering the development of a large domestic market.

Thirdly, increasing secondary distribution efforts is crucial, and this requires a significant increase of government social spending.

Cross-country data reveal a clear trend—previously mentioned as Wagner's Law. Considering China's goal of increasing GDP per capita from $12,000 to $23,000 in the next 13 years, and recognizing the general pattern of accelerated government social spending during this phase, it is clear that expanding social expenditures is vital. Only by significantly increasing social spending can China provide universal, full-lifecycle public services, thereby achieving an important objective of secondary distribution.

Fourthly, tertiary distribution, which supplements primary distribution and secondary distribution, holds significant potential for allowing individuals, businesses, and society to fully develop their capabilities. Tertiary distribution includes charitable activities, volunteer actions, corporate social responsibility, and more. Beyond these, it's essential to emphasize that businesses must adopt a people-centered approach to development and operations, especially in the application of technology, innovation, and algorithms. This remains one of the most crucial yet underemphasized aspects of tertiary distribution. To be specific, enterprises must rethink their objectives and innovatively integrate considerations for employees, users, suppliers, communities, society, and the environment into their operational models. This approach will enable Chinese enterprises to continuously generate creative solutions while also generating substantial returns that benefit both the market and society at large.

Here's an example of how businesses can drive social mobility. It is widely recognized that the age group between 20 and 35 represents prime years for both childbearing and peak labor productivity. In China, individuals in this age group are typically on an upward career trajectory, peaking around 35 before entering a gradual decline. However, this period also coincides with a steady increase in household labor burdens—particularly related to childcare and domestic responsibilities. This creates a critical tension between career and family development. The severe scarcity of household resources—time, energy, and income—contributes to China's low fertility rates and low willingness to have children. This constraint also restricts the improvement of employment quality which in turn impedes the enhancement of social mobility in the country. The notorious "996" work culture further exacerbates this resource squeeze. Yet businesses possess significant power to recalibrate this dynamic. Through "innovation for good"—such as family-friendly scheduling or flexible remote work policies—employers can help employees achieve balanced career and family development, ultimately fostering both personal and societal mobility.

Share the Outcomes of Productivity: High-Quality Development and Common Prosperity for All

The goal of achieving common prosperity through high-quality development not only declares the ultimate aim of Chinese-style socialist modernization but also outlines the essential pathway to achieving this goal. In economic terms, this unified statement of goal and path can be understood as the equitable sharing of the benefits of increased productivity. Over the past four decades of reform and opening up, China has relied on the liberation of productive forces to create the miracle of rapid economic growth. This growth has fueled the development of social productive forces, enhanced comprehensive national strength, and significantly improved people's living standards. In the new development stage, China faces new challenges characterized by growing pains and the complex issues that come with rapid expansion. These challenges present both difficulties and opportunities. People-centered high-quality development serves as the fundamental solution to these challenges. Furthermore, deepening reforms and expanding opening up are vital to securing new opportunities and achieving common prosperity for all.

This paper explores the interplay between high-quality development and common prosperity through an economic lens, demonstrating that advancing common prosperity is fundamentally about sharing the fruits of productivity growth. It examines the distinct roles and main responsibilities of primary, secondary, and tertiary distribution (primarily corporate social responsibility), identifying critical reform measures needed in each domain and their potential dividends. Here are the core conclusions. First, primary distribution serves as the incentive and efficiency mechanisms for continued productivity growth, thus holding a fundamental position in the distribution system. Second, secondary distribution is an essential means of improving income distribution and enhancing people's well-being, requiring continual strengthening in response to changes in the development stage. Third, tertiary distribution, centered around corporate social responsibility, presents many opportunities for advancement. Unleashing these opportunities can better achieve the integration of productivity growth with its fair distribution.

Primary Distribution: The Fundamental Mechanism for Enhancing Productivity

Growing the economic pie is the material prerequisite for sharing it equitably. The performance of economic growth is a function of various resources and production factors, while productivity gains stem from their reallocation and more efficient use. Different from secondary distribution and tertiary distribution, primary distribution relies more heavily on the decisive role of the market in allocating resources and places a greater emphasis on efficiency and incentives. Given these characteristics, primary distribution serves as the foundational mechanism in the distribution system. It supports the principle of doing one's best within one's capacity in the pursuit of common prosperity. By leveraging market-based incentives, it mobilizes enthusiasm across various groups for employment and entrepreneurship, promotes balanced and prosperous development across industries and regions, and lays the groundwork for shared productivity gains. This approach helps avoid secondary distribution that exceeds the current development stage, prevents overpromising social welfare, and steers clear of impractical approaches such as enforced equal prosperity or simultaneous prosperity. It also avoids penalizing high performers or discouraging individual initiative.

Because primary distribution determines the returns to various production factors, it dictates the incentives available to factor owners and the strength of those incentives. This, in turn, influences the reproduction, participation rate, adequacy, and quality of production factors. In light of its role in determining compensation, forming incentives, and reallocating resources, primary distribution occupies a fundamental position among the three forms of distribution. The owners of production factors are also the participants in primary distribution. These include workers with physical labor, technical skills, or managerial capabilities; capital investors; operators with land-use rights; entrepreneurs who combine production factors; and governments that provide public goods. Each of these participants receives returns commensurate with their contributions through primary distribution. Their confidence and motivation are essential for boosting productivity and economic growth.

Under the basic socialist economic system, the owners of production factors and market entities operate in a market environment where they are legally guaranteed equal access to resources and production factors, participate in competition fairly and justly, and receive equal legal protection. That is to say, once the ownership structure of production factors is established—within a framework where public ownership remains the mainstay while allowing multiple forms of ownership to develop side by side—the basic structure of primary distribution is also formed. This structure broadly aligns with the principle of distribution according to labor as the mainstay, supplemented by multiple coexisting distribution methods. The specific distribution outcomes depend on the actual contributions of the owners of production factors and participants in resource allocation. Economic theory suggests that once the initial allocation of resources and factors is completed, as long as property rights are clearly defined, the subsequent reallocation process focuses primarily on improving resource allocation efficiency—a process that unfolds within the domain of primary distribution.

As a goal of Chinese-style socialist modernization, common prosperity must be achieved through high-quality development and the shared benefits of increasing productivity. From the perspective of economics, transforming common prosperity into the sharing of productivity gains means that rising productivity must be matched by rising levels of shared benefits—essentially, synchronizing economic growth with increases in residents' incomes. Highlighting this point is necessary because such synchronization does not occur automatically. Figure 2 shows the actual growth rates of GDP per capita and per capita disposable income. Since the labor force is a component of the total population, GDP per capita can be used as a proxy for labor productivity, while per capita disposable income reflects the extent to which residents share in productivity gains. Data analysis shows that from 1978 to 2020, GDP per capita and per capita disposable income maintained complete synchronicity, both growing at an average annual rate of 8.2%.

However, as Fig. 2 illustrates, GDP per capita and per capita disposable income have not grown in lockstep at all times over the past four decades. For instance, between 1985 and 2000, the synchronicity was relatively weak: GDP per capita grew at an average annual rate of 6.9%, while per capita disposable income grew at 6. 1%. During this period, the income gap between urban and rural residents widened, with urban income growing at 5.9% annually and rural income at just 4. 1%. Since the 18th CPC National Congress in 2012, the synchronicity between economic growth and income growth has significantly improved. Residents' incomes have grown faster than GDP expansion, and rural incomes have outpaced urban incomes, helping to narrow the previous disparities. For example, from

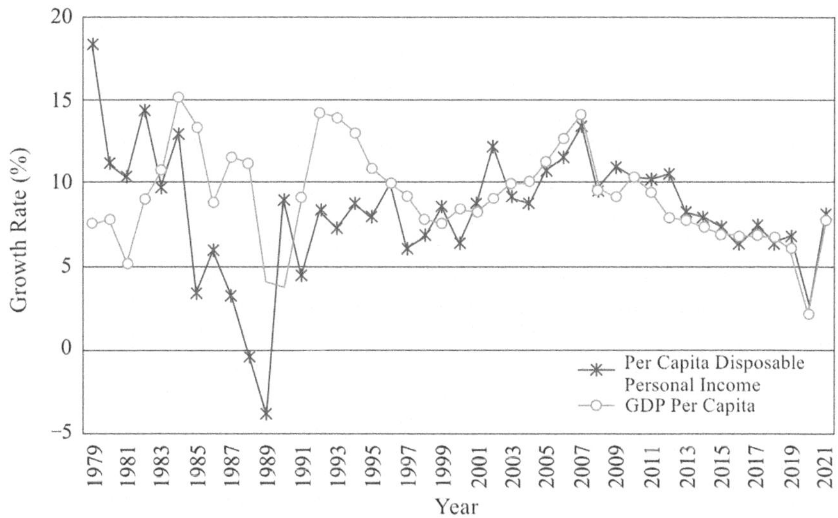

Fig. 2 Synchronicity of economic growth and growth in residents' incomes. Source: "National Data," National Bureau of Statistics of China

2010 to 2020, the annual growth rate of GDP per capita was 6.3%, while per capita disposable income reached 7.2%; urban and rural incomes grew at 6.2% and 7.8% per year, respectively.

The fifth Plenary Session of the 19th CPC Central Committee set the qualitative goal of building China into a moderately developed country by 2035, alongside the quantitative goal of doubling GDP from 2020 to 2035. Taking into account demographic trends and the need to synchronize economic and income growth, China has set the goal of doubling its per capita GDP and per capita disposable income during this period, which implies an average annual growth rate of approximately 5%. Achieving these targets will require advancing reforms in various fields. Among these, promoting people-centered urbanization through reform of the household system is not only an effective measure but also one that yields dual benefits on both the supply and demand sides.

In 2021, China's urbanization rate based on the permanent population was 64.72%, while the urbanization rate based on household registration stood at only 46.7%, a gap of about 18 percentage points. The practical significance and potential effects of household registration system reform lie in the fact that narrowing or eliminating this gap can immediately boost the potential growth rate. Furthermore, this reform would grant urban household registration (*hukou*) to approximately 260 million rural migrants living in cities (most of whom are migrant workers). The reform dividends from both the supply and demand sides would be enormous, proportional to the large population involved.

On the supply side, registering migrant workers as urban residents would improve job stability and extend their working years, sending clear incentive signals and encouraging the continued migration of the rural labor force into urban areas, significantly increasing the supply of non-agricultural labor. For example, in 2020, agricultural labor accounted for 23.6% of the workforce. Reducing this share would allow the non-agricultural labor force to expand further. On the demand side, household registration system reform centered on migrant workers would drive new urbanization, significantly boosting both urban construction investment and consumer demand. The two stages of urban-to-rural migration would have a multiplier effect on household consumption. A simulation study by the research team of the Organisation for Economic Co-operation and Development showed that rural workers who move to cities increase their consumption by 30% even before obtaining urban household registration (*hukou*). Once they obtain it, their consumption can rise by another 30%, assuming all other factors remain constant.

Secondary Distribution: A Necessary Path to Sharing Productivity Outcomes

Ensuring a fair distribution of the pie is essential to making the pie bigger. Primary distribution alone does not encompass the full process of income allocation, and realizing the sharing of productivity gains requires a robust secondary distribution mechanism. Therefore, building common prosperity demands heightened emphasis on fairness in secondary distribution. The belief that primary distribution alone can resolve income imbalances between capital factor owners and labor factor owners stems from laissez-faire ideology, which has persisted since the origins of Western economics. This perspective gained particular prominence through the neoliberal economics that prevailed from the 1980s onward, with three major ideological schools exerting significant policy influence. The first is trickle-down economics represented by Milton Friedman, who argued that the ethically sound principle of income distribution is that everyone should ultimately receive the output generated by their own factors and means of production—thus implying that the market mechanism can inherently resolve income distribution issues. The second is the "big tradeoff" theory championed by Arthur Okun, which posits an inherent tension between efficiency and equity, suggesting that the two cannot be simultaneously maximized. The third is the irrelevance theory promoted by Robert Lucas, which goes even further by rejecting not only the necessity and effectiveness of redistributive policies but also any correlation between growth and distribution. According to this view, studying income distribution is of little practical value.

These representative theories, together with the broader influence of neoliberal economics, had profound effects on secondary distribution policies globally. They contributed to setbacks in the development of the welfare system, leading to their decline worldwide, and even major regressions in some pioneering countries. As a result, many developing countries—and even some developed ones—have experienced worsening income inequality, economic polarization, social fragmentation, and political division. Economists and policymakers must base their beliefs on empirically observable significant facts and abandon deeply entrenched conventional notions—particularly trickle-down economics.

Yet empirical research itself has yielded two starkly opposing observations: the famous Kuznets inverted-U curve and Piketty's theory of inequality. Kuznets, drawing on data from early industrialized countries, observed that income inequality initially rises with economic development, peaks at a certain level (the Kuznets turning point), and then declines—forming an inverted U-shaped curve. In contrast, Piketty's analysis of large-scale, long-term historical data across multiple countries demonstrates that the rate of return on capital (r) consistently outpaces economic growth and wage increases (g), a relationship he formalized as "Piketty inequality." This finding critically negates the existence of a Kuznets curve or turning point, instead suggesting that widening income disparities are an inherent, self-reinforcing trend that cannot reverse spontaneously.

However, effective secondary distribution can alter the Piketty inequality dynamic and enable countries to reach a Kuznets turning point at an appropriate stage of development—meaning that an inverted U-shaped pattern of income distribution remains possible. It should be noted that both institutional arrangements in primary distribution and policy efforts in secondary distribution can contribute to shaping a socially acceptable and reasonable income distribution pattern. Cross-country comparative studies show that the foundation of income distribution lies in the policy orientation and institutional arrangements of primary distribution, while secondary distribution plays a crucial corrective role. According to OECD data, in high-income member states, secondary distribution reduces the Gini coefficient from primary distribution by an average of 35%, significantly narrowing income gaps. In addition to direct redistribution through taxation and transfer payments, government spending on social welfare also meaningfully improves income distribution. Data from 39 countries and regions (including OECD member states) reveal a strong negative correlation between the proportion of public social spending in GDP and the Gini coefficient.

Evidently, the scope of secondary distribution exceeds far beyond direct income adjustments such as taxes and transfers. In line with China's developmental philosophy of ensuring and improving people's well-being through development and responding to evolving developmental realities, the essence of secondary distribution policy lies in providing more adequate, equitable, and universally accessible basic public services that cover all citizens throughout their entire lifecycle. Thus, the central task of secondary distribution today is to build and enhance this system of service delivery—in other words, to construct a welfare system with Chinese characteristics. As a national commitment, China is committed to establishing a social welfare system that provides essential public services within a clearly defined framework. This includes specifying the government's responsibilities, scope, and service standards, as well as normatively and accurately defining the content and implementation of secondary distribution policies.

The principle of "doing one's best within one's capacity" requires, on the one hand, defining the goals that secondary distribution policies are intended to achieve in line with the concept of shared development—clearly specifying what should and should not be undertaken—and, on the other hand, determining the appropriate intensity of secondary distribution at each stage of development. Theoretically, this dual principle can be encapsulated in a single equation for the provision of basic public services or a social welfare system. Within this equation, "doing one's best" and "within one's capacity" are reflected, respectively, in the requirement that the intensity of secondary distribution should neither fall short of nor exceed the available resources. At any given stage of development, a consensus is usually attainable regarding the ideal form of this equation.

However, in terms of the content and extent of basic public service it defines, any addition may risk exceeding available means, while any reduction may fall short of achieving intended goals.

Once a country defines its social welfare commitment and designs its social welfare configuration based on its development philosophy and national conditions, secondary distribution measures become a matter of national regulation, endowed with greater enforceability and clearer boundaries. Generally, the effectiveness of secondary distribution can be assessed based on its impact in three areas: expanding the proportion of household income in national income, optimizing the overall income distribution, and raising the general level of social welfare. These three outcomes also form the essential foundations for building its social welfare system. In Fig. 3, we use the physical transaction flow-of-funds table compiled by the National Bureau of Statistics of China to calculate the ratio of total disposable income (after secondary distribution) to total primary income. This enables observation of changes in the income status of the three main parties in national income distribution—enterprises, government, and households—before and after secondary distribution.

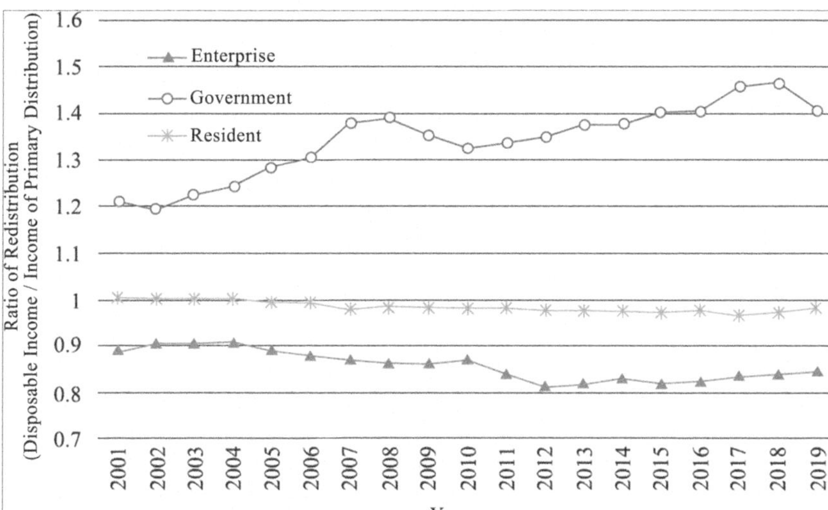

Fig. 3 Secondary distribution of enterprises, governments, and residents. Data Source: "National Data" from National Bureau of Statistics, National Bureau of Statistics Website

As Fig. 3 illustrates, the government's level of disposable income increases significantly following secondary distribution compared to its income at the stage of primary distribution, with the corporate sector being the primary source and target of this adjustment. Here, the secondary distribution ratios (the ratios of disposable income to primary distribution income) of the government and corporate sectors exhibit a seesaw relationship. In the meantime, despite increased government efforts to promote secondary distribution, the income share and secondary distribution ratio of the household sector have shown only limited improvement. In other words, the increased share of government income has not been fully converted into gains in households' disposable income. Based on this data alone, it is difficult to assess the actual state of social welfare provision. If secondary distribution does not ultimately lead to improved levels and greater equalization of basic public services, its original intent becomes ambiguous and difficult to justify.

Establishing a basic public service system that covers the entire population and spans the full lifecycle is essential to building a welfare system with Chinese characteristics. This also constitutes the fundamental function and primary task of secondary distribution. As emphasized at the 20th CPC National Congress, the country must work continuously to ensure access to childcare, education, employment, medical services, elderly care, housing, and social assistance—serving as both the political declaration and formal expression of this task. The urgency and necessity of this endeavor stem from two critical aspects. First, it is a response to the serious challenges confronting China's development. Improving the adequacy and parity of basic public services will alleviate residents' concerns about future expenditures and stimulate domestic demand, thereby supporting sustained economic growth. Second, it aligns with the general rule of economic and social development. According to World Bank data, the scale and proportion of social welfare expenditure typically increase alongside income per capita. In the development window where GDP per capita increases from $10,000 to $25,000, the average proportion of government social expenditure in GDP grows significantly—from approximately 26–37%—signaling the completion of welfare system construction. China is currently within this critical development stage and thus faces an urgent need to accelerate the building of a social welfare system.

Social Responsibility: An Indispensable Booster for Sharing Productivity Gains

Primary distribution and secondary distribution focus on narrowing disparities in personal income and access to basic public services. As key measures to improve people's well-being, they center on establishing systems, laying down mechanisms, and creating incentives to advance the goal of common prosperity. This process, rooted in reform, falls within the scope of formal institutional arrangement and is intended to develop a crucial main driving system for achieving this goal. Conducting top-level design for reform means proactively establishing comprehensive and stable foundational structures and new mechanisms. These measures include integrating a series of social welfare indicators into medium- and long-term development plans to improve overall quality of life; formulating and issuing national basic public service standards aligned with the goals of ensuring access to childcare, education, employment, medical services, elderly care, housing, and social assistance; and advancing reforms in related sectors, guided by the new development philosophy—with a specific focus on the principle of shared development. All these efforts are integral to constructing the main driving system.

However, even if this main driving system is basically established, the strength and smoothness of its operation can vary significantly depending on the existence and strength of a supportive environment beyond formal institutional arrangements. The extent to which this environment provides a boosting effect is critical. In mainstream economics, the purpose of establishing formal institutional arrangements is to create predictable patterns through which economic agents respond to fundamental incentive signals in the market. For example, consumers make purchasing decisions based on product prices; workers decide whether to participate in employment based on compensation and opportunity costs; enterprises make production decisions based on supply and demand conditions; and governments make public expenditure decisions based on national capacity and fiscal conditions. Yet, recent research—particularly in behavioral economics—has shown that this economic paradigm, which assumes agents act solely in response to incentive signals, is insufficient to fully explain behaviors and outcomes in reality.

In practice, numerous factors reinforce or interfere with outcomes, determining whether incentive signals are correctly conveyed and interpreted, whether decisions or choices are reasonable and appropriate, and whether the results align with the intended goals of mechanism design. Behavioral economist Richard Thaler argues that a multitude of "nudge" factors influence ultimate decisions and outcomes. According to Thaler and his collaborators, such nudging forces operate within an informal environment beyond formal institutional arrangements, characterized by their non-coercive nature, minimal behavioral side effects, and greater reliance on individuals' "prosocial" motivations. Evidently, nudges conducive to sharing productivity gains are most likely to emerge in the domain of tertiary distribution.

Tertiary distribution generally includes charitable activities, volunteer work, and the social responsibility of enterprises and social organizations. Discussions of tertiary distribution often focus on how many resources it can mobilize for poverty alleviation and income distribution, and through which channels. However, when defining the connotation and extension of these available resources, such analyses often exclude certain nudging factors that do not rely solely on material resources. In reality, formal institutional arrangements and their designed incentive signals are often insufficient to achieve expected changes—they must be complemented by nudging forces emerging from informal environments.

Just as major technological inventions are often accompanied by countless small, user-friendly innovations that make daily life and production more convenient, alongside major formal institutional innovations, there must also exist—indeed there are already—various small-scale or even micro-level institutional innovations, or institutional "nudges." These informal institutional arrangements not only reduce the transaction costs of institutional operations but also bring institutional design closer to human experience. If small technological inventions primarily leverage people's physiological needs, institutional nudges mainly cater to psychological tendencies, making people more comfortable and compliant with the institutional environment. Moreover, just as there is no strict boundary between major and minor technological inventions, there is no fixed line between formal institutional innovations and institutional nudges. Once proven effective and necessary, such nudges can often evolve into formal institutional arrangements.

In the domain of tertiary distribution—particularly in the fulfillment of social responsibilities by enterprises and organizations—there exists considerable potential for nudging interventions. These can not only help formal institutional arrangements operate more effectively but also compensate for their deficiencies. For example, when the household registration system reform is initiated, how to equitably share the benefits and costs between the central government and local governments, as well as between urban residents and migrant workers awaiting registration, becomes critical; when the three-child policy is adopted, how to ease the resource constraints faced by young couples balancing career development and childbearing, parenting, and children's education is vital to raising their fertility willingness; with the policy of gradually delaying retirement age underway, how to enhance the skills and labor market adaptability of elderly workers is essential for increasing their actual labor force participation; and as public education spending and its share of GDP rise, how to align input structures with the public good attributes of different stages and types of education is key. All of these factors determine the effectiveness of policy implementation and reflect the substantial demand for nudging measures.

There is both urgent demand and latent supply for nudges that facilitate sharing the gains of productivity. In fact, with the current level of technological advancement, market maturity, and business management capacity, almost all operational difficulties and bottlenecks hindering institutional functioning can be addressed. What is lacking are the motivations and incentives for relevant actors to provide such nudges. In other words, designing low-transaction-cost economic interaction mechanisms, developing effective nudging techniques, and cultivating an environment conducive to the smooth functioning of formal institutions are all behaviors with positive externalities that face free-rider problems and incentives incompatibilities. Thus, one of the key tasks in coordinating institutional arrangements across primary, secondary, and tertiary distribution is to foster an institutional and social environment—through laws and regulations, social norms, public opinion guidance, and a robust social integrity system—that encourages all market participants to internalize social responsibility into their behavior, advancing "science for good," "management for good," and "innovation for good."

Reform Dividends

From the perspective of theory, policy, and practice, the proposition of sharing productivity gains helps to unify the promotion of high-quality development with the realization of common prosperity. It aligns the goals and pathways of Chinese-style socialist modernization. It also reconciles the principles of doing our best and acting within our means in safeguarding and improving people's well-being. Furthermore, it coordinates the urgency and sustainability of building a social welfare system that covers the entire population and the full lifecycle. In doing so, the imperative to promote common prosperity for all through high-quality development can be logically integrated with a series of other major goals and strategic arrangements for the new development stage.

As foundational institutional arrangements that are mutually coordinated and supportive in advancing the goal of common prosperity, the three domains of distribution—primary, secondary, and tertiary—face pressing reform tasks and each harbors significant opportunities for reaping reform dividends. These anticipated reform dividends, characterized by increasing returns, can serve as powerful incentives for advancing reforms in critical areas. The actual gains achieved through each step of reform, and the reasonable sharing of those gains among all stakeholders, contribute to achieving incentive compatibility, thereby fostering deeper and broader reforms. In this way, reform and opening up drive high-quality development, which in turn promotes the sharing of productivity gains, establishing a virtuous circle in which high-quality development continually advances the goal of common prosperity for all.

While reforms undeniably pursue shared and multifaceted objectives, their social benefits—or reform dividends—primarily manifest across both supply-side and demand-side dimensions. On the supply side, breakthroughs in key areas of reform can significantly increase the availability of production factors and enhance overall productivity, thereby stabilizing or even raising China's potential growth rate. On the demand side, progress in other critical reform areas can boost household incomes and ease consumption-related burdens, thereby expanding domestic demand through increased consumer spending. This, in turn, helps balance overall social demand and ensures that the actual growth rate remains aligned with the potential growth rate. Furthermore, certain reforms produce simultaneous effects on both the supply and demand sides—both improving the economy's potential growth and creating a more favorable demand environment to support its realization.

Chief Expert of National High-End Think Tank at the Chinese Academy of Social Sciences (CASS) and Former Vice President of the CASS
BeijingChina

Cai Fang

Contents

List of Tables

CHAPTER 1

Scientific Connotation and Essential Requirements of Chinese Modernization

Yao Yang, Liu Shouying, Huang Hanquan, Zeng Zheng, Ren Baoping, Zhang Qian, and Zou Yinan

Chinese Modernization and Its Global Significance

Yao Yang

How to understand the relationship between the Party and Chinese modernization? This is an important topic among modern Chinese intellectuals. We need to examine the Party's century-long history within the context of modernization in latecomer countries and explore the Chinese path to modernization that the CPC has pioneered, as well as its significance for the world, especially for latecomer economies.

Y. Yang (✉)
National School of Development, Peking University, Beijing, China

L. Shouying
School of Economics, Renmin University of China, Beijing, China

H. Hanquan
Price Cost Investigation Center, National Development and Reform Commission, Beijing, China

C. Fang et al., *Modernization in a Chinese Style*,
https://doi.org/10.1007/978-981-95-6919-9_1

Throughout the world, modernization contains two dimensions of transformation and development. In terms of transformation, modernization pursues open and liberal social, political, and economic systems of modern societies while abandoning those rigid and oppressive social, political, and economic systems of ancient societies. Regarding development, modernization aims to increase personal income and enhance national strength. But these two dimensions are hardly consistent all the time and may even constrain each other. Latecomer countries are confronted with greater challenges because they need to achieve transformation and development within a shorter timeframe. They must catch up as soon as possible with the social, economic, and political development of the first-mover countries, while simultaneously contending with potential shocks or even aggression from these established modern countries.

The CPC emerged during the process of Chinese intellectuals seeking a "holistic" solution to the problem of transformation and catching up.[1]

[1] Lin Yusheng. Anti Traditionalism Trends and Chinese Utopianism in 20th-Century China [M]// Liu Junning et al. Economic Democracy and Economic Freedom: Res Publica. Beijing: SDX Joint Publishing Company, 1997. This article is reprinted from: Xu Jilin. Discussion on History of Chinese Thought in 20th Century: First Volume [M]. Beijing: Orient Publishing Center of China Publishing Group Co., Ltd., 2000.

Z. Zheng
Institute of Market and Price, National Development and Reform Commission, Beijing, China

R. Baoping
Chang Jiang Scholars Program under the Ministry of Education, Beijing, China

School of Digital Economy and Management, Nanjing University, Nanjing, China

Z. Qian
Research Institute on Economy and Development of Western China at Northwest University, Xi'an, China

Z. Yinan
Economics Teaching and Research Department, Party School of the CPC Central Committee (National Academy of Governance), Beijing, China

Its original intention was to transform China's political, social, and economic structures through class struggle, ultimately striving to create a new, egalitarian society. During the initial three decades following the founding of the People's Republic of China, the Party led the Chinese people in pursuing socialist revolution and construction, accelerating the nation's transformation and modernization. After the beginning of the reform and opening up, the Party leveraged excellent components from traditional Chinese culture to furnish critical philosophical and institutional backing for the rapid economic takeoff of the country. The Party has thus guided China along a distinctive trajectory of modernization that holds global relevance. To be specific, this path proves to be of global significance in four key aspects. Firstly, as a large latecomer country accomplishing peaceful transformation and catch-up, it is unprecedented in global modernization. Secondly, Chinese modernization prioritizes human development, resulting in enhanced educational and health levels of the common people. Thirdly, it takes a pragmatic approach, making tangible efforts to improve both economic and institutional frameworks. Finally, the ruling party demonstrates broad representation, maintaining a neutral stance on societal issues, allowing it to focus on the long-term development of the entire nation.

Birth of the Communist Party of China

If the Glorious Revolution of 1688 is taken as the starting point, modernization has gone through more than 300 years worldwide; if we define the conclusion of World War II as the endpoint of Western modernization, this process has extended beyond 200 years. However, nations that are late to modernize will not take such lengthy timelines because they have already seen the outcomes of modernization. Their imperative for economic advancement necessitates a strategy of catching up with modernized countries. First-mover countries basically adopted a gradual, incremental approach to economic development, primarily utilizing market mechanisms. Latecomer countries aspiring to elevate their living standards to those of developed countries must consider unconventional strategies. But realizing catch-up is an uphill struggle. In the past 70 years, after World War II, only 11 economies, including Japan and some Southern

European nations, have successfully transitioned from middle or low-income classifications to the living standards characteristic of developed countries. Only four Asian economies—South Korea, Singapore, China's Taiwan region, and China's Hong Kong region—have successfully transitioned from impoverished conditions to developed high-income status. They are collectively known as the "Four Asian Tigers." The process of economic catch-up is profoundly challenging and represents a low-probability endeavor.

The challenges of social and political reform parallel those associated with economic development, yet are even more profound. Ancient societies were characterized by rigid stratification, where upper classes would not easily forfeit their privileges. Also, these societies were marked by ideological inflexibility, with dominant social classes resistant to relinquishing their status. Although ancient Chinese society exhibited relatively high mobility, its institutional frameworks and ideologies remained rigid. In contrast, modern societies are defined by open systems and liberal ideologies, which inevitably conflict with the structures of ancient societies. The transformation from ancient to modern society is bound to be a painful process. Historical precedents in Europe illustrate that major nations, such as Britain and France, had to go through revolutions before they started their modernization process, whereas nations that circumvented revolutions faced alternative forms of struggle. For instance, Germany emerged as the most successful nation in economic catch-up during the nineteenth century, opting for militarism over social revolution.[2] This parallels Japan, which emerged as the leading nation in economic catch-up during the twentieth century.

China embarked on its modern transformation after 1860. Just as Li Hongzhang said, in the late nineteenth century, China was going through great changes of a magnitude not seen in 3000 years. The nation had never experienced such a profound external influence as that exerted by Western civilization throughout its 3000-year recorded history. The last significant cultural shock had been the introduction of Buddhism, which took the country approximately a millennium to assimilate fully. The impact of Western civilization was not only more extensive but also more

[2] Babara Tuchma. The Guns of August [M]. Translated by Zhang Daiyun et al. Shanghai: SDX Joint Publishing Company, 2018.

profound than that of Buddhism. This raised concerns among the Chinese intelligentsia and officials regarding the potential duration required for complete assimilation.

Chinese modernization went through three phases from 1860 to 1919. The initial phase, known as the Westernization Movement, yielded notable achievements. By the onset of the First Sino-Japanese War, China had established the largest navy in Asia—the Beiyang Fleet. But the defeat of this war led to a critical realization among reformers that mere technical advancements were insufficient; institutional reform was also imperative. China thus embarked on the second phase of modernization, characterized by the emergence of two forces: revolutionary movements and political reform initiatives. The former was represented by the Revive China Society (Xing Zhong Hui) led by Sun Yat-sen, while the latter was the Hundred Days' Reform spearheaded by Kang Youwei. The reform ultimately failed, giving rise to the Republic of China (1912–1949) through revolutionary efforts. Nevertheless, the revolution did not fulfill its intended objectives, leading to Yuan Shikai's imperial restoration, the fragmentation of the nation by warlords, and foreign oppression. Around the Hundred Days' Reform, Social Darwinism gained traction in China, facilitated by the translation and editing of *Evolution and Ethics* by Yan Fu, as well as the dissemination of ideas through *Qingyi Bao* (*The China Discussion*) and *Xinmin Congbao* (*Xinmin Series Newspaper*), both published by Liang Qichao in Japan.[3] As the revolution failed to elevate China to a respected status within the global community, intellectuals began to explore alternative solutions, setting the stage for the New Culture Movement. Since neither technological advances nor institutional reform proved adequate, the root cause was deemed to be the cultural framework. Advocates of the New Culture Movement therefore began to focus on the transformation of public sentiment and cultural paradigms, with the prominent theme of anti-traditionalism encapsulated in the slogan "Down with Confucianism." The May 4th Movement further radicalized the New Culture Movement. Radical intellectuals like Chen Duxiu and Li Dazhao began to introduce Marxism. They were inspired by the October Revolution in Russia and realized that a socialist revolution could provide

[3] Social Darwinism had been one of the dominant political ideologies in Japan since the Meiji Restoration. Liang Qichao was deeply influenced by this ideology. See: Hazama Naoki. Liang Qichao · Meiji Japan · West [M]. Beijing: Social Sciences Academic Press (China), 2012.

a holistic solution for building a strong China. Following World War I, Western intellectuals began to express a pessimistic view of their own culture, a sentiment echoed by Chinese scholars. In this context, Marxism surfaced as a counterpart to the mainstream of Western culture, resonating with the critical perspectives of Chinese radicals toward the West.

Meanwhile, the ongoing cultural revolution at home thirsted for a radical doctrine to guide its trajectory, making the introduction of Marxism particularly timely. The localization of Marxism in China began. The CPC's acceptance of Marxism was driven by both idealistic and pragmatic considerations, the latter proving more consequential in practice. Class struggle became a pivotal instrument for the Party's social transformation efforts, as it endeavored to carry out social transformation via class struggle wherever possible.[4] From the angle of modernization, class struggle at that time was a mechanism for modernization and transformation. The focus of class struggle was directed at property owners and authorities that represented the political, social, and economic structures of the ancient regime, ultimately resulting in the establishment of a new modern order.

Why was the Kuomintang (Chinese Nationalist Party, KMT) unable to undertake the task of China's modern transformation? This was because they fundamentally lacked the required qualities and capabilities for such a mission. The revolution led by Sun Yat-sen was rooted in nationalism. Later, he subsequently proposed the Three Principles of the People to unify Tongmenghui (the Chinese Revolutionary Alliance) and the KMT. During the initial collaboration between the KMT and the Communist Party, Sun Yat-sen was convinced that the Principle of the People's Livelihood (one of the Three Principles of the People) aligned with the communist goal of improving welfare for the common people. This perceived alignment allowed for the incorporation of communist ideas within the broader framework of his own doctrine. He employed this argument to promote cooperation with the Communist Party among the right-wing factions of the KMT.[5] However, Sun Yat-sen was staunchly opposed to class struggle in China because he contended that there were no class

[4] The CPC had been under the leadership of the Communist International led by the Soviet Union since its inception. Although the ultimate goal of the Communist International was to achieve a socialist revolution in China, the Soviet Union often selectively supported and restrained the revolutionary activities of the CPC in favor of its own benefits. See: Yang Kuisong. Revolution in "Intermediate Zone" [M]. Taiyuan: Shanxi People's Publishing House, 2020.

[5] Yang Kuisong. Kuomintang "Works with the CPC" and "Fights against the CPC" [M]. Nanning: Guangxi Normal University Press, 2016.

distinctions in China. This viewpoint indicates that Sun lacked historical insight and failed to recognize that the Communist Party was strategically leveraging class struggle as a means to overthrow the old system. Initially, Chiang Kai-shek endorsed collaboration with the Communist Party and expressed empathy toward the Russian Revolution, even leading a delegation to Russia for an exploratory mission. His shift in viewpoint was a complex evolution. First, he developed a rift with the Communist Party due to the "Zhongshan Warship Incident." Additionally, his appetite for power grew as the Northern Expedition (1926–1927) progressed from victory to victory. Furthermore, the Communist Party's land reform initiatives in rural areas and their attempts to seize power in the cities challenged his conservative boundaries. The April 12 Anti-Revolutionary Coup (1927) allowed Chiang Kai-shek to consolidate control over the KMT while systematically purging communists. Ultimately, this transformation rendered the KMT counter-revolutionary, diminishing its appeal to progressive young people. This is the reason why youths with lofty ideals rushed to Yan'an in Shaanxi rather than Chongqing from 1935 to 1948; while Chongqing represented a refuge, Yan'an in Shaanxi symbolized a pathway to the promising future of a new China. They keenly perceived the moral decline of the KMT. In this context, the KMT had forfeited its role as a vanguard for the Chinese revolution and modernization.

According to Li Zehou, the period from 1919 to 1949 represents a dual variation of enlightenment and national salvation,[6] with the latter being more dominant. However, framing this historical phase exclusively through the lens of enlightenment presents an incomplete narrative; it necessitates a contextualization within the broader framework of modernization. Enlightenment is only one facet of modernization, whereas the revolutionary efforts aimed at societal transformation hold greater significance. Therefore, national salvation not only overshadowed the process of enlightenment but also obscured the revolutionary movements, and the latter could only be actualized following the founding of the People's Republic of China.

[6] Li Zehou. Dual Variation of Enlightenment and Salvation [M]//Towards the Future: Issue No. 1. Chengdu: Sichuan People's Publishing House, 1986. Reprinted in: Xu Jilin. Discussion on History of Chinese Thought in the 20th Century: Volume One [M]. Beijing: Orient Publishing Center of China Publishing Group Co., Ltd., 2000.

Socialist Revolution and Its Significance

Following the establishment of the People's Republic of China, the CPC stayed true to its original aspiration and began to carry out the socialist revolution, including land reform (and the subsequent organization of people's communes), socialist transformation of capitalist industry and commerce, women's liberation, and the building of a new socialist culture. In addition, the CPC was devoted to promoting education and improving public health. With the exception of organizing people's communes and the transformation of capitalist industry and commerce, which were more in the service of socialist construction, these efforts gave a strong push to the process of Chinese modernization.

Land Reform

Some studies have relied on localized data from certain regions to suggest that agrarian relations were not particularly tense in old China.[7] However, the survey made by the Resource Committee of the national government of the Republic of China in the early 1930s showed that the proportion of owner peasants across the country was only 41.7%, a figure that fell to 27.2% in the southern region. Among non-owner peasants, there were more hired peasants in the northern region and more tenant peasants in the southern region.[8] These data reveal the extreme tension in pre-1949 agrarian relations. The breaking of such old agrarian relations has a two-fold significance.

The first aspect is the liberation of productive forces. There are two reasons why the old agrarian relations constrained productivity. Firstly, peasants' motivation for production was diminished because they did not possess the land and thus did not reap the full fruits of their labor. Hired peasants, having no land at all, lived on the meager wages provided by landlords, and thus had little motivation to work hard. Tenant peasants typically had to surrender 50% of their harvest to landlords, which also discouraged their motivation for production. Secondly, tenant peasants had very little wealth and were vulnerable to risks, but they had to endure

[7] For example, Qin Hui and Jin Yan, using the Guanzhong region as a case study, proposed the judgment that there were no landlords in Guanzhong. See: Qin Hui, Jin Yan. Pastoral Poetry and Rhapsody [M]. 3rd Edition. Nanjing: Jiangsu Phoenix Literature and Art Press, 2019.

[8] Yao Yang. Development Economics [M]. 2nd Edition. Beijing: Peking University Press, 2018.

the consequences of natural disasters. Under fixed rental contracts in particular, they were responsible for all losses from reduced yields, further undermining their motivation to produce. Ensuring that "land to the tiller" can entirely eliminate efficiency losses caused by the first factor and significantly reduce losses resulting from the second.

The second aspect is a kind of personal dependence fostered by feudal agrarian relations. Whether hired peasants or tenant peasants, they were bound to landlords in a relationship of personal attachment. An example of this is found in *White Deer Plain*, where Bai Jiaxuan and his long-term hired hand Lu San share such a bond. The existence of various forms of personal dependencies in political, social, and economic spheres is one of the counterpoints to modernization. In an agricultural society, land is the most basic production factor, and agrarian relations decide other social relations. Therefore, breaking up the old agrarian relations is a crucial step toward modernization.

Research has shown that land reform plays a crucial role in fostering long-run economic growth in a country or region.[9] In Latin American countries, land distribution was highly unequal, and agriculture was dominated by large plantations. The politics of these countries were controlled by large estate owners, which seriously hindered the development of these countries. On the contrary, South Korea and Chinese Taiwan carried out more thorough land reforms, which substantially facilitated their industrial development.[10] Land reform in the Chinese mainland was more extensive and profound, which enormously increased grain yield and advanced modernization in rural areas.

Women's Liberation

In almost all ancient societies, the status of women was very low. The emancipation of women in first-mover countries had come a long way, with most countries not granting women the right to vote until after World War I. Latecomer countries needed to liberate women in a much shorter period of time. From its very founding, the CPC has attached great importance to women's liberation. During the Soviet area Period in China from

[9] Deininger, Klaus; and Lyn Squire. "New Ways of Looking at Old Issues: Inequality and Growth," Journal of Development Economics, Vol. 57 (1998): 259-287.

[10] According to Lee Teng-hui's doctoral dissertation, 40% of industrial capital accumulation in Taiwan during the 1950s came from the extraction of agricultural surplus. See: Lee, Teng-hui. Intersectoral capital flows in the economic development of Taiwan, 1895-1960, Ithaca: Cornell University Press, 1971.

1927 to 1937, the CPC mobilized women to work to compensate for the labor shortages caused by men going to war. During the Yan'an period from 1935 to 1948, the focus of women's liberation shifted toward literacy and political participation. Studies found that these measures had lasting impacts. At that time, the gender ratio in Soviet area counties was more balanced compared to surrounding counties, and the female labor force participation rate was higher.[11] Although women's educational level was generally lower than men's at the time, this situation was somewhat better in the Shaanxi-Gansu-Ningxia Border Region than in the surrounding areas.[12] The CPC advanced the cause of women's liberation through revolutionary means after the founding of the People's Republic of China. The Marriage Law was promulgated prior to the promulgation of the Constitution in an effort to abolish past customs that constrained women's status, such as foot-binding, arranged marriage, and polygamy, thereby legally establishing gender equality within families. In the meantime, women were mobilized to take part in local political activities, significantly enhancing their social status. These actions produced a lasting effect. In the counties with a higher proportion of female Party members in 1950, women's educational levels relative to men were higher, and the gender ratios were more balanced by the 1980s.[13] Under the commune system, women's labor participation rates increased substantially, and this tradition persisted even after the implementation of the household contract responsibility system. Even though the labor force participation rate of women slightly descended over the past two decades, it still remains above 60% nowadays, which is much higher than the world's average of 50%.

Build a New Socialist Culture

Ancient Chinese society was characterized by geographical relationships and blood lineage. The majority of people, excluding scholar-bureaucrats, had their social circles only within the bounds of their local community and family network. Just as Fei Xiaotong pointed out, the social

[11] He Erlong, Yao Yang. Long-term Impact of the Soviet Republic of China on Participation Rate of Female Labor Force and Sex Ratio at Birth. CCER Working Paper, C2022001.

[12] He Erlong. Long-term Impact of the Shaan-Gan-Ning Border Region on Women's Education. School of Marxism, Peking University.

[13] Yao Yang, and Wuyue You. "Women's Political Participation and Gender Gaps of Education in China: 1950-1990." *World Development*, 2018, 106: 220-237. Wuyue You, Yao Yang. Women's Political Status and Sex Ratio at Birth—Based on Empirical Research of County-level Data during 1950-2000 [J]. Chinese Social Sciences, 2020 (4).

relationships of Chinese people are like ripples spreading outward from a stone dropped into a pond, with one individual in the middle and others spreading out like ripples according to the proximity of geographical and blood relations. This individual-centric social relation framework in ancient China meant that, beyond geographical and blood connections, there were few functional social organizations, which starkly contrasts with Western societies. In Western countries, religion is central to people's lives, and the role of religious communities is very visible, connecting people through their religious beliefs.

Religious beliefs can unite a much wider range of people than geographical proximity or blood ties, and are therefore more likely to foster a sense of community even among strangers. China was different. For the vast majority of Chinese people, "China" holds cultural significance rather than political meaning. Social governance at the grassroots level may depend exclusively on geographical relationships and consanguinity. The role of the state was only to defend itself against foreign invasion and to maintain domestic tranquility. Chinese "collectivism" resembled the Hobbesian sense of collectivism: the state, acting as a "Leviathan," was viewed as a protector of social stability, and the people acquiesced to the actions of the state. The ordinary people took the state as an external authority to which they must submit rather than an organic part of society.

Modern society is just contrary to ancient Chinese society: a modern state may encompass multiple cultures, but what unites its people is a shared political identity and a unified government built upon that identity. One of the key tasks of Chinese modernization has been to establish the political identity of the Chinese people and build the nation upon a unified understanding of politics and governance. The CPC's approach to achieving this goal was to build a new socialist culture and establish the political identity of the Chinese people within the framework of socialism. The institutional changes brought about by the socialist revolution were themselves part of this process. Never in Chinese history had there been such a thorough social transformation as the socialist revolution. The Party reached out to every corner of society through tight organization and brought every Chinese person into the process of modernization. In comparing the KMT and the CPC, Huang Renyu noted that the KMT's way of governing was top-down, whereas the CPC's approach was bottom-up.[14] The socialist revolution led by the CPC profoundly transformed

[14] Huang Renyu. Yellow River and Blue Mountains: Memoir of Huang Renyu [M]. Beijing: Jiuzhou Press, 2019.

Chinese society from the grassroots level, fundamentally altering the structure and operational dynamics of local communities. This transformation significantly advanced the political identification of the general populace with the state. On this basis, the Party made further efforts to strengthen the public's political identity through a wide array of means, including publicity, education systems, and literary and artistic works. The following is a demonstration of how the CPC constructed people's political identity through literary and artistic works, using the film *Five Golden Flowers* as an example.

Five Golden Flowers is a color movie produced in 1959, telling the story of Ah Peng, a young man of the Bai ethnic group, in search of his beloved Jinhua (Golden Flower). During the March Fair, Ah Peng encounters the beautiful Jinhua by the Butterfly Spring. The following year, carrying the love token she gave him, Ah Peng returns to the Butterfly Spring and searches throughout Cangshan Mountain and Erhai Lake for her. Along the way, he meets four young women also named Jinhua, all active members of the commune, before finally finding the girl of his dreams, who turns out to be the deputy director of the commune. Ah Peng and Jin Hua joyfully reunite at the Butterfly Spring. Other girls named Jin Hua and their lovers gather around them to celebrate the moment with a final chorus. The cinematography is highly poetic, and several songs from the film remain widely sung to this day. However, for the purposes of this analysis, the political message conveyed by the film is of paramount importance.

First of all, both protagonists are members of the Bai ethnic group, clearly promoting the concept of a unified multiethnic Chinese nation. The southwestern region of China had long been under the rule of the Tusi system, and the identification with the central plains was very weak. In the film, the stunning landscapes of Dali, along with the vigorous young men and beautiful women of the Bai minority, leave the audience with a positive impression of China's ethnic minority regions, naturally igniting a passion for national unity. Secondly, throughout Ah Peng's journey to find Jinhua, the film showcases the joyous transformations brought about by the people's commune in people's lives. Regardless of the context of the time, this portrayal subtly immerses the audience in a sense of political identification with the nation. Lastly, the five Jin Hua (Golden Flower) that Ah Peng encountered are all active members of the commune. This highlights the depth and breadth of women's liberation in ethnic minority areas. The restrictions on women in ethnic minority areas were not as severe as in Han-inhabited areas, and each of the five Golden Flowers in the film is portrayed as cheerful and lively, exhibiting a boldness and openness that surpasses that of Han women. While such portrayals do carry elements of romanticized imagination of minority groups, they play a positive role in promoting women's liberation. Women's liberation is an important part of socialist cultural values. This film's use of romance to promote women's liberation extends its significance beyond the liberation of women alone and contributes to the fostering of the country's political identity.

The interpersonal relationship was changed significantly in the course of the socialist revolution and construction. Such changes were reflected in the way strangers addressed each other, with comrade becoming a standard appellation for strangers. The term "comrade" signifies shared ideals and was previously used only within the Party. Its use among strangers implies a common aspiration or goal, which, in the context of China at that time, was the building of a socialist China. Comrade, therefore, became an important symbol of national political identity translated to the individual level. Today, this form of address has largely disappeared from interactions between strangers, which may also indicate that China's national political identity has been fully realized.

Socialist Construction

After the founding of the People's Republic of China, the Party not only carried out a socialist revolution but also embarked on a vigorous socialist construction, establishing an industrialization path led by heavy industry. There were many reasons for choosing this path. The first was the lessons of history. Beginning with the Westernization Movement, several generations of Chinese intellectuals and leaders have been convinced that backwardness invited aggression, and only building China's own industry could make the country strong enough to avoid aggression. Mao Zedong followed this philosophy. Secondly, the international environment at that time was unfavorable to China's participation in the global division of labor. On the one hand, China's economy was basically isolated from the West due to the economic blockade imposed by the latter; on the other hand, the Soviet Union intended to position China as an agricultural nation in the socialist camp, which Mao Zedong resolutely opposed and persuaded the Soviet Union to help China develop industrialization. Thirdly, the popular advice to developing countries by international academic and policy circles at the time was also to develop their own industries by means of import substitution policies. One of the central themes of the emerging discipline of development economics was the concept of economies of scale in industrial development. Under economies of scale, enterprises had to reach a minimum efficient scale of production in order to survive, which gave rise to the policy of so-called "protection of infant industries." Meanwhile, Raúl Prebisch's "core-periphery" hypothesis highlighted the distinctions between manufacturing-based core countries and raw material-based periphery countries. As a general principle, advancements in manufacturing technology within core nations ought to enhance the trade conditions of peripheral countries. But Prebisch did not find this to be the case.[15] This hypothesis was later developed into the dependency theory, in which periphery countries were caught in the trap of raw material production and became dependent on core countries. The newly built People's Republic of China, at the forefront of anti-imperialism and anti-colonialism, could easily accept such a theory.

The assistance from the Soviet Union played a crucial role in China's industrialization in the 1950s, with the establishment of 156 civilian projects funded by the Soviet Union laying a solid foundation for China's heavy industry, and some of these enterprises are still functioning today. But capital accumulation in China was a more pressing question. The aid from the Soviet Union was mostly in the form of loans, so China must accumulate the capital needed for industrialization. Under the circumstances, the only possible source for capital accumulation was rural areas. Just as what the Soviet Union did, China adopted the method of depressing the prices of agricultural products. This is an important background of communization and planned purchase and supply by the state.[16] While it was hard for the state to control agricultural production and prices in decentralized farming systems, the establishment of people's communes could facilitate the unification of agricultural production. This, coupled with a planned purchase and supply system, could enable the centralized purchase and sale of agricultural products, thereby allowing for price control. Once capital was available, it had to be concentrated and used in strategic sectors approved by the state, and the socialist transformation of capitalist industry and commerce served this purpose.

All in all, China's industrialization adopted an unconventional catch-up strategy. How to evaluate this strategy? Yao Yang and Zheng Dongya provided a qualitative simulation study.[17] This study is based on the premise

[15] Prebisch, Raúl. *The Economic Development of Latin America and Its Principal Problems.* New York: United Nations Press, 1950.

[16] Bo Yibo. A Review of Several Major Decisions and Events [M]. Beijing: CPC Party History Press, 2008.

[17] Yao Yang, Zheng Dongya. Heavy Industry and Economic Development: The Chinese Planned Economy Revisited [J]. Economic Research, 2008 (4): 26–40.

that heavy industry has a technological externality on other industries, with its technological advancements leading to reduced production costs across industries. Given the existence of such externalities, it is justified for the government to subsidize heavy industry. We calculated the optimal subsidy rate and the optimal subsidy time and discovered that the optimal subsidy rate was 33%, while the actual subsidy rate measured by our model was 36.7%, which is not much different from each other. However, we calculated the optimal subsidy time to be 12 years, in stark contrast to the actual implementation period of 25 years. In conclusion, the catch-up strategy itself is not inherently flawed, but the problem lies in the prolonged execution. In addition, when implementing the catch-up strategy, the Party made the critical mistake of hastily advancing initiatives like the "Great Leap Forward," a lesson worth learning by future generations.

While pushing ahead with economic development, the Party also emphasized the expansion of education and the improvement of public health. Studies have shown that the educational attainment of individuals in the late 1940s and 1950s exhibited the weakest correlation with that of their parents,[18] which implies that in the initial three decades following the founding of the People's Republic of China, the focus was on extending education to the general population, thereby enhancing intergenerational educational mobility. For public health, the commune-based basic healthcare system enabled the general public to get access to basic medical services and reduced infant mortality rates. The patriotic health campaign and vaccination efforts eradicated many infectious diseases, leading to a steady rise in life expectancy among the population.

Table 1.1 gives a comparison of China and India around the year 1978, reflecting China's achievements in modernization. The two countries are comparable in many respects. India gained independence in 1947, and the People's Republic of China was established in 1949. The two countries had similarly large populations. In particular, India, like China, adopted the import substitution policy to boost its heavy industry. However, Table 1.1 shows that apart from GDP per capita and gross enrollment ratio in higher education, India lagged far behind China in adult literacy rate, infant mortality rate, people's life expectancy, and industrial development. The reason for India's higher per capita GDP at the time lay in China's comparatively lower starting point, while China directed the bulk of its capital accumulation toward heavy industry. By 1992, China's GDP

[18] Hu, Zhi-An, and Yang Yao. "The Great U Curve—Education Mobility in China in the Period 1930-1985." China Center for Economic Research, Peking University, 2017.

Table 1.1 Comparison of China and India (1978)

	China	*India*
GDP per capita (in dollars unchanged in 2000)	155	206
Adult literacy rate (%)	65.5	40.8
Gross enrollment rate of higher education (%)	0.7	4.9
Life expectancy (years)	66	54
Infant mortality rate (‰)	54.2	106.4
Proportion of manufacturing value added in GDP (%)	40.0	17.0
Proportion of manufacturing employment (%)	17.3	13.0

Note: China and India's adult literacy rates were collected in 1982 and 1981, respectively (Yao, Yang. "The Chinese Growth Miracle." *Handbook of Economic Growth*. Chapter 7, Vol. 2, pp. 943–1032. Amsterdam: North-Holland, 2014)

per capita had surpassed that of India. The fact that India had a higher gross enrollment rate in higher education was related to the situation that China just restored the college entrance examination at that time. During this period, India attached more importance to higher education, while China put more emphasis on basic education. Given the low-income levels and high illiteracy rates in both countries at that time, it was obvious that basic education should be a national priority. In retrospect, China's investment in basic education played a significant role in the development of an export-oriented economy after the reform and opening up, while India's lower education level has been a constraint on its industrial development.

Reform and Opening Up: Reconciling with Chinese Tradition

The socialist revolution changed China in a stormy way, bringing it to the threshold of modernization. This revolution aimed at enhancing construction and laid the groundwork for social construction. On the one hand, the hierarchical structure of Chinese society was broken down, and social and political equality reached a higher level, greatly enhancing the people's political identity with the state. On the other hand, socialist construction established an industrial foundation and improved the education and health of the people. Following the onset of the reform and opening up, the Party redirected its focus toward economic development, leading to a pragmatic departure from the radical approaches of the socialist revolution period. The Party also started to re-examine its relationship with traditional values. Two critical considerations emerge. Firstly, the socialist revolution primarily operated in the political, social, and economic spheres without encroaching upon the family and its associated private domains.[19] In rural areas, families owned land and raised poultry and livestock; in urban areas, although families did not possess their own industries, they remained cohesive social units akin to those in rural regions. Chinese traditional culture was thus kept through the family. Economic construction needed the mobilization of individual initiative, while respect for traditional culture, as well as the patterns of individual behaviors derived from it, was essential for stimulating personal motivation. Secondly, the Party needed to find new ideological resources and practices to anchor its actions after abandoning radical ideas and practices. It was only natural for the Chinese to embrace the excellent aspects of their traditional heritage. The Party's return to three key aspects of Chinese fine tradition: pragmatism, meritocracy, and market economy. By integrating these traditions with the long-established theories and practices of a Marxist political party, the Party laid the philosophical and political foundation for the rapid economic growth that followed the reform and opening up.[20]

Pragmatism

On a practical level, the most distinctive feature of Chinese culture is pragmatism. From people's daily life to political practices, pragmatism was the most prominent characteristic of ancient China. The most important reason for the emergence of pragmatism in China is the absence of an indigenous religion, coupled with the early focus of Chinese ancestors on tangible realities. *The Book of Songs* originated in the early Western Zhou Dynasty (1046–771BC), a period when Chinese ancestors were already praising love in verse. At the same time, Greece remained in its so-called "Age of Myths," exemplified by the Trojan War, which was fought over an abducted woman. By then, Chinese ancestors had already established a pattern of peaceful living on this land, celebrating love and the joys of earthly life. This embodies a distinctive characteristic of Chinese civilization.

At the philosophical level, pragmatism encompasses two basic principles. Firstly, the legitimacy of the means can be reasonably inferred from

[19] Friedman, Edward. *Chinese Village, Socialist State*. New Haven: Yale University Press, 1993.

[20] The Party's return to Chinese tradition can be seen as a practice of adapting Marxism to Chinese conditions, which is a broad topic in itself, and for the purpose of this article, the author will not expand on it here.

the legitimacy of the ends. One of the prerequisites of revolution is the establishment of opposing factions. Consequently, the focus shifts to means, encapsulated in the slogan "Better to have the grass of socialism than the seedlings of capitalism." Pragmatism is goal-oriented; as long as the objective is achieved, the means may be considered legitimate. Deng Xiaoping's "cat theory" is a vivid reflection of this principle. "Reasonable infer" herein is crucial. One must use his or her own knowledge system, moral standards, and logic to think if he or she tries to justify the means, or else he or she will resort to unscrupulous means. Secondly, there is no eternal truth. Practice is the only criterion for testing truth. Chinese people do not believe in the existence of eternity. A very important idea in traditional Chinese philosophy is that the only unchanging law in the universe is that everything changes. The Chinese firmly believe that practices produce true knowledge and only practice can test whether knowledge is true or not. The Chinese term "实践 (*shijian*)" is generally translated into practice in English, but it is not accurate. The word "practice" implies that a model already exists, and one practices according to that model to gain proficiency. "*shijian*" (实践), however, is different in that it involves a cycle of "exploration-theory building-application-exploration," for which there is no exact equivalent in English.

Pragmatism has facilitated the initiation of reform and advanced the reform agenda. Consider this: what reforms might have been possible had we remained entangled in discussions surrounding various ideologies and absolute truths? Whether it is rural reform, state-owned enterprise reform, or price reform, each of these initiatives challenges the theoretical certainties of the past. Deng Xiaoping's principle of "no debate" has guided the Party toward a result-oriented philosophy of action. Under this philosophical guidance, the legitimacy of a system is no longer assessed by its attributes but by its ability to enhance productivity and contribute to the great rejuvenation of the Chinese nation. It was only in this way that institutional reform could take place.

Meritocracy

China has a long-standing tradition of meritocracy. Already in the Western Zhou Dynasty (1046–771BC), the Imperial College had been established to cultivate talents. The practice of selecting and using the virtuous and capable was institutionalized during the reign of the Emperor Wu of the Han Dynasty (141–87BC). In the Sui dynasty (581–618), the imperial examination system was invented to provide a way for commoners to ascend the social hierarchy. The philosophical foundation of meritocracy was rooted in the pre-Qin Confucian view of human nature. Unlike Western notions of fixed and monolithic human traits, pre-Qin Confucianism viewed human nature as diverse, malleable, and adaptable. It asserts that an individual's potential for virtue and competence is contingent upon their cultivated efforts and the surrounding environment.[21] Since the number of political positions is limited, and economic development requires incentives for people to contribute, the political structure of a society must identify and designate the virtuous and capable, while the economic system must provide appropriate incentives for these individuals. At the practical level, the contribution of Mohism to meritocracy was even greater. By the time of the Western Han Dynasty (202BC–8AD), when Confucianism became the dominant thought, it had absorbed the ideas of Mohism. Eventually, through the teachings of Dong Zhongshu, meritocracy became a constitutional principle of China's bureaucratic monarchy.[22] From a modern perspective, this constitutional principle can act as an alternative to the ballot system of electoral democracy and is sufficient to correct the problems of the ballot system, particularly its populist tendencies and its use by those with ulterior motives to incite and demagogue the people.

The Party has upheld the tradition of choosing and designating the virtuous and capable during reform and opening up. From the beginning of the1980s, when the Party proposed the building of pioneering, youthful, knowledgeable, and specialized cadres, it has attached great importance to the cultivation and selection of cadres. Research revealed that the Party's system of cadre selection was consistent with the principle of choosing and designating the virtuous and capable. Officials with greater capabilities were more likely to be promoted, and they tend to achieve higher lifetime accomplishments. In addition, the Party places significant emphasis on the training of cadres, and one way of doing so is to improve the skills and capabilities of talents by dispatching them to various posts.[23]

The principle of meritocracy, as enshrined in the constitution, remains of theoretical and practical importance today. The CPC is composed of

[21] Yao Yang, Qin Zizhong. Difference in Human Nature and Political Structure of Confucianism [J]. Open Times, 2017(6): 146–165.

[22] Su Li. Constitutional Systems of Great Powers: Institutional System of China in History [M]. Beijing: Peking University Press, 2018.

[23] Yao Yang, Xi Tianyang, Li Lixing et al. Selection, Cultivation and Incentives-Evidence from CCER Officials Database [J]. China Economic Quarterly, 2020 (3): 1017-1040.

exemplary members drawn from the populace, underpinned by the principle of meritocracy, which confers a constitutional status upon its leadership. The Party proposes overarching policy and legislative ideas, while the people's congresses serve as platforms for the Party to cultivate consensus. The authoritative function of the people's congresses is evident in their deliberation and voting on the Party's nominations for personnel and general policies, as well as in their role in finalizing legislation based on the Party's proposals.

Return to Market Economy

Deng Xiaoping said the market economy is not exclusive to capitalism. It, as a matter of fact, is not unique to the West either. By the Northern Song Dynasty (960–1127), China had already completed the construction of a market economy. During this period, the market economy was relatively well-developed, with the establishment of private land ownership, significant industry and commercial growth, and even the invention of paper money and securities trading, marking the dawn of modern finance.[24] The main feature of Western capitalism is not the market economy, but rather the machine-based mass production and the resultant nearly unrestricted capital accumulation. China's development of a market economy after the reform and opening up seemed at the time to be learning from the West, but in fact it was a return to its own tradition. To a large extent, Chinese practices of market economy have their distinctive characteristics, which are highly related to China's development stage and the cultural mentality of its people. The Party has guided the whole nation toward the establishment of a uniquely Chinese market economy.

In a market economy, the principles of distribution according to production factors, rewarding diligence while penalizing idleness, and adhering to the principle of survival of the fittest are essential for maintaining market efficiency. This aligns with the Chinese tradition of meritocracy and does not conflict with the labor-based distribution principle. On the one hand, factor-based distribution encompasses distribution according to labor; on the other hand, factor-based distribution is, fundamentally, labor-based distribution, as capital is ultimately derived from labor.

[24]Wu Gou. Song: Dawn of Modernity [M]. Nanning: Guangxi Normal University Press, 2019.

Revisiting the Significance of Revolution

Future historians will certainly refer to the reform and opening up when they write about Deng Xiaoping's historical achievements. But historians with a sense of historical depth will emphasize that his primary achievement was to bring the Party "back" to China. The birth of the Party was an outcome of the eastward diffusion of Western thought—a political organization founded by radical Chinese intellectuals embracing progressive Western ideas during the May 4th Movement. Just as stated earlier, the Party consciously became an instrument of Chinese modernization, guiding China into the modern world in a stormy way. This process inevitably involved the grand issue of absorbing and fusing Chinese culture with Western culture. During the revolutionary period, the Party largely practiced Western revolutionary theory, but as a political party rooted in China, the Party had to eventually confront the significant question of integrating Chinese and Western cultures.

At present, this topic is being addressed within the framework of adapting Marxism to the Chinese context. But, for future historians, the more important question is Deng Xiaoping's role in guiding the Party back to Chinese tradition, setting it on the path to liberating China from a century-long reliance on cultural importation. At the level of *Shu* (or technique), the reform and opening up was a way of learning from the West, but at the level of *Tao* (or principle), it marked the beginning of a process of returning to Chinese tradition. It should be noted that the planned economy was also a learning from the West, and the reform and opening up was simply a shift from learning one kind of Western model to another. However, in this latter process of learning, the Party's guiding ideology and code of conduct were distinctly Chinese. In this sense, the Party replicates the situation where traditional Chinese values fully utilize modern Western institutions and technology. China has indeed returned to the principle of "Chinese Essence and Western Means." For a civilization with 3000 years of written records, it is entirely understandable and necessary to adhere to its own "essence." But the contemporary "essence" differs significantly from that of over a century ago, as it has preserved its core while eliminating its impurities. It has evolved into a value system and a logic of action that are appropriate to the times. In the process of introducing the "Western means," it was impossible for China to avoid the values and codes of conduct that it had brought with it. Therefore, the practice of "Chinese Essence and Western Means" since the reform and opening up must be the integration of Chinese tradition and the modern Western value system, rather than a superficial juxtaposition, as seen during the Westernization Movement.

A question naturally arises: Was the revolution of the twentieth century a detour, given the eventual return to Chinese tradition? The answer is no. First of all, the revolution accelerated the process of Chinese modernization, bringing the country from a stubbornly antiquated society to the threshold of modernity in a relatively short period of time. Secondly, the return to Chinese tradition at this time is a return at a higher level. The revolution purged China's tradition of its decayed elements, allowing this current return to select the excellent elements to be inherited and carried forward. Finally, international comparisons show that latecomer countries that bypassed revolution encountered significant difficulties in their modernization process, hindering their economic catch-up.

The Philippines is a case in point. In 1980, the Philippines' per capita GDP was more than five times that of China, but by 2020, China's per capita GDP was almost four times that of the Philippines. In 40 years, the two countries reversed their positions by a factor of 20. Why did the Philippines end in failure? Philippine democracy has been uninterrupted since the fall of the Marcos dictatorship in 1986, and appears to possess a self-correcting capacity, as evidenced by the impeachment of President Estrada. But Philippine democracy operates within a social structure that has never changed, and as several Philippine scholars have noted, "the great Philippine enigma has thus arisen: the most vivid electoral politics unfolds atop Asia's most iniquitous class structure that has remained unchanged through the ages."[25] The class structure in the Philippines originates from the plantation economy left by the Spanish colonizers, with the owners of large plantations dominating the economy and politics. To this day, the politics of the Philippines still bears strong traces of family politics. In other words, party affiliation does not matter as much as loyalty to powerful politicians. Since 1988, most presidents have come from prominent family backgrounds, with the exception of the impeached Estrada (a well-known actor before his election) and another president (a former national defense minister). The recently elected president is the son of Marcos, and the vice president is the daughter of the recently retired

[25] Bello, Walden, Marissa de Guzman, Mary Lou Malig, and Herbert Docena. *The Anti-Development State: The Political Economy of Permanent Crisis in the Philippines*. p. xvi. Manila: Zed Books, 2005.

Duterte. This is exactly the dependency politics that Fukuyama argues has led to the downfall of democratic politics.[26] Dependency politics is also a main factor hindering economic growth because it leads to nepotism, enabling a select few to monopolize economic opportunities and resources.

Revolution is inherently painful, but it can establish long-term political stability at the cost of short-term suffering. The vast majority of latecomer countries had experienced colonization, and the colonizers left behind systems of electoral politics, compelling these nations to carry out social transformation within a democratic framework. The result of democracy is always a compromise among various forces, but social transformation requires the deprivation of power and resources from certain dominant groups. This inherent contradiction renders the social transformations in post-colonial countries an extremely arduous and protracted undertaking. For instance, the Philippines initiated land reform during the American occupation, but it was not completed until the first decade of the twenty-first century, and land was sold to landless peasants rather than being given to them for free. Land reform in India was even more difficult. Although the country enacted the Land Reform Act at the onset of independence, the act had been barely implemented even after 70 years. In West Bengal, which had been under the rule of the Communist Party of India for several decades, more than 30% of peasants had no land.[27] A paradox of the transition to modernization is that an effective social transformation often necessitates violence to achieve short-term results. China serves as a successful example, while many postcolonial countries have failed.

World Significance of the Chinese Path

Revisiting the dual challenges of transformation and catch-up development raised at the beginning of this paper, we find that the Chinese path offers a solution to this challenge. From the perspective of transformation and catch-up, countries and regions over the past 200 years can be classified into three types: those whose transformation lags behind catch-up, those whose transformation and catch-up occur simultaneously, and those where neither transformation nor catch-up has taken place.

[26] Francis Fukuyama. Political Order and Political Decay [M]. Translated by Mao Junjie. Nanning: Guangxi Normal University Press, 2015.

[27] Yao Yang. Development Economics [M]. 2nd Edition. Beijing: Peking University Press, 2018: References for Chapter 19 and this Chapter.

Germany and Japan, before World War II were typical examples of the first type. Both countries were the most successful countries in catch-up in the nineteenth and twentieth centuries, respectively, but both countries eventually turned militaristic because they failed to achieve social transformation. Their economic success, in fact, was a major factor delaying their political and social transformation. Germany's economic and military success fueled national pride. For Germans, Russian culture was seen as inferior, French culture as decadent, and British culture as full of cunning. Only German culture represented nobility and greatness, and therefore, Germany should dominate Europe. Germany, the German Emperor Kaiser Wilhelm II in particular, was indignant at the perceived "disrespect" from other Europeans. He coveted the prosperity of Paris on the one hand, and on the other hand, detested the condescension he faced from Britain, the motherland of his mother. He hoped to win Paris by winning the war, earning the respect he believed he "deserved."[28] Japan essentially repeated what Germany did. After the Meiji Restoration, Japan's national power was enormously enhanced. It easily defeated its former mentor, China, in the First Sino-Japanese War of 1894–1895 and vanquished Russia, the "Road Roller of Europe," in the Russo-Japanese War (1904–1905). Japan thought it was mighty enough to fight against the white race on behalf of the yellow race. Japan even declared itself the originator of Chinese culture and referred to China as "Shina." Ultimately, both Germany and Japan faced total destruction in the war. The root cause was that, despite their economic advancement to the forefront of modern society, they were still caught between antiquity and modernity in terms of ideology, politics, and society. The governing of the most advanced technologies by a pre-modern mindset and behavioral logic was bound to yield anti-modern outcomes.

The Four Asian Tigers, especially South Korea and Chinese Taiwan, were typical examples of the second type. During the colonial period, Japan intentionally suppressed the elites of industry and commerce in South Korea and Taiwan. After World War II, both regions implemented land reform, resulting in more egalitarian societies that eliminated powerful groups that had previously impeded social reforms. This provided the political and social foundation for their governments to kick-start economic growth. Singapore, a city-state, experienced rapid modernization

[28] Babara Tuchma. The Guns of August [M]. Translated by Zhang Daiyun et al. Shanghai: SJPC, 2018.

of its social structure, significantly bolstered by Lee Kuan Yew's wisdom and strong governance capabilities, which greatly facilitated economic development. The commonality among these countries and regions is their preceding social transformation, which laid a foundation for the execution of government power in a neutral way.

The majority of developing countries fall into the third type. In these countries, slow political and social transformation was the main primary factor hindering their ability to catch up rapidly. Most developing countries were colonies of European and American powers, and before colonization, they were in ancient or even primitive societies. Rather than changing these ancient or primitive social structures, the colonizers used them for their own purpose, thus ossifying the existing social and political structures. The departure of the colonizers left these countries with a modern electoral democratic system, extremely reducing the room for social reform. These countries could only hope to promote social and political transformation through market forces in the course of development. This dynamic, however, entrapped them in a vicious cycle: incomplete political and social transformation shackled economic development, while stagnant economic downturn restricted further political and social transformation.

However, Germany and Japan seem to be two counterexamples. The reason may lie in the fact that both Germany and Japan had strong regimes capable of mobilizing resources to achieve economic catch-up in a short period of time, whereas most developing countries have not developed such strong governments. The transformation and economic catch-up of developing countries must be endogenous to the process of social development, and both will undergo a lengthy historical process.

China resembles the "Four Asian Tigers" more in that it has experienced transformation and catch-up simultaneously. Yet, as a major country, China's path to modernization holds greater global significance. Specifically, China's path to modernization encompasses the following four dimensions of world significance.

Firstly, the transition from antiquity to modernity occurred within a relatively brief timeframe. The British Revolution lasted half a century, while the French Revolution and its subsequent repercussions spanned over 100 years. If the period of Japanese invasion is excluded, China's revolution (including socialist revolution) in the twentieth century also lasted half a century, which is not particularly long in comparison. Just as the English Revolution and the French Revolution ushered England and

France into the modern world, the Chinese revolution brought China into the modern era. From the angle of economic catch-up, the revolution facilitated the establishment of an egalitarian society in China without class distinctions, providing the necessary guarantees for China's economic takeoff. Although we do not expect other developing countries to realize political and social transformation through revolution, they must prioritize the promotion of equality as a central task of their political reform. Otherwise, they can hardly maintain long-term and stable economic growth.

Secondly, China's modernization path emphasizes human development. As summarized in Table 1.1, the CPC focused on improving the educational standards and health conditions of the general populace during the socialist revolution and construction. In comparing the different economic performances of China and India, Amartya Sen, a renowned Indian economist, said that China was better prepared for human development than India.[29] People are the primary productive force, and education and health are the main indicators of people's productivity. Improving people's education and health enhances their productivity. Distinct from other developing countries, China paid more attention to the education and health of ordinary people. This not only embodies the philosophy of egalitarianism upheld by the CPC but also aligns with the general logic of economic development, which posits that it is more likely to stimulate economic development by enhancing the capabilities of the majority rather than improving the capabilities of the minority.

Thirdly, pragmatism should be a philosophy of action. National pride is an important ideological source of national cohesion, but many developing countries have pushed it to the extreme, rejecting actions that might compromise their national "prestige." Regarding economic development, this is manifested in the refusal to develop labor-intensive industries and the focus on high-end industries because the elites of developing countries believe that labor-intensive industries are undignified and exploitative. Only high-end industries, they believe, can enable them to be on equal footing with developed countries. Concerning institutional construction, those countries are unwilling to compromise with national realities and stubbornly persist in the so-called "optimal" system, even though these systems fail to function effectively. China is different. In the early stages of

[29] Amartya Sen. Development as Freedom [M]. Translated by Ren Zuo, Yu Zhen. Beijing: China Renmin University Press, 2002.

its economic takeoff, China readily accepted labor-intensive industries transferred from developed economies to accumulate capital and technology, which ultimately led to the establishment of the world's largest and most resilient manufacturing system, positioning itself at the forefront of various technological fields. In terms of institution-building, China did not pursue a perfect system, but rather adopted a gradual approach by first establishing a "useful" system and then continuously improving it in practice. As a result, China's institutional transformation has avoided the pains of institutional transformation in the Soviet Union and Eastern Europe and has provided the conditions for steady economic development. China's pragmatism and success are of great importance to the world.

Fourthly, the ruling party plays the role of a central pillar in society. The CPC possesses extensive representativeness, with more than 90 million members from all walks of life and all social strata. The Party has become a focal point for consolidating social consensus. Under the principle of democratic centralism, the Party gathers ideas from various social classes and representative groups to formulate national policies. Hence, the Party and the government can transcend the interests of social groups, maintaining neutrality in the face of potential social conflicts and dedicating themselves to the long-term development of China as a whole.[30] In other developing countries, governments often exhibit the trait of insularity. They are either swayed by interest groups or coerced by populism, and consequently, resources fail to flow toward their optimally efficient allocation. Although many countries do not have a ruling party as strong as the CPC, they can still learn from China's experience of building a neutral government. Through reasonable institutional arrangements, it is possible, even in an electoral democracy, to establish a neutral government. The neutrality of the state is a notion highlighted by Adam Smith as early as in his *The Wealth of Nations.* China exactly embodies Smith's notion of a state, and this is why Giovanni Arrighi named his monumental work on the world system *Adam Smith in Beijing*.[31]

China is still on the road to modernization, and the next 30 years will be a critical sprint phase. If it can complete political and social

[30] Yao Yang. Neutral Government: An Explanation for China's Economic Success during the Transition Period [J]. Economic Review, 2009(3): 5–13.

He Daxing, Yao Yang. Social Equality, Neutral Government and China's Economic Growth [J]. Economic Research, 2011(1): 4–17.

[31] Giovanni Arrighi. Adam Smith in Beijing [M]. Translated by Lu Aiguo, Huang Ping, Xu Anjie. Beijing: Social Sciences Academic Press (China), 2009.

transformation and catch up with the income level of developed countries by 2049, the 100th anniversary of the founding of the People's Republic of China, it will not only have achieved the great rejuvenation of the Chinese nation but also carved out a path of modernization that is uniquely Chinese yet holds global significance. Up to now, China has been the only major country that has not sought external expansion during the peak of modernization, and future historians are destined to write about this at length. Moving forward, China will remain committed to a path of peaceful development and will make a greater contribution to the world.

The Unique Path of Chinese Modernization

Liu Shouying

Modernization is the greatest change in human society since the advent of the written language, marking a departure from traditional social structures. It not only brought about a scientific and technological revolution, a leap in social productivity, and the cumulative growth of the modern economy, but also achieved ideological revolution, institutional innovation, and social transformation. The classic path made Britain and its followers modern countries. But, latecomer countries, as followers, in their pursuit of modernization, have encountered numerous challenges, setbacks, violence, and turmoil while attempting to adopt the institutions and models of predecessors, often falling into various traps from which they could not extricate themselves. As Chinese President Xi Jinping, also General Secretary of the CPC Central Committee, pointed out, "Given the varied historical conditions, it is only natural that different countries may choose different paths of development."[32] The modernization of the Chinese nation commenced under the bombardment of the Western powers, undergoing phases of the transplantation of Western technologies and institutions as well as the adoption of the Soviet model. Ultimately, under the leadership of the CPC, China arduously blazed its path to modernization by adapting Marxism to the Chinese context and adopting a problem-oriented and practice-based approach.

[32] Xi Jinping's Speech at Arab League Headquarters (Full Text) (Chin. ed.) [OL]. [2016-01-22]. http://www.xinhuanet.com/world/2016-01/22/c_1117855467.htm.

The Path to Modernization Is Not Uniform

Modernization Is the Most Intensive, Profound, and Radical Social Change

Modernization is a worldwide phenomenon that began in Western Europe in the fourteenth and fifteenth centuries. Some regions emerged from feudal fragmentation to establish unified modern nation-states, thereby providing the prerequisites for modernization in Western Europe and becoming the starting point of modernization for humanity. The Industrial Revolution in Britain in the eighteenth century led humanity into industrial civilization and also triggered the global impact of modernization—from Western Europe to Central and Eastern Europe, North America, then to West Asia and North Africa, and on to South Asia, East Asia, and South America. By the twentieth century, modernization had become an irreversible trend.[33] It is more than a change of social economy and formation, namely, the profound shift from an agriculture-based society with a low per capita income to an urbanized and industrialized society with a strong emphasis on the use of science and technology.[34] It is a gradual establishment of a brand-new form of civilization (industrial civilization), representing the transformation of human civilization from an agricultural civilization to an industrial civilization. Therefore, modernization is an all-encompassing revolutionary transformation of mankind in all aspects, not only in the economy, but also in politics, society, culture, values, and ideology.

Modernization Is Not Synonymous with Westernization

There are only forerunners and latecomers to modernization, and all economies that are not forerunners are latecomers. Forerunners tend to export their models, while latecomers tend to follow the models and paths of the forerunners. Since the West was the forerunner of modernization, modernization was often unfortunately equated with Westernization, which led to setbacks in the path of modernization for many latecomers. The study of modernization began in the 1950s in the United States with a set of criteria for modernization, labeling those states that met these criteria as "modern" and those that did not as "traditional." According to these criteria, only Western societies were modern, and all other countries were regarded as traditional. When countries that had just emerged from colonial rule began to pursue national construction and transformation,

[33] Edited by Qiang Chengdan,The History of Britain, Volume VI. Jiangsu China: Jiangsu People's Publishing House, 2016.

[34] Edited by Gilbert Rozman,The Modernization of China. New York: The Free Press, 1981.

they could only be considered modern when they aligned with Western standards. Modernization was even given a strong ideological coloring.

Diversified Models and Paths of Modernization

Modernization has taken different models and pathways in different countries and regions, due to vast differences in culture and historical traditions, variations in temporal and environmental conditions, different agents and circumstances involved, and varying ways of thinking and solutions. The pace and model of modernization of a country or region are primarily determined by internal and external factors and the interaction between them. Internal factors reflect the unique historical background of a country or a region, while external factors can exert a great influence on latecomers. While forerunners of modernization mainly rely on the gradual transformation of internal factors, latecomers tend to rely on external factors to accelerate the transformation of internal factors. Modernization itself is the process in which internal and external factors mutually affect and integrate. The commonality of external factors and the particularity of internal factors are intertwined to form a complex and rich picture of modernization in the world.[35] The success of a country or region's modernization depends on whether it can find a path of its own. Paths and models of modernization are affected by various elements. Local culture and history influence the path to modernization; however, similar cultural and historical backgrounds may yield different models, while different cultures and histories may follow similar paths. There is no single "model" that is absolutely right or "good," nor is there a single path that is universally applicable.

Connotation Expansion of Chinese Modernization

After the CPC came to power, China truly began the modernization of this ancient agricultural country, bidding farewell to its rural past.

Transformation from an Agricultural to an Industrial Country

The 7th National Congress of the CPC in 1945 and the 2nd Plenary Session of the 7th CPC Central Committee in 1949 proposed that the goal of constructing a new China, following the victory of the revolution, was to steadily transform China from an agricultural to an industrial country and build China into a great socialist society. Mao Zedong put forward a two-step strategic plan: first, to develop productive forces through industrialization, recover the national economy, complete the transition

[35] Same to footnote 34.

from a semi-colonial and semi-feudal economy to a new-democratic economy and lay the foundation of productive forces and material conditions; second, to achieve the leap from a new-democratic economy to a socialist economy through mutual aid and cooperation as well as collectivization, once socialist elements had accumulated to a certain extent and all the necessary conditions were in place.

Four Modernizations of Industry, Agriculture, Science and Culture, and National Defense

Mao Zedong and other leaders began planning for the modernization of the country after its transition from an agricultural country to an industrial one. At the 1st Session of the 1st National People's Congress in September 1954, Mao Zedong proposed the implementation of several 5-year plans aimed at transforming economically and culturally backward China into "a great industrial country with a high degree of modern culture."[36] In 1954, Zhou Enlai, in his Report on the Work of the Government, explicitly pointed out for the first time that the modernization China sought to achieve encompassed "strong and modernized industry, modernized agriculture, modernized transportation, and modernized national defense."[37] At the 3rd Session of the 1st National People's Congress in June 1956, Li Xiannian characterized a modern China as "a fully modernized and prosperous socialist industrial country."[38] At the 4th Session of the 1st National People's Congress in June–July 1957, Zhou Enlai, in his Report on the Work of the Government, underscored the formidable challenge of "building China into a socialist country with modernized industry and agriculture," pointing out that "achieving victory in this struggle would require not just years, but decades."[39] At the enlarged 11th Session of the Supreme State Conference in February 1957, Mao Zedong expanded the concept of modernization to include science and culture, envisioning the

[36] Mao Zedong. Strive to Build a Great Socialist Country (September 15, 1954) [M]// Documentation Research Office of the CPC Central Committee. Collected Works of Mao Zedong: Volume 6. Beijing: People's Publishing House, 1999.

[37] Zhou Enlai. Report on the Work of the Government (Chin. ed.) [OL]. [2008-03-06]. http://www.gov.cn/test/2008-03/06/content_910658.htm.

[38] Li Xiannian. Reports on the 1955 National Accounts and the 1956 National Budget (Chin. ed.) [OL]. [2008-03-06]. http://www.gov.cn/test/2008-03/06/content_911631.htm.

[39] Zhou Enlai. Report on the Work of the Government (Chin. ed.) [OL]. [2008-03-07]. http://www.gov.cn/test/2008-03/07/content_912288.htm.

establishment of "a socialist country with modern industry, modern agriculture and modern science and culture."[40] From December 1959 to February 1960, when Mao Zedong was reading the Soviet *Textbook on Political Economy*, he clarified all aspects of the four modernizations proposed by the first generation of leadership, stating that "the construction of socialism originally required industrial modernization, agricultural modernization, and modernization of science and culture, and now it must also include modernization of national defense."[41] The 3rd Session of the 2nd National People's Congress in March–April 1962 proposed to "build an independent, complete, and modernized national economic system."[42] The 4th Session of the 2nd National People's Congress in November–December 1963 called on the people of all ethnic groups to "strive to build our country into a powerful socialist country with modern agriculture, modern industry, modern national defense, and modern science and technology."[43] At the First Session of the 3rd National People's Congress, held from December 1964 to January 1965, the proposal was formally put forward to achieve the four modernizations in two stages: "Starting from the beginning of the 3rd Five-Year Plan, China's national economic development can be considered in two steps: first, building independent and relatively complete systems of industry and national economy; second, fully achieving modernizations of agriculture, industry, national defense, and science and technology, positioning our economy at the forefront of the world."[44] At the 1st Session of the 4th National People's Congress in January 1975, Zhou Enlai reiterated the two-step scheme in the Report on the Work of the Government: "first, constructing independent and relatively complete systems of industry and national

[40] Mao Zedong. On the Correct Handling of Contradictions among the People (February 27, 1957) [M]// Documentation Research Office of the CPC Central Committee. Collected Works of Mao Zedong: Volume 7. Beijing: People's Publishing House, 1999.

[41] Conversations on the Soviet Union's *Textbook of Political Economy* (Excerpt) (December 1959–February 1960) [M]// Documentation Research Office of the CPC Central Committee. Collected Works of Mao Zedong: Volume 8. Beijing: People's Publishing House, 1999.

[42] Successful Conclusion of the 3rd Session of the 2nd National People's Congress (Chin. ed.) [OL]. [2008-03-07]. http://www.gov.cn/test/2008-03/07/content_912986.htm.

[43] Press Releases of the 4th Session of the 2nd National People's Congress (Chin. ed.) [OL]. [2008-03-10]. http://www.gov.cn/test/2008-03/10/content_915134.htm.

[44] Zhou Enlai. Major Tasks of National Economic Development (December 21, 1964) [M]// Literature Editorial Committee of the Central Committee of the CPC. Selected Works of Zhou Enlai: Volume 2. Beijing: People's Publishing House, 1984.

economy within 15 years, that is, by 1980; second, fully achieving modernizations of agriculture, industry, national defense, and science and technology within this century, advancing our national economy to the forefront of the world."[45]

Chinese Modernization
After the 3rd Plenary Session of the 11th CPC Central Committee, Deng Xiaoping repeatedly stressed that modernization was crucial to the future and destiny of the country and the Chinese nation. For the first time, he put forward the concept of "Chinese modernization," pointing out, "Our modernization construction must be based on China's realities"[46] and "we must develop a path of modernization that is suitable for China's circumstances."[47] Chinese modernization, first and foremost, must be socialist modernization. He noted, "Many people discuss modernization, yet they forget that the modernization in question is socialist modernization."[48] "Chinese modernization can only rely on socialism, not capitalism."[49] The second aspect is all-around modernization. Deng Xiaoping stressed that our modernization was all-around modernization of the economy, politics, and culture. For the first time, the Report of the 13th CPC National Congress put forward the idea of "building China into a socialist modernized country that is prosperous, democratic and culturally advanced." The third aspect is that modernization encompasses achieving "a moderately prosperous society." Deng Xiaoping explained, "Chinese-style modernization means setting the standards a bit lower. The gross national product, in particular, is not going to be very high in terms

[45] Zhou Enlai. Report on the Work of the Government (Chin. ed.) [OL]. [2008-03-10]. http://www.gov.cn/test/2008-03/10/content_915335.htm.

[46] Deng Xiaoping's Opening Speech at the 12th National Congress of the CPC (Chin. ed.) [OL]. [2012-09-27]. https://fuwu.12371.cn/2012/09/27/ARTI1348710255841791.shtml.

[47] Deng Xiaoping. Adhere to the Four Cardinal Principles (March 30, 1979) [M]// Deng Xiaoping. Selected Works of Deng Xiaoping: The 2nd Volume. 2nd Edition. Beijing: People's Publishing House, 1994.

[48] Deng Xiaoping. China Can Only Follow the Socialist Path (March 3, 1987) [M]// Deng Xiaoping. Selected Works of Deng Xiaoping: Volume 3. Beijing: People's Publishing House, 1993.

[49] Deng Xiaoping. Learn From Historical Experience and Prevent Erroneous Tendencies (April 30, 1987) [M]// Deng Xiaoping. Selected Works of Deng Xiaoping: Volume 3. Beijing: People's Publishing House, 1993.

of per capita value."[50] "The so-called 'moderately prosperous', in terms of the gross national product, means reaching $800 per capita per year."[51] To this end, the three-step strategy was proposed: first, doubling the gross national product compared to 1980 and solving the problem of food and clothing; second, reaching a moderately prosperous standard of living by the end of the twentieth century; third, basically achieving modernization by the mid-twenty-first century.

Comprehensive, Coordinated Modernization with Scientific Development
With the remarkable progress made in the reform and opening up and the substantial improvement in the material living standards of the people, China's modernization embraces a richer connotation and a bigger goal. The first is modernization with comprehensive and coordinated development. This not only highlights modern economy, politics, and culture, but also advocates for "mutual coordination and comprehensive development," stating that "not only should the economy improve, but the moral, scientific, and cultural quality of the people, as well as social order and social ethos, must also be enhanced." The second is a moderately prosperous society at a higher level in all respects. The 15th National Congress of the CPC put forward the goal: "on the basis of economic development, to enable all people to achieve a moderately prosperous life, and gradually advance to a higher level." The 16th National Congress proposed that "When human society steps into the twentieth century, China will enter a new development stage of building a moderately prosperous society in all respects and accelerating the advancement of socialist modernization." As a result, the "new three-step strategy" and "Two Centenary Goals" were introduced. The 15th National Congress of the CPC declared that "In the first decade, the GNP should be doubled compared with that of 2000, and people will lead a better-off life by the time of the Party's centenary. The national economy will be more developed and various systems will be further improved; by the middle of the century, that is, upon the 100th anniversary of the founding of the People's Republic of China, we will have basically realized modernization and built a prosperous, democratic, and

[50] Deng Xiaoping. Some Opinions on Economic Work (October 4, 1979) [M]// Deng Xiaoping. Selected Works of Deng Xiaoping: Volume 2. 2nd Edition. Beijing: People's Publishing House, 1994.

[51] Deng Xiaoping. Build Socialism with Chinese Characteristics (June 30, 1984) [M]// Deng Xiaoping. Selected Works of Deng Xiaoping: Volume 3. Beijing: People's Publishing House, 1993.

culturally advanced country." The 16th National Congress of the CPC reiterated that "In the first two decades of this century, we will concentrate on building a well-off society of a higher standard in an all-round way benefiting more than one billion people."

As modernization deepened and the problems of imbalance and inconsistencies in socio-economic development came to the fore, the CPC Central Committee, with Comrade Hu Jintao at its core, set forth the scientific outlook on development, "which is people-oriented and calls for comprehensive, balanced and sustainable development," promoting the all-round development of the economy, society and humanity. The first key element is "five aspects of coordination." The 3rd Plenary Session of the 16th CPC Central Committee called for "promoting a balanced growth between urban and rural areas, different regions, economic and social undertakings, man and nature as well as domestic progress and opening-up to the world." This approach emphasizes the coordinated development of socio-economic factors and the relationship between humans and nature, based on the development of productive forces, thereby deepening and broadening the connotation of socialist modernization. Social construction, along with economic, political, and cultural construction, is included in the scope of the social modernization drive. The Constitution of the Communist Party of China, as amended after the 17th CPC National Congress, proposed the goal of "building China into a great modern socialist country that is prosperous, strong, democratic, culturally advanced, harmonious, and beautiful." The second key element is building a moderately prosperous society in all respects. The 17th CPC National Congress highlighted the objectives of "continuing to build a moderately prosperous society in all respects and accelerate socialist modernization, and accomplishing the lofty mission bestowed by the times." The third key aspect is to adhere to the Two Centenary Goals. The 17th CPC National Congress reaffirmed that: "We have made steady progress toward the goal of building a moderately prosperous society in all respects set at the 16th National Congress, and we will continue to work hard to ensure its attainment by 2020."

Building China into a Great Modern Socialist Country in All Respects
Since the 18th CPC National Congress, the CPC Central Committee, with Comrade Xi Jinping at its core, has made a major judgment based on domestic and international situations. Socialism with Chinese characteristics has entered a new era. Since then, socialist modernization has been

endowed with new connotations and richer content. The first is the proposal of the harmonized development of industrialization, informatization, urbanization, and agricultural modernization. The 18th CPC National Congress stated, "We should keep to the Chinese-style path of carrying out industrialization in a new way and advancing informatization, urbanization and agricultural modernization. We should promote integration of informatization and industrialization, interaction between industrialization and urbanization, and coordination between urbanization and agricultural modernization, thus promoting harmonized development of industrialization, informatization, urbanization and agricultural modernization." The second is the proposal of a modern civilization. The construction of an ecological civilization, together with economic, political, cultural, and social construction, was incorporated into socialist modernization, and the 19th CPC National Congress put forward the goal of "a modern socialist country that is prosperous, strong, democratic, culturally advanced, harmonious, and beautiful." The third is to build a moderately prosperous society in all respects. General Secretary Xi Jinping declared that "By 2020, the GDP and per capita income of urban and rural residents will double that of 2010, and a moderately prosperous society benefiting more than a billion people will be built in all respects."[52] The fourth is the rural revitalization strategy. The 19th CPC National Congress designated the rural revitalization strategy as "a major historical task for securing the success of building a moderately prosperous society in all respects and fully building a modern socialist China." The 19th CPC National Congress proposed a two-step strategic plan for building China into a great modern socialist country in all respects in the new era. "The first stage, from 2020 to 2035, is to build on the foundation of the moderately prosperous society and work hard for another 15 years to basically realize socialist modernization. The second stage, from 2035 to the middle of the twenty-first century, will see us building on having achieved basic modernization and working hard for a further 15 years to develop China into a great modern socialist country that is prosperous, strong, democratic, culturally advanced, harmonious, and beautiful."

[52] Xi Jinping's Keynote Speech at the Fifth BRICS Summit (Chin. ed.) [OL]. [2013-03-28]. https://www.12371.cn/2013/03/28/ARTI1364400205944353.shtml.

Dynamics of Chinese Modernization

An important driving force behind Chinese modernization is the achievement of modernization catch-up through structural construction and continuous institutional reform.

Promoting the Transformation of an Agricultural Country Through the New-Democratic System

The CPC ascribes the crisis of modern China to the semi-colonial and semi-feudal nature of its society. To change the impoverished and weakened state of old China, it was essential to "change the status of the present colonial, semi-colonial and semi-feudal society."[53] In December 1939, Mao Zedong defined the new-democratic nature of the Chinese revolution as follows: "The present bourgeois democratic revolution in China is a new type of special bourgeois democratic revolution ... which we call the new democratic revolution." "Economically, it takes over capitalistic enterprises operated by imperialists and traitors and reactionaries under state management, allocates landlords' land to peasants, and preserves private capitalistic enterprises in general while not abolishing the economy of the wealthy peasants."[54] In January 1940, Mao Zedong elaborated on the economic forms of the new democracy. "The state-owned economy under the leadership of the proletariat of the new democratic republic is socialist in nature and is the leading force in the national economy as a whole. However, the new democratic republic does not confiscate other forms of capitalist private property, nor does it prohibit the development of capitalist production that is 'incapable of manipulating people's livelihood'"; in rural areas, "socialist agriculture is not yet generally established, but various forms of cooperative economies developed on the basis of 'land to the tiller' also contain socialist elements." Additionally, "necessary measures will be taken to confiscate landlords' land and distribute it to landless peasants or those with little land," while "the economy of wealthy peasants will also be permitted to exist."[55] In December 1947, Mao Zedong explained the economic structure of the new democracy. "In general, the new China's economy encompasses: (1) State-owned economy, which is the

[53] Mao Zedong. Chinese Revolution and the Communist Party of China (December 1939) [M]// Mao Zedong. Selected Works of Mao Zedong: Volume 2. 2nd Edition. Beijing: People's Publishing House, 1991.

[54] Same to footnote 50.

[55] Mao Zedong. On New Democracy (January 1940) [M]// Mao Zedong. Selected Works of Mao Zedong: Volume 2. 2nd Edition. Beijing: People's Publishing House, 1991.

leading element; (2) Agricultural economy that is gradually developing from individual to collective ownership; (3) The economy of small independent industrialists and businesses, and small and medium-sized private capitalist economy. These elements collectively defined the entire national economy of the new democracy."[56] In September 1948, Mao Zedong further delineated the relations among various economic components of the new democracy. "This country is led by the proletariat, so all these economies are socialist in nature. Although the rural individual economy and the urban private economy are numerically large, they do not play a decisive role. The state-owned economy and the public sector, which is smaller in quantity, play a decisive role. It is better to refer to our socio-economic system as the 'New Democratic Economy.'"[57] In January 1949, Mao Zedong underscored the institutional features of the new-democratic economy. On the one hand, we must guard against the misconception that the new-democratic economy is neither a planned economy nor one moving toward socialism, for it is absolutely wrong to regard it instead as a system of free trade and free competition leading to capitalism. On the other hand, we must be highly vigilant and prudent, avoiding rushing into socialization.[58] The CPC began the construction of a new-democratic system around the time of its revolutionary victory. The 2nd Plenary Session of the 7th CPC Central Committee formulated the policies of the new democracy, which included: confiscating bureaucratic capital to the ownership of the People's Republic, establishing and vigorously developing a socialist state-owned economy; utilizing while restricting the private capitalist economy; transforming landlord landownership into a peasant landownership system through land reform; and, guiding peasants toward collaboration and collectivization in a "prudent, gradual and active" manner; and implementing unified management of foreign trade. Through the establishment and construction of the new-democratic system, the semi-colonial and semi-feudal economic structure was dismantled, and socialist

[56] Mao Zedong. The Present Situation and Our Tasks (December 25, 1947) [M]// Mao Zedong. Selected Works of Mao Zedong: Volume 4. 2nd Edition. Beijing: People's Publishing House, 1991.

[57] Mao Zedong. Report and Conclusion at the Meeting of the Political Bureau of the CPC Central Committee [M]// Documentation Research Office of the CPC Central Committee. Selected Works of Mao Zedong: Volume 5. Beijing: People's Publishing House, 1996.

[58] Mao Zedong and the 2nd Plenary Session of the 7th CPC Central Committee (Chin. ed.) [OL]. [2019-12-05]. http://dangshi.people.com.cn/n1/2019/1205/c85037-31491454.html?ivk_sa=1025883i.

elements were integrated into the economic system. This laid the material basis and conditions for the establishment of a socialist economic structure and ultimately facilitated the transformation from an agricultural country to an industrialized one.

Advancing National Industrialization Through the Socialist System and Planned Economy

After the founding of the People's Republic of China, the rapid recovery of the national economy, coupled with changes in the international environment, led the first generation of Party leaders, with Comrade Mao Zedong at its core, to decide to follow China's own path. The goal was to catch up with developed countries through the "four modernizations." China opted for an economic development strategy focused on heavy industry and the accelerated construction of a national economic system. To achieve this, China pursued heavy-industry-oriented national industrialization, guided by socialist ideals and goals. In 1953, China began its transition toward socialism and initiated the establishment of a centralized planned economy. The socialist system was essentially established through the "three socialist transformations." In September 1952, Mao Zedong developed the general line for the transition period. In December 1953, he stated, "This is a transition period, from the founding of the People's Republic to the basic completion of the socialist transformation. The general line and task of the Party for this transition period is to gradually accomplish China's socialist industrialization, as well as the socialist transformation of agriculture, the handicraft industry, and capitalist industry and commerce, over a fairly long period of time."[59] In February 1954, after the 4th Plenary Session of the 7th CPC Central Committee, the socialist transformation was formally launched. This transformation included: the socialist transformation of individual agriculture through the gradual formation of agricultural cooperatives, starting with mutual-aid groups followed by primary cooperatives, and eventually advanced cooperatives; the socialist transformation of individual handicrafts through the transition from production groups to supply and marketing cooperatives,

[59] Strive to Mobilize All Forces to Build China into a Great Socialist Country—Outline for the Study and Publicity of the Party's General Line During the Transition Period [M]// Documentation Research Office of the CPC Central Committee. Selected Important Documents Since the Founding of the People's Republic of China (1949–1965): Volume 4. Beijing: Central Party Literature Press, 2011.

and then to fully socialist production cooperatives; and the transformation of capitalist industry and commerce through public-private partnership. Between 1949 and 1956, China had largely completed the socialist transformation of agriculture, the handicraft industry, and capitalist industry and commerce, thus uprooting the system that had sustained a rural China for thousands of years. This transition marked a shift from a new democracy to socialism for a large Eastern country with a relatively backward economy and culture, ultimately establishing a socialist system. Furthermore, a socialist planned economic system was established. After the establishment of the socialist system, the country chose a highly centralized planned economy to carry out the four modernizations of industry, agriculture, national defense, science and technology, in order to accumulate the necessary capital for industrialization as quickly as possible. The main measures included: the abolition of the capitalist economy and private economies, replaced by a single socialist system of public ownership; the implementation of a unified distribution system according to labor; the implementation of a highly centralized planned economy, which abolished commodities and markets and created national plans; and the implementation of agricultural collectivization, through the establishment of a "three-level ownership and group-based" collective ownership system. The establishment of the socialist planned economy laid an institutional foundation for national industrialization.

Promoting Chinese Modernization Through Socialist Market System Reform

The highly centralized planned economic system severely impeded the development of social productive forces, leading to widespread poverty and a widening gap between China and developed countries. China was on the verge of "being expelled from the game." The 3rd Plenary Session of the 11th CPC Central Committee marked the beginning of economic reforms, initiating the transformation of the socialist market system and setting China on a monumental journey toward Chinese-style modernization, with the socialist system with Chinese characteristics serving as the fundamental framework for this advancement. In December 1978, the 3rd Plenary Session of the 11th CPC Central Committee reaffirmed the ideological line of "emancipate the mind and seek truth from facts." In September 1982, in his opening speech at the 12th CPC National Congress, Deng Xiaoping proposed the idea of "building socialism with

Chinese characteristics."[60] In October 1984, the 3rd Plenary Session of the 12th CPC Central Committee outlined that the socialist planned economy was "the planned commodity economy based on public ownership," making it clear that China would remain in the primary stage of socialism for a long period of time. This session set the institutional framework for this stage. The first aspect of this framework was to uphold and improve the basic economic system, with public ownership as the mainstay and multiple forms of ownership developing together. The 15th CPC National Congress emphasized that "public ownership being dominant and diverse forms of ownership developing side by side is a basic economic system at the primary stage of socialism in China." The 16th CPC National Congress further proposed to "unwaveringly consolidate and develop the public-owned economy" and "unswervingly encourage, support and guide the development of the non-public sector of the economy" ; the 17th CPC National Congress proposed "we need to ensure equal protection of property rights, and create a new situation in which all economic sectors compete on an equal footing and reinforce each other." The second aspect was to uphold and improve the socialist market economy system. China's economic system reform evolved from a dominant planned economy supplemented by market regulation, to a socialist planned commodity economy, and ultimately toward the internal unity of economic planning and market mechanisms. The 14th CPC National Congress established the target model for the socialist market economy system; the 3rd Plenary Session of the 14th CPC Central Committee further put forward the basic framework for the socialist market economy system; the 15th CPC National Congress and the 5th Plenary Session of the 16th CPC Central Committee linked the development of the market economy with the realization of economic marketization under the primary stage of socialism, making a breakthrough in the reform of the socialist market economy system. The 17th CPC National Congress emphasized the need to give the market forces a "basic role" in allocating resources. The third aspect was to adhere to and improve the system, whereby distribution according to labor remains the predominant model while coexisting with various other models. This included allowing some regions and people to get rich first and helping others to achieve prosper-

[60] Deng Xiaoping. Opening Speech at the 12th CPC National Congress (September 1, 1982) [M]// Deng Xiaoping. Selected Works of Deng Xiaoping Volume 3. Beijing: People's Publishing House, 1993.

ity, thereby gradually moving toward common prosperity. The goal was to gradually form a system that combines distribution according to labor with distribution according to the factors of production. This system would involve improving the distribution of income in accordance with labor, capital, technology, managerial expertise, and other production factors, based on their respective contributions. The aim was to strike a balance between fairness and efficiency and to rectify the distribution order and gradually reverse the trend of widening income disparities by safeguarding legitimate income, adjusting excessive income, and prohibiting illegal income. The identification of the primary stage of socialism and the deepening of reform in the market economy system mobilized the enthusiasm of all parties and entities, raised the efficiency of resource allocation, and provided an institutional guarantee for Chinese modernization.

Developing the Institutional Foundation for a Great Modern Socialist Country: Based on General Secretary Xi Jinping Thought on Socialism with Chinese Characteristics for a New Era

Since the 18th CPC National Congress, the CPC Central Committee, with Comrade Xi Jinping at its core, has adhered to the direction of reforming the socialist market economy, continuously advanced the development and improvement of the socialist market economy, and reformed the relationship between the socialist ownership structure and the market economic system, and refined the relationship between the market and the government in various ways. It was made clear that the basic economic system, in which public ownership is the mainstay and economic entities of diverse ownership develop together, is a major pillar of the socialist system with Chinese characteristics and an essential requirement for improving the socialist market economic system. The CPC Central Committee has consistently upheld the principle of "unswervingly consolidating and developing the public sector, and encouraging, supporting and guiding the development of the non-public sector," fostering a complementary and mutually reinforcing relationship among all forms of ownership for common development. The CPC Central Committee has also made it clear that the market plays the decisive role in resource allocation, while the government should better fulfill its role. These two elements are not mutually exclusive or contradictory, but rather are compatible and unified. The 19th CPC National Congress established the guiding position of General Secretary Xi Jinping's thought on socialism with Chinese characteristics for a new era, strengthening the Party's centralized guidance and unified leadership on economic work. It emphasized the people-centered development philosophy, adhered to adapting to, grasping and guiding the new normal in economic development, and advanced supply-side structural reform as the main focus of economic work. In doing so, it concentrated on solving problems and deploying a new strategy for economic development. With the goals of General Secretary Xi Jinping's thought on socialism with Chinese characteristics for a new era and the vision of building a moderately prosperous society in all respects, efforts were made to promote material, political, cultural and ethical, social, and ecological progress. These efforts aim to create a new form of human civilization and develop China into a great modern socialist country.

Unique Features of Chinese Modernization

The greatest challenge of a country's modernization is to achieve and even expand universality through its distinctive characteristics. Chinese modernization is a journey in which China constantly recognizes and leverages its particularities to reach the goal of modernization.

Characteristics and Role of the Communist Party of China

National capacity is a necessary condition for a country's modernization. The CPC plays a pivotal role in the course of Chinese modernization by virtue of its exceptional organizational and leadership abilities. The first is its unique values. Since modern times, the Chinese nation has been confronted with two historical tasks: achieving national independence and liberation, as well as building a strong and prosperous nation and ensuring the well-being of its people. The CPC has undertaken the historical mission of "seeking happiness for the Chinese people and rejuvenation for the Chinese nation" since its establishment. It is this mission that has enabled the CPC to surmount unimaginable risks, challenges, and hardships throughout the arduous journey of Chinese modernization, ultimately transforming the state of total disunity and warlord domination that existed in modern China. The second is its unique organizational capability. The CPC gathers excellent members from society through strict organizational procedures and screening mechanisms, providing space for their growth and development through distinctive personnel selection and training systems. Unlike the Western political electoral party system, the party-state regime with Chinese characteristics secures the core position of the CPC in leading the country's modernization and development strategies. To guarantee the scientific decision-making and "ensure that the Party will never change its nature, its aspiration, or its character"[61] has become a key to maintaining the organizational advantages of the CPC for a long time. The CPC's solutions to these challenges are that it relies on democratic centralism to address organizational deliberation and decision-making challenges, and it relies on self-supervision and self-purification to maintain vitality. General Secretary Xi Jinping pointed out, "A hallmark that distinguishes the Communist Party of China from other political parties is its courage in undertaking self-reform."[62]He also emphasized, "Uncompromisingly practice effective self-supervision and exert full and rigorous Party self-governance"[63] and "Ensure that the Party always remains at the forefront of the times even as profound changes sweep the global landscape, and stands firm as the backbone of the nation throughout the process of risks and challenges at home and abroad."[64] The third is exceptional leadership. The CPC maintains and enhances its leadership in advancing Chinese modernization by adapting Marxism to China's realities, focusing on problem-solving, formulating and employing programs, paths, principles, and policies, and adhering to the principle that development is of primary importance to China and that development is for the people. This ensures the Party's directional positioning, cohesion, and advanced nature.

China's National Condition Based on a Huge Population

The biggest constraint affecting the success of a country's modernization is its national conditions. Countries that failed in modernization either neglected their national conditions at the outset or deviated from them in the process of modernization. China's modernization represents a transformation within its basic national context, characterized by a huge population that has nurtured an agricultural civilization for thousands of years. The main obstacle facing Chinese modernization is the need to reduce excessive dependence on land within the existing man–land relationship.

[61] Resolution of the Central Committee of the Communist Party of China on Major Achievements and Historical Experience of the Party over the Past Century (Chin. ed.) [OL]. [2021-11-16]. http://www.gov.cn/zhengce/2021-11/16/content_5651269.htm.

[62] Same to footnote 58.

[63] Xi Jinping. Speech at a Ceremony Marking the Centenary of the Communist Party of China (Chin. ed.) [OL]. [2021-07-01]. http://www.gov.cn/xinwen/2021-07/01/content_5621847.htm.

[64] Same to footnote 50.

On the one hand, the Party has put great emphasis on issues concerning agriculture, rural areas, and farmers, recognizing the well-being of rural people as central to national stability and development, particularly prioritizing land-related issues as central to Chinese modernization. During the revolutionary period, the land revolution reconstructed the relationship between peasants and landowners, enabling peasants to acquire land, thereby winning both power and the support of peasants. After coming to power, the CPC mobilized the majority of peasants through land reform, laying an institutional foundation for agricultural production recovery and the organization of agricultural cooperatives. During the reform and opening up, the reform of the household contract responsibility system and the long-term stability of land tenure provided institutional guarantees for rural development and the transformation of peasants. In the new era, the reform separating rural land ownership rights, contract rights, and management rights, along with the unified market of urban–rural land, laid the foundation for the modernization of agriculture and rural areas. In addition to winning the support of the people through land-related measures, the Party has continuously stressed the importance of the issues pertaining to rural people and rural areas, increasing the proportion of national expenditure on agriculture and rural areas, striving to break down the urban–rural dual system, and resolving issues such as employment, social security, healthcare, and elderly care for rural people. This promotes equitable access to basic public services in urban and rural areas. The rural vitalization strategy was elevated to the level of a national strategy. On the other hand, the Party has leveraged China's distinctive land system to foster development, striving to free rural people from the constraints imposed by land and accelerate industrialization and urbanization in China. In the early stages of the reform and opening up, rural people were allowed to use collective land to run township enterprises, thereby initiating rural industrialization and providing a channel for rural people to engage in non-agricultural employment and increase their incomes. After the late 1990s, the Party leveraged land capitalization to accelerate urbanization. Endeavors were made to set up industrial parks on low-priced land, creating a global manufacturing hub that enabled the inter-regional mobility of rural people and allowed them to share the fruits of industrialization. Entering the new era, the Party has made concerted efforts to promote people-centered new urbanization, granting farmers with urban rights, facilitating their integration into urban life, and advancing China's historical transformation from an "rural China" to an "urban–rural China."

China's Pursuit of Its Own Path of Development

Global experience shows that transplanting institutions and models cannot achieve a country's modernization smoothly. Chinese modernization is a journey seeking, exploring, and building its own path, ultimately forming a unique socialist path with Chinese characteristics. During the revolutionary period, the Party's leadership in the Chinese revolution frequently encountered "left-wing" and "right-wing" subjectivism. After August 1927, the Chinese revolution faced a choice between two paths: one was to blindly replicate the model of the Russian October Revolution and pursue a city-centered uprising; the other was to, based on China's specific conditions, adopt the strategy of "encircling the cities from the countryside and seizing power through armed struggle." The first generation of leaders, with Comrade Mao Zedong at its core, combined the basic principles of Marxism with China's realities and pioneered a revolutionary path of "encircling the cities from the countryside and seizing power through armed struggle." This laid the foundation of political power for Chinese modernization. After the establishment of the People's Republic of China, the Party faced a new and formidable task: how to complete the socialist revolution and how to lead national construction. The Soviet Union, the first socialist country in human history, undoubtedly provided valuable historical experience for socialist construction, which was worth learning from. However, the shortcomings and problems of the Soviet model were introduced to China, leading to setbacks in the country's economic construction as it "copied Soviet methods." On February 25, 1956, Mao Zedong clearly stated, "In the past, we avoided some mistakes by learning from their experiences and lessons; now we must be even more cautious and learn from their mistakes."[65] At the 20th Congress of the Communist Party of the Soviet Union, Nikita S. Khrushchev exposed the flaws and mistakes of the Soviet socialist construction model, which accelerated the CPC's exploration of its own path to modernization. The CPC shifted from "learning from the Soviet Union" to "taking the Soviet Union as a cautionary example." Taking into account China's unique development stage and characteristics, it began building a comprehensive industrial system, laying the material foundation for Chinese modernization.

[65] Mao Zedong. On the Ten Major Relationships (April 25, 1956) [M]// Mao Zedong. Selected Works of Mao Zedong: Volume 5. Beijing: People's Publishing House, 1977.

After the end of the Great Cultural Revolution (1966–1976), the Chinese Communists, with Comrade Deng Xiaoping as their chief representative, deeply analyzed and understood the characteristics of the era of peace and development. It accurately assessed China's national conditions, thoroughly reviewed both the positive and negative experiences of China's socialist construction, and drew lessons from global socialist history. The Party made the historic decision to shift the focus of the Party and the state work toward economic development and to implement the reform and opening up policies. It also developed a deep and accurate understanding of the essence of socialism, established the basic line for the primary stage of socialism, and explicitly put forward the idea of taking China's own path to build socialism with Chinese characteristics. Regarding questions like "how long will the red flag last?," where the CPC was headed, and whether the road of socialism with Chinese characteristics could continue, comrade Jiang Zemin emphasized, "Chinese socialism is neither the Soviet Union model nor the Eastern European model, but socialism with Chinese characteristics. This path is the historical choice made by the Chinese people after more than a century of struggle and exploration."[66] As China's reforms have entered deeper waters, various contradictions and problems have surfaced, including an irrational economic structure, unscientific patterns of growth, development restricted by limited environmental resources, and unfair distribution. Comrade Hu Jintao put forward the "people-centered" scientific outlook on development and the Five-Sphere Integrated Plan, addressing the central question of the times: "What kind of development should we pursue, and how should we achieve it?" In the new era, the CPC, with Comrade Xi Jinping at its core, adopted a forward-thinking perspective. Based on a renewed understanding of principal social contradictions, the Party formulated a strategic plan for the development of socialism with Chinese characteristics in the new era, proposing the supply-side structural reform as the main line for building a modern economic system. Grounded in a new stage of development, implementing the new development philosophy, and navigating the new development paradigm, the Party achieved a comprehensive victory in the fight against poverty and the historic achievement of building a moderately prosperous society in all respects.

[66] Documentation Research Office of the CPC Central Committee. Annual Compilation of Jiang Zemin Thought: 1989~2008 [M]. Beijing: Central Party Literature Press, 2010.

For the People, By the People

General Secretary Xi Jinping pointed out, "This country is its people; the people are the country. As the Communist Party of China has led the people in fighting to establish and develop the People's Republic, it has really been fighting for their support."[67] He also stated, "The people are both the creators and the observers of history and both its protagonists and playwrights."[68] Whether leading revolution, promoting development, or advancing reform, the Communist Party of China has always relied on the people and worked for the people; likewise, Chinese modernization is also carried out by the people and for the people. During the revolutionary period, the Party gained power by resolving the land issues of peasants. In the period of social construction, the Party relied on the accumulated wealth of the peasants and the low wages of urban residents to ensure the implementation of the country's industrialization strategy. During the reform period, the Party gave full play to the wisdom and strength of the people, sparking the creativity of the masses, resulting in the world-renowned "Chinese Miracle." The Party, adhering to a people-centered development approach, in the new era, has achieved historic milestones of eliminating absolute poverty and building a moderately prosperous society in all respects. The fundamental purpose of Chinese modernization is to serve the people. The people are the most crucial subject of Chinese modernization. Chinese modernization ensures that the benefits of development are more equally distributed among the population, keeping pace with people's ever-growing needs for a better life.

To secure the interests of the people, the Party, through reforms, regional poverty alleviation, and targeted poverty alleviation, has made a great historic achievement of eradicating the world's largest scale of absolute poverty and reached the goal of building a moderately prosperous society in all respects. China's structural transformation has urbanized 64.72% of its total population and quickened the urbanization of rural migrant workers. Meanwhile, the Party has paid attention to well-rounded human development. At the inception of the People's Republic of China, 80% of the population was illiterate, and the enrollment rate for

[67] Xi Jinping. Speech at a Ceremony Marking the Centenary of the Communist Party of China (Chin. ed.) [OL]. [2021-07-01]. http://www.gov.cn/xinwen/2021-07/01/content_5621847.htm.

[68] Xi Jinping. Remarks at a Conference on Literary and Artistic Work (Chin. ed.) [OL]. [2015-10-14]. http://www.xinhuanet.com/politics/2015-10/14/c_1116825558.htm.

school-age children was less than 20%. By 2021, there were 2,756 regular colleges and universities throughout the country, with a total enrollment in various forms of higher education reaching 44.3 million, resulting in a gross enrollment rate of 57.8%. The average life expectancy at that time was only 35 years; by 2019, this indicator had risen to 78.2 years, with urban residents exceeding an average life expectancy of 80 years. Key health indicators are surpassing the average levels of middle-income countries globally. The social security system has gradually been established, with its coverage continually expanding and a multi-tiered social security framework being continuously improved. The basic medical insurance scheme now covers more than 1.3 billion people, while the basic pension insurance scheme extends to nearly 1 billion people.

After achieving the First Centenary Goal of building a moderately prosperous society, China is now pursuing the Second Centenary Goal of building a modern socialist country. The 19th CPC National Congress made a two-stage strategic arrangement for the Second Centenary Goal. To achieve this goal, China must take a path of its own, building a modern country that is respected worldwide and makes a significant contribution to human civilization. To this end, China must overcome the challenges that hinder its modernization in the new journey ahead.

The first challenge is how to achieve comprehensive modernization. Most countries pursuing modernization take industrialization and urbanization as their ultimate goals, often leading to a lag in agricultural modernization and unresolved issues related to rural populations. In the process of modernization, China also encountered accelerated industrialization and urbanization alongside the delayed modernization of agriculture and the urbanization of its rural population. On this new journey, the Party has called for the synchronous development in industrialization, urbanization, informatization, and agricultural modernization—collectively known as the "Four Modernizations"—to prevent structural imbalance in modernization. For a country like China, with a huge population and a high proportion of rural residents, the synchronous modernization of agriculture and rural populations is particularly crucial.

Instead of taking the old development model of 'pollute first, clean up later' or transferring pollution elsewhere. We must pursue a path of green development that aims for a harmonious coexistence between humanity and nature. To surpass the traditional capitalist model of industrial civilization, it is imperative to fundamentally transform the conventional approach to development and implement a sustainable development strategy by respecting, adapting to, and protecting nature, in order to promote a comprehensive green transformation of economic and social development.

Some countries that have already achieved or are pursuing modernization often regard a certain level of material well-being as the sole criterion for modernization, neglecting the importance of spiritual and cultural development, which can lead to alienation and distortion in the course of modernization. For modernization to succeed, we must balance material and spiritual advancement. It is not enough for people to have sufficient food and other daily needs; they must also live with dignity and a strong sense of morality. Achieving this balance is a key goal for modern societies, but it is also extremely difficult. To attain it, we must shift away from a singular focus on GDP and place greater emphasis on values, cultural soft power, and the spiritual pursuits of individuals.

The second challenge is how to achieve well-rounded human development and common prosperity for all. Polarization is the ultimate challenge faced by all modern countries and stands as the greatest difficulty in China's new development journey. Common prosperity is the fundamental principle and ultimate goal of scientific socialism, and it is also the main task of socialism with Chinese characteristics in the new era. In our quest for common prosperity in the new journey to build a modern socialist country, we certainly cannot promote egalitarianism at the expense of the motivation of the majority of workers, nor implement redistributive policies that compromise individuals' aspirations for wealth accumulation. We must not impose a one-size-fits-all approach to equalize incomes and property among different groups and classes, or pursue the impractical goal of uniform development across various regions. The common prosperity we strive for includes two aspects. The first is "prosperity," which refers to the comprehensive improvement of people's living standards. The second is "common," which encompasses a reduction in inequality, a notable decrease in urban–rural and regional disparities, a significant narrowing of income and property gaps among residents, the equalization of basic public services, the expansion of the middle-income group, and, after all, the benefits of economic development being shared by all citizens.

The third challenge is how to construct a modern country and modernize China's governance system and capacity. For any country, the most challenging task in modernization is how to build a modern state that fits its national context. Every country aspiring to become modern must address the institutionalization of public power. Chinese civilization has a long history of centralized governance, spanning over 2000 years. The

CPC, with its unique organizational and leadership characteristics, achieved effective governance during the periods of revolution, construction, and reform. In the course of building a modern country, the construction of a modern national governance system under the leadership of the CPC is the key to the Second Centenary Goal. Not every country will achieve modernization, but the common feature of every fortunate one is the establishment of open access orders within its borders. In order to realize the Second Centenary Goal, China must uphold the leadership of the CPC and continuously improve the system of socialism with Chinese characteristics, realizing the construction of a modern state in China by the institutionalization of open rights.

Connotation and Requirements of China's Economic Modernization

Huang Hanquan

Building a modernized economic system is a major strategic decision made by the CPC Central Committee from the perspective of the overall development of the Party and the country. It aims to achieve the "Two Centenary Goals" and meet the new requirements of socialism with Chinese characteristics as the country enters a new era. General Secretary Xi Jinping pointed out that a strong country requires a strong economy. The construction of a modernized economic system is not only a key component but also a determining factor in building a strong modern socialist country. Only with a modernized economic system can China better adapt to the trend of modernization, seize the initiative in international competition, and provide an economic foundation and strong support for modernization in other fields. China is now embarking on the new journey of building a strong socialist modern country and advancing the great rejuvenation of the Chinese nation through Chinese-style modernization. It is of great significance to keenly understand the position and role of economic modernization within the broader context of Chinese modernization, accurately grasp its connotations and requirements, and identify effective points of action and implementation pathways to ensure the smooth progress of China's modernization efforts.

Modernization of the Economic System Is a Crucial Foundation for the Chinese Modernization

Modernization has been a sweeping historical change in human society since the Industrial Revolution. It encompasses both the modernization of productive forces and the modernization of production relations, involving all aspects of the economy and society. As Karl Marx pointed out, the production of material goods is the basis for the existence and development of human society. Economic modernization plays a fundamental role in the overall strategy of modernization. Throughout the history of global modernization, the central task of all modernization efforts has been the development of productive forces. Without strong economic power and the capacity to drive growth, it is impossible to establish a material basis for a great modern country, and the modernization of other fields will lack economic support. It can be said that economic modernization is not only the main battlefield and core content of a country's modernization but also a vital source of momentum for the entire modernization process.

As far as China is concerned, the modernization of the economic system serves as a crucial foundation for Chinese modernization. Modernization is a common pursuit of all developing countries, but it varies from country to country due to differences in development stages, political systems, economic systems, cultural backgrounds, and others. Not all countries follow the same path to modernization. Chinese modernization will not only abide by the general laws of modernization but will also have its own features. General Secretary Xi Jinping pointed out, "Western developed countries underwent a 'sequential development' model, progressing through industrialization, urbanization, agricultural modernization and informatization in linear order over two centuries to reach their current level. As a latecomer, China must overtake them and reclaim the lost two centuries. This is why China must follow a 'parallel-track' process, where industrialization, informatization, urbanization and agricultural modernization must progress simultaneously in an overlapping manner."[69] The modernization of the economic system exactly exemplifies the features of parallel modernization, embodying the characteristics of a Chinese-style modernization.

[69] Documentation Research Office of the CPC Central Committee. Compilation of Xi Jinping's Remarks on Socialist Economic Construction [M]. Beijing: Central Party Literature Press, 2017.

Furthermore, building a modernized economic system is an urgent requirement for overcoming critical challenges and the only way to achieve high-quality development. According to the Report from the 19th CPC National Congress, China's economy has been transitioning from a phase of rapid growth to a stage of high-quality development. This is a pivotal stage for transforming the growth model, improving the economic structure, and fostering new drivers of growth. It is essential to recognize that China still faces a series of risks and challenges, such as low development quality, significant contradictions between resources and the environment, considerable regional and urban–rural gaps, and bottlenecks in economic circulation. To resolve these contradictions and facilitate the transition, China must base itself on the new development stage, fully implement the new development philosophy, create a new economic dynamic, make substantial progress in high-quality development, promote common prosperity, and coordinate development and security. These are central to building a modernized economic system.

The Modernized Economic System: A More Systematic and Complete Framework

The modernized economic system is a concept put forward in the context of Chinese modernization, conveying a more holistic, systematic, and coordinated connotation. On January 30, 2018, during the 3rd collective study session of the Political Bureau of the CPC Central Committee, General Secretary Xi Jinping pointed out that the modernized economic system is an organic whole that comprises the interrelationships and intrinsic connections among all links, levels, and fields of social-economic activities.[70] It requires the integrated construction and advancement of the *industrial system, the market* system, the income distribution system, the urban–rural and regional development system, the green development system, the comprehensive opening system, and the economic system. This charts the correct course for building a modernized economic system. Naturally, as the situation evolves and practice deepens, the connotation of a modernized economic system becomes more systematic and complete.

[70] Xi Jinping. Accelerating Economic Modernization (January 30, 2018) [M]// Xi Jinping. Xi Jinping: The Governance of China: Volume 3. Beijing: Foreign Languages Press, 2020.

In light of new circumstances and requirements, a modernized economic system should have the following features.

Innovation is the primary force for driving development. The innovation-driven development is among the most notable features of a modernized economic system. A modernized economic system underscores that innovation is the first impetus behind development. We must rely on innovation to promote transformations in quality, efficiency, and dynamics, thereby enhancing total factor productivity. China must put a high value on basic research and implement the strategy for invigorating China through science and education, the strategy for developing a quality workforce, and the innovation-driven development strategy, to achieve a high level of scientific and technological self-reliance and strength. China must focus on the in-depth integration of science and technology with the economy, actively utilizing new technologies, new business patterns, and new models to transform and upgrade traditional industries, continuously boost emerging industries, accelerate the development of the digital economy, and foster new growth drivers.

The modernization of the industrial system is the core content. The industrial system is the core of the economic system. The modernization of the economic system is first and foremost the modernization of the industrial system, which requires placing the focus of economic development on the real economy. Efforts should be centered on improving the quality and efficiency of the supply system, as well as on ensuring the coordinated development of the real economy, technological innovation, modern finance, and human resources, to continuously strengthen, improve, and expand the real economy. Industry, agriculture, and services are the pillars of the real economy. Efforts must be made to modernize industry, agriculture, and services simultaneously and promote the integrated development of these industries, advancing the industrial structure. The industrial chain is the foundation of the real economy. It is necessary to upgrade industrial foundations and modernize the industrial chain, facilitating the transformation and upgrading of industries, particularly manufacturing, toward higher-end, smart, and green development.

An effective and smooth economic cycle is a basic prerequisite. The unimpeded flow of economic factors is fundamental for the normal operation and development of a modernized economic system. In terms of internal and external linkages, it is necessary for China to insist on boosting domestic demand and promoting high-standard opening up, to establish a "dual circulation" development pattern in which the domestic economic cycle plays a leading role while the international economic cycle remains an extension and supplement. Concerning regional coordination, the implementation of regional development strategies, especially those for major regional development, is required to establish a development pattern that highlights advantages and ensures coordinated linkage. In the area of urban–rural integration, it is necessary to implement the new urbanization strategy and the rural revitalization strategy to create a pattern of urbanization with urban agglomerations as the mainstay, with coordinated development among large, medium, and small cities as well as small towns, alongside the integrated urban–rural development.

Green, low-carbon, and circular development represents a universal paradigm. Green, low-carbon, and circular development is an intrinsic feature of the modern economic system. Green development requires the firm establishment of the concept that "lucid waters and lush mountains are invaluable assets," the emphasis on ecological priority and environmental protection, the development of a green economy, and the harmonizing development of economic growth with resource and environmental sustainability. Low-carbon development closely aligns with the goals of carbon peak and carbon neutrality, advocating for the advancement of a low-carbon economy and the establishment of a clean, low-carbon, safe, and efficient energy system, and an energy-saving and eco-friendly industrial system of clean production. For circular development, it is necessary to underline the efficient use and recycling of resources, develop a circular economy, and develop a production-living style of "Reduce, Reuse, and Recycle."

Promoting the gradual realization of common prosperity is an essential requirement. Realizing common prosperity for all is an essential requirement of socialism, and an important feature of the Chinese-style modernization. Building a modernized economic system must implement a people-centered philosophy of development and conform to the requirements of gradually achieving common prosperity for all. On the one hand, it requires to focus on developing an incentive mechanism conducive to improving efficiency and wealth creation, maximizing the enthusiasm, initiative, and creativity of all parties, and making the economic pie bigger. On the other hand, China must strive to establish a distribution system conducive to narrowing income gaps and dividing the economic pie fairly, so that the people can experience a greater sense of fulfillment, happiness, and security.

Strong economic security is a significant characteristic. Economic security is the foundation of national security. A modernized economic system should be able to resist all kinds of domestic and international risks and shocks. Building a modernized economic system requires integrating development and security, enhancing the resilience of economic growth and the level of safety, proactively guarding against all kinds of risks, guaranteeing the safe supply of primary commodities like food, energy, and important resources, and ensuring the autonomy of and control over the industrial chain and supply chain, to firmly safeguard the bottom line of national food security, energy security, as well as the industry chain and supply chain security.

A well-developed and mature economic system serves as a fundamental institutional guarantee. A modernized economic system requires robust institutional support. Building a modernized economic system requires correctly handling the relationship between government and market, enabling the market to play a decisive role in resource allocation while enhancing the government's effectiveness. This involves establishing a systematic, mature, and high-level socialist market economy and building a high-standard market system that is unified, open, orderly and competitive, well-established, and well-governed. Additionally, efforts should be made to improve basic market economy institutions, including property rights protection, market access, fair competition, and social credit. The goal is to foster a synergy between an effective market and a proactive government, to ensure the free flow of factors, flexible prices, fair and orderly competition, and natural selection among enterprises.

Building a Modernized Economic System: The "One Body and Two Wings" Framework of Industrial Economy, Innovation, and Finance

The construction of a modernized economic system is a systematic endeavor requiring identifying key priorities, pinpointing effective leverage points, and clarifying the main areas of focus. Strategic placement in critical areas is necessary. By emphasizing the "One Body and Two Wings" framework, China can target specific points and lines, thus driving the modernization of the economic system forward in a steady and progressive manner.

The term "one body" refers to the industrial system. It is essential to prioritize the modernization of the industrial system as a driving force to accelerate the modernization of industry, agriculture, and services. Efforts should focus on vigorously developing advanced manufacturing, modern agriculture, and modern services, while fostering and expanding strategic emerging industries and speeding up the development of the digital economy. All efforts must be aimed at consolidating the groundwork and foundation of a modernized economic system. Industrial modernization should prioritize manufacturing. In accordance with the goals of new industrialization, China is actively promoting the extensive application of information technologies in industrialization, integrating manufacturing and services, and combining digital technology and manufacturing technology. This will facilitate the upgrading of manufacturing to higher-end, more intelligent, and greener standards, continuously enhancing the level and quality of new industrialization, and providing powerful support for building China's strength in manufacturing, science and technology, product quality, aerospace, transport, cyberspace, and digital technologies. By comparison, the modernization of agriculture remains a weak link in China's overall modernization efforts. Therefore, it is crucial to comprehensively implement the rural revitalization strategy to accelerate the construction of an agricultural powerhouse. This includes advancing agricultural technology, mechanization, standardization, and scaling up operations to transition from traditional to modern agriculture. The modernization of the service sector should focus on transforming and upgrading traditional services, vigorously developing the modern service industry, promoting the specialization and high-end transformation of productive services, and enhancing the quality and diversity of life services. This will improve labor productivity in the service sector, overcome the "Baumol's Cost Disease," and facilitate the transition from a major service nation to a strong service nation.

The "two wings" are technological innovation and institutional innovation. The modernization of science and technology is a core content and a typical indicator of productivity modernization and also serves as a driving force for the broader modernization of the economic system. It is essential to uphold the core role of innovation in China's modernization drive and seize the opportunities presented by the new round of scientific and technological revolution and industrial transformation. This involves focusing on the frontiers of science and technology, the primary battlefield of the economy, major national demands as well as people's lives and health, China must strengthen fundamental research, applied fundamental research and applied research to enhance its independent innovation capability, increase the level of transformation of scientific and technological achievements into industry, and accelerate the building of a strong scientific and technological country. A sound and vigorous economic system is essential for safeguarding economic modernization. It is necessary to align with the requirements for the modernization of China's governance system and governance capabilities, push ahead with institutional and systemic innovation, and uphold and improve the basic socialist economic system. Efforts should focus on improving the property rights system, ensuring the market-based allocation of production factors, and organically integrating these efforts with the deepening of the supply-side structural reform. The goal is to accelerate the construction of a high-level socialist market economy. We aim to build a high-standard market system that provides effective institutional support for vigorously driving productivity development, thereby safeguarding the construction of a modern economic system.

How Did China Successfully Avoid "Development Traps"

Zeng Zheng

General Secretary Xi Jinping pointed out that Chinese modernization is the modernization of a massive population, the modernization of common prosperity for all, the modernization of both material and cultural-ethical advancement, the modernization of harmony between humanity and nature, and the modernization of peaceful development.[71] This framework serves as scientific guidance and a strategic arrangement, formulated based on China's national realities, lessons drawn from human history, insights from the development experiences of other nations, and a comprehensive assessment of global trends. It fully embodies the Party's vision of modernization, providing a clear direction and practical pathway for advancing socialist modernization. Looking at modern and contemporary human history, although the paths of economic development vary across

[71] Hold High the Great Banner of Socialism with Chinese Characteristics and Strive in Unity to Build a Modern Socialist Country in All Respects—Report to the 20th National Congress of the Communist Party of China (Chin. ed.) (October 16, 2022) [N/OL]. People's Daily, [2022-10-26]. http://paper.people.com.cn/rmrb/html/2022-10/26/nw.D110000renmrb_20221026_3-01.htm.

countries, most major countries have encountered various contradictions and challenges in their modernization process, often falling into different development traps. Some countries struggle to overcome development traps, resulting in economic stagnation. Others may appear to have successfully surpassed these traps, yet shifted the costs and burdens onto domestic groups or other nations. Chinese modernization represents a remarkable innovation in the history of human development. It not only enables China to transcend development traps but also ensures an inclusive approach to global development. This unique path will contribute a new model of economic and social development and social progress, paving the way for a new trajectory in human civilization.

Transcending the Comparative Advantage Trap: Avoiding Low-End Development Lock-In Caused by Global Division of Labor

Historically, some latecomer countries relied on resource advantages to achieve economic takeoff but fell victim to the "resource curse." These countries failed to establish a comprehensive industrial system, becoming trapped in a state of "Immiserizing Growth." Meanwhile, some other countries leveraged latecomer advantages, such as cheap labor, to rapidly integrate into the global division of labor and fuel domestic industrialization. However, they became locked at the low end of the global value chain. Combined with other institutional factors, their GDP per capita stagnated at the middle-income level, leading them to fall into the middle-income trap.

Both types of nations excessively relied on comparative advantage for economic growth and failed to transition their economic development models at the appropriate time, ultimately falling into the so-called comparative advantage trap. Over the past four decades of reform and opening up, China has fully participated in the global division of labor. By leveraging its vast population and low labor costs, China effectively harnessed its demographic dividend, achieving the longest period of rapid economic growth in human history. It is now on the verge of elevating the world's most populous country into the ranks of high-income countries.

Since the international financial crisis in 2008, there has been an ongoing debate about the gradual loss of China's industrial comparative advantages. Many Western politicians, scholars, and media outlets have expressed skepticism about China's economic transformation. But China has accelerated its shift in development patterns, deepened the supply-side structural reform, promoted high-quality development, and comprehensively implemented an innovation-driven strategy. These efforts have significantly enhanced its global industrial competitiveness. China has transitioned from a passive participation in the global division of labor, based on comparative advantages, to a proactive role grounded in comprehensive competitive advantages. Both its industrial and technological structures in trade have been notably optimized, and its position in the global value chain has rapidly ascended. The proportion of high-tech products in China's total export trade increased from 29. 1% in 2008 to 45% in 2021. At the same time, according to value-added trade data released by the OECD/WTO (World Trade Organization), the value-added rate of China's export products rose from 70% in 2008 to over 80% in recent years. Furthermore, China's GDP per capita increased from $3468 in 2008 to $12,551 in 2021.

In recent years, China has adhered to the basic principle of "self-supporting, controllable, safe, and efficient," focusing on the development of the real economy. Efforts have intensified to improve a new system concentrating nationwide efforts and resources on key national undertakings, in line with the socialist market economy. China is actively advancing breakthroughs in core technologies in key fields, upgrading its industrial base, and modernizing its industrial chain. On the basis of continuously improving the quality of development, China has worked to stabilize the proportion of the manufacturing industry while strengthening its competitive edge, aiming for high-quality development in manufacturing. At the same time, China has advanced its people-centered urbanization strategy, fostering an urban system based on city agglomerations and metropolitan areas to promote coordinated and distinctive development among large, medium, and small cities, as well as small towns, thereby enabling more people to enjoy a higher quality of urban life. Through coordinated efforts in new industrialization and people-oriented urbanization, China aims to skip over the comparative advantage trap and gradually achieve modernization on a massive population scale.

Transcending the Latin American Trap: Avoiding the Widening Income Gap Caused by Rapid Economic Growth

While economic growth alone does not bridge the income gap, overly rigid welfare provisions can preclude sustainable economic expansion. Therefore, balancing economic growth with income distribution is a common challenge faced by all countries. Historically, some Latin American countries failed to address income distribution issues during their rapid development phase. When economic growth slowed, their implementation of welfare policies disrupted the critical balance between development and equity, ultimately precipitating a fall into the "Latin American trap." Over the past four decades, China has adhered to a system in which distribution according to work serves as the mainstay, with multiple forms of distribution existing alongside it. Efforts have been made to increase the share of personal income in the distribution of national income, gradually improving the distribution structure. During this period of economic growth, China has successfully avoided the trend of widening income disparity.

It must be admitted that for a long period after the reform and opening up, although the Chinese government adopted various policies to effectively curb excessive income inequality, the overall trend of income disparity continued to expand. China's Gini coefficient peaked at 0.491 in 2008, an increase of 0. 174 compared to 1978. Similarly, the ratio of per capita disposable income between urban and rural residents increased from 2.55:1 in 1979 to 3.31:1 in 2008. In recent years, while maintaining steady economic growth and avoiding excessive welfare policies, the Chinese government has successfully implemented targeted poverty alleviation programs, accelerated reforms in key areas such as finance and taxation, and institutionalized anti-monopoly measures. These efforts have effectively prevented the disorderly expansion of capital and, to some extent, curbed the further widening of the income gap. As of 2021, China's Gini coefficient had declined to about 0.46, and the ratio of per capita disposable income between urban and rural residents had dropped to 2.5:1.

To achieve the goal of basically realizing socialist modernization by 2035, China is committed to ensuring that personal income growth keeps pace with economic growth and that workers' compensation rises in tandem with labor productivity. Efforts will be made to continuously raise the income of low-income groups while expanding the middle-income group, with a more proactive approach to promoting common prosperity for all. In primary distribution, China will continue to uphold the principle of distribution according to labor as the mainstay, while allowing multiple modes of distribution to coexist. The goal is to increase the proportion of labor remuneration. In secondary distribution, adjustments to taxation, social security, and transfer payments will be intensified and made more precise. Meanwhile, the role of charity and other public welfare initiatives in tertiary distribution will be leveraged to improve the distribution pattern of income and wealth. By establishing a foundational institutional framework that ensures coordination and complementarity between primary, secondary, and tertiary distribution, China aims to avoid the Latin American trap and achieve modernization characterized by common prosperity for all.

Transcending the Materialism Trap: Avoiding the Spiritual Emptiness in an Age of Affluence

Economic development is the foundation for moral progress, yet it does not automatically cultivate spiritual pursuits. Without proper guidance, it may instead result in spiritual emptiness and moral decay. Historically, some Western developed countries, after achieving material prosperity, faced a lack of proper social guidance, which led to widespread spiritual emptiness. For instance, the United States in the 1960s fell into the "Beat Generation" trap. Since the launch of the reform and opening up, while adhering to the principle of prioritizing economic development, China has also recognized the construction of socialist cultural and ethical civilization as a critical factor in the success of socialism. The country has upheld the strategic policy of attaching equal importance to both material and spiritual civilizations. By strengthening cultural and theoretical development, China has made significant progress in cultural and ethical civilization, dramatically increasing the production and supply of cultural and artistic works and enriching its spiritual and cultural wealth.

In recent years, some Western politicians, scholars, and media outlets have continued to equate Western civilization with modern civilization, aggressively promoting the concept of "universal civilization." This perspective has gradually shifted from a subject-centered theory to egocentrism, and in extreme cases, into a form of solipsism. Some have even attempted to reshape other civilizations, exacerbating global cultural conflicts. In the meantime, some Western politicians and scholars have baselessly criticized that China's modern culture has deviated from their so-called self-centered cultural system. In response to these baseless accusations, China has firmly upheld its "Four Confidences"—confident in the path, theory, system, and culture of socialism with Chinese characteristics—while establishing a strategy for the coordinated development of both material and cultural-ethical progress. China has championed the leadership of socialist core values in mass cultural and ethical civilization activities, implementing in-depth civic moral construction projects, strengthening the ideological and moral development of society, and promoting ideals and beliefs. The country has also strengthened the promotion of socialism with Chinese characteristics and the Chinese dream. These efforts have significantly advanced the creation of mass cultural and ethical civilization, leading to a substantial improvement in cultural and ethical civilization alongside steady economic growth.

In the coming years, China will enter a crucial phase in the construction of a cultural and ethical civilization and the cultivation of a new generation of socialist successors. The country will continue to uphold Marxism as the guiding ideology and insist on leading cultural construction with core socialist values. It will foster public support for socialism, nurture a new generation with sound values and ethics, promote Chinese culture, and enhance China's global image. Efforts will be made to enhance ideological and moral education, promote philosophy and social sciences with Chinese characteristics, and inherit and carry forward China's excellent traditional culture. Additionally, China will continue to improve the civilization of its citizens, promote the unity of meeting people's cultural needs and strengthening their spiritual vitality, thereby fostering ideological concepts, spiritual outlooks, civilized styles, and behavioral norms that meet the requirements of the new era. By building a strong socialist culture, China will avoid the "Beat Generation" trap and achieve modernization that harmonizes material and cultural and ethical civilization.

Transcending the Environmental Kuznets Trap: Avoiding the Environmental Curse of Industrialization

According to classical theories of modern economics, environmental degradation is often seen as an inevitable stage of economic development, independent of subjective awareness or failures in institutions, strategies, and policies. However, historical experience shows that, without appropriate policy constraints and guidance, economic development at advanced stages does not immediately lead to improvements in resource conservation and environmental protection. Some Western countries, despite achieving high levels of economic development, have failed to make remarkable progress in environmental improvement. Some countries, driven by the dogma of "development first and protection later," only began to emphasize environmental protection after reaching the high-income stage, and paid a high price for environmental governance. Since the launch of the policy of reform and opening up, China has adhered to a proactive approach of prevention-first and comprehensive governance, strengthening pollution control and ecological protection from the outset. Starting with early initiatives targeting the "three wastes" (wastewater, exhaust gas, and solid waste), China has progressively integrated environmental capacity constraints and total emissions control into economic and social planning. This has evolved into an emphasis on the coordinated development of environmental protection, economic growth, and social well-being. As a result, China's per capita emissions and cumulative per capita emissions remain significantly lower than those of most developed countries. China has forged a path of resource-efficient and environmentally friendly development, characterized by simultaneous progress in protection and governance.

However, due to prolonged periods of rapid economic growth and weak environmental awareness in some regions, China still has a deficit in ecological conservation and governance. Over the past decade, China has made greater efforts to promote ecological civilization and build a beautiful China. A series of environmental protection projects, including environmental governance and protection efforts for mountains, rivers, forests, farmland, and lakes, has led to transformational changes. China has made remarkable strides in its green and low-carbon transformation. In 2021, the average PM2.5 concentration in China's prefecture-level cities reached the first-stage transition value set by the World Health Organization, making China the fastest-improving country in air quality. From 2013 to 2021, the proportion of surface water bodies rated Class I-III improved by 23.3 percentage points, and black and odorous water bodies in prefecture-level cities were largely eliminated. Additionally, China's forest area increased by 7. 1%, reaching 227 billion hectares. China has become the world's leading force in afforestation.

In recent years, China has embraced the fundamental strategy of promoting green development and fostering harmony between humanity and nature. The country is strengthening the implementation of sustainable development strategies and reinforcing campaigns for cleaner air, water, and soil. It has improved the overall coordination mechanism in the field of ecological civilization, constructing a comprehensive system for ecological conservation, upgrading the quality and stability of ecosystems, and enhancing environmental quality and capacity. The country strives to promote a comprehensive green transformation of economic and social development, building a beautiful China of high quality and contributing new and greater solutions to global challenges and common problems faced by humanity. By constructing a community of harmony between humanity and nature, China aims to circumvent the Kuznets trap and achieve a model of modernization where economic progress and ecological balance coexist in harmony.

Transcending the Colonization Trap: Avoiding External Exploitation Associated with Superpower Development

Colonization has historically served as both the condition and the basis for the rise of capitalism, acting as the driving force behind its expansion. Historically, the development of the capitalist commodity economy required not only the global dumping of goods and the plundering of raw materials but also the export of surplus capital to foreign markets. As a result, the rise of traditional industrialized countries is largely a history of bloody colonial conquests. Colonialism has been a vital strategic pillar for the establishment, expansion, and consolidation of capitalism. Since the launch of its reform and opening up policy, China has upheld an independent foreign policy of peace, refraining from forming exclusive alliances, engaging in bloc politics, or carving out spheres of influence. Instead, China has pursued a win–win strategy of opening up, with the promotion of common development alongside national interests as the fundamental principle in managing economic and trade relations with other countries. By strengthening international economic and technological exchanges, actively participating in global trade divisions, and providing foreign aid to the best of its ability, China has contributed to shared development and global prosperity. In achieving its own growth, China has played a significant role in promoting the prosperity and supporting the rise of latecomer countries.

However, some Western politicians, scholars, and media outlets maliciously fabricate misleading narratives such as the "China threat theory" and "Chinese neocolonialism" in an attempt to undermine China's international image and hinder its reform and opening up. In response to these false accusations, China has made great efforts in recent years to construct a comprehensive, multi-level, and three-dimensional diplomatic layout while actively engaging in promoting reform and development in the global governance system. On the basis of high-standard opening up, China continues to support economic globalization, continuously expanding imports, and advancing high-quality cooperation under the Belt and Road Initiative. Over the past decade, China has signed more than 200 cooperation documents under the Belt and Road Initiative with 149 countries and 32 international organizations. Additionally, the number of free trade agreements signed by China has increased from 10 to 19. These efforts have opened new frontiers for major-country diplomacy with Chinese characteristics, marking historic achievements in the country's reform and opening up. By deepening global engagement, China has offered greater market, investment, and growth opportunities for global businesses, ensuring that the benefits of its economic and social development are shared by people worldwide.

The forthcoming period represents a pivotal moment for China's external engagement and opening up. The country will accelerate efforts to foster a new pattern of development that is focused on the domestic economy, with positive interactions between domestic and international economic flows. China will actively participate in the reform and development of the global governance system, advancing a broader agenda of opening up across more areas and in greater depth. The goal is to build a higher-level system for an open economy. China will leverage its super-large market advantage to attract global commodities and resources, creating new international cooperation and competitive advantages. Additionally, it will promote the high-quality development of the Belt and Road Initiative, push forward the deepening of multilateral and bilateral cooperation, and create greater market opportunities to achieve mutual benefits and win–win outcomes. Through the vision of building a community of common destiny for mankind, China seeks to transcend the historical pitfalls of colonization and pursue modernization through peaceful development.

Constructing an Evaluation Index System for Chinese Modernization

Ren Baoping and Zhang Qian

Chinese modernization not only shares common characteristics with global modernization but also distinctly embodies the fundamental feature of the socialist development path with Chinese characteristics. It represents an innovative model of modernization that integrates the universal principles of modernization with China's specific national conditions, development stages, and contemporary realities. This creative path of modernization requires a scientific and rational evaluation index system to measure and assess its level of modernization. Such a system is essential for understanding the basic trends and principal contradictions of Chinese modernization, which in turn enables more targeted strategic planning for its further advancement. This endeavor carries significant theoretical and practical value. Therefore, constructing a scientifically sound evaluation index system for Chinese modernization, based on fundamental facts and key characteristics of this unique path, is both necessary and urgent.

Statistical Dimensions of the Evaluation Index System for Chinese Modernization

Based on the fundamental logic and key characteristics of Chinese-style modernization, this analysis examines the essential statistical dimensions for evaluating it, thereby constructing an evaluation index system that aligns with China's national conditions and reflects Chinese characteristics.

Globally, several representative evaluation index systems for modernization exist, including the Black modernization index, the Ingles index system of modernization, and the United Nations Human Development Index (HDI). Domestically, various institutions have developed their own modernization index systems based on different dimensions. For instance, the Chinese Academy of Social Sciences proposed an index system encompassing economic development, social progress, population quality, and living standards. The Sustainable Development Strategy Group of the Chinese Academy of Sciences developed an index system based on driving forces for modernization, modernization quality, and social equity. Additionally, local governments and development planning departments also have formulated modernization evaluation systems tailored to regional characteristics. Except for the UN's HDI, most international and domestic studies adopt a multi-indicator approach to comprehensively assess a country's modernization from various dimensions and perspectives. Professor Hong Yinxing and his research team (2014) expanded upon previous index systems, creating a relatively scientific and reasonable index system that includes five key dimensions: economic modernization, urban and rural modernization, social modernization, ecological civilization modernization, and political civilization modernization. This system systematically addresses major fields and aspects crucial to the development and construction of modernization, making it a valuable theoretical and practical reference for future research on Chinese modernization.

In alignment with the 14th Five-Year Plan for economic and social development and the long-range objectives for 2035, Chinese modernization must integrate modernized structures into economic construction, social progress, and people's livelihoods, achieving a new level of modernization. The expanded framework for modernization emphasizes five core dimensions: economic modernization, social process modernization, urban–rural regional modernization, ecological civilization modernization, and governance capability modernization. These five dimensions comprehensively address fundamental aspects of people's living needs and embody the people-centered philosophy of modernization. Therefore, the construction of an evaluation index system for Chinese modernization should begin with these five dimensions.

Economic Modernization

Economic modernization is both the foundation and core of Chinese modernization, providing the material basis for modernization development. Following the general rule of modernization, both China and other countries have pursued modernization through rapid economic growth. Theoretical research on modernization shows that economic modernization, as a starting point, plays a fundamental role in the overall modernization process. In responding to the essential requirements of high-quality economic transformation in the new era, China's modernization must not only increase total economic output but also achieve significant progress in high-quality economic development and technological strength, positioning China among the forefront of innovative nations. The process of economic modernization must focus on reshaping new drivers of growth, leveraging digital development as a key pathway to enhance productive forces, and advancing a new pattern of all-around opening up as a key component. These efforts aim to build an economic modernization path with Chinese characteristics, in line with China's unique conditions.

First, the endeavor must begin with the core requirement of economic modernization: reshaping the drivers of economic growth. This involves fostering new sources of growth, transforming the economic growth model, optimizing the economic structure, and improving economic efficiency to boost overall economic modernization.

Second, accelerating digitalization and innovation in industrial layouts has become an urgent necessity for economic modernization. The integration of digital technology, innovation, and productive force will inject fresh vitality into a new round of technological revolution. This will drive profound transformations in the science and technology industries, promoting the deep integration of digitalization and innovation with manufacturing and service industries. Transforming traditional economic development models to strengthen the modern industrial system serves as a crucial force in advancing economic modernization.

Finally, fostering a new pattern of comprehensive openness is another important aspect of economic modernization. A high-level open economy is indispensable for achieving economic modernization. On the one hand, a unified, open, and well-ordered market system is a fundamental requirement. On the other hand, ensuring an efficient and virtuous cycle between domestic demand and global division of labor enhances the efficiency of resource allocation within market mechanisms, serving as an essential pathway to realizing economic modernization.

Modernization of Social Processes

As a people-oriented model of modernization, the evaluation dimension must integrate modern development into social development. This approach reflects the core principle of prioritizing human well-being, ultimately aiming for human modernization. The fundamental goal of achieving basic modernization for a nation or region, be it the improvement of its overall national strength, the strengthening of its economic strength, or the optimization of its resource and environmental management, is to meet the people's need for a better life. Therefore, the evaluation dimension of modernization should be grounded in the fundamental logic of improving the quality of people's lives, and the modernization of social progress should be taken as a primary evaluation dimension of Chinese modernization.

The modernization of social progress follows the trajectory of economic modernization and is a continuous, dynamic historical process that must remain closely connected to the people. As such, the modernization of social progress encompasses critical public concerns, including healthcare, basic social security, the allocation of social resources, population education and quality, social organization, and cultural accessibility. Since Chinese modernization is an innovative and people-oriented path, the realization of a great modern country cannot be separated from the modernization of social progress. It must instead prioritize the comprehensive coordination and integration of both economic and social modernization, which should be explicitly reflected in the index system. To assess the degree and level of basic modernization, particular emphasis should be placed on the modernization of social progress, evaluating fundamental social issues such as human development, social security, and income distribution.

Urban–Rural and Regional Modernization

An analysis of China's modernization challenges reveals that a significant gap between urban and rural areas in terms of development is evident. The pronounced dual structural contradictions between these areas cannot be ignored, so coordinating urban–rural relationships and promoting integrated urban–rural development are critical to the strategy of China's modernization. Regarding the pathway for Chinese modernization, the country has pioneered a multi-dimensional, parallel model of development. A closer examination of this parallel modernization model reveals that agricultural modernization has always been a crucial component of China's broader modernization efforts. Advancing the modernization of agriculture, rural areas, and farmers in a comprehensive manner is of significant importance for China to achieve its goal of becoming a fully modernized country. From a problem-oriented perspective, the modernization of urban and rural areas is not only a key strategic component of Chinese modernization but also a critical pathway for achieving integrated urban–rural development. This is why it should constitute a key dimension in the evaluation index system for Chinese modernization.

The modernization of urban and rural areas focuses on strategic planning and policies that emphasize urban–rural coordination and integration, the interactive development between cities and towns, and the interconnection of basic public services and infrastructure.

First, the level of urbanization is a critical factor in assessing urban–rural relations, as a determining factor in both urban modernization and human development. The continuous enhancement of a city's capacity and administrative status promotes the quality of urban functions, creates more livable environments, and fosters the sustainable development of resources and the environment. This, in turn, facilitates a new model of inclusive and shared development, where cities and towns mutually reinforce each other's progress.

Second, urban and rural modernization aims to narrow the income gap between urban and rural residents. A significant income disparity not only affects social harmony and people's living standards but also constrains investment and consumption optimization in both urban and rural areas.

Lastly, ensuring equitable access to basic public services and facilities in urban and rural areas allows residents to enjoy equal public service rights and facilitates the smooth flow of modern production factors across regions. This is crucial for market-oriented resource allocation and, as a result, promotes positive regional interactions and reinforces the deep integration of urban and rural development.

Ecological Civilization Modernization

As a latecomer to modernization, China benefits from certain advantages compared to first-mover countries. However, it also faces stricter constraints on natural resources. In the early stages of modernization, the excessive pursuit of economic growth led to environmental degradation and resource depletion. As China enters the new era, ecological civilization has become both an essential component and a necessary requirement of Chinese modernization. This shift is driven by the need for high-quality development, the goals of carbon neutrality and carbon peak, and the growing prominence of environmental challenges in the modernization process. Modernization cannot come at the cost of ecological destruction; instead, economic, social, and ecological development must be integrated into a unified trinity. Enhancing ecological civilization and promoting sustainable development are critical prerequisites for achieving modernization. Therefore, given the pressing resource and environmental constraints during modernization, the modernization of ecological civilization, as an integral part of Chinese modernization, should be included in the evaluation dimensions of Chinese-style modernization.

The modernization of ecological civilization is grounded in a balanced approach to natural resources and ecosystems. While ensuring continued economic growth, it emphasizes green benefits and sustainable output, advancing modernization through the coordinated promotion of environmental protection and high-quality development. By protecting and improving ecosystems, productivity can be enhanced, thereby fostering the sustainable development of Chinese modernization. According to the fundamental connotations of ecological civilization modernization, its evaluation system should measure not only static resource endowments but also dynamic changes. This includes key aspects such as resource endowment, resource consumption, environmental quality, pollution emissions, pollution control, and the level of green development.

Governance Capability Modernization

The modernization of governance capacity serves as the cornerstone of Chinese modernization. This requires leveraging the effectiveness of the national governance system by relying on institutions, mechanisms, policies, and technology to achieve democratic and scientific decision-making, law-based enforcement, coordinated and balanced regulation, and interactive collaboration. Together, these efforts contribute to advancing the modernization of China's governance capacity.

Looking at the historical process of Chinese modernization, it is clear that the modernization of governance capacity and the governance system is a key guarantee for building Chinese-style modernization. It has played a vital role in ensuring social stability, strengthening the rule of law, and enhancing public security. Under the leadership of the CPC, Chinese modernization has demonstrated a remarkable ability to sustain long-term social stability while achieving rapid economic growth—an ability that is directly linked to the continuous advancement of governance modernization. From the perspective of institutional guarantee, the modernization of the governance system and governance capacity is an indispensable part of institutional modernization. The modernization of governance capacity not only constitutes a fundamental component of Chinese modernization but also serves as a critical safeguard throughout the modernization process. Therefore, when evaluating the progress of Chinese-style modernization, governance capability modernization should be regarded as a key dimension of the assessment framework. To build a scientific and reasonable evaluation index system for Chinese modernization, it is crucial to carefully consider the level of governance modernization. This includes analyzing various aspects such as government efficiency, digital government construction, administrative personnel capacity, Party conduct and integrity, rule of law, and public security.

In conclusion, economic modernization serves as the core foundation of Chinese modernization. The modernization of social progress is a key component of Chinese modernization. Urban–rural modernization provides a practical solution to the challenges of a dual-structured society. Ecological civilization modernization is crucial for addressing resource and environmental constraints in the modernization drive. Governance capability modernizing acts as a fundamental safeguard for modernization efforts. Therefore, it is imperative to build a scientific and reasonable evaluation index system for Chinese modernization based on these five key dimensions.

Building the Evaluation Index System of Chinese Modernization

Based on theoretical analysis of Chinese modernization, a scientific and reasonable evaluation index system should encompass the fundamental dimensions of: economic modernization, social progress modernization, urban–rural and regional modernization, ecological civilization modernization, and governance capability modernization. In line with the theoretical understanding of these dimensions, appropriate indicators should be selected that align with their defined connotations, in order to construct a scientifically sound and rational evaluation index system for Chinese-style modernization, as shown in Table 1.2.

Index System for Economic Modernization

Expanding on the connotations of Chinese modernization and aligning with the requirements for high-quality economic development in the new era, the assessment of economic modernization should extend beyond mere quantitative economic growth. It must also encompass factors such as improvement in economic efficiency and technological advancement, optimization of the economic structure, enhancement of information and innovation-driven economic strength, and the deepening of an open economy.

Based on the key aspects of economic modernization, per capita regional GDP can serve as a primary indicator for measuring the overall scale of economic output. Other indicators, such as the proportion of value added by the service industry, agricultural labor productivity, and total agricultural machinery power, can be selected to evaluate the modernization of economic structure and efficiency. Industrial structure, production efficiency, and agricultural modernization can be used to reflect the ongoing transformation of the economic development model. The proportion of R&D expenditure, the proportion of business volume in technology market transactions, and the number of effective patents per 10,000 people should be considered to assess innovation capacity and R&D strength. The proportion of e-commerce sales can be used to

Table 1.2 Evaluation index system for China's modernization

Primary dimension	*Sub-dimension*	*Basic indicator*	*Unit*	*Indicator attribute*
Economic modernization	Economy quantity and scale	Per capita regional GDP	CNY	Positive
	Economic structure and economic efficiency	Proportion of service industry value added in regional GDP	%	Positive
		Agricultural labor productivity	–	Positive
		Total agricultural machinery power	10,000 kilowatts	Positive
	Innovation capability and R&D strength	Proportion of R&D (scientific research and experimental development) expenditure in regional GDP	%	Positive
		Proportion of technology market transaction volume in regional GDP	%	Positive
		Number of effective patents per 10,000 people	Items	Positive
	Information application level	Proportion of e-commerce sales	%	Positive
	Level of opening	Proportion of total import and export of goods by foreign-invested enterprises in the regional GDP	%	Positive
	Development strength of cultural industry	Proportion of operating revenue of cultural manufacturing enterprises above the designated size in the regional GDP	%	Positive

(continued)

Table 1.2 (continued)

Primary dimension	*Sub-dimension*	*Basic indicator*	*Unit*	*Indicator attribute*
Social process modernization	Residents' health level	Average life expectancy	Year	Positive
	Basic social security	Coverage rate of urban and rural basic pension insurance	%	Positive
		Coverage rate of urban and rural basic medical insurance	%	Positive
		Coverage rate of unemployment insurance	%	Positive
		Proportion of housing security expenditure in the fiscal expenditure	%	Positive
		Number of nursing beds per 1000 elderly	Bed	Positive
	Comprehensive human resource capability	Full-time equivalent of R&D personnel in industries and businesses above the designated size	Person	Positive
		Average number of students in secondary and higher education per 100,000 students	Person	Positive
	Modern education level	Average years of education of the regional population	Year	Positive
	Information resource penetration	Internet penetration	%	Positive
	Social organization	Number of social organizations per 10,000 population	Number	Positive
	Cultural and sports public facilities	Library floor space per 10,000 population	Square meter	Positive

(continued)

Table 1.2 (continued)

Primary dimension	*Sub-dimension*	*Basic indicator*	*Unit*	*Indicator attribute*
Urban–rural and regionalmodernization	Urban agglomeration capacity	Urbanization rate	%	Positive
	Urban and rural public infrastructure construction	County-level natural gas penetration rate	%	Positive
	Urban public transportation and service level	Per capita urban road area	Square meter	Positive
		Passenger volume of urban public transport	10,000 people	Positive
		Passenger volume of urban rail transit	10,000 people	Positive
	Urban and rural incomes	Per capita disposable income of urban residents	RMB	Positive
		Per capita disposable income of rural residents	RMB	Positive
	Urban–rural income gap	Theil index of income of urban and rural residents	–	Negative
Ecological civilization modernization	Energy consumption	Electricity consumption per unit of regional GDP	kWh/RMB	Negative
	Pollutant emissions	Chemical oxygen demand emission	10,000 tons	Negative
		Sulfur dioxide emission	10,000 tons	Negative
		Ammonia nitrogen emissions	10,000 tons	Negative
		Nitrogen oxide emissions	10,000 tons	Negative
	Comprehensive quality of ecological environment	Number of days above the secondary standard of urban air quality	%	Positive
	Resource reserves	Water resources per capita	m^3/person	Positive
	Environmental governance	Area of soil erosion control	1000 ha	Positive
		Daily treatment capacity of urban sewage	10,000 m^3	Positive
	Greening level	Forest coverage rate	%	Positive
		Coverage rate of the built green space	%	Positive

(continued)

Table 1.2 (continued)

Primary dimension	*Sub-dimension*	*Basic indicator*	*Unit*	*Indicator attribute*
Governance capacity modernization	Government efficiency	Proportion of public service expenditure in GDP	%	Positive
	Digital government	Digital service penetration level	%	Positive
	Party integrity construction	Frequency of searches for party integrity construction	Times	Positive
	Rule of law construction	Frequency of searches for the rule of law construction	Times	Positive
	Public safety construction	Proportion of public safety expenditure in the fiscal expenditure	%	Positive

(indicate the level of informatization in economic modernization, while the proportion of total imports and exports by foreign-invested enterprises reflects the level of openness. In addition, the culture industry, as a new knowledge-based modern service economy, plays a crucial role in enriching economic modernization. Therefore, revitalizing the economy through cultural development is essential for increasing product value and upgrading the industrial structure. From the perspective of increasing added value through industrial upgrading, the development of the cultural industry is indispensable for economic modernization. Therefore, the proportion of operating revenue from cultural manufacturing enterprises above a designated size can serve as an indicator of cultural industry development strength. Together, these elements form the comprehensive evaluation index system of Chinese economic modernization.

Index System of Social Progress Modernization

Drawing from the fundamental evaluation dimensions of social progress modernization and guided by the human-centered logic of the Chinese path to modernization, this study uses the degree of people's modernization as the starting point for assessing the modernization of social progress. Therefore, the modernization level of people's comprehensive development capabilities and the modernization of their lifestyles are key indicators for assessing the modernization of social progress in China.

To assess the modernization of comprehensive human development capabilities, the following indicators can be chosen. First, the average life expectancy can be selected to indicate residents' health level, which is also a basic condition for people's development capabilities. Second, indicators such as the coverage rate of basic pension insurance in urban and rural areas, the coverage rate of basic medical insurance in urban and rural areas, the coverage rate of unemployment insurance, the proportion of housing security expenditure in fiscal expenditure, and the number of nursing beds per 1000 elderly, can be used to assess the level of basic social security. These reflect the government's efforts in providing essential public services and ensuring basic protection for citizens. Third, indicators such as the full-time equivalent number of R&D personnel in industrial enterprises above a designated size, and the average number of students in secondary and higher education per 100,000 population can reflect the comprehensive human resource capacity. Finally, the level of modern education can be evaluated by the average years of education for the population in a region. These four categories of indicators comprehensively reflect the capabilities of people's well-rounded development within the context of social modernization. Regarding people's modern lifestyles, indicators such as the Internet penetration rate, the number of social organizations per 10,000 population, and the library floor space per 10,000 population can be chosen. These indicators respectively reflect the level of access to information and technology, the development of social organizations, and cultural and sports facilities. These indicators together measure the level of modernization in people's lifestyles.

Index System of Urban–Rural and Regional Modernization

Urban–rural and regional modernization is a strategic planning and policy orientation that focuses on urban–rural integration, interactive coordination between cities and towns, and the interconnected development of basic public services and infrastructure. Its index system should align with its basic connotations and assess modernization from two key dimensions: urban development status and the urban–rural gap. The level of urban development can be further categorized into urban agglomeration capacity and urban public service capacity, while the urban–rural gap can be assessed based on income levels and the income gap between urban and rural residents. These dimensions collectively provide a comprehensive evaluation of urban and rural modernization.

In terms of specific indicators, the urbanization rate can be used to indicate urban agglomeration capacity. The county-level gas penetration rate can be chosen to reflect the sharing and service capacity of urban and rural public infrastructure construction; the per capita area of urban roads, passenger volume of urban public transportation, and passenger volume of urban rail transit together reflect the quality and accessibility of urban public transportation and services. The per capita disposable income of urban residents, the per capita disposable income of rural residents, and the Theil index collectively measure the income levels and disparities between urban and rural residents. Among them, the Theil index specifically measures the inequality across regions. As a negative indicator, a higher Theil index signifies a larger rural–urban income gap and the more serious constraints related to unequal distribution among regions.

Index System of Ecological Civilization Modernization

Ecological civilization modernization is a key measure for addressing resource and environmental constraints in the process of modernization. The selection of its indicators must consider two dimensions: static resource stock and dynamic changes. A comprehensive index system should be established by integrating static and dynamic aspects, drawing on multiple dimensions such as energy consumption, pollution emissions, environmental governance, resource endowment, pollution control, and green development.

In the sub-dimension of ecological civilization construction, electricity consumption per unit of regional GDP can reflect regional energy consumption. Emission levels of pollutants such as chemical oxygen demand, sulfur dioxide, ammonia nitrogen, and nitrogen oxides can serve as indicators of regional pollutant discharge. The proportion of days meeting the secondary standard of urban air quality and per capita water resource availability can respectively reflect the overall quality of the ecological environment and the level of resource reserves. The area of soil erosion control and daily urban sewage treatment capacity can measure a region's capability and effectiveness in pollution control. The forest coverage rate and the greening coverage rate in built-up areas can reflect a region's efforts in improving greenery.

Index System of Governance Capacity Modernization

The construction of an index system for governance capacity modernization needs to take into account basic contents of governance capacity modernization and focus on five primary dimensions: enhancing government efficiency, advancing digital government, promoting social harmony and stability through Party conduct and clean government, strengthening legal development to ensure the rule of law and public safety, and improving public safety through regional public security initiatives. This framework will establish a scientific indicator system that embodies the connotations and reflects the core requirements of governance capacity modernization. Within the sub-dimension of governance modernization, improvements in government efficiency can be reflected by the proportion of public service expenditure in GDP. While the digital transformation of government can be assessed by the penetration rate of digital services. The level of Party conduct and clean government and the capacity for rule of law construction can be evaluated using the search frequency of the terms "Party conduct and clean government" and "rule of law construction" in the Baidu Index, based on data availability. The efficiency of public safety governance can be reflected by the proportion of public safety expenditure in fiscal expenditure.

In a word, by integrating the five fundamental dimensions of economic modernization, social progress modernization, urban–rural and regional modernization, ecological civilization modernization, and governance capacity modernization, and based on the availability of data and the consistency in indicator definitions, a scientific and rational index system for Chinese modernization can be constructed.

The Spatial-Temporal Characteristic and Practical Logic of Chinese Modernization

Zou Yinan

General Secretary Xi Jinping pointed out, "China's modernization is very different from that of Western developed countries. The development process of Western developed countries is a 'sequential' progression, in which industrialization, urbanization, agricultural modernization, and informatization have developed step by step, and it has taken more than 200 years for them to reach their current level. As a latecomer, China must overtake them and reclaim the 'lost two hundred years.' This is why China must follow a 'parallel' process, in which industrialization, informatization, urbanization, and agricultural modernization must progress simultaneously in an overlapping manner."[72] The "parallel" process of modernization represents the most significant spatial-temporal difference between China and Western countries in terms of their paths to modernization. This characteristic directly influences variables in China's modernization drive, including its development tasks, cycles, requirements, and strategies. A deep understanding of the spatial-temporal characteristics of China's parallel modernization and an accurate recognition of their impact on the development path and model are crucial for the new journey of building a socialist modernization country in all respects.

Development Tasks Are Highly Overlapped in Chinese Modernization

The "parallel" spatial-temporal characteristics of Chinese modernization imply that multiple development tasks must be carried out concurrently or even simultaneously. For China, this overlapping of modernization tasks not only presents the opportunity to shorten the development process by leveraging the achievements of modern civilization but also brings the risk of accumulated contradictions, as issues from each development stage may remain unresolved. Therefore, it is essential to accurately grasp the spatial-temporal features of Chinese modernization in order to seize opportunities while managing challenges.

Overlapping Development of Industrialization, Urbanization, Agricultural Modernization, and Informatization

Industrialization, urbanization, agricultural modernization, and informatization are essential tasks for any country aiming to achieve modernization. In Western countries, these tasks were completed over a span of more than 200 years in a serial order, with clear divisions between stages and a smooth progression from one task to the next. This formed a "sequential" development process. Western modernization began with

[72] Documentation Research Office of the CPC Central Committee. Compilation of Xi Jinping's Remarks on Socialist Economic Construction [M]. Beijing: Central Party Literature Press, 2017.

the Industrial Revolution in mid-eighteenth-century Britain. Early industrialization focused on labor-intensive industries, and the labor demand in urban industrial sectors led to the migration of the rural population to cities, a trend that continued until the mid-twentieth century. Urbanization caused a shortage of the agricultural labor force, which in turn spurred technological advancements in agriculture to conserve labor, gradually completing the modernization of agriculture through mechanization. After World War II, breakthroughs in information technology spurred significant growth in productivity, transforming the socio-economic structure, ushering in the era of informatization.

Unlike Western countries, China must complete its modernization in less than a century, which requires the overlapping development of industrialization, urbanization, agricultural modernization, and informatization. At certain stages, some of these tasks may even need to progress simultaneously. Consequently, there is no clear division between stages, and often the development tasks of one stage must begin before the previous stage is fully completed. During specific historical periods, the order of these tasks may even need to be reversed. This means that any textbook on modernization based on the Western "sequential" model cannot serve as a directly applicable template for Chinese modernization. For instance, Western modernization did not confront the task of informatization until the later stages of industrialization, and it did not need to address the integration of informatization and industrialization. However, by the time China began its industrialization, the information industry had already profoundly changed the development logic and operational methods of industrial development. Under these circumstances, China must advance industrialization and informatization in tandem, promoting the deep integration of the two processes.

Overlapping Development Is an Opportunity for "Corner Overtaking"

The vivid metaphor of "corner overtaking" for a latecomer in modernization refers to it leveraging existing achievements in human civilization and knowledge at key historical junctures to find shortcuts for development. This approach shortens the time needed to complete various stages of modernization and helps to reduce the gap with developed countries until eventually surpassing them. In the "sequential" modernization process of Western countries, each stage requires the full maturation of various modernity elements within society before progressing to the next. This results in a prolonged duration for each stage. For example, the industrialization process in Western countries generally incorporates three stages: the dominance of the consumer goods industry, a balance between consumption and capital goods industries, and the dominance of the capital goods industry. Each of these stages spans several decades. This development law is encapsulated in Hoffmann's Industrialization Law. Besides industrialization, Western countries followed a step-by-step approach to advancing urbanization, agricultural modernization, and informatization, forming a development pattern through continuous exploration.

Unlike Western countries, China began its process of modernization after observing the entire development of developed countries. The experiences of Western countries in overcoming development bottlenecks and the lessons learned from their falling into development traps became valuable knowledge for China's modernization path. By building on this knowledge and considering its own unique circumstances, China has been able to avoid detours and achieve breakthroughs at critical points in its development. For example, during the socialist construction period, China, guided by Marxist political economy theory prioritizing the development of means of production, and inspired by Western industrial practices emphasizing "capital accumulation as the essence of industrialization," established systems and mechanisms that facilitated capital accumulation, particularly in heavy industry. This enabled China to bypass the consumer goods industry stage and directly enter the capital goods industry-dominant stage. As a result, a complete industrial system was rapidly established, significantly shortening the process of industrialization. While this strategy of prioritizing heavy industry came at a great cost, it played an important role in helping China rapidly catch up with global industrialization.

The Social Risks of Excessive Development Task Overlap

The shift from tradition to modernization involves not only a profound change in the model of material production but also a revolution in ways of thinking. This transformation typically requires a long period of time and may even need to be accomplished through intergenerational change. In Western countries, the "sequential" approach to development allows for gradual societal change, in which both adventurous youths and older generations with traditional views can find space for survival and development in the same era. Whether transitioning from rural to urban civilization or from industrial to information-based thinking, Western countries have had sufficient time to absorb the shocks brought by modernization to their traditional societies. As a result, social contradictions and risks caused by development can be relatively easy to mitigate.

In contrast, the highly overlapping tasks of China's modernization mean that it frequently faces the situation where development phases often begin before previous phases are fully completed. The difficulty of implementing this multi-task, multi-objective parallel model, as well as the risk it poses to society, is far greater than that of the "sequential" modernization model adopted by Western countries. For example, in Western countries, agricultural modernization typically follows the completion of industrialization and urbanization. The impact of machines replacing manual labor through industrialization, along with the reduction in the rural labor force due to urbanization, naturally paves the way for agricultural modernization.

However, in China, agricultural modernization was pursued alongside industrial modernization, and significant progress was made in agriculture while urbanization was still in its early stages. By the time over 200 million migrant workers had not fully integrated into the industrial sector and the cities, agriculture and rural areas had already significantly reduced their reliance on labor. As a result, China was compelled to accelerate urbanization while also preserving migrant workers' rural identities and land rights in order to minimize social risks caused by the parallel modernization drive.

The Timeframe of Chinese Modernization Is Significantly Compressed

The "parallel" spatial-temporal characteristics of Chinese modernization imply a shortened development cycle. This means the same journey must be completed in a much shorter period, requiring a relatively rapid pace of progress. Since the growth momentum changes at different stages of development, it is crucial to timely shift the development model to maintain continuous and stable growth in the course of modernization.

A 300-Year Journey in Just 100 Years

Although the modernization processes of Western countries are not identical, most have gone through a "sequential" development process over more than 200 years. British modernization, if the Industrial Revolution is taken as the starting point, dates back to the mid-eighteenth century and ended in the early twentieth century, lasting about 250 years. France, while completing its industrialization by the early nineteenth century, was considered to begin its modernization with the 1789 Revolution. France completed its modernization by the mid-twentieth century, spanning roughly 160 years. The United States started modernization after gaining independence in 1776 and completed it by the 1930s, taking approximately 150 years. Germany's modernization started with the Industrial Revolution in the 1830s, but was delayed by its prolonged national unification. It experienced several setbacks and was finally completed after the reunification of East and West Germany at the end of the twentieth century. It took about 160 years.

In theory, China's modernization can be traced back to the Westernization Movement during the late Qing Dynasty. Yet, this movement did not lead to a full-scale industrial revolution and was mostly limited to importing military equipment and machinery from Western countries. The true process of modernization began with the establishment of the People's Republic of China in 1949. If China achieves basic modernization in 2035, the whole process will take 85 years. Even if it stretches to 2050, it will still be under 100 years. In comparison, China's modernization will only take about one-third to two-thirds of the time taken by Western countries. If we include the information revolution after World War II and the ongoing digital revolution in the scope of modernization, and assume that both China and the Western countries complete their modernization at the same time, Western modernization will span about 300 years, far longer than China's 100 years. That means China will complete a journey that took Western countries 300 years in just 100 years.

The modernization process of any country must go through three social stages: agricultural society, industrial society, and post-industrial society. Western countries took about 300 years to progress through these stages, allowing each stage to fully develop and giving sufficient room for the contradictions arising from these transitions to be addressed. However, China's "parallel" modernization model compresses this 300-year process into roughly 100 years. This results in a situation where China must simultaneously contend with regions at different stages— agricultural, industrial, and post-industrial societies—while managing the complexities of new contradictions from the next stage, even as unresolved issues from previous stages persist. Samuel P. Huntington, a well-known political scientist, once said, "Modernity breeds stability, but modernization breeds instability." When the accumulation of different types of contradictions exceeds the tolerance of society, mass incidents can erupt, leading to social instability and hindering the progress of modernization. Therefore, the risks and contradictions that China faces in its modernization journey are unparalleled by those experienced by Western countries that have already completed their modernization. This places even higher demands on China's leadership to coordinate reform, development, and stability in the process of modernization.

Compressed Development Time Requires a Higher Economic Growth Rate

The compressed timeframe for China's modernization demands that the country maintain a higher economic growth rate, one that must significantly exceed that of developed Western countries. Only in this way can China ultimately achieve comparable levels in core indicators such as total social output and GDP per capita. Over the more than 70 years since the founding of the People's Republic of China, the country has consistently maintained faster economic growth than Western countries, with an annual growth rate of GDP averaging 8.3%. In 1949, China's total social output and GDP per capita were only $12.3 billion and $23, respectively, while the United States boasted figures of $267.3 and $1,882. China's figures represented only 4.6% and 1.2% of the US metrics, respectively. By 2020, China's total social output and GDP per capita had risen to $14.73 trillion and $11,300, while the United States reached $20.94 trillion and $63,500, respectively. At this point, China's figures amounted to 70.3% and 17.8% of those of the United States. Looking back over the past 70 years of modernization, China's rapid growth has significantly narrowed the gap with developed countries.

Going forward, China must continue to maintain a relatively high rate of economic growth. At the 5th Plenary Session of the 19th CPC Central Committee, it was announced that China's GDP per capita will reach the level of a moderately developed country by 2035. According to the median level among 70 high-income countries, the country currently in this position is Portugal, with a GDP per capita of about $21,000. Assuming Portugal maintains an average annual GDP growth rate of 2.5% in the next 15 years, China will need to achieve an average annual GDP growth rate of 4.7% to catch up by 2035. These are the baseline requirements for achieving basic modernization. Given China's current growth trend, it is not easy to achieve this target, requiring scientific planning and painstaking efforts.

High-Quality Development Contributes to a Higher Economic Growth Rate

The 6th Plenary Session of the 19th CPC Central Committee adopted the Resolution on the Major Achievements and Historical Experience of the Party over the Past Century (hereinafter referred to as the Resolution). The Resolution underlines that China will realize high-quality development in which innovation is the primary driving force, coordination is an endogenous feature, go-green is a prevailing mode, openness is the only path, and sharing is the fundamental goal. High-quality development does not mean abandoning the pace of growth. In fact, the relationship between the economic growth rate and development quality is dialectically unified. The most important hallmark of high-quality development is still maintaining a high economic growth rate, but this requires a profound transformation in terms of quality, efficiency, and the driving forces behind growth. Advancing economic and social development in an ever-changing environment is, in itself, a basic feature of parallel modernization.

The key to high-quality development lies in enhancing total factor productivity. First, technological advancement is the most effective way to raise total factor productivity. The high accumulation of production factors played a significant role in China's economic growth, and the high growth of the Chinese economy during the first 30 years after the reform and opening up largely relied on the accumulation of labor, capital, and land. Nowadays, given that the transfer of surplus rural labor has been completed, the role of loans in driving economic growth has diminished, and land-driven development is no longer sustainable, China must increase total factor productivity through technological advances. By focusing on technological progress, China can explore opportunities for increasing the rate of total factor productivity. To achieve this, China should prioritize independent innovation and establish a market-oriented, enterprise-led technological innovation system that integrates industry, academia, and research. Leveraging the advantages of a new type of national system, China should concentrate national efforts and resources on key technological breakthroughs. Efforts must be focused on critical fields where China is relatively weak, such as industrial machinery, critical materials, precision instruments, high-end components, and basic software and hardware, to break bottlenecks in the industrial chain and achieve high-level self-reliance and strength. Second, institutional optimization is also an important source of improving total factor productivity. It is essential to remove institutional barriers that restrict the value creation of various production factors. A market-oriented approach must be adopted to unlock dormant resources, optimize resource allocation through competitive mechanisms, and ensure the free flow of innovation.

Chinese Modernization Represents a Multifaceted Coordination of Development Requirements

The "parallel" spatial-temporal features of Chinese modernization mean that the country's development must move beyond a singular focus on material civilization. It requires coordinating material civilization with political, cultural, social, and ecological civilization in the development process. By adhering to the Five-Sphere Integrated Plan, China aims to drive comprehensive social progress and create a new form of human civilization.

The Window of Opportunity for Focusing on Material Civilization Has Closed

Continuously improving social productivity to create abundant material wealth is at the core of modernization. In Western developed countries, the "sequential" mode of development not only created the conditions for accomplishing all tasks of material civilization in order but also provided an extended window of opportunity for a "single-minded" focus on material civilization. In the early stages of modernization, people's awareness of rights was still emerging, and the concept of harmony between humans and nature had not yet taken deep root. As a result, Western countries did not need to consider the coordinated development of material civilization, political civilization, cultural and ethical civilization, social civilization, and ecological civilization. They could focus primarily on material civilization and shift their focus to other objectives after the primary goal is achieved. For example, Western countries generally underwent the "pollute first, clean up later" process, which led to far-reaching ecological damage in the pursuit of economic development. To a large extent, material civilization was achieved by sacrificing ecological well-being.

In contrast, the window of opportunity for focusing solely on material civilization had long closed by the time China began its modernization. The "pollute first, clean up later" model was no longer viable. In 1972, the international organization The Club of Rome, known for its research into the future of global development, released a report titled *The Limits to Growth*. This report, based on resource and environmental constraints, proposed a "zero growth" scheme for the global economy, which caused a global stir. While The Club of Rome's call may not have had substantial influence on China's industrialization, *The Paris Agreement* in 2016 marked a global commitment to climate change. China, as a responsible major power, made a solemn pledge to reduce emissions, setting the goal of reaching peak carbon emissions by 2030 and achieving carbon neutrality by 2060. Thus, China's economic development is now rigorously constrained by resource and environmental limits.

Coordinating Multiple Development Requirements Needs the Five-Sphere Integrated Plan

As a latecomer to modernization, China must not only deepen its understanding of the sustainable development of its economy and society, as well as the perpetual utilization of natural resources, but also constantly readjust its relationship with the world. This includes promoting exchanges and mutual learning between Eastern and Western civilizations, and enhancing mutual understanding and inclusiveness. Chinese modernization must be guided by the "present progressive tense" requirements of contemporary global modernization, coordinating progress across all fields rather than adhering to the "past tense" developmental logic of Western modernization. Therefore, the Five-Sphere Integrated Plan is an inevitable choice for China's modernization drive.

The strategic layout for coordinating the development of material civilization, political civilization, cultural-ethical civilization, social civilization, and ecological civilization has evolved from its initial formation to its eventual refinement over just 30 years, highlighting the "parallel" development characteristic of Chinese modernization. The 12th CPC National Congress in 1982 first proposed the strategy of attaching equal importance to the development of material and spiritual civilization. This marked the initial form of China's integrated modernization layout. The 16th CPC National Congress in 2002 expanded this approach to include "political civilization," thus evolving the concept from the development of "two civilizations" to the development of "three civilizations." The 17th CPC National Congress in 2007 further integrated "social construction" into the goal of building a moderately prosperous society in all respects, extending the model from three to four aspects. The 18th CPC National

Congress in 2012 included "ecological civilization" in the overall layout, forming the Five-Sphere Integrated Plan for building a moderately prosperous society in all respects. It can be seen that the formation and maturation of the Five-Sphere Integrated Plan is an accelerating historical process. Rooted in the logic of "parallel" development, it conforms to the fundamental requirement for the well-coordinated progress of material, political, cultural-ethical, social, and ecological civilizations, and points the way forward for Chinese modernization.

Create a New Form of Human Civilization

General Secretary Xi Jinping has pointed out that China's population exceeds the combined population of all developed countries. Achieving full modernization in China would mean more than doubling the world's current developed population. If the Chinese population were to follow the current resource consumption model of developed countries, the world could not bear the burden. So, China must transform its growth model through scientific and technological innovation. The shift in the growth model is, in essence, a transformation in the form of civilization. Chinese modernization is one of a huge population, one of common prosperity for all, one of material and cultural-ethical advancement, one of harmony between humanity and nature, and one of peaceful development. This is the direction that China must stick to in its modernization drive, and it also serves as a model for other developing countries striving for modernization.

Nowadays, global changes of a magnitude not seen in a century have profoundly altered the relationships between countries and civilizations, as well as the relationship between humanity and nature. Uncertainties like extremism, terrorism, pandemics, extreme poverty, and ecological crises pose significant threats to human survival and development. Under these circumstances, Chinese modernization is not only the realization of China's national rejuvenation but also a promising blueprint for the future of all humanity. The Chinese people have long embraced the noble tradition of caring for the world and building a human community with a shared future. The creation of a new form of civilization—one in which all human beings share the same destiny—is the aspiration of the Chinese people today. This new form of civilization is a civilization in which people from all countries live in harmony, cooperate for mutual benefits, and share the fruits of development. It is a contemporary civilization that aligns with the aspirations of people worldwide and ushers in a new era for human development.

Chinese Modernization Follows a Catch-Up Development Strategy

The "parallel" spatial-temporal feature of Chinese modernization means that the country's development will gradually transition from lagging behind the global trend to following, catching up with, and even leading the world. The catch-up strategy in itself embodies China's strong aspiration for national rejuvenation, with the CPC shouldering the inevitable mission and socialism with Chinese characteristics serving as the necessary institutional arrangement for this strategy.

Chinese Modernization as a Response to Strong Historical Challenges

The "sequential" modernization of Western countries evolved through the development of economic, political, and cultural elements. Developed free from external pressure, this process follows an orderly sequence according to certain laws, with internal social contradictions acting as the fundamental driving force. While Western countries formed nation-states early and pursued self-reliance and self-strengthening, and national rejuvenation as part of their modernization, it represented a spontaneous and bottom-up development and evolution process.

In contrast, Chinese modernization is a forced response to the existential threats China faced during its semi-colonization and later under the oppression of superpowers. The whole society was impacted by external shocks, sparking both ideological and institutional transformation, which extended into economic reforms. This aligns with the "shock-reaction" model proposed by John King Fairbank or the "challenge-response" model by Arnold Joseph Toynbee. Therefore, Chinese modernization has, from the very beginning, carried the strong historical demand of China since the modern era, that is, liberation from oppression, and this process was marked by distinct national and popular characteristics. Consequently, the formulation of the modernization strategy clearly exhibits a clear tendency toward catching up.

Socialism with Chinese Characteristics as an Inherent Institutional Feature of the Catch-Up Strategy

The implementation of a catch-up development strategy requires a specific institutional arrangement. At the outset of China's modernization, agriculture dominated the national economy, and the rural population occupied nearly 90% of the total population. Transforming this underdeveloped economic structure and quickly achieving industrialization in an agricultural society was the greatest aspiration of China's first generation of national leaders. If China had adopted the industrialization path of Western countries—beginning with handicrafts, progressing to workshop production, and eventually moving to modern mechanical industry—it would have faced a long and arduous journey, which was unacceptable given the urgency of the situation. This is why the first generation of China's national leaders chose a development strategy that prioritized heavy industry without hesitation, and accordingly matched it with a set of factor price systems conducive to capital accumulation, and implemented a highly regulated micromanagement mechanism. This approach resulted in a planned economy under the classic socialist system, which effectively accelerated China's industrialization and laid the industrial foundation for overtaking developed countries. After the 1980s, in response to new domestic and international circumstances, China resolutely implemented the reform and opening up policy and boldly pushed forward the restructuring of the economy and the reform of the economic system. China integrated labor-intensive industries, supported by the transfer of surplus rural laborers, into the global economic system. This created an economic miracle, making significant strides toward catching up with the times. The system of socialism with Chinese characteristics was revitalized and adapted to new realities.

After the 18th CPC National Congress, China's economy faced challenges arising from the "three-overlapping phases"—a combination of slowing economic growth, structural adjustment, and digesting stimulus policies. The reform of the economic system became an arduous and complex task, while the process of opening up encountered headwinds from economic globalization. Internal and external contradictions are intertwined, giving rise to a multifaceted situation. In response, the CPC Central Committee, with Comrade Xi Jinping at its core, demonstrated immense strategic courage and political wisdom in advancing socialism with Chinese characteristics in the new era. On the one hand, the Party comprehensively deepened reform, addressing long-standing issues accumulated from more than 30 years of high-speed growth. On the other hand, it pushed for a transformation in the mode of development, transitioning from high-speed economic growth to high-quality development. In response to Western countries' attempts to contain China's catch-up, efforts were made to break through technological bottlenecks by concentrating national efforts and resources on key national projects. The Party also implemented powerful policies to expand domestic demand, creating a super-large-scale market. Meanwhile, China unswervingly leveraged its role in economic globalization, creating new opportunities for economic development and demonstrating the institutional advantages of coordinating all efforts for major national undertakings. Under the guidance of the system of socialism with Chinese characteristics, China is now closer than ever to the center of the global stage, increasingly nearing the realization of national rejuvenation.

The CPC's Inevitable Role in China's National Rejuvenation

In line with endogenous and spontaneous evolution of the "sequential" development process, Western party politics is also an institutional arrangement designed to accommodate the expression of diversified social interests. Rooted in a culture of distrust, capitalist political systems and bourgeois parties acting as representatives of capital, since their inception, have prioritized the protection of their own groups as the sole objective for political survival. These parties have failed to provide a long-term vision that unites society in a shared cause, struggling to address the immediate demands of the populace. Instead, they often become mired in a quagmire of interest competition, party infighting, and class antagonism.

In stark contrast, from the moment of its founding, the CPC has embraced lofty political ideals and ambitious development goals. The Party's distinct mission-oriented characteristics resonate strongly with the historical aspirations of the Chinese nation, leading to a mutually reinforcing commitment to a "parallel" modernization development path. Over the past century, the CPC has devoted itself to creating a new form of social development that overcomes feudalism, transcends capital dominance, fosters unity among various parties, improves people's well-being, and strives toward human liberation. Looking into the second centenary, the CPC will continue to shoulder the historical responsibility of national rejuvenation. By leveraging the institutional advantages of socialism with Chinese characteristics, the Party will harness the diligence, wisdom, and courage of the Chinese people, tapping into the immense potential of China's human resources and vast market. In doing so, China will carve out a new path for Chinese modernization in the twenty-first century.

General Secretary Xi Jinping has pointed out, "We must follow our own path. This is the bedrock that underpins all the theories and practices of our Party. More than that, it is the historical conclusion our Party has drawn from its struggles over the past century."[73] According to the "parallel" spatial-temporal features of Chinese modernization, the modernization led and built by the CPC must, subjectively, be a distinctly different path from that of Western countries. Objectively, it also provides a set of Chinese solutions for modernization, offering a diverse array of models for other developing countries. It opens up new possibilities for the theory and practice of modernization in the world. Understanding and mastering the "parallel" spatial-temporal features of Chinese modernization, and implementing targeted measures to maximize its advantages and avoid its disadvantages, is an essential theoretical tool for successfully building a modern socialist China and achieving the Second Centenary Goal.

[73] Xi Jinping. Speech at a Ceremony Marking the Centenary of the Communist Party of China (Chin. ed.) [OL]. [2021-07-01]. http://www.gov.cn/xinwen/2021-07/01/content_5621847.htm.

CHAPTER 2

High-Quality Development and Chinese Modernization

Huang Qunhui, Yu Miaojie, Zhu Keli, and Guan Qingyou

Path Selection and Strategic Layout of Chinese Economic Modernization

Huang Qunhui

The Report of the 20th CPC National Congress stressed that "We must fully and faithfully apply the new development philosophy on all fronts, continue reforms to develop the socialist market economy, stick to high-standard opening up, and accelerate efforts to foster a new pattern of development that is focused on the domestic economy and features

H. Qunhui (✉)
School of Economics, Chinese Academy of Social Sciences,
Beijing, China

Y. Miaojie
Chang Jiang Scholars Program under the Ministry of Education, Beijing, China

Liaoning University, Liaoning, China

C. Fang et al., *Modernization in a Chinese Style*,
https://doi.org/10.1007/978-981-95-6919-9_2

positive interplay between domestic and international economic flows."[1] At the opening ceremony of the seminar for principal provincial- and ministerial-level leading cadres studying and implementing the guiding principles of the 5th Plenary Session of the 19th CPC Central Committee, General Secretary Xi Jinping pointed out that entering a new stage of development, applying the new development philosophy, and fostering a new pattern of development are determined by the theoretical, historical, and practical logic of China's economic and social development.[2] He further emphasized that creating a new pattern of development clarifies the path for China's economic modernization. So, what is the theoretical logic and implementation mechanism of this path of economic modernization under the new pattern of development? To understand this requires an in-depth study and accurate comprehension from the perspective of economic modernization theory.

Logic of Modernization Theory for Fostering a New Pattern of Development

Modernization theory provides a rational understanding of the characteristics and laws governing modernization, articulated through a structured logical framework. While modernization is generally understood as the

[1] Hold High the Great Banner of Socialism with Chinese Characteristics and Strive in Unity to Build a Modern Socialist Country in all Respects—Report at the 20th National Congress of the CPC (Chin. ed.) (October 16, 2022) [N/OL]. People's Daily, [2022-10-26]. http://paper.people.com.cn/rmrb/html/2022-10/26/nw.D110000renmrb_20221026_3-01.htm.

[2] Xi Jinping gives an important speech at the opening ceremony of a seminar where principal provincial- and ministerial-level leading cadres study and implement the guiding principles of the 5th Plenary Session of the 19th CPC Central Committee. We must thoroughly study and fully implement the guiding principles of the 5th Plenary Session of the 19th CPC Central Committee and get off to a good start in fully building a modern socialist country (Chin. ed.). [N/OL]. People's Daily, [2021-01-12]. http://paper.people.com.cn/rmrb/html/2021-01/12/nw.D110000renmrb_20210112_1-01.htm.

Z. Keli
China Institute of New Economy, Beijing, China

G. Qingyou
School of Economics, Hainan University, Haikou, China

Reality Institute of Advanced Finance, Beijing, China

historical process through which human society transitions from traditional to modern states, it specifically includes both the profound changes experienced by developed countries since the Industrial Revolution and the process through which developing countries catch up to the world's advanced economies to become developed countries. Given the complexity of modernization, modernization theory has evolved into a vast knowledge system encompassing numerous schools of thought. Among these, three theoretical consensuses are particularly noteworthy.

The first theory is the dynamics of modernization. According to the well-known Marxist assertion that the economic base determines the superstructure, the driving force of social change is economic growth and structural transformation. In the context of modernization, the driving force is economic modernization. Classical modernization theories posit that the core process of economic modernization is industrialization, to the extent that economic modernization can be equated with industrialization. This means that modernization is essentially a process of social change driven by industrialization. Economic theory suggests that industrialization is an industry-driven process in which a country or region achieves higher per capita income and undergoes a structural shift from an agriculture-dominated economy to an industry-dominated one. In essence, it is a process of successive breakthroughs in the combination of key production factors in the national economy, progressing from lower to higher levels of development. In other words, economic modernization is a process of sustained economic growth as an economy undergoes a transition from traditional to modern. Industrialization and economic growth constitute the core topics of development economics and economics as a whole. In this sense, many economic theories can be understood as theories of economic modernization and theories of modernization dynamics.

The second theory pertains to the stages of modernization. Modernization is a process that can be divided into different stages. Notably, Walt Whitman Rostow's theory categorizes modernization into "six stages": traditional society, preconditions for economic take-off, take-off, drive to maturity, age of high mass consumption, and pursuit of the quality of life. Additionally, Hollis B. Chenery's framework outlines "five stages" of economic modernization: pre-industrialization, early industrialization, mid-industrialization, late modernization, and post-industrialization. Furthermore, the World Bank classifies economies into "four categories" based solely on per capita national income: low-income economies, lower-middle-income economies, upper-middle-income economies, and high-income economies. This classification can be interpreted as representing the economic modernization process of a given economy. It is also noteworthy that the transition from middle-income to high-income status is often fraught with challenges, leading to the concept of the "middle-income trap" within the modernization discourse.

The third theory pertains to the models of modernization. Modernization is a process with multiple paths and models, and it is also influenced by path dependency. Although countries share the common modernization goal of becoming developed countries, their paths and models of development can vary significantly due to differences in resource endowments, social structures, and historical-cultural contexts. This is particularly true for latecomer countries, whose modernization trajectories differ from those of advanced countries. These latecomer countries can leverage "latecomer advantages" to achieve what is often referred to as "catch-up" development. For instance, in terms of driving force, economic modernization can be categorized into three models: market-driven, government-driven, and hybrid approaches combining both government and market forces. The United Kingdom, the United States, and France are generally classified as market-driven economies. Germany and Japan follow a hybrid model, where both government and market forces play significant roles. The Soviet Union and China, under the planned economy, can be broadly categorized as government-driven economies. Following the reform and opening up, China has pursued market-oriented reforms, transitioning its economic modernization from a purely government-driven model to a hybrid model jointly driven by both government and market forces.

In his speech at the 20th CPC National Congress, General Secretary Xi Jinping stressed that the accelerating efforts to foster a new pattern of development that is focused on the domestic economy and features positive interplay between domestic and international economic flows is a major strategic task in promoting China's overall development. This aligns with *The Outline of the 14th Five-Year Plan for Economic and Social Development and the Long-Range Objectives through the Year 2035*. Achieving this goal requires a comprehensive understanding and proactive advancement from a holistic perspective. The key to creating a new development pattern lies in ensuring unimpeded economic cycles, and the most essential feature of this process is to achieve a high level of self-reliance and self-improvement. Based on the three areas of consensus in modernization theory discussed above, the logic of modernization theory for fostering a new pattern of development can be summarized in three main dimensions.

Understand the New Development Pattern Based on Modernization Stages

Based on the theory of modernization stages, constructing a new pattern of development is an inevitable prerequisite for advancing to the new stage of Chinese-style socialist modernization. It represents an economic modernization path that aligns with this new stage of modernization.

The 14th Five-Year Plan period marks the first 5 years of China's new journey toward achieving its Second Centenary Goal, having already fulfilled the First Centenary Goal of building a moderately prosperous society in all respects. This period signifies China's transition into a new development stage. General Secretary Xi Jinping emphasized that "The new stage of development where we now stand is a certain point in the primary stage of socialism. Also, this is the stage from a new starting point after several decades of accumulation."[3] At this new stage of development, the Party will lead the Chinese people in making a historic leap—from standing up and growing prosperous to becoming strong.

According to modernization stage theory, China's new stage of development represents a new phase in the cause of socialism. After several decades of accumulation, China has completed the historic transformation from standing up and growing prosperous to becoming strong. That signifies the start of a new stage in China's modernization process, marking the beginning of a new journey toward fully building a modern country. If we refer to Rostow's six stages of modernization, Chinese society has already taken off, completed its transition to maturity, and is now advancing toward the stage of high mass consumption and the pursuit of a higher quality of life. Most literature indicates that China is currently in the stage of high mass consumption, and that the new stage of development signals a transition toward enhancing the quality of life. From the perspective of economic growth, the first three stages—the preconditions for take-off, the take-off, and the drive to technological maturity—can be categorized as a period of rapid economic expansion. The subsequent two stages—the age of high mass consumption and the pursuit of life quality—represent a shift toward high-quality development. The new development stage indicates China's shift from high-speed growth to high-quality development. If we apply Chenery's five-stage model, a comprehensive evaluation of indicators such as per capita GDP, industrial output, urbanization rate,

[3] Xi Jinping. Acquire a better understanding of the new development stage, act on the new development philosophy, and create a new economic dynamic [J]. Qiushi, 2021 (9).

manufacturing share, and the proportion of employment in the primary industry suggests that China has already entered the late stage of industrialization. The new stage of development signifies that China is transitioning from late-stage industrialization to a post-industrial economy. This new stage is characterized by high-quality industrialization, including the synchronous development of new industrialization, urbanization, informatization, and agricultural modernization. Essentially, this new stage of development represents the "final sprint" toward achieving modernization, marked by quantitative accumulation leading to a qualitative leap.

At the new stage of development, or the "sprint" phase of modernization, China's economy must successfully navigate three crucial milestones: first, bypass the "middle-income trap" and become a high-income country by around 2025; second, achieve basic modernization and become a moderately developed country by 2035; and third, build a great modern socialist country that is prosperous, strong, democratic, culturally advanced, harmonious, and beautiful by 2050. While China's potential growth rate suggests that it can achieve these milestones on schedule, this is clearly "not a spontaneous, passive, or effortless stage that can be passed through naturally."[4] This new stage of development necessitates a corresponding new development path and modernization strategy focused on high-quality development. Accelerating the formation of a new pattern of development that is focused on the domestic economy and features positive interplay between domestic and international economic flows requires a new economic modernization strategy that fits this new stage of development and is guided by the new development philosophy. At this new stage, China has already completed the stage of "getting rich," laying a solid material foundation. It now possesses one of the world's strongest comprehensive national strengths and an economic base as a large, advanced economy. Whether from the perspective of production supply or the vast market potential of its 1.4 billion people, China already has the basic conditions for a domestic economic cycle. In addition, China's low-cost, export-oriented industrialization strategy, which has played a crucial role in its economic catch-up since reform and opening up, is becoming less suitable for the new stage of development. The drawbacks of this strategy, such as limitations in core technologies and the urgent need to expand domestic demand, have become increasingly apparent. Considering the

[4] Xi Jinping. Acquire a better understanding of the new development stage, act on the new development philosophy, and create a new economic dynamic [J]. Qiushi, 2021 (9).

challenges faced by and trends in economic globalization, accelerating the construction of a new development pattern of "dual circulation," with the mainstay being the realization of a large domestic economic cycle at a higher level of openness, has become an inevitable choice for the path of economic modernization in the new stage of development.

Understand the New Development Pattern Based on Modernization Models

From the perspective of modernization model theory, China's new development pattern is an exploration based on its resource endowments and historical development trajectory. It represents an economic modernization model characterized by self-reliance and self-strengthening, overcoming dependency on core technologies, and establishing viable substitution.

For China, as a latecomer country seeking to catch up and achieve modernization, it is essential to fully leverage its "latecomer advantage" and explore an economic modernization model suited to its unique social, economic, natural, historical, and cultural conditions. Drawing on the "great breakthrough" theory of Russian-American economist Alexander Gerschenkron, economic modernization with Chinese characteristics is inherently "substitutional." In other words, China's modernization model differs from the so-called standard or ideal model of advanced countries. These differences represent the "substitution" of corresponding elements from the economic modernization models of developed countries.

Latecomer countries possess their own unique advantages in constructing modernization models. On the one hand, they can extensively learn from the modernization experiences and lessons of developed countries, thereby fostering innovation based on their own development and achieving broad "substitution" in their modernization models. On the other hand, they can introduce, digest, learn from, and absorb advanced technologies from developed countries, distinguishing their models and paths from those of advanced nations. Of course, these "latecomer advantages" can only be effectively utilized to discover an alternative modernization model on the condition that latecomer countries have a correct understanding of their national conditions and economic backwardness, along with a strong determination to advance their economic modernization process. It can be said that China's economic modernization journey to date has demonstrated the successful use of its latecomer advantages. By allowing the market to play a decisive role in resource allocation while better utilizing government functions, China has successfully followed a path of socialist economic modernization with distinctive Chinese characteristics, under the leadership of the CPC. China's modernization process has now entered a new stage focused on high-quality development in pursuit of improved living standards.

However, latecomer countries also face their "latecomer disadvantages" in the process of economic modernization. While they benefit from the experiences and technologies of advanced countries, they also become dependent on these countries in areas such as technology, trade, and capital. Nowadays, based on the global value chain division of labor, latecomer countries are often locked into the middle and lower ends of the value chain. Within the world economic rules and the international economic order set by advanced countries, latecomer countries are often in an unequal position. When the modernization process of latecomer countries reaches a certain level, that is, when their international competitiveness grows, their economies expand rapidly, and their international economic status improves significantly, trade frictions between latecomer countries and advanced countries are likely to occur, thus restricting the modernization development of latecomer countries. Radical scholars of development economics use the concept of "dependency" to describe the "dependent relationship" that developing countries have with developed countries within the global economic system. Although radical theories have been heavily criticized and may not always be accurate in the context of globalization, global modernization history shows that the issue of "dependency" has existed to some degree in most developing countries. If latecomer countries reach a certain stage of modernization and are unable to break through such dependence through independent technological innovation, their modernization is likely to stagnate or be completely interrupted. In fact, the inability of many developing countries to become high-income countries and their entrapment in the so-called "middle-income trap" is a reflection of this unbreakable dependency, or perhaps an inevitable outcome.

In China's modernization process, its economic development also faces an innovation bottleneck. The weak capacity for scientific and technological innovation has become the Achilles' heel of China's high-quality economic development. Although China's capacity for scientific and technological innovation continues to improve, and it has become the leading country in terms of research and development (R&D) personnel investment and the second-largest in R&D expenditure, the industrial foundation—represented by the "four fundamentals" (core parts and components, basic processes, basic materials, and industrial technology)—and the modernization of the industrial chain are in urgent need of improvement. There are still many "bottleneck" technologies that need to be overcome. A significant number of core and key technologies remain heavily dependent on foreign countries. If such dependency on core technologies cannot be effectively overcome, it will directly constrain China's high-quality economic development and the advancement of its modernization drive. The trade tensions between China and the United States in 2018, the COVID-19 epidemic in 2020, and the strong backlash against economic globalization further highlight the necessity and urgency of breaking this dependency on core technologies. General Secretary Xi Jinping pointed out, "The new development pattern is essentially self-reliance and self-strengthening. We must place greater emphasis on independent innovation."[5] This means that the new development pattern is a model of economic modernization centered on promoting domestic economic circulation and seeking to break free from the dependency of core technologies. To a certain extent, it represents a shift away from the low-cost export-oriented industrialization development model. Of course, pursuing a new pattern of development doesn't mean rejecting opening up and globalization. On the contrary, it calls for a high level of opening up, focusing on enhancing the efficiency and quality of domestic circulation through the international economic cycle, shaping new advantages in global cooperation and competition, improving the quality and allocation of production factors, and boosting China's innovation capacity as well as industrial transformation and upgrading. In other words, constructing a new pattern of development is about overcoming the dependency on core technologies within the context of economic globalization and establishing an economic modernization model with Chinese characteristics.

[5] Xi Jinping gives an important speech at the opening ceremony of a seminar where principal provincial- and ministerial-level leading cadres study and implement the guiding principles of the 5th Plenary Session of the 19th CPC Central Committee. We must thoroughly study and fully implement the guiding principles of the 5th Plenary Session of the 19th CPC Central Committee and get off to a good start in fully building a modern socialist country (Chin. ed.) [N/OL]. People's Daily, [2021-01-12]. http://paper.people.com.cn/rmrb/html/2021-01/12/nw.D110000renmrb_20210112_1-01.htm.

Understand the New Development Pattern Based on Modernization Dynamics

Based on the theory of modernization dynamics, fostering a new pattern of development is an economic modernization strategy aimed at smoothing the economic cycle and fully leveraging the economic advantages of a major power.

Productive forces determine production relations, and the economic foundation determines the superstructure. Economic modernization is both the driving force and foundation of national modernization as a whole. Although economic development cannot be directly equated with the process of economic modernization, how to promote economic growth and optimize the economic structure, as well as how to facilitate the transformation of the traditional economic structure into a modern one, undoubtedly forms the core of the economic modernization strategy. As the path to achieving economic modernization at the new stage of development, building a new development pattern is also a strategy for economic modernization for this new stage.

The keyword for the new development pattern is "economic circulation." Economic activity, in essence, is a process of circulation in which information, capital, and goods (including services) flow among different actors, such as residents, businesses, and governments, based on the economic division of labor and value addition. Throughout the history of economic thought, the idea of using circulation and flow to describe economic activities can be traced back to Francois Quesnay's *Tableau Economique* published in 1758. Karl Marx, in his *Das Kapital,* introduced the theory of social reproduction, describing it as an economic cycle consisting of production, distribution, exchange, and consumption. Additionally, he presented three processes and formulae in the cycle of industrial capital: from money to commodities, from commodity purchase to the production of new commodities, and from new commodities back to money. On this basis, Wassily Leontief proposed replacing the theory of scarcity with the theory of reproducibility—an economic theory rooted in circulation and flow—and suggested it should serve as the cornerstone of economic theory. Therefore, describing the new development pattern from the perspective of economic circulation not only captures the essential features of economic development but also enriches and develops contemporary Marxist political economy.

Fostering the new development pattern hinges on unimpeded economic circulation so as to guarantee continuous social reproduction, ensure sustained economic growth, and promote the ongoing optimization of the economic structure. This is also a core requirement of economic modernization at the new stage of development. Currently, factors hindering the smooth circulation of China's economy include both structural factors on the supply side and the failure to effectively unleash the potential of domestic demand on the demand side, as well as the growing impact of the uncertainty and instability of the international environment brought about by global changes of a magnitude not seen in a century. This situation necessitates strategic and policy adjustments: deepening supply-side structural reform to better align supply with domestic demand; enhancing demand-side management to effectively stimulate demand; balancing the internal and external dynamics of economic growth on the basis of opening up to the outside world at a higher level; forming a positive interplay between domestic and international economic flows; and striking a balance between economic efficiency and economic security to build a more efficient and secure industrial system and regional layout.

From the perspective of modernization strategy, fostering a new pattern of development that is focused on the domestic economic circulation and features positive interplay between domestic and international economic flows has its theoretical logic established in the unique characteristics of the industrialization of major powers. Simon Smith Kuznets, in his *Economic Growth of Nations: Total Output and Production Structure*, classifies sample countries into 22 large nations and 35 smaller ones based on population. His empirical analysis shows that, at the same GDP per capita level, large countries tend to have a larger proportion of industrial output, particularly in manufacturing. Similarly, in *Development Pattern: 1950—1970,* Hollis B. Chenery and others elucidated the differences in development patterns between large and small powers. Although there are many differences, the most general feature of large countries' economic development is an inward economic orientation due to their large populations and huge market capacities. If Kuznets's study supports the fact that China's rapid industrialization since the reform and opening up has established it as the world's largest manufacturing power, then the studies by Chenery and others provide a theoretical basis for China's endeavor to foster a new pattern of development centered on domestic circulation. At the beginning of the reform and opening up, although China had a huge population, its low GDP per capita precluded the existence of a large market capacity. During this period, China actively participated in international economic flows, sourcing its raw materials for production from abroad and selling finished products in foreign markets. It was reasonable to adopt the strategy of export-led industrialization. Today, China's GDP per capita has exceeded $10,000, and it has a middle-income group of more than 400 million people. This makes China an enormous market. Additionally, the value added in China's manufacturing sector now surpasses the sum of the United States, Japan, and Germany. Given these supply and demand conditions, it is logical to foster a new pattern of development focused on the domestic economic circulation. Of course, this does not mean neglecting international circulation. On the contrary, international circulation must be based on domestic circulation, with both domestic and international circulations mutually reinforcing each other.

Finally, it should be noted that economic modernization encompasses industrialization, urbanization, informatization, and agricultural modernization, among other aspects. As a modernization strategy, the new development pattern focuses on smoothing domestic economic circulation. This can be manifested through the deep integration of information technologies and industrialization, the positive interaction between industrialization and urbanization, and the coordinated development of urbanization and agricultural modernization. The synchronous development of industrialization, informatization, urbanization, and agricultural modernization is both the inherent requirement and a fundamental principle of modernization in the contemporary era. It is also an inevitable demand of the strategy for high-quality economic development, guided by the new development philosophy at the new stage of development.

Accurately Grasp the Fostering of the New Development Pattern from a Comprehensive Perspective

Accelerating efforts to foster a new pattern of development, focused on the domestic economy and featuring positive interplay between domestic and international economic flows, is a major strategic plan made by the Central Committee with Comrade Xi Jinping at its core. This strategy takes into account the overall situation of the great rejuvenation of the Chinese nation and global changes of a magnitude not seen in a century, and is based on a thorough assessment of the current situation while keeping an eye on the long-term future. It is a systemic and deep-level transformation, which is of great significance for China's high-quality development and the world's economic prosperity. General Secretary Xi Jinping's series of important remarks on accelerating efforts to foster a new pattern of development are characterized by profound vision, broad and deep insights, a comprehensive system, and rigorous logic. These ideas form a critical component of General Secretary Xi Jinping's economic thought and are major theoretical contributions to the political economy of socialism with Chinese characteristics. This strategy must be accurately understood and thoroughly implemented from a comprehensive perspective.

Fundamental Basis, Realistic Logic, and Major Significance of Fostering a New Pattern of Development

It is essential to correctly understand the historical position and development stage of socialism with Chinese characteristics. This understanding serves as the foundation for the Party to define central tasks and formulate lines and strategies accordingly. After successfully building a moderately prosperous society in all respects and embarking on the journey to fully build a modern socialist country, China has entered a new stage of development. Grasping this new development stage is the practical basis for implementing the new development philosophy and constructing a new economic pattern. At this new stage of development, China's economic strength, technological capabilities, comprehensive national power, and people's living standard have all reached new heights. With a per capita GDP surpassing $10,000, China has become a super-large economy with the second-largest economy in terms of total economic output and the largest in terms of total manufacturing output in the world. Both in terms of supply capacity and demand potential, China now possesses the conditions and foundations to foster a new pattern of development that is focused on the domestic economy, which supports and drives positive interplay between domestic and international economic flows. Meanwhile, with major changes in the demand structure and production functions, problems such as the disconnection between supply and demand, and poor circulation caused by bottlenecks in technology supply and imperfections in the market system and mechanism, have become increasingly prominent. The previous development model, characterized by export-oriented industrialization based on the low-cost advantage of labor and other factors, and participation in the international cycle with raw materials sourced from abroad and the finished products sold in foreign markets, is increasingly ill-suited to the new development stage. Additionally, the international environment has become more complex and uncertain due to unprecedented global changes. A series of significant variables such as the new round of scientific and technological revolution and industrial transformation, trade disputes between China and the United States, the COVID-19 pandemic, and the Russia–Ukraine conflict have profound and far-reaching impacts. The trend of economic de-globalization is becoming increasingly clear, and global patterns, as well as industrial and supply chain layouts, are facing tremendous shocks. Under these circumstances, it is imperative for China to further smooth domestic circulation and enhance the independence and sustainability of its economic development. The new stage of development demands a stronger and more resilient national economic circulation system. Therefore, speeding up efforts to construct the new development pattern is China's proactive response to the major changes across various aspects of the new stage.

Fostering a new development pattern is a strategic path for economic modernization at the new stage of development, carrying both practical implications and profound historical significance. In the face of profound global economic and political changes and the new characteristics of the modernization process in China, the Central Committee, with Comrade Xi Jinping at its core, made the major strategic decision to accelerate the formation of a new economic pattern. This strategy aims at national rejuvenation amid global changes of a magnitude not seen in a century. This is a primary strategic task for China's overall development. It represents a continued deepening of supply-side structural reforms, a holistic enhancement of China's economic development strategy, and a forward-looking layout for gaining the initiative in future development. It is also a major historical task to be accomplished at the new stage of development. Given that China is a socialist country with a large population and an enormous market, the new development stage faces unprecedented challenges and risks. To address these challenges and risks, it is imperative to expedite the formation of a new economic pattern to ensure smooth domestic circulation, build self-reliance and resilience, and create a robust domestic economic circulation system and a solid foundational base. At the same time, China must also enhance its attraction to global factors and resources, while continuously improving the efficiency and quality of domestic economic flow through the global economic cycle. By doing so, China will be able to foster higher-quality, more efficient, fairer, more sustainable, and safer economic growth. The great rejuvenation of the Chinese nation will proceed without delay or interruption. Therefore, accelerating the construction of the new development pattern is of immense and far-reaching significance for China's high-quality development and for realizing the Chinese Dream of national rejuvenation.

Scientific Connotation, Key Aspects, and Essential Characteristics of the New Development Pattern

The basic connotation of the new development pattern is that it is centered on domestic circulation, with the domestic and international circulations reinforcing each other. To scientifically understand this paradigm, several aspects need to be considered. The first is its comprehensiveness. On the one hand, focusing on the domestic economy does not mean closing off the country from the world. It is about leveraging domestic demand potential and ensuring a better connection between domestic and international markets. The strategy does not advocate an extreme focus solely on domestic circulation or a drastic reduction in opening up to the outside world. On the other hand, China has already moved beyond the stage of economic growth mainly driven by foreign capital and trade. The new development pattern requires a shift from cost-driven, export-oriented, high-speed industrialization to innovation-driven, domestic-demand-oriented, and high-quality industrialization. This means moving away from the outdated model of "two ends abroad" and massive import-export operations. The second is a holistic approach. It must be fully understood that the new development pattern is a major strategic shift in China's economic development and path, and it is a crucial strategic deployment for the long-term security and stability of the nation, encompassing a nationwide unified large cycle and large market that includes various links such as production, circulation, distribution, and consumption. It is essential not to focus only on smaller local markets or regional circulation, nor to engage in low-level logistics cycles. The third is coordination. The construction of a new development pattern requires effective synergy between strengthening demand-side management and deepening supply-side structural reform. It is a misconception to view the establishment of a new development pattern solely as an expansion of domestic demand and the formation of a large domestic market, while neglecting the deepening of supply-side structural reforms. Likewise, it is also erroneous to consider the construction of a new development pattern merely as a further deepening of supply-side structural reforms, overlooking the importance of enhancing demand-side management and the long-term perspective on expanding domestic demand. The fourth is the systematic understanding. The new development stage, the new development philosophy, and the new development pattern must not be considered in isolation. It is crucial to recognize that entering a new development stage, implementing the new development philosophy, and fostering a new development pattern are determined by the historical, theoretical, and practical logic of China's economic and social development. Grasping the new development stage serves as the practical basis for applying the new development philosophy and fostering the new development pattern. The new development philosophy provides a guiding framework for understanding the new development stage and fostering the new development pattern, which, in turn, is a strategic choice to address the opportunities and challenges posed by the new development stage and to implement the new development philosophy. In conclusion, the new development stage, the new development philosophy, and the new development pattern must be viewed as an integrated and systematic whole. Only by understanding and applying them together can we fully appreciate their profound implications.

The key to fostering the new development pattern lies in ensuring the smooth flow of the economic cycle. The entire process of economic activity can be divided into various links, such as production, distribution, circulation, and consumption. A sound economic cycle, which supports reasonable growth, requires that production factors and products circulate smoothly among links and within each link. Fostering a new pattern of development requires focusing on the domestic economy, which is the core essence of this new pattern, while the smooth internal circulation led by domestic demand is the crux of the domestic macrocycle. Therefore, fostering a new pattern of development must adhere to the strategic focus of expanding domestic demand. Currently, the main reason for the stagnation in domestic economic circulation and the hindrance to expanding domestic demand is that China's domestic demand system is still incomplete and needs to be further improved. To address this, it is necessary to speed up the construction of a complete domestic demand system and further release the potential of domestic demand. To improve the domestic demand system, reforms are needed in several areas, including the construction of a modernized market system, a modernized industrial system, an income distribution system, and a new type of consumption system. In particular, the key contradiction between domestic supply and demand is that the supply side cannot fully adapt to the transformation and upgrading of demand, resulting in the failure of supply and demand to properly match and form an economic cycle. This challenge requires deepening supply-side structural reforms and making it the main line and strategic direction. Of course, for domestic circulation to be smooth, international circulation must also contribute to improving efficiency and the overall level of the economic cycle.

The most essential attribute of the new pattern of development is achieving high-level self-reliance and self-strengthening. The focus on the domestic economy in the new pattern doesn't simply refer to a greater proportion of domestic circulation in economic growth in quantitative terms. This isn't the essence of the new pattern of development. According to analytical measurements, in terms of GDP, China's economic cycle has long been dominated by domestic circulation, with the leading role of the domestic economy already well-established. General Secretary Xi Jinping pointed out that "The most essential attribute of fostering a new pattern of development is achieving high-level self-reliance and self-strengthening. We must attach greater importance to independent innovation."[6] This means the new pattern of development is one in which high-level independent innovation plays a major role in ensuring the smooth flow of the economic cycle. As China enters a new stage of development, the country's national economic conditions have undergone significant changes. The comparative advantage of low-cost labor is gradually diminishing, and the outdated combination of production functions is no longer sustainable. There is an urgent need for innovation to create a new combination of production functions. At the same time, global economic trends are shifting against the current of globalization, and the low-cost, export-driven industrialization model is no longer viable. Core technologies in key sectors remain controlled by others, and economic security risks are increasing. Many new bottlenecks and obstacles have emerged in China's economic cycle. Whether it is from the perspective of promoting an unimpeded economic cycle or cultivating new growth drivers to advance

[6] Xi Jinping gives an important speech at the opening ceremony of a seminar where principal provincial- and ministerial-level leading cadres study and implement the guiding principles of the 5th Plenary Session of the 19th CPC Central Committee. We must thoroughly study and fully implement the guiding principles of the 5th Plenary Session of the 19th CPC Central Committee and get off to a good start in fully building a modern socialist country (Chin. ed.) [N/OL]. People's Daily, [2021-01-12]. http://paper.people.com.cn/rmrb/html/2021-01/12/nw.D110000renmrb_20210112_1-01.htm.

economic growth, it is necessary to deepen the supply-side structural reform and institutional innovation to cultivate a high level of independent technological innovation capacity, break through industrial development bottlenecks, comprehensively optimize and upgrade the industrial structure, enhance innovation capacity, competitiveness, and comprehensive strength, and develop a more effective and higher-quality input–output relationship. This is essential to ensure the smooth flow of the economic cycle and achieve a higher level of dynamic balance between supply and demand.

Strategic Layout, Major Initiatives, and Policy System for Fostering the New Development Pattern

To foster the new pattern of development, the first priority is to uphold the central role of innovation in the overall modernization process. Self-reliance and self-strengthening in science and technology must be positioned as the strategic support of for China's development. It is necessary to focus on the real economy, accelerate the development of a modern industrial system, and enhance China's capabilities in science and technology, manufacturing, product quality, cyberspace, and digitalization. The second priority is to maintain the strategic focus on expanding domestic demand, fostering a complete domestic demand system. The construction of a super-large domestic market should become a sustainable historical process. This requires combining the expansion of domestic demand with deepening the supply-side structural reform, generating and meeting new demands through innovation and high-quality supply. The third is to accelerate further reforms in key areas and critical links, constructing a high-level socialist market economy. It is necessary to continue implementing a broader, more profound opening up across more areas, establishing a driving mechanism that focuses on the smooth functioning of domestic economic circulation and features positive interplay between domestic and international economic flows. The fourth is to speed up coordinated development between urban and rural areas, as well as across regions. This includes ensuring the synchronous development of new industrialization, urbanization, informatization, and agricultural modernization, while accelerating ecological civilization construction, optimizing the industrial and spatial layouts of the domestic economy, and promoting green, low-carbon, and circular development. The fifth is to adhere to a holistic approach to national security. National security must be integrated into all fields and links, strengthening the ability to dynamically safeguard national security in a complex environment.

There are several major initiatives for fostering the new pattern of development. The first is to establish a macro-governance mechanism that effectively coordinates supply-side structural reform and demand-side management, while continuously improving the macroeconomic regulation system. Upholding the principle of focusing on supply-side structural reform, prioritizing domestic economic circulation, and ensuring the decisive role of the market in resource allocation, China must accelerate the formulation of an economic operation mechanism that maintains a dynamic balance between supply and demand, coordinates reforms, and management effectively, improves the mutual advancement of domestic and international circulation, and integrates market mechanisms with government roles. The second initiative is to enhance China's strategic capacity in science and technology, as well as enterprises' capabilities for technological innovation. By focusing on upgrading the industrial foundation and modernizing supply chains, China will make greater efforts to revitalize the industrial foundation and advance the construction of new infrastructure. Additionally, China aims to strengthen and expand its digital economy, boost emerging strategic industries, and support the modernization of the service industry. The third initiative is to thoroughly implement the strategy of expanding domestic demand. This includes actively advancing the construction of a unified national market by improving systems for production, market, distribution, and consumption. It is necessary to focus on smoothing the domestic circulation and promoting positive interplay between domestic and international economic flows. Comprehensive efforts should be made to boost consumption, reinforcing its fundamental role in economic growth, and optimize investment structures, leveraging effective investment to improve the supply structure. The fourth initiative is to build a high-level socialist market economy and a new open economic framework, so that the market can play a decisive role in resource allocation, while the government can better perform its role. China will adhere to the principle of "two unwavering commitments"—that is, unswervingly consolidating and developing the public sector and unswervingly encouraging, supporting, and guiding the development of the non- public sector—thereby promoting the healthy development of non-public enterprises and entrepreneurs. This involves creating a market environment in which all ownership entities have equal legal access to resources, can compete fairly, and are equally protected by law. This will stimulate the vitality of all market participants. Additionally, it is necessary to establish a modern system of property rights and lay the foundation for the ownership structure that supports the growth of a contemporary socialist market economy and modern economic development. The fifth initiative is to promote the integrated development of urban and rural areas, regions, and industries, achieving strategic synergy in new industrialization, people-centered new urbanization, and rural revitalization. This requires comprehensive advancement in green production and consumption transformation to achieve stable and efficient growth of the green economy. The sixth initiative is to further integrate development and security, especially by consolidating the foundation of economic security. On the one hand, China must safeguard the real economy and industrial development centered on the supply chain. On the other hand, it is necessary to maintain financial security to prevent systemic risks. To this end, the country should continue the supply-side structural reform of the financial sector and ensure that finance returns to its essence of supporting the real economy. By focusing on these critical points, China will uphold a holistic approach to national security, implement national security strategies, and prevent and mitigate major risks in the course of China's modernization.

From the perspective of accelerating the fostering of a new pattern of development, it is necessary to gradually form a policy system that pursues progress while ensuring stability. Since the 18th CPC National Congress, General Secretary Xi Jinping has repeatedly emphasized the general principle of pursuing progress while ensuring stability, which has become an important principle in China's governance philosophy and a methodology for economic work. Fostering a new pattern of development requires a policy framework that pursues progress while ensuring stability. Stability is the keynote and the big picture, focusing on policies to stabilize economic operations, ensuring that no systemic risks arise in economic operations. Progress refers to proactive policies in various key fields for building a new development pattern on the basis of stability. Stability and progress are organically integrated and mutually reinforcing. The policy framework of pursuing progress while ensuring stability consists of seven overall requirements: steady and effective macro policies; micro policies leashing the vitality of market entities; structural policies smoothing the cycle of the national economy; concrete and feasible technology policies; policies of reform and opening up liberating development momentum; regional policies highlighting balance and coordination; and social policies satisfying people's basic needs. To be specific, the policy framework of pursuing progress while ensuring stability puts emphasis on the following aspects. First, active fiscal policies and prudent monetary policies should be coordinated, and cross-cyclical and counter-cyclical macroeconomic measures should be organically integrated, with a strategic focus on boosting domestic demand while addressing structural issues, to ensure that macroeconomic policies are more targeted and effective. Second, microeconomic policies must be accurately grounded in the relationship between industrial policies and competition policies. These policies must facilitate deepening reform and opening up, aligning with the development trend of the digital economy, and continuously stimulating the vitality of market entities, boosting their confidence, and creating a favorable environment where businesses of all types of ownership can compete and grow. Third, efforts should be made to deepen the supply-side structural reform, focusing on facilitating the circulation of the national economy and removing supply-side bottlenecks, while continuously strengthening and refining structural policies, particularly by accelerating the solid implementation of technology policies to establish a modern industrial system characterized by a virtuous circle among technology, finance, and industry, ultimately fostering a new pattern of development defined by high-level self-reliance and self-strengthening in science and technology. Fourth, it is crucial to correctly understand and grasp the strategic objectives and practical pathways for achieving common prosperity. This means advancing both economic development and people's well-being in a coordinated way, while improving the balance and coordination of regional development policies. Social policies must ensure the protection of people's basic livelihoods, and regional development policies must work effectively in conjunction with social welfare policies.

Build a Strong and Resilient Circulation System of the National Economy

On April 29, 2022, the Central Political Bureau held a meeting and analyzed the current economic situation and economic work. The meeting pointed out that risks and challenges had increased due to the COVID-19 pandemic and the Ukraine crisis. The complexity, severity, and uncertainty of China's economy had risen, with new challenges in stabilizing growth, employment, and commodity prices. It emphasized that ensuring economic stability and improving people's livelihoods were of critical importance. The meeting called for strengthening confidence and overcoming difficulties to ensure the effective implementation of the policies set by the CPC Central Committee. Building a strong and resilient circulation system of the national economy is a key initiative of the Central Government to accelerate the construction of a new development pattern based on the current economic situation and through effectively coordinating epidemic control with economic and social development.

Building a Strong and Resilient Circulation System of the National Economy as an Inherent Requirement for Fostering the New Development Pattern

A strong and resilient circulation system of the national economy is characterized by two main aspects. On the one hand, it features abundant, high-end production factors, an unimpeded economic cycle, a reasonable and modern economic structure, steady and huge economic output, and the ability to maintain strong competitiveness in the international economic arena. On the other hand, it possesses the capacity to withstand significant external shocks, ensuring that the economic system can quickly absorb such shocks and return to normal circulation. Against the backdrop of the unprecedented global changes of the past hundred years and the rise of reverse globalization, global macroeconomic governance has entered uncharted territory. The latest round of scientific, technological, and industrial revolutions, with intelligence, digitalization, informatization, and green development as the main trends, is reshaping the global economic foundation and industrial layout. The global economic environment is becoming increasingly complex, with considerable uncertainties and instabilities. From the perspective of coordinating the overall strategy for the great national rejuvenation and the great changes that have not been seen in the world in a century, China needs to build not only a strong and competitive national economic cycle but also a resilient one that can withstand massive external shocks.

General Secretary Xi Jinping proposed accelerating the construction of a new pattern of development that focuses on the domestic economy and features positive interplay between domestic and international economic flows. He pointed out that the key to fostering the new development pattern lies in the unimpeded flow of the economic cycle and that the most essential feature is the realization of a high level of self-reliance and self-strengthening. In this context, the new development pattern does not only reflect a situation where the domestic economic circulation accounts for a high share of the overall economic cycle; more importantly, it embodies an unobstructed economic cycle driven by high-level independent innovation at home, the continuous expansion of domestic demand to increase the flow of economic circulation, and the dominant role of the domestic economy in facilitating the positive interplay between domestic and international economic flows. In other words, the domestic economy as the mainstay of the new pattern of development is not solely about the high share of domestic economic flow; it is more about the "mainstay" that focuses on high-level independent innovation, expanding domestic demand, and leveraging the dominant role of domestic circulation. This new development pattern can effectively coordinate economic efficiency and security. It lays a solid foundation for the circulation system of the domestic economy, attracts global resources, and ensures that China's economy maintains strong competitiveness in the face of fierce international competition. At the same time, it enables the country's economic layout to effectively withstand external shocks, quickly absorb risks, and ensure a safer, more efficient economic cycle. Therefore, building a strong and resilient circulation system for the national economy, in essence, is an inherent requirement for fostering a new pattern of development.

Improving the Modernization of the Industrial Chain as a Critical Task for Building a Strong and Resilient Circulation System of the National Economy

In the circulation system of the national economy, the industrial system plays a pivotal role in production and reproduction, serving as the driving force that ensures the smooth flow of the economic cycle. Since the onset of reform and opening up, China has rapidly advanced its industrialization process and actively participated in the global value chain, becoming the world's largest country in industry and trade. As a crucial participant in the division of labor in the global value chain, China holds an important position in the global industrial chain and supply chain. In particular, as the largest manufacturing country with a complete production system, China's value-added manufacturing output is already greater than the combined total of the United States, Japan, and Germany, which has, to a large extent, effectively supported the country's economic resilience. According to the *Industrial Development Report 2022* published by the United Nations Industrial Development Organization, countries with well-developed manufacturing systems are better equipped to withstand economic crises, and manufacturing capability is vital for economic resilience. In the wake of the COVID-19 pandemic, China's well-developed manufacturing system has played a major role in safeguarding economic stability.

In the face of global changes of a magnitude not seen in a century, the global industrial chain is facing major challenges of restructuring. China's industrial chain and supply chain are confronted with multiple pressures, characterized by factors such as industrial transformation under the new industrial revolution, substantial fluctuations in primary product supply, shortages in breakthroughs in "bottleneck" technologies, as well as the impacts of reverse globalization and "decoupling." These overlapping issues have led to considerable uncertainties regarding industrial security. Nowadays, the key to global economic competition lies in the industrial chain. Some Western countries are overtly suppressing China's industrial chain and attempting to sever China's links within the global industrial chain through various institutional arrangements. This situation underscores the urgency of safeguarding China's industrial chain and highlights the critical importance of establishing a resilient circulation system for the national economy.

To build a strong and resilient circulation system of the national economy, it is imperative to address the "capability shortfalls" in China's manufacturing sector by upgrading the industrial base and modernizing the industrial chain. This is one of the primary goals of industrial development during the period of the 14th Five-Year Plan. The modernization of the industrial chain largely depends on improving the capacity for scientific and technological innovation. This requires continuously improving the overall environment for industrial innovation and development, and constructing an industrial innovation ecosystem that is conducive to enhancing the industrial foundation and the level of the industrial chain. From a policy perspective, it is essential to properly manage the relationship between industrial policies and competition policies, leveraging the fundamental role of competition policies in improving the capability of the industrial foundation and the level of the industrial chain. The 14th Five-Year Plan outlined three major initiatives aimed at modernizing the industrial chain: the industrial foundation reinforcement project, the leading enterprise cultivation project, and the industrial competitiveness survey and evaluation project. Beyond these initiatives, two additional crucial measures are necessary to modernize the industrial chain and build a strong and resilient circulation system of the national economy. On the one hand, at the production and manufacturing level, it is necessary to integrate elements, optimize processes, and cultivate talents to enhance China's industrial base. On the other hand, through the establishment of a cross-institutional coordination mechanism linking enterprises (chain-leading enterprises), research institutions, statistical departments, industry associations, government regulatory authorities, and government decision-making departments, and under the premise of breaking down the barriers of data sharing and resolving the problem of data confidentiality, a set of normalized foundational analysis frameworks and a mechanism for information collection, feedback and processing should be established to respond to the dynamic changes of the industrial chain. This will facilitate the maintenance of industrial chain security as well as the accurate analysis and assessment of economic resilience.

Fostering a High-Standard Market System as an Important Element in Building a Strong and Resilient Circulation System of the National Economy

In the circulation system of the national economy, the market system is a system in which production factors, products, and services are exchanged among various entities on the basis of the division of labor, and the price mechanism ensures that supply meets demand. Whether the market system is perfect or not is a decisive factor in the smooth flow of the economic cycle. A strong and resilient circulation system of the national economy requires a high-standard market system that features a huge capacity, a reasonable structure, efficient operation, unification, openness, active participants, and orderly competition. Since reform and opening up began, China has carried out market-based reforms, gradually establishing a socialist market economy and improving its market system. Especially since the 18th CPC National Congress, China has made tremendous progress in market system development, which has played a foundational role in supporting the healthy development of the economic cycle.

The successive promulgations of the *Opinions of the CPC Central Committee and the State Council on Improving System and Mechanism for Market-based Allocation of Factors* and the *Opinions of the CPC Central Committee and the State Council on Accelerating the Construction of a Unified National Market* are of great importance in establishing a high-standard market system and fostering a strong and resilient circulation system of the national economy. By improving the system and mechanisms for market-based allocation of factors, China can expand the scope of market-driven resource allocation, enhance the factor market system, improve institutional constructions, and eliminate the barriers hindering the market-based allocation of production factors. This will ensure market-determined factor prices, autonomous and orderly economic flow, and efficient and fair allocation of factors, thus laying a solid institutional foundation for the construction of a high-standard factor market system and a smooth economic cycle. Accelerating the construction of a unified national market can create a stable, fair, transparent, and predictable business environment. It will help reduce institutional transaction costs, effectively eliminate industrial and regional barriers, promote the orderly flow and rational allocation of innovative elements, and enable the market's scale and agglomeration effects to fully play out. This will facilitate smooth and efficient domestic market operations, continuously expand its capacity, and help cultivate a strong domestic market, which will, in turn, maintain and enhance China's attraction for global enterprises and resources, ultimately contributing to the development of a powerful and resilient circulation system.

Adhering to High-Level Opening Up as an Effective Guarantee for Building a Strong and Resilient Circulation System of the National Economy

Building a strong and resilient circulation system of the national economy does not imply ensuring economic security and economic resilience through a closed domestic economic cycle. Instead, it requires achieving a high-level opening up through an open domestic and international dual-cycle system. With a strong domestic economic circulation system and a solid foundation, China can attract global factor resources, enhance its competitiveness in fierce international competition, and drive global resource allocation. This will enable China to continuously strengthen its new advantages in international economic cooperation and competition by constructing a mutually beneficial, diversified, balanced, safe, and efficient open economic system, thereby ensuring economic security and enhancing economic resilience in the context of economic globalization.

To advance high-level opening up based on a strong and resilient circulation system of the national economy, the first step is to emphasize institutional openness, aligning with the standards of a high-level international business environment. China must intensify openness in regulations, rules, management, and standards, especially in connection with the markets, rules, and standards of countries along the Belt and Road. Second, China must actively participate in the reform of the global economic governance system, contribute to rule-making in emerging fields, and propose more Chinese initiatives and solutions in the creation of higher-level international economic and trade rules. Third, China should actively promote opening up by building an open innovation ecosystem, improving its capacity for scientific and technological innovation, and propelling opening up. Whether a country's national economic cycle is strong and resilient is fundamentally determined by its innovation capacity, which can be improved not only by increasing investment in innovation but also by building an open innovation ecosystem. The opening up of the manufacturing and service industries should focus on the development of an open innovation ecosystem to promote the enhancement of innovation capacity. Fourth, it is necessary to improve the policy mechanisms supporting high-level opening up and integrate development with security. As opening up expands, the country needs to strengthen its review mechanisms for foreign investment, antitrust and unfair competition, national technology security list, and unreliable entities list.

We advance a robust and resilient national economic circulation system through high-level opening up, and it is essential to leverage the role of Pilot Free Trade Zones. Since August 2013, when the China (Shanghai) Pilot Free Trade Zone was officially inaugurated, China has set up a total of 21 Pilot Free Trade Zones in six batches, creating a coordinated network of free trade zones that spans the east, west, south, north, and central regions, integrating land and maritime strategies. These Pilot Free Trade Zones have played a pioneering role in China's socialist modernization. As China enters the new stage of development, Pilot Free Trade Zones must redefine their roles in the new pattern of development and contribute to building a strong and resilient circulation system of the national economy. These zones must gradually develop into central nodes of the domestic economic cycle, and strategic links in the interplay between domestic and international economic flows. First, Pilot Free Trade Zones should become hubs of high-level independent innovation, playing a significant role in upgrading China's industrial base and modernizing industrial chains. Second, they should serve as high-quality hubs for gathering top-tier global resources, with the capacity to attract global high-end elements, such as digital resources, knowledge, talent, and capital. Third, they must develop into testing grounds for high-standard economic and trade rules. By conducting stress tests on advanced economic and trade regulations within these zones, China can advance institutional openness in terms of rules, regulations, management, and standards. This will help create an effective buffer against the impacts of new global economic rules, ultimately enhancing the resilience of China's economic circulation system.

Simultaneously Advancing New Four Modernizations and Building a Modern Economic System

The 5th Plenary Session of the 19th CPC Central Committee set the long-term goal of basically achieving socialist modernization by 2035 and included "basically realizing new industrialization, informatization, urbanization, agricultural modernization, and building a modernized economic system" as one of its objectives. This follows the 18th CPC National Congress, which proposed that China "should keep to the Chinese-style path of carrying out industrialization in a new way and advancing informatization, urbanization and agricultural modernization, and that we should promote integration of informatization and industrialization, interaction between industrialization and urbanization, and coordination between urbanization and agricultural modernization, thus promoting harmonized development of industrialization, informatization, urbanization and agricultural modernization." The 19th CPC National Congress further underscored that "new industrialization, informatization, urbanization, and agricultural modernization go hand in hand" and, for the first time, proposed a specific timeline for the basic realization of the "New Four Modernizations." This also marked the first time a clear deadline was set for building a modern economic system, following the Party's strategic deployment of applying a new vision of development and fostering a modernized economy. Achieving new industrialization, informatization, urbanization, and agricultural modernization is a fundamental pathway to building a modern socialist country. It is also a pivotal strategic initiative in launching the new journey toward the comprehensive realization of socialist modernization.

Simultaneously Advancing the New Four Modernizations and Building a Modern Economic System: An Essential Requirement for Basically Achieving Socialist Modernization

The modernization of a country's national economy is fundamentally driven by the interactive development of industrialization and urbanization. Industrialization provides the economic foundation and growth momentum, while urbanization facilitates the concentration of key production factors and creates a broad demand market for industrialization. From a development economics perspective, industrialization is essentially a process of economic growth in which critical production factors in the national economy undergo successive advancements, transitioning from low-level to high-level combinations, which further fuel increases in per capita income and economic restructuring. As industrialization and economic growth progress, production factors like labor and capital gradually shift from rural areas to urban areas, leading to city expansion and accelerated urbanization. In turn, rapid urbanization further drives the transformation of economic structures and the increase in per capita income. Nowadays, the world is experiencing an era of informatization, driven by groundbreaking developments in information technology. This has sparked a new wave of technological revolution and industrial transformation, making informatization a defining feature of modernization. The deep integration of informatization with industrialization constantly enriches the connotation of urbanization. The interactive development of industrialization and urbanization plays a key role in advancing agricultural modernization. As agricultural productivity improves, surplus rural labor is increasingly absorbed into urban areas, reinforcing urbanization. This dynamic cycle highlights the interdependence of industrialization, informatization, urbanization, and agricultural modernization. Thus, in the modern era, achieving national modernization inherently requires the synchronous advancement of these four key areas.

Based on the understanding of the above requirement and principle, the 18th CPC National Congress proposed the synchronous development of new industrialization, informatization, urbanization, and agricultural modernization. At the 19th CPC National Congress, following the significant judgment that China's economy had shifted from a phase of rapid growth to a stage of high-quality development, it further stressed that the "New Four Modernizations" must go hand in hand. This strategic focus is essential for China's transition to high-quality development.

High-quality economic development must align with the principles of the new development philosophy, prioritizing innovation as the primary driving force, emphasizing endogenous coordination, and pursuing inclusive, green, and sustainable growth. Unlike traditional industrialization, new industrialization is a course of economic modernization in which industrialization and informatization are mutually promoted, featuring high technological content, good economic efficiency, low resource consumption, low environmental pollution, and the optimal utilization of human resources. The harmonized development of the New Four Modernizations fully reflects the requirements of the new pattern of development. On the one hand, scientific and technological innovation serves as the primary driving force of modernization, guiding the expansion of informatization and green development—both of which are global modernization trends. On the other hand, this approach acknowledges existing imbalances and inadequacies in China's modernization process, highlighting the need for coordinated development among production factors, among industries, between industries and regions, between urban and rural areas, and between humanity and nature. Therefore, actively promoting the strategy of new industrialization, achieving deep integration between informatization and industrialization, fostering a positive interaction between industrialization and urbanization, and ensuring synergy between urbanization and agricultural modernization are fundamental requirements for building a modern economic system and realizing high-quality development.

In alignment with the strategic deployment of the 19th National Congress and the 5th Plenary Session of the 19th Central Committee, the 14th Five-Year Plan marks the beginning of China's new journey toward building a modern socialist country in all respects. Achieving socialist modernization inherently requires the synchronous development of the New Four Modernizations. Meanwhile, a modern socialist country must also have a modernized economic system, which includes a modern industrial system driven by innovation and collaborative development, as well as an urban–rural and regional development system that highlights complementary advantages and coordination. The realization of these systems is a natural outcome of advancing industrialization and urbanization. Recognizing this, the Report of the 19th CPC National Congress proposes to promote the harmonized development of the New Four Modernizations, and at the same time identifies the construction of a modernized economy as a strategic goal for China's long-term development. On this basis, the 5th Plenary Session of the 19th CPC Central

Committee set the goal of basically achieving the New Four Modernizations and completing the construction of a modernized economy by 2035.

Advancing the Harmonized Development of the New Four Modernizations and Achieving Economic Modernization Must Tackle Problems of Imbalances and Inadequacies in Development

Since the founding of the People's Republic of China, the CPC has led the Chinese people in actively exploring their own path to industrialization. Over time, the Party has introduced a series of interconnected yet distinct development strategies, including industrialization, the four modernizations, new industrialization, and the harmonized development of the New Four Modernizations. Since the launch of reform and opening up, China, guided by the theory of socialism with Chinese characteristics, has undergone rapid industrialization. Over more than 40 years, China has progressed from the early to the later stages of industrialization and from widespread poverty to prosperity in all respects. Entering the new era of socialism with Chinese characteristics, China's economic development now prioritizes quality over sheer speed. Notable progress has been made in fields such as informatization, urbanization, agricultural modernization, and the building of a new socialist countryside. However, it should be noted that China's modernization, driven by a "catching-up" approach, has been characterized by high-speed industrialization and urbanization, inevitably leading to significant imbalances and inadequacies. The quality of economic development still has room for improvement. As required by the goals of the New Four Modernizations, several key areas require attention.

First, industrialization remains imbalanced, and the integration of industrialization and informatization is insufficient. The driving forces behind industrialization exhibit an imbalance between internal and external factors. For a long time, China's high-speed industrialization strategy, characterized by low costs and export orientation, has resulted in a high degree of external dependency and an urgent need to expand domestic demand. This, in turn, has led to prominent challenges such as increasing economic security risks, a shortage of core technologies, and pressures to upgrade industrial structures. These challenges significantly hinder China's transition from high-speed growth to high-quality development. From a regional perspective, industrialization levels show a clear gradient decline from the eastern to the central and western regions. For example, Shanghai,

Beijing, Jiangsu, Guangdong, and Zhejiang have already entered the stage of post-industrialization, while most other eastern provinces remain in the late stages of industrialization, and a significant portion of central and western provinces are still in the mid-stage of industrialization. Regarding industrial structure, industries such as steel, petrochemicals, and building materials face serious overcapacity issues. Meanwhile, the development of high-end industries and the upper segments of the value chain remains insufficient. Fields like key equipment, core components, and basic raw materials are heavily reliant on imports and foreign enterprises, while there is a shortage of high-quality, customized, complex, and high-value-added products. In terms of resources and environment for industrialization, there is a growing imbalance between the speed of industrialization and the carrying capacity of China's natural resources and the environment. The speed of industrialization is outpacing the carrying capacity of China's resources and ecosystem. In terms of the relationship between industrialization and informatization, the integration of the two must be further improved. The convergence of the Internet, big data, artificial intelligence, and the real economy needs to be deepened. China must enhance informatization in manufacturing and improve its intelligent manufacturing capabilities. Additionally, China's industrial software development lags behind, with most industrial software still provided by foreign companies. Addressing this issue is an urgent priority.

Second, new people-centered urbanization must be improved, and the interaction between urbanization and industrialization remains insufficient. Since reform and opening up, especially after the 18th CPC National Congress, China's urbanization has accelerated significantly. By 2021, the urbanization rate of China's permanent population was 64.72%, an increase of 46.8 percentage points from 1978, 12.15 percentage points from 2012, and 8.62 percentage points from 2015. However, by the end of 2021, the urbanization rate of registered residents was only 46.7%, still far behind that of the permanent population. To improve the quality of people-centered urbanization, the first priority is to enhance the urbanization of the rural migrant population and ensure they can enjoy equal rights as citizens. The second priority is to coordinate the construction of networks across large, medium, and small cities to strengthen industrial development, public services, employment opportunities, and population agglomeration in cities and towns. This requires a more harmonious interaction between urbanization and industrialization. Currently, there is insufficient interaction between the two in China, which is mainly manifested in a dual misalignment of "temporal dissonance" and "spatial non-interaction" between industrial development and urban growth. On the one hand, the lag in public services in cities and towns affects the normal industrial transformation and upgrading. On the other hand, the industrial clustering is not sufficiently effective, which constrains the capacity of cities to support further growth. If industrialization and urbanization do not interact effectively, industries could become isolated due to a lack of urban synergy, while cities could become hollow without industrial support. In the future, efforts should be made to establish a model of positive interaction between urbanization and industrialization—one that promotes the mutual promotion of industrial and urban development as well as the coordinated development of urban and rural development. This will facilitate the scientific coordination of industrial growth and regional spatial allocation. Furthermore, efforts should be made to develop urban agglomerations and clusters.

Third, agricultural modernization remains a weak link in China's modernization, and its coordination with industrialization and urbanization is still insufficient. Currently, agricultural modernization lags behind new industrialization, informatization, and urbanization. There is an urgent need for improvement in mechanization, scientific advancement, water conservancy, electrification, industrialization, green development, and informatization. China's agricultural development level is not in sync with its overall industrialization. Problems such as structural imbalances in agricultural supply, extensive development methods, non-point source pollution, and risks related to the quality and safety of agricultural products must be addressed through further agricultural modernization. The 5th Plenary Session of the 19th CPC Central Committee emphasized the importance of implementing a comprehensive rural revitalization strategy, strengthening the support of industry for agriculture and the support of urban areas for rural areas, and promoting a new type of relationship between industry and agriculture, as well as between urban and rural areas. This strategy should foster mutual promotion, complementary development, coordinated growth, and shared prosperity, while accelerating the modernization of agriculture and rural areas. This directive is crucial. On the one hand, improving agricultural modernization requires leveraging industrialization and modern technologies, as well as transferring surplus agricultural labor through urbanization. On the other hand, advancing agricultural modernization will fully unleash agricultural labor, further promoting the development of industrialization and urbanization. In the future, efforts should be made to advance the coordinated development of agricultural modernization, industrialization, and urbanization, promote deep integration among the primary, secondary, and tertiary industries, and facilitate urban–rural integration. In addition, it is necessary to cultivate new growth drivers for agricultural and rural development, paving the way for a path of agricultural modernization with Chinese characteristics—one that features efficient output, product safety, resource conservation, and environmental protection.

Advancing the Harmonized Development of the New Four Modernizations and Achieving Economic Modernization Must Apply the New Development Philosophy

Innovation-driven, coordinated, green, open, and inclusive development for the benefit of all is the guiding principle of China's modernization in the new era. As an important strategy and pathway for China's modernization, promoting the harmonized development of the New Four Modernizations must adhere to the new development philosophy. This is also an essential requirement of high-quality development. In light of the prominent imbalances and inadequacies previously mentioned, advancing the harmonized development of the New Four Modernizations under the guidance of the new development philosophy must focus on three key policy priorities.

First, it is necessary to prioritize innovation as the primary driving force and promote the harmonized development of the New Four Modernizations through technological innovation, thereby building an innovation-driven modern economic system. To achieve modernization in China, the role of technological innovation must be central. Technological innovation should serve as the fundamental driving force behind new industrialization, informatization, urbanization, and agricultural modernization. In the current era, technological innovation must firmly embrace the major direction of informatization, which is a defining technological feature of modernization. Since the first technological revolution, human society has progressed through various phases: the early mechanical era, the steam engine and railway era, the electricity and steel era, the oil and automobiles era, and the information and communication era. Since the latter half of the twentieth century, significant breakthroughs have been made in areas such as computer chip processing technology, data storage technology, network communication technology, and analytical and computational techniques. These innovations have led to exponential growth in information technologies, information products, and methods for information acquisition and processing, primarily characterized by computers, the Internet, mobile communication, and big data. The deep integration of informatization and manufacturing technologies has driven the innovation and expansion of smart, digital, and networked manufacturing technologies, resulting in the emergence of a complex technological system within the new industrial revolution. The 14th Five-Year Plan marks an accelerated phase of scientific and technological revolution and industrial transformation, providing China with a unique opportunity for "corner overtaking" in modernization. The level of the New Four Modernizations in China has already reached a considerable base, coinciding with a new wave of technological and industrial revolution opportunities. China is closer than ever to achieving the goal of building a strong modern socialist country in a comprehensive manner and realizing the great rejuvenation of the Chinese nation. China must seize this rare historical opportunity through innovation.

Second, China must align with the general trend of integrated innovation-driven development to promote the coordinated development of the New Four Modernizations and build a modern economic system that ensures the coordinated development of all factors. Promoting the harmonized development and simultaneous realization of the New Four Modernizations reflects China's understanding of the systemic features of modernization. Achieving national modernization is the result of coordinated efforts across various elements, industries, and regions. Nowadays, the world is experiencing an irreversible trend of integrated innovation-driven development across the primary, secondary, and tertiary industries, as well as between science and technology and between technology and industry. The integration of informatization into manufacturing and service-oriented manufacturing is accelerating, and the deep integration of the Internet with all three industrial sectors has become the core source of efficiency and the direction of technological innovation. Within this trend of integrated innovation-driven development, the continuous emergence of new industries, business models, and patterns further strengthens the new driving forces of economic development. Grasping and promoting this trend is crucial for advancing the harmonized development of new industrialization, informatization, urbanization, and agricultural modernization. Currently, the main obstacles to China's integrated innovation-driven development include the insufficient supply of generic technologies for precompetitive technology and a shortage of interdisciplinary talents. Therefore, it is essential to increase investment in the innovation of general-purpose and generic technologies, as well as in the training of versatile and interdisciplinary talents.

Third, China must uphold and improve the basic socialist economic system, overcome institutional bottlenecks in domestic economic circulation, and create a favorable institutional environment for the harmonized development of the New Four Modernizations and the establishment of a modern economic system. For this purpose, it is necessary to leverage the decisive role of market forces in resource allocation while also better utilizing the role of government, ensuring a proper balance between an effective market and a capable government. China must also invigorate all types of market participants, firmly consolidate and develop the public sector, and consistently encourage, support, and guide the development of the non-public sector. Proactive action must be taken to build an efficient, well-regulated, and unified domestic market that adheres to high standards. Necessary institutional support will ensure equal access, fair competition, impartial oversight, openness, orderliness, good faith conduct, and legal compliance. China must improve macroeconomic governance and establish a governance system that is guided by the national development plan, supported by a modern fiscal, taxation, and financial system, with fiscal and monetary policies as the main instruments. This system should better coordinate policies on employment, industries, investment, consumption, environmental protection, specific regions, and so on, setting clearer objectives, ensuring a reasonable division of functions, and boosting efficient collaboration. China must accelerate the transformation of government functions and continue to improve the market-based international business environment that respects the rule of law. Without a high level of marketization and a full-fledged market economic system, real economic modernization cannot be achieved. Therefore, advancing the harmonized development of the New Four Modernizations and building a modern economic system require the accelerated improvement of the socialist market economy, particularly in the areas of the property rights system and the market-based allocation of production factors.

New Philosophy and Pattern of Chinese High-Quality Development

Yu Miaojie

China's economy is currently facing a situation of "three overlapping phases." The first is the slowdown in economic growth, which is determined by the objective laws of economic development. The second is the pain of structural adjustment, a proactive effort to accelerate the transformation of the economic development model. The third is the process of digesting the effects of previous economic stimulus policies, an inevitable stage in addressing the deep-rooted contradictions that have accumulated over the years. At the same time, China is facing global changes of a magnitude not seen in a century, compounded by the unprecedented impact of the COVID-19 pandemic.

Despite these challenges, China's economy has entered a new stage, primarily characterized by high-quality development. The following discussion explores this transformation from three key perspectives. First, what are the indicators that confirm China's economy has entered this new stage, and in what ways does it manifest high-quality development? Second, based on the spirit of the 6th Plenary Session of the 19th CPC Central Committee, China must fully implement the five new development visions of innovation, coordination, green development, opening up, and sharing. This means making innovation the primary driving force, green development the prevailing model, openness the necessary path, sharing the fundamental goal, and coordination an intrinsic feature. How can China specifically implement this new development philosophy? Third, at the core of the new development pattern is the "dual circulation" strategy. How can China foster a new pattern of development that focuses on the domestic economy and features positive interplay between domestic and international economic flows?

What Is "New" About the New Development Stage?

Why is China's economy now in a stage of high-quality development? In my view, this can be understood through the following six aspects.

First, the increase in product value added. Nowadays, almost every country has been integrated into the global economy and trade. If a country's products generate higher value added, this reflects an improvement in economic quality at the micro level.

Value added can be measured by using two approaches: a time-series comparison and an inter-sectoral comparison.

From a time-series perspective, China's exports can be classified into two categories: general trade and processing trade. The value added of general trade is higher than that of processing trade, so shifts in product additional value can be assessed by analyzing changes in the proportion of general trade. From 1995 to 2007, processing trade accounted for the majority of China's foreign trade. However, since the 2008 financial crisis, the proportion of processing trade (involving customer-supplied materials) has been declining, while general trade has been steadily increasing. This indicates that the value added of China's exports is on the rise.

When comparing different industrial sectors, the processing trade initially revolved around the "Three-plus-one" trading-mix (custom manufacturing with supplied materials, designs, or samples, as well as compensation trade) and labor-intensive products such as clothing, shoes, and hats. Now, however, the processing trade has increasingly shifted toward capital-intensive products, such as electromechanical equipment, transportation equipment, and optical devices, which generally have higher value added.

Second, the evolution of China's export products' quality. Enhancing product quality is another key indicator of China's high-quality development. The year 2021 marked the 20th anniversary of China's accession to the World Trade Organization (WTO). From 2001 to 2012 (before the 18th CPC National Congress), the quality of China's export products increased by approximately 30%. Since the 18th CPC National Congress, the quality has further improved by an additional 25–30%. Overall, the quality of China's export products has seen a significant increase over the past two decades.

Third, the increase in enterprises' total factor productivity. Total factor productivity (TFP) is a crucial measure of economic development. Paul R. Krugman, the 2008 Nobel laureate in Economics, once stated that while TFP is not everything, it is nearly everything in the long run. To assess an economy's transformation and progress, enterprise-level TFP is one of the most important indicators. This indicator essentially reflects the performance of enterprises, such as the time required to manufacture a pair of shoes.

A comparison of China's TFP with that of the United States reveals that significant progress is evident. In 2000 or 2001, before China joined the WTO, China's TFP was about 30% of the US level. By 2015, this figure had risen to 45%, representing a 50% increase.

To put this into perspective, China's TFP at 45% of the US level means that if it takes one hour to manufacture a pair of shoes in the United States, it would take slightly more than two hours in China. But a more comprehensive analysis is needed.

While China's technology and efficiency may not be on par with that of the United States, its labor costs are only about 1/5 to 1/6 of those in the

United States. From this perspective, China's products still hold a competitive advantage. Of course, more importantly, Chinese enterprises' TFP is steadily increasing, gradually narrowing the gap with the United States.

Fourth, China's economy features a complete industrial chain. China is the only country in the world that possesses all industrial sectors classified under the United Nations' industrial classification system. According to the National Bureau of Statistics, China has 41 major industrial categories and 666 sub-categories. Namely, China embraces a complete industrial system.

China is the world's largest exporter. The diversity of its exports further reflects its industrial completeness. In 2020, China exported approximately 10,850 types of products according to the eight-digit International Harmonized System (HS). If classified according to the ten-digit HS codes, the number of product types increases to around 14,000.

Fifth, China's economy benefits from industrial clustering. China's industrial cities do not aim to develop all industries; instead, each major city specializes in its own signature industry. For instance, Shenzhen specializes in electronics, Shantou in toys, Langfang in furniture, and Xingtai in cashmere.

The advantages of industrial clustering include resource concentration, cost reduction, and economies of scale. Furthermore, it generates positive spillover effects for upstream and downstream industries, further enhancing business profitability.

Sixth, from a broader industrial perspective, China's economy is undergoing continuous transformation and upgrading. Currently, the proportion of primary, secondary, and tertiary industries in China's economy are 7%, 38%, and 55%, respectively. This reflects China's position as both a global manufacturing powerhouse and a world factory. The growing proportion of the tertiary industry is a clear indication of high-quality development.

China's primary industry share is similar to that of most countries, including developed ones. However, the key difference lies in the balance between the secondary and tertiary industries. In 2013, the tertiary industry surpassed the secondary industry in size, and by 2020, their proportions had shifted to 55% (tertiary) and 38% (secondary). Personally, I believe that maintaining a relatively large secondary industry is essential. At this stage of development, a strong real economy is crucial to sustaining China's role as the world's factory. Only with a solid manufacturing base can the national economy be stable and healthy. The primary role of the virtual economy is to support and complement the real economy, rather than replace it. As the saying goes, "Without the skin, where will the hair attach?"

The above points clearly demonstrate that after the 19th CPC National Congress, China's economy has indeed entered a new stage of high-quality development.

How to Apply the Five New Visions of Development?

Despite significant progress, China's economy still confronts multiple challenges. So, what measures should be taken to address these challenges? One prerequisite is to maintain high-quality development of the national economy, which requires a deep understanding and application of a new philosophy of innovation, coordination, green, open, and shared development.

First Vision: Innovation

Innovation encompasses both narrow and broad dimensions. In the narrow sense, innovation refers to self-reliance and self-strengthening in science and technology, including both technological progress and scientific innovation. These two concepts, however, are distinct. Technological progress allows enterprises—large and small—to improve their performance through enhanced management efficiency and technological capabilities. However, scientific innovation typically requires collective efforts from large research institutions to tackle key technological problems.

Achieving innovation relies primarily on two metrics: input and output. Input mainly refers to expenditure on research and development (R&D). To promote high-quality development, China must increase R&D investment. From this perspective, R&D can be divided into product R&D and process R&D. Product R&D focuses on new product development, while process R&D concentrates on gradual improvements in production methods. On these two points, the *2021 Report on the Work of the Government* clearly outlined quantitative targets to improve R&D intensity, the proportion of R&D expenditure to GDP. In general, OECD members' average is around 2.6%, while China's R&D intensity was 2.2–2.3% in 2020, with a target of 3%.

R&D investment intensity varies significantly across provinces, leading to disparities in innovation capacity among cities. For example, Beijing's R&D intensity reached 6%, and Shenzhen was 4.1% in 2020, and both are expected to rise further. These figures suggest that with effort, it is entirely possible for China to reach the goal of an average R&D intensity of 3%.

R&D can be divided into basic R&D and applied R&D. The proportion of basic R&D expenditure is now required to be more than 8% of total R&D expenditure. To achieve self-reliance and self-strengthening in science and technology, it is essential to focus on the ten key industries outlined in "Made in China 2025" and resolve 35 bottleneck technologies, such as the lithography machine in the semiconductor industry. Nowadays, there is a more important project, "Technological Innovation 2030," which aims to expand the integration channels of industry, academia, research, and application, ensuring that R&D occupies a more prominent position in national investment.

Of course, innovation encompasses more than the narrow sense previously mentioned. In a broad sense, it is more important. It involves innovation in rules, regulations, and standards. Here are three examples to illustrate.

The first example is the establishment of Pilot Free Trade Zones. China has established 21 Pilot Free Trade Zones since 2013, and these zones primarily focus on four key tasks. The first task is to ensure that foreign enterprises enjoy pre-establishment national treatment, supplemented by a negative list. In other words, they are treated the same as domestic enterprises. The negative list essentially means "everything which is not forbidden is allowed," and the reform direction is to reduce the number of items on this list. The second is to implement a trade policy characterized by "frontline liberalization, second-tier control." The third is to streamline the administration, delegate power, improve government services, optimize the business climate, and facilitate investment. The fourth is to promote reforms related to capital markets and capital projects, particularly in the financial sector. So far, significant progress has been made in these four areas. Regarding the development of Pilot Free Trade Zones, it is hoped that by 2025, the end of the 14th Five-Year Plan, China will achieve full coverage of Pilot Free Trade Zones in the provinces east of the Hu Huanyong Line. At present, there are only four provinces in this area that have not set up a Pilot Free Trade Zone: Jilin and Shanxi in the north, and

Guizhou and Jiangxi in the south. However, these places are expected to set up Pilot Free Trade Zones in the near future.

The second example is the Hainan Free Trade Port, which represents a more advanced and demanding model of openness than the traditional Pilot Free Trade Zone. In June 2020, China released the *Overall Plan for Hainan Free Trade Port,* which outlines two phases: an early harvest by 2025 and full openness by 2035. The early harvest focuses on promoting the free flow of products and factors, which include not only land, capital, and personnel but also transportation and data, the two new forms of factors. Efforts must be directed toward liberalizing trade and facilitating investment. Notably, the Hainan Free Trade Port's strengths lie in its innovative measures during the full openness phase, including innovations in rules and regulations, such as zero tariffs, low tax rates, and tax reduction policies. The concept of zero tariffs is straightforward, while a low tax rate entails learning from regions like Hong Kong and Singapore by reducing the corporate income tax rate and the personal income tax rate to 15%. The Hainan Free Trade Port provides a lower tax rate that is different from the progressive tax rate in the Chinese mainland. In addition, there is a strong emphasis on addressing three critical areas: combating trade smuggling, preventing financial fraud, and safeguarding public health. These aspects highlight the significant innovations in regulatory practices within the Hainan Free Trade Port.

The third example is free trade ports. The concept of a free trade port extends beyond its literal interpretation as a maritime or river harbor. In a broader sense, it encompasses inland aviation hubs—such as major airports in landlocked provincial capitals—that lack traditional coastal or border advantages. How can they prepare themselves for openness? One potential solution is to consider establishing free trade airports in certain qualified cities. That is to say, if a city is relatively large and has more than one airport, it can facilitate high-quality service trade. By implementing high-quality service trade projects, it can effectively work toward the establishment of free trade airports, thereby fostering high-quality economic development.

Second Vision: Green Development

At the United Nations General Assembly in 2020, Chinese President Xi Jinping made a solemn commitment for China to achieve its "dual carbon" goals, meaning it aims to peak carbon emissions by 2030 and reach carbon neutrality by 2060. It should be noted that this commitment reflects the responsibility of a major developing country. Why? According to the current plan, China intends to take 30 years to go from carbon peaking to carbon neutrality, while developed countries typically require 50–70 years to accomplish the goal. In other words, China has a shorter time frame and thus faces a heavier task.

China is an important supporter of the three international conventions on climate. The first is the *United Nations Framework Convention on Climate Change* (UNFCCC), where China is one of the 10 signatories. China also actively supports the implementation of the *Kyoto Protocol* and the *Paris Agreement*. China put forward the core concept that all countries must jointly shoulder the responsibility for climate change and carbon dioxide emission reduction. It emphasizes two points: the concept of per capita emission and the concept of cumulative emission. For instance, developed countries, which account for one-quarter of the global population, have emitted three-quarters of the total carbon dioxide since the Industrial Revolution. Therefore, the concept of cumulative emission must be applied to understand this issue. Furthermore, because these countries have smaller populations, the perspective of per capita emissions must also be applied. They should bear more responsibility. Even with this understanding based on the two concepts, China has taken the lead in setting an example. To achieve the goal of carbon peaking and carbon neutrality, China has set several targets. First, by 2030, carbon dioxide emissions per unit of GDP will be reduced by more than 65%. This is a stringent target. Second, energy consumption and carbon dioxide emissions per unit of GDP must decrease by 13.5% and 18%, respectively.

For instance, the proportion of non-fossil fuel consumption in primary energy consumption is currently 15% in China, and the goal is to reach 25% by 2030. The current 15% includes 2% from nuclear power, 8% from hydropower, and 4.7% from renewable energy like photovoltaic and wind power. Achieving the 25% target in just 10 years is undoubtedly a daunting challenge.

Third Vision: Coordination

This vision consists of three main components: urban–rural coordination, regional coordination, and industrial coordination. At present, the focus is on regional coordination.

At present, one of the main tasks is to ensure the integration of the New Four Modernizations, which means realizing new industrialization, informatization, and urbanization on the basis of agricultural modernization.

Industrialization and urbanization must complement each other and develop in coordination. If not, problems may arise. For example, what happens if an industrialized country fails in urbanization? Many people will flood into cities in search of employment, wages will rise rapidly, and as a result, businesses will face reduced profits, which threatens their sustainable development. Conversely, some countries, such as South Africa, have been modernized but without industrialization. While many people move to cities to look for jobs, there are not enough job opportunities, which can lead to the emergence of slums and exacerbate the wealth gap, thereby increasing the potential for social instability. Therefore, China emphasizes the coordinated development of urbanization and industrialization, with informatization empowering both processes.

To achieve this, there is a current emphasis on developing "large cities and large countries." Namely, urbanization is not about expanding every small city into a large metropolis. Rather, the goal is to build large urban clusters, focusing on the development of nine major urban agglomerations, with five of these agglomerations as a starting point.

The map of nighttime urban light intensity clearly shows three particularly bright regions: the Guangdong–Hong Kong–Macao Greater Bay Area, the integrated Yangtze River Delta, and the coordinated Beijing–Tianjin–Hebei region. The Chengdu–Chongqing economic belt and the Yangtze River middle reaches economic belt follow in brightness. The Chengdu–Chongqing economic belt currently only consists of the cities of Chengdu and Chongqing, and it will take time to form a cohesive urban cluster. Wuhan, Changsha, and Nanchang along the middle reaches of the Yangtze River are relatively isolated, highlighting the necessity for coordinated development.

Apart from these five urban agglomerations, there are other urban clusters. To the north of the Yangtze River, there are the Shandong Peninsula urban cluster, the Liaoning Central and Southern urban cluster, and the central plain urban cluster. To the south of the Yangtze River, there is the Cross-Strait urban cluster. While focusing on the development of the five or nine urban agglomerations, revitalizing the northeast and promoting development in the northwest must also remain top priorities.

Fourth Vision: Shared Prosperity

The vision of sharing encompasses three aspects.

First, China has secured a complete victory in the battle against extreme poverty. One-fifth of the global population has been completely lifted out of poverty, which is a remarkable achievement. The international community regards China's economic development and its success in poverty alleviation as two remarkable miracles created by the country's economic and social progress.

Second, China must promote the effective implementation of rural revitalization. One important approach is encapsulated in the old Chinese saying, "Give a man a fish and you feed him for a day; teach him to fish and you feed him for a lifetime." For rural areas to be revitalized, it is essential to foster industrial development to stimulate economic growth in relatively impoverished regions. How can this be achieved? One proposal is to facilitate the gradual relocation of the processing trade. Currently, due to rising labor costs, the costs of processing trade in coastal areas are also increasing, making it less suitable for development. In this circumstance, how should the processing trade be transferred from coastal areas? Should it be moved overseas or to inland provinces? My personal understanding is that different industries should be treated differently. Labor-intensive industries should be transferred to foreign countries. Although inland provinces offer lower wages than coastal areas, labor costs are still relatively higher compared to other developing countries, so countries like Bangladesh and Vietnam have a comparative advantage. Capital-intensive industries should be relocated to inland provinces. Unlike labor-intensive industries, capital-intensive industries require the entire industrial chain, which countries like Bangladesh, Vietnam, or those in Africa cannot provide. Shifting capital-intensive industries from coastal areas to inland provinces aligns with the inherent characteristics of economic development.

Third, China must achieve the goal of common prosperity. The 10th Meeting of the Central Committee for Finance and Economics on August 17, 2021, repeatedly emphasized the need to solidly promote common prosperity, which has also been highlighted in various central government documents. Common prosperity does not simply mean equal distribution of wealth. The core of common prosperity, in my view, is to create wealth through innovation and hard work. The goal is to form an olive-shaped distribution structure, where the middle class is larger, and the extremes at both ends are smaller, thereby increasing the proportion of the middle-income group. Common prosperity cannot be achieved merely through intergenerational wealth transfer; it must be realized through innovation and diligence, while avoiding the emergence of a rentier class similar to that in Britain.

Fifth Vision: Opening Up

Opening up is essential for economic development.

To understand the concept of opening up, we first need to assess whether there has been a fundamental shift in the global trend of globalization. The answer varies, leading to different approaches. My personal opinion is that the globalization trend has not fundamentally changed; rather, its form has evolved.

There are two aspects to determine whether globalization still retains its basic features. One is the diversification of production locations, and the other is the maintenance of multilateral trade. If both are present, we can affirm the existence of economic globalization; if not, the opposite is true. Despite some countries adopting trade protectionism, the result is limited to increasing the costs of imports or raising the costs of China's exports. Fundamentally, this has not altered the localized production and multilateral trade patterns. Products are still manufactured with various components sourced from multiple countries and then assembled in places like China, Vietnam, or elsewhere, before being exported all over the world. This trend has not undergone any significant changes.

Therefore, we can conclude that globalization is still ongoing, but its manifestations have changed dramatically. Previously, the goal of the global economy was driven by the multilateral economic and trade cooperation structure promoted by the WTO. However, today, it has shifted to one of tripartite confrontation. Around the year 2000, before China joined the WTO, the global economic and trade structure consisted of two primary blocks: one was the European Union with Germany as the central node, and the other was the Asia-Pacific economic and trade circle or trans-Pacific economic sphere, centered around the United States. Now, the pattern of tripartite confrontation clearly has taken shape. The Germany-centered EU still exists, the North American Free Trade Area remains focused on the United States, but its influence has mostly shrunk to Canada and Mexico, while China has gradually emerged as the central hub of the Asia-Pacific economic and trade region. It must be underscored that this pattern of tripartite confrontation does not imply isolation; these regions remain interconnected.

This pattern of tripartite confrontation is supported by various economic and trade/free trade agreements. For example, the EU region is supported by the economic and trade integration framework, North America by the North American Free Trade Area, which has now transitioned to the USMCA (United States–Mexico–Canada Agreement), and in the Asia-Pacific region, the recently signed RCEP (Regional Comprehensive Economic Partnership) serves as a foundational support. Of course, these regions are interlinked. For instance, the CPTPP (Comprehensive Progressive Trans-Pacific Partnership) is being negotiated between Asia-Pacific and North America, China is working with the EU on the China–EU Comprehensive Investment Agreement to enhance bilateral ties, and there is the Transatlantic Trade and Investment Partnership (TTIP) between the United States and the European Union.

Foster the New Development Pattern Through Economic Dual Circulation

How to construct a new development pattern? One key focus is the economic dual circulation. In May 2020, the Standing Committee of the Political Bureau of the CPC Central Committee first proposed that China should fully leverage the advantages of its super-large market and domestic demand potential, constructing a new development pattern that features positive interplay between domestic and international economic flows. Both statements are critically important. The first statement, "fully leverage the advantages of its super-large market and domestic demand potential," signals that China's core competitiveness is no longer the comparative advantage of labor costs but the unified national market. Whether China can successfully construct a unified national market and better unleash domestic demand potential is the fundamental guarantee for the successful implementation of the dual circulation strategy and the construction of the new development pattern. The new development pattern of dual circulation signifies a synergistic relationship between domestic and international economic flows; neither aspect should be prioritized at the expense of the other.

To enhance domestic circulation, several aspects need to be addressed.

First of all, the market-based allocation of production factors should be promoted based on the principles of openness, fairness, and impartiality. To build a socialist market economy, the first step is to strengthen and expand state-owned enterprises and the state-owned sector. The 6th Plenary Session of the 19th CPC Central Committee, held in November 2021, clearly outlined that efforts should be made to enhance the competitiveness, innovation, domination, influence, and risk-resistance capacities of state-owned enterprises and state-owned capital. At the same time, it is necessary to encourage, support, guide, and develop the private economy, transforming it from a "beneficial supplement" to an "important component" of the economy. In fact, the private economy has already become an essential part of China's national economy, as reflected in the commonly cited "5-6-7-8-9" model. The private economy contributes 50% of GDP, 60% of taxes, 70% of innovation, 80% of employment, and 90% of enterprises, which highlights its significance in the national economy from various perspectives. The next step is to advance the market-based reform under the principle of openness, fairness, and impartiality, particularly focusing on the reform of the factor market.

Second, efforts should be made to advance trade liberalization by building a new pattern of comprehensive opening up, and to facilitate investment by improving the business environment. These two points can be understood together. Their goal is to ensure stability in employment, financial operations, foreign trade, foreign investment, domestic investment, and expectations. This is of paramount importance. The foundation of these "six stabilities" is ensuring stable expectations. Domestically, China faces a situation of "three-period overlap," while globally, there is the challenge brought about by profound changes of a magnitude not seen in a century. In terms of policy expectations, it is necessary to strengthen the continuity and predictability of policies. The ultimate goal is to stabilize employment. If employment is unstable, everything else will be problematic, potentially escalating into a huge challenge. Achieving stable employment requires stability in foreign trade, foreign investment, financial operations, and domestic investment. What specific measures should be taken? In August 2020, the General Office of the State Council issued the *Opinions on* Further *Stabilizing Foreign Trade and Foreign Investment*, making clear that efforts must be made to stabilize foreign trade, foreign investment, finance, and investment to ensure the "six stabilities."

Third, the most important task in internal circulation is to stimulate domestic demand and boost consumption. While this objective is relatively easy to state, implementing it requires substantial effort. The key tools to achieve this are proactive fiscal policies and prudent monetary policies aimed at stimulating demand and expanding consumption.

The underlying logic centers on two fundamental principles. First, to stimulate domestic demand and boost consumption, the top priority must be to ensure stable employment. If people face unemployment, how can they contribute to stimulating domestic demand or boosting consumption? This is not realistic. Ensuring employment requires stabilizing market entities. Second, as mentioned earlier, more than 80% of employment opportunities are created by the private sector, predominantly through micro-, small-, and medium-sized enterprises (MSMEs). Therefore, ensuring employment requires supporting MSMEs. Currently, these enterprises are facing significant challenges due to factors such as the COVID-19 pandemic. Therefore, prudent monetary policies, such as re-lending and re-discounting, should be introduced to alleviate their financial difficulties. As long as these businesses can access funding, they will be able to recover. This is the rationale behind adopting prudent monetary policies.

In recent years, there have been three key policy statements. The first is that "prudent monetary policy shall be more flexible, moderate, and precisely targeted." This means that China does not follow the US approach of large-scale stimulus ("flooding the market"). In fact, this statement provides a clear indication of the direction of the Renminbi (RMB). If the Federal Reserve adopts a loose monetary policy while China does not, overseas investors will be less inclined to invest in the United States because of the falling interest rates on the US dollar and lower returns on investment. As demand for the dollar decreases, the dollar will naturally depreciate, while the RMB will appreciate. Understanding this logic, it can be precisely judged that the RMB will appreciate starting in the second half of 2020, with some fluctuations, but the general trend remains unchanged. The second statement emphasizes the need to "maintain a reasonable growth in money supply and social financing scale." The so-called "reasonable growth" does not refer to massive growth. The third statement is "to ensure that newly increased financing should be directed toward manufacturing, micro-, small-, and medium-sized enterprises, and supporting the real economy." To put it more bluntly, the focus on supporting the real economy is being emphasized more strongly. Previously, loans to micro-, small-, and medium-sized enterprises were primarily provided by small and medium-sized banks, and while these banks continue to do so, large commercial banks are now also participating in such lending. This approach can be seen as "using a sledgehammer to crack a nut." To sum up, prudent monetary policy aims to help micro-, small-, and medium-sized enterprises overcome difficulties during the epidemic.

So, how should we understand the proactive fiscal policy? To boost consumption, the disposable income of the people must steadily rise. To achieve this, on one hand, tax and fee reductions are needed (which means lower revenues for local governments), while on the other hand, local governments must continue to be responsible for necessary infrastructures and public expenditures. This requires a proactive fiscal policy. This is the underlying logic for using proactive fiscal policy to stimulate domestic demand and increase consumption. To understand this fiscal policy, it is essential to clarify two fundamental questions: first, how much funding is available, and second, how it should be allocated. Generally speaking, the total available funds are around RMB 28 trillion. This includes general fiscal revenue of RMB 20 trillion, a fiscal deficit of RMB 3.76 trillion in 2020, special treasury bonds of RMB 1 trillion, and local government bonds of RMB 3.75 trillion. The current situation is similar. Though there are fewer financial arrangements, the base is growing, so the total amount is about RMB 28 trillion. Regarding fund allocation, the priority must be on employment, people's livelihoods, and market entities. The newly increased RMB 2 trillion should be allocated entirely to the county-level grassroots. Every year, emphasis is placed on the local and grassroots levels, but now the focus is specifically on the county level, which is why ensuring the smooth operation of the special transfer payment mechanism is crucial. In addition, money should also be directed to new industrial facilities, new urbanization, and major water conservancy and transportation projects. These are the main priorities of fiscal policy.

To strengthen external circulation, I believe six key areas should be addressed.

First, the diversification of export destinations. Companies should not always target mature markets in Europe and America. While these markets have well-established rules and Chinese enterprises are more experienced in these areas, the increasingly complex China–US relations make these markets less suitable as the primary export targets. Companies should prepare for future challenges by expanding trade with newly industrialized countries. While it may be difficult at first to break into these markets or maintain a certain market share, this should not deter businesses. They must persist and push forward little by little, much like trying to crack a tough nut.

Second, import expansion. Imports have become an important part of China's trade growth. The China International Import Expo, which has been held five times, and the China Import and Export Fair (Canton Fair) particularly highlight the expansion of imports. Here are three reasons for increasing imports. The first is that the import of high-quality consumer goods will enhance people's sense of well-being and happiness. The second is the import of intermediate products, which, as a result of tariff reductions, will lower import costs for enterprises, increase their profits, and support their sustainable development. The third is that the import of final products, such as automobiles, will naturally intensify domestic competition in the short term, but, in the long run, will drive enterprises to turn pressure into motivation, improving the overall competitiveness of the industry through a process of "survival of the fittest."

Third, the diversification and digitalization of service trade. China's service trade is lagging behind its commodity trade in volume and exhibits a deficit trend. My suggestion for the service trade is to expand its volume, adjust its structure, and build distinctive features. First, it is essential to increase the total volume of service trade, which currently stands at only RMB 600 billion—far too small. Second, structural adjustments must target the four major industries of transportation, tourism, education, and healthcare, whose development in China is currently hindered by funding deficits. By improving these key areas, many other aspects, particularly those related to soft power, such as improving the business environment, can be better implemented, leading to an enhancement in service trade. Finally, establishing unique characteristics involves developing flagship industries with comparative advantages, such as South Korea's success in the medical aesthetics industry.

The digitalization of service trade is another crucial feature. As a new economic form, the digital economy will play an increasingly important role in economic growth. The digitalization of service trade should focus on three key areas. The first is digital trade, such as e-commerce. The second is digital service trade, such as software outsourcing services. The third is data trade, such as Huawei Cloud and Alibaba Cloud. The digitalization of service trade is bound to be a major development direction.

Fourth, the diversification of outward investment. In 2020, China became the world's largest foreign investor, with outward foreign direct investment totaling $135 billion. Outward investment is not just about "going global," but more importantly about "embedding locally." This means that when investing in other countries, China must consider the social and economic features of each country and integrate more into local communities. By taking on more social responsibilities, Chinese enterprises can gain greater recognition from local societies, which is more conducive to long-term development.

Fifth, differentiated development under the Belt and Road Initiative. China must move forward with a dual strategy, developing both the overland and maritime Silk Roads, but with differentiation. Countries along the overland Silk Road often have complex geopolitical relations. For Chinese enterprises, it is more practical to engage in simple economic and trade cooperation, such as imports and exports, rather than direct investment, as they may face more geopolitical constraints in these regions. In contrast, countries along the Maritime Silk Road have a significantly higher level of economic and trade cooperation with China. Therefore, Chinese economic and trade cooperation with the countries on the Maritime Silk Road should not be limited to simple imports and exports, but can also encourage enterprises to invest in these countries.

Sixth, progressive regional trade and economic cooperation. China has already signed the Regional Comprehensive Economic Partnership (RCEP) with 15 countries, which will bring China closer to ASEAN countries in terms of trade and economic links. Following this, China will walk with both eggs—signing the China–EU Comprehensive Agreement on Investment (CAI) with the EU and joining the Comprehensive and Progressive Agreement for Trans-Pacific Partnership (CPTPP). China has expressed a strong interest in joining the CPTPP and has negotiated with 11 countries. Unlike RCEP, CPTPP emphasizes more integrated rules with less flexibility, meaning that joining the CPTPP will require higher standards from China. China's stance toward the CPTPP is one of proactive engagement, although the related negotiations will require time.

From my perspective, the current top priority should be the implementation of the CAI. Although this agreement is currently at a standstill, the EU will soon realize that its economic development is closely tied to China's, as China offers a larger market compared to other nations. Once the EU acknowledges this, I am confident that the future of this agreement remains bright and both parties will likely work together to bring it to fruition.

The analyses above outline six reasons why it can be asserted that the Chinese economy has entered a new stage of high-quality development. At this stage, China must continue to uphold the five new visions of development and utilize the "dual circulation" strategy as a catalyst to foster a new pattern of development based on dual circulation. I believe that as long as this approach is maintained, China's economy will keep improving, and the great rejuvenation of the Chinese nation will soon be realized.

Examining New Trends in the Lower-Tier Markets Under the New Development Pattern

Zhu Keli

In this discussion on the Chinese economy, lower-tier markets, and the expansion of domestic demand, I would like to share some preliminary insights and reflections.

If we consider that changes in the behavior of each economic agent often stem from a broader array of choices, I hope these reflections will aid in our understanding of the underlying realities behind these choices, such as policies, technologies, and market dynamics. This understanding will enable us to embrace future business and life with a more expansive framework and a broader perspective.

Tapping the New Potential of China's Economy

From the perspective of the new development pattern, what new driving forces and potential exist for tapping into the domestic demand of China's economy?

Since the outbreak of COVID-19, China's economy has faced significant challenges, but it is important to recognize that the contribution of consumption to economic growth has been increasing, reaching 54.3% in 2020, which is a historically high proportion. Looking further back, from 2011 to 2019, the average annual consumption share was 53.4%. The increase in 2020 compared to the past 9 years serves as direct evidence that China's economy grew against the trend during the pandemic.

In the next 5 or more years and even beyond, there will be four main sources of new potential for the Chinese economy, particularly in terms of consumption dynamics.

Coordinated Urban–Rural Development

As China's urbanization rate surpasses 60%, the country has entered a new stage where urbanization and rural revitalization are working in tandem. At this stage, urbanization remains a crucial driver of economic growth.

From a policy perspective, it is an inevitable trend to place rural revitalization at a high priority. However, it is important to note that rural revitalization is not a policy that stands in opposition to urbanization.

If the rural population continues to decrease, will rural revitalization become more challenging? This issue has been frequently raised in policy discussions. I firmly believe that urban and rural strategies should not be treated as separate and opposed to each other. They should be understood in an integrated, coordinated way. China must center on the urbanization of the urban population, enhancing urbanization policies and promoting the development of urban agglomerations and metropolitan areas, in order to drive rural revitalization through new urbanization.

Another point to emphasize is that only by unswervingly advancing new urbanization and enabling more rural residents to integrate into cities can more space be freed up to make better preparations for rural revitalization.

Enhancing Supply Capacity

The CPC Central Committee has emphasized the need to simultaneously address supply-side reform and demand-side management. From the perspective of economic logic, this means creating a cycle where demand drives supply and supply generates new demand.

Investigations show that, in recent years, many factories have made progress in digital transformation, process reengineering, and supply chain management. New forms and models, such as platform economy, sharing economy, and C2M (Customer-to-Manufacturer), are providing more value channels, opening up larger markets, and strengthening business empowerment.

These endeavors have created sustainable conditions for the improvement of supply capacity. In the past, "Made in China" was often associated with low quality at low prices. Today, the possibility of high quality at low prices is emerging.

Optimizing Consumption Structure

Expanding domestic demand and promoting consumption are key priorities in current economic policies. In the early stages of China's reform and opening up, people's needs were primarily basic sustenance. Today, however, they are increasingly concerned about life quality and the pursuit of a better life. While there is a general upward trend in consumption, differences at specific levels remain. On the one hand, trends like diversified consumption structures, varied consumer markets, and personalized consumption characteristics coexist. On the other hand, differentiation and divergence in consumption are widely observed, mainly across different regions, demographic groups, and urban–rural areas.

In fact, optimizing and upgrading the consumption structure is a process that requires continuous reform and evolution.

New Technology and New Economy

The application of new technologies is driving the emergence of new industries, new business forms, and new business models, forming the basic logic behind the creation of a new economy.

China has increasingly emphasized innovation in science and technology. In addition to breakthroughs in chokepoint technologies and core R&D domains, critical enabling technologies such as big data, cloud computing, artificial intelligence, and blockchain are empowering transformative growth. Intelligent manufacturing, for example, is an industrial-scale application of these new technologies.

New business forms and models derived from new technology, new products, and the integration of online and offline innovations have quickly become powerful drivers of economic growth. Whether it is like AI-powered robots and autonomous driving or online office solutions and smart healthcare facilitated by digital platforms, these technologies have demonstrated their capabilities, especially during the pandemic.

Following the new development pattern of dual circulation, the potential in these areas—whether in new urbanization that enhances supply capacity, optimizes consumption structure, or fosters new technologies and business forms—creates substantial space for the future development of the Chinese economy through the synergistic effects of these various drivers.

Understanding New Trends in Lower-Tier Markets

What is the lower-tier market? It refers to the vast potential market that needs to be activated in the future, including 200 prefecture-level cities, 3000 counties, and 40,000 villages and towns beyond third-tier cities.

As the primary area for tapping into new consumption, the lower-tier market's new trends can be summarized in five pivotal "New" dimensions: New Frontier, New Users, New Policies, New Pillars, and New Countryside.

New Frontier

Looking at the overall capacity of China's lower-tier market, it encompasses more than 900 million people across 200 prefecture-level cities, 3000 counties, and 40,000 villages and towns. It is roughly three times as large as the American market. No other country in the world has a market of such magnitude.

In addition to the vertical lower-tier market, there is also a related dimension concerning communities within various cities. From a broader perspective and business logic, communities and the lower-tier market can intersect in many ways. In the future, the business opportunities in communities will combine with those in the lower-tier market to create a new market synergy. Additionally, in the lower-tier market, communities in cities below the third tier and rural towns represent new frontiers.

New Users

As previously mentioned, the lower-tier market encompasses more than 900 million people, accounting for over 60% of the total population and half of the country's total mobile phone users, with every 100 people owning more than 90 mobile phones. In addition, Internet platforms have seen rapid user growth. For instance, a representative C2M platform has over 1.2 million merchants, 500,000 manufacturers, and 300,000 foreign trade factories.

These numbers, including the population size as well as the Internet user base and user growth in the lower-tier market, all point to the tremendous potential of new users from different aspects.

New Policies

From targeted poverty alleviation to the expansion of domestic demand, and now to comprehensive rural vitalization, along with new urbanization strategies, the government has provided policy guarantee and momentum for the development and growth of the lower-tier market.

With the strong backing of these policy initiatives, the lower-tier market is expected to be effectively activated, transforming from a latent market into a vibrant one in the future.

New Pillars
New technologies, business forms, platforms, and models are providing essential new pillars for the development of the lower-tier market.

New platforms and business models serve as the bridge between factories and users, creating a bilateral market tailored to the lower-tier segments. This approach, supported by big data, enables more precise supply-demand matching, offering new users and businesses more choices and more efficient connections, thereby stimulating fresh vitality in the lower-tier market.

New Countryside
Rural revitalization, in line with policy objectives and market trends, can be understood as an effort to activate and uplift the lower-tier market, enabling the majority of users to enjoy a lifestyle more aligned with modern civilization.

As the central government's primary policy document regarding the lower-tier market, this policy undoubtedly serves a significant purpose. In the digital age, it is precisely these new platforms that build a bridge between new townships and rural areas. Of course, as time progresses, even more innovative business models will emerge to serve the lower-tier market and new villages.

Stimulating New Dividends from a Massive Market

After analyzing the new potential of China's economy and emerging trends in the lower-tier market, it is finally necessary to explore a path to unlocking a trillion-scale market dividend. Below are several fundamental observations based on the logic of empowering the lower-tier market with new models.

Good Supply Replaces Bad Supply
With growing customer demands and stricter regulations, the market is showing a decreasing tolerance for low-quality, low-priced products. However, there are some localized instances of reverse trends emerging. A report from the China Consumers Association highlighted that counterfeit, substandard, and expired products are reappearing in rural markets.

This suggests that the vast opportunities in the lower-tier market have also attracted some individuals who fail to provide products that genuinely reflect the pursuit of a better life. As a result, high-quality producers or merchants who truly offer superior products are being driven out, creating a crowding-out effect.

But poor-quality goods will not dominate forever. Good products will eventually shine through. If new business models can enable more users to have more choices, then such business models are not only viable but should also become increasingly mainstream within market mechanisms.

From Low Quality, Low Price to High Quality, Low Price

The practical foundation for this shift lies not only in technological support but also in China's supply chain advantages. A flexible supply chain is a key enabler of high-quality, affordable products. Especially when new business models enable users to directly contact factories, many intermediate links, including sales, distribution, and inventory, are eliminated, allowing for production to be tailored to actual demand.

As a result, the costs previously imposed on consumers through intermediate links are reduced. The old notion that low price equals poor quality has been overturned. Now, consumers can enjoy high-quality products at low prices. This change is mainly driven by cost reductions through new business models.

Advancing the Supply-Side Reform of the Manufacturing Industry

A few years ago, the central government proposed the promotion of the supply-side reform. At that time, it was embarrassing but somewhat typical to see Chinese citizens traveling abroad to purchase basic goods like smart toilet lids. Why is supply-side reform necessary? One of the key reasons is the recognition that China's manufacturing industry is large but lacks strength, and it has reached a point where transformation is required.

One of the factors contributing to this lack of strength is the presence of too many intermediate links in the past. Although supply-side reform was not officially introduced as a key policy initially, it was seen as a market-driven behavior. However, it has now become imperative to implement such policies. These policy initiatives, like supply-side reform and market-oriented allocation reform, can contribute to achieving high-quality development. In terms of the market, new business models can help improve quality, reduce costs, and increase efficiency in China's manufacturing industry, thereby advancing the supply-side reform of the manufacturing sector.

Facilitating a Breakthrough for the Industrial Belt Amid Economic Headwinds

The COVID-19 pandemic posed a major challenge to China's manufacturing industry. In the past, with a favorable macroeconomic environment, it was relatively difficult to push ahead with transformation, even though many problems were recognized. However, under the pandemic, some issues have come to the fore, presenting new and greater challenges, with a large number of foreign trade factories facing a crisis of survival. In such a situation, is there any room for the market to break out against the trend?

In the context of the new development pattern, this may indeed present an opportunity. Amid the epidemic-induced lockdown, foreign trade has faced significant difficulties. The shift from foreign trade to domestic sales, which drives domestic circulation, has become a necessary path forward. At this moment, can China seize the market demand points arising from environmental changes and leverage digital platforms and models to promote the transformation of tens of thousands of coastal industrial belts through this shift from foreign trade to domestic sales? This is a truly historic opportunity.

Of course, while the lower-tier market may be vast, the adage remains true—opportunities only come to those who are prepared. If Internet platforms based on new business models have strategic reserves in commercial infrastructure, technology, business forms, and data, then when a "black swan" event, such as the pandemic, occurs, they will be able to guide and help factories and merchants in the industrial belt to pull themselves together and achieve great results against the trend based on such models and platforms.

Economy, Policy, and Investment Under the New Development Pattern of Dual Circulation

Guan Qingyou

The 20th CPC National Congress proposed the top-level design for Chinese modernization, with the dual circulation being a crucial requirement and key path for achieving it. This article will explore the economy, policy, and investment under the new development pattern of dual circulation from three dimensions. First, looking at the long-term historical cycle, the world is undergoing changes of a magnitude not seen in a century, and China is, and will remain, in a period of strategic opportunities for a long time. Second, from the perspective of industrial upgrading and technological evolution, China continues to experience rapid development. Investment institutions need to identify strong players in the right sectors while managing risks and seizing critical opportunities. Third, from the perspective of asset allocation, the asset pool of Chinese residents is shifting, and the financial industry has entered a new stage. The insurance industry, in particular, is entering its golden age.

China Remains, and Will Long Remain, in a Period of Strategic Opportunity

Let us first look at China's economy and development from a broad historical perspective. China faced trade frictions in 2018, the COVID-19 pandemic in 2020, and financial risks after 2017. As high-net-worth individuals, it is estimated that a considerable number of people feel anxious, and I myself was once anxious as well. Over the years, whether due to asset price fluctuations or changes in the external environment, China finds itself at a critical juncture, marked by the transformation of its development patterns and industrial upgrading. While numerous new problems need to be solved and emerging trends must be analyzed, this article will look at China's future trajectory and economic outlook from a longer historical cycle and multiple perspectives.

From a macro-historical perspective, how should we understand the unprecedented global changes China is facing today? About 300 years ago, during the height of the Industrial Revolution, China was in the prime of the Kangxi-Qianlong era of the Qing Dynasty, perceiving itself as the Celestial Empire. According to the Economist Intelligence Unit (EIU), China's overall strength was relatively robust at that time, though it is difficult to estimate the total economic output accurately. However, the country's strength was largely driven by national ambitions, particularly in terms of industrial and manufacturing capabilities. EIU data show that China's share of global economic output peaked around 1820, during the 25th year of Emperor Jiaqing's reign, approximately 200 years ago. After that, there was a steady decline. China's share of the world's economy began to rise again after reform and opening up, marking a significant turning point. 300 years ago, China closed itself off from the outside world, leading to a gradual national decline. About 150 years ago, during the Westernization Movement, the Chinese began to feel external pressure, which spurred the country's modernization efforts of the late Qing dynasty. Approximately 80 or 90 years ago, the Kuomintang (KMT) also attempted to push the country toward modernization, but this effort was ultimately interrupted by Japan's full-scale invasion in 1937. Looking at China's development from various historical perspectives offers different insights into its trajectory.

Recently, I have been reflecting on the limitations of economics in addressing certain issues, particularly in relation to long-term cycles. Economists tend to focus on short-term data fluctuations, and while there is research on long-term economic cycles, it is difficult to verify such extended periods. This is why I hope to present a clearer picture using historical comparisons and key concepts, as well as some important factors, even if only as a broad outline. Looking at a 40-year cycle, China has experienced a period of rapid growth. In 2010, China's economy ranked second globally, surpassing Japan. This is a milestone event. If we consider a 20-year cycle, China underwent a new round of globalization, becoming the world's largest trading nation and a major beneficiary of globalization.

Experts have debated the impact of long-term economic imbalances on China–US relations since China's WTO accession. This suggests that economists were already concerned about the potential effects of economic imbalances on the bilateral relationship a decade ago. But, predicting the exact moment when economic tensions would lead to a qualitative shift in bilateral relations has proven elusive. It is well known that economic imbalance can lead to changes in the political attitudes and economic interests of different social strata in both countries. The United States, for example, has faced significant industrial hollowing, while economies like China and Vietnam have become the "world's factory."

If we look at the 10-year cycle, China has experienced three rounds of fiscal easing and several rounds of asset bubbles. From the standpoint of national macroeconomic management, asset bubbles represent risks. But for investors, they present significant opportunities. Economists and investors approach problems from different perspectives. Economists often focus on risk, which is why they seldom profit, whereas investors may not always be right, but they can still make money. As the saying goes, "Listen to both sides, and you'll be enlightened." Different people have different perspectives on thinking and analyzing issues. For investors, whether high-net-worth individuals or professionals, it is crucial to understand the risks posed by asset bubbles. We must ensure that, when bubbles burst, we are not left as passive bystanders. This is a key point.

If we consider a timeframe of 3–4 years, this period represents a gradual defusing of financial risks. Financial rectification refers to measures aimed at preventing a systemic financial crisis by adjusting the financial regulatory framework and partially defusing financial risks. From the financial rectification in 2017 to the beginning of the China–US trade disputes in 2018, the asset market faced severe challenges. Few people were making money, and the acceleration of financial risk release led to liquidity issues for many listed companies. In my opinion, the financial rectification in 2017 was both necessary and successful. The financial rectification in 2021 focused on two main areas: one targeting entities that experienced sudden defaults and financial blowups, and the other addressing the platform economy, including the introduction of anti-monopoly regulations aimed at platform businesses. Clear regulation of the platform economy is likely to be prioritized over the next 2 or 3 years, and it is essential.

Based on the current pace of development, China is expected to surpass the United States in total economic output by 2030, or at the latest, 2035. According to purchasing power parity, China's total output had already exceeded that of the United States as early as 2014. At present, China's economy is roughly two-thirds the size of the US economy. However, when measured by exchange rates, disparities remain across various sectors between China and the United States. Since 2018, various social sectors have also engaged in extensive reflection and deliberation on this issue. From the perspective of economic imbalance, this is easy to understand. Economic globalization has encountered difficulties in distribution. The global economic pie has indeed grown, and according to Adam Smith's theory, China stands as a beneficiary of the world economy, with the United States also reaping benefits. However, the uneven distribution of globalization's benefits has caused a loss of profits for many social classes in the United States. For instance, many manufacturing hubs in the United States are in decline, and Detroit has become a "ghost town." This illustrates the severe hollowing out of American industry. Viewed through the lens of global economic imbalance, the qualitative shift in China–US relations becomes more understandable.

From a political standpoint, competition among major powers often leads to overlapping and conflicting goals, suggesting that geopolitical competition among major powers will intensify over the next decade. China must avoid two major risks: one is disruption caused by external forces, and the other is being dragged into conflicts that excessively deplete its own strength. As long as these two scenarios are avoided, China's development trajectory should remain secure.

China Remains on the Track of Rapid Development

China has gone through four stages since the beginning of reform and opening up.

The first stage is marketization. In the first 20 years of reform and opening up, China underwent labor marketization, and the first wave of entrepreneurs emerged. In 1984, after Comrade Deng Xiaoping's first southern tour talk, the "84 generation" of entrepreneurs appeared, followed by the "92 generation" after Deng's second southern tour talk. During this period, China also underwent capital marketization, marked by the first public share offering by FEILO ACOUSTICS, and Deng Xiaoping presented its stock certificate to the chairman of the New York Stock Exchange in person. This period also saw the first acquisition case and a gradual opening to foreign investment.

Simultaneously, China launched the first round of market-oriented reform of land. In the new development pattern of dual circulation, the market-oriented reform of production factors, with a focus on land reform, is crucial. Traditionally, the factors of production were land, labor, and technology, but now data have been added as a key production factor.

The second stage is industrialization, spanning from the late 1990s to 2008. During this time, there was an upsurge in exports, infrastructure development, and real estate. This stage benefited from several waves of dividends, especially the role China assumed as a pillar of the global labor force following its accession to the WTO in 2001. It is unrealistic in the short term to expect any country to replace China in terms of labor force size, market volume, or the completeness of its manufacturing ecosystem. After the COVID-19 pandemic, many orders were redirected from Southeast Asia and India due to their poor epidemic control, and China possesses the most complete industrial chain and manufacturing system. Experts in international relations have pointed out that China has not experienced industrial transfer; instead, some Chinese industries have spilled over into Vietnam, but Vietnam still relies heavily on the industrial ecosystem of China's Pearl River Delta. Countries like Vietnam have not undergone the stage of heavy chemical industry that China, Japan, and South Korea have already completed. The stage of heavy chemical industry is very important. China underwent this process in two distinct phases: the first during the planned economy in the initial 30 years after the establishment of the People's Republic of China, and the second over the more than 40 years following the launch of the reform and opening up, particularly after China's accession to the WTO. This has been vital for the integrity of the system and the establishment of an industrial base. Therefore, China has fully embraced the dividends of globalization over the past 20 years.

In addition, there is the dividend of urbanization. Although China's urbanization has slowed down and faces various institutional obstacles that need to be gradually addressed in the context of constructing a "dual circulation" economy, particularly in activating domestic circulation—significant potential remains. China's urbanization rate has just surpassed 60%. Based on Japan's urbanization standard of 75%, China still has a development space of 15–20 percentage points. Moreover, the number of individuals who have migrated to urban areas and can access public services as citizens does not exceed 50%, indicating that urbanization remains a major driver of future economic growth. The ongoing global changes, coupled with the changes in China's domestic development pattern and industrial structure upgrades, have set increasingly high demands for domestic reform. Recent agreements like the Regional Comprehensive Economic Partnership (RCEP) and the ongoing negotiations for China to join the Comprehensive and Progressive Agreement for Trans-Pacific Partnership (CPTPP) serve as catalysts for deeper domestic reform and opening up. Given the foundation built over the past 40 and 70 years, along with the current state of opening up, China's future development remains assured.

The third stage is financialization. China's stage of financialization occurred from 2009 to 2016, during which the fastest-growing sectors in China were the financial industry, real estate, and mobile Internet. A common characteristic of these sectors was the use of leverage, and the core concept of this era is also leverage. Both the international community and China, including governments and the general population, were increasing leverage during this age. For financial professionals and high-net-worth individuals, this was absolutely a golden age. But from the perspective of the national macroeconomic environment and financial regulation, it implies risks. After 2008, the global wealth disparity has sharply amplified, with affluent cohorts capturing an expanding share. In the United States, the "Occupy Wall Street" movement emerged, and in several countries, there were protests against rapidly rising housing prices. These phenomena were closely related to the increased use of leverage. In 2018, many enterprises lost control due to the tightening of the liquidity environment and changes in external conditions, as well as a lack of understanding of regulatory and liquidity policies. Some enterprises made mistakes by stepping on the wrong foot or did not have enough time to adjust after recognizing the problems.

Financial institutions have increased their leverage during this period. From the perspective of financial business, a loose monetary environment provided opportunities for some individuals and organizations. On the whole, the years after 2008 represented a golden age for the bond market.

Residents increased their leverage, with a particular upsurge in personal housing loans. At this stage, the property market was also characterized by high leverage and a high turnover rate. Real estate developers made money from capital turnover rather than rising housing prices. This means real estate was developing according to the model of the financial industry. In 2020, with the introduction of the "three red lines" policy, real estate developers began transitioning to a model based on the manufacturing industry. Therefore, it is imperative to remove the financialization attribute from real estate.

During the fourth stage and the most recent stage, the year of 2017 marked an important point. The fourth stage has the following features. First, China is moving away from being the world's factory. The country's position as the "world factory" is facing new challenges, such as rising costs of labor, energy, and environmental protection. Second, the model of excessive financialization has gone forever. The value added by the financial sector as a percentage peaked at 8.35% in 2015, which was higher than that of the United States and Japan before the financial crisis. This indicates that China's economy is highly prosperous. The 2017 financial rectification process commenced with the Central Political Bureau Meeting in late July 2016, which explicitly called for measures to "curb asset bubbles." The tightening of liquidity and strengthening of regulations after 2017 were actually a large-scale rectification. Third, there has been a shift away from an over-reliance on asset-based models, with the 2017 financial rectification indirectly impacting the real estate sector. Fourth, China is breaking free from excessive dependence on infrastructure construction.

The dual circulation, a new pattern of development that is focused on the domestic economy and features positive interplay between domestic and international economic flows, was first proposed in May 2020. From an academic perspective, the purpose of dual circulation is to stimulate domestic demand. While large economies still need external markets, it is crucial to activate the internal market. Although China has activated the domestic market since2008, this was done passively through a debt-driven model. The debt-driven model solved problems after 2008 but has many aftereffects.

Why does the monetary policy need to be normalized? There were lessons to be learned from the past decade. A former Japanese central banker once said that Japan's economy lost 30 years mainly because the country had implemented the wrong economics. At that time, because of the pressure from the United States, including the appreciation of the *yen* after the *Plaza Accord*, Japan needed to balance international trade by activating domestic demand, but it adopted inappropriate loose monetary policies. China must avoid following Japan's path. To activate domestic circulation and boost domestic demand, China must rely on reform. Reform is inherently challenging, and while China's reform has now entered the deep-water zone, the potential for reform is vast. Japan's efforts to reform its economy were hindered by its distinctive postwar economic structure, in which financial-industrial conglomerates held a dominant position. Japan's experience offers a critical lesson: national leaders must exercise firm control over these powerful financial groups, rather than be influenced by them. Leveraging its institutional advantages, China is able to readjust its financial structure. To foster the new development pattern, China must remain committed to expanding its openness and deepening reforms. China possesses the necessary conditions to succeed. There are still gaps between the east and west, north and south, urban and rural areas, and bridging these gaps will unlock the economic growth potential.

In a word, the dual circulation model encompasses six key concepts. The first is the parallel world. China has signed the RCEP agreement with many countries and is considering joining the CPTPP. Now, China and the United States are pulling together their respective groups. China is ready to be a member of the CPTPP, while it remains uncertain whether the United States will rejoin the TPP (*Trans-Pacific Partnership Agreement*) or renegotiate with European allies. Since China has successfully established its network through RCEP, it would be advisable to invite the United States to join as well, so that the two countries can support each other in addressing any challenges they may face.

The second is the expansion of domestic demand. To achieve this goal, it is essential to carry out in-depth market-oriented reforms of factors of production. Reforms must deepen across essential factors such as labor, capital, and land, demanding bolder ideological emancipation. To those questioning the feasibility, I maintain its viability. In my opinion, the core issue of this reform is to enable farmers to become property owners. Peasants have been making contributions since the founding of the People's Republic of China. For the first 30 years, there was a price scissors gap between industry and agriculture, and this gap persisted for the next 40 years as well. Therefore, China must implement land system reforms to enable farmers to own properties, which will stimulate their enthusiasm. Public service also needs attention. The real disparity in big cities is not only in wealth but also in the quality of public services.

The third is a unified market. It refers to the need to unify market management, industry management, transport management, logistics management, and many other areas, eliminating local protectionism, improving efficiency, and reducing costs. A unified market is crucial for improving economic efficiency and lowering costs.

The fourth is the digital economy or new infrastructure. The construction of digital infrastructure is a visible and tangible opportunity for industrial development. Regardless of the dimension of entry into the digital economy, whether through enterprises or investments through the primary and secondary markets, it is important not to miss this opportunity. Meanwhile, China must address the so-called "bottleneck" technological issues. While there are different opinions about China's scientific research environment, on the whole, there is real pressure from the outside, and China is at the same time in this stage of development. I am still optimistic about China's technological progress, despite challenges from sluggish domestic demand and external pressure, but I do not recommend trying to do everything on our own. The United States is working to decouple from China in technology and strike blows to Chinese technology enterprises like Huawei. But I am convinced that China will have more enterprises like Huawei and remain committed to domestic substitution and independent innovation.

The fifth is changes in regional economic geography. Since 2008, central cities have been rising and developing more rapidly than coastal cities. The digital economy offers an opportunity for an overall infrastructure upgrade.

The sixth is the deep integration and restructuring of the industrial chain. For example, Suzhou and Shanghai are closely collaborating to forge a closer partnership. There is a new round of industrial extension and restructuring coming out of the all-round cooperation of finance, R&D, production, and manufacturing between Suzhou and Shanghai. This is what we refer to as the "hypercycle."

Financial Industry Enters a New Era

Regarding economic performance, although China's economy has entered the "new normal," the development trend is basically steady. Now, China is faced with two forces. One is external pressure, namely negative interest rates. For example, for insurance companies, the real golden age is just beginning. Over the past 40 or 20 years, insurance companies have not experienced bubbles, compared to other sectors of finance, especially for practitioners, and without bubbles, there are no opportunities. Of course, we must also capitalize on favorable market conditions, state-owned institutions in particular. For another example, why do people invest in gold? When the price of gold per ounce rose from $1300 to $2000, it reflected the relative value of negative interest rates. China has entered the stage of lower returns on assets, yet foreign institutions are still struggling to access this market; China remains one of the few major economies where asset returns remain positive. Whether considering the trend of an aging population or the objective reality of 40 years of rapid economic growth, China is bound to gradually enter an era of zero or negative interest rates.

China's reform potential is greater than that of Japan and South Korea. From an investment perspective, this presents a once-in-a-lifetime opportunity. In the long run, China will be a key asset hub among the world's major economies.

The other is the reform dividends. Taking the stock market as an example, China is experiencing a transformation from the so-called "supply and marketing cooperative" model to the "supermarket" model. It is imperative to accelerate the implementation of the registration system. This necessitates several critical tasks to fully realize the registration system. First of all, supervision and review must be separated. Exchanges should operate as corporate entities, and personnel appointments should not be controlled by the China Securities Regulatory Commission. Second, the registration system must replace the current trading system. Currently, the trading market still adheres to a T + 1 trading mechanism, and it is essential to introduce mechanisms such as short-selling. Third, there are certain loopholes that need to be addressed in the implementation of the registration system. For instance, stock market differentiation is inevitable and will likely worsen. But there is no corresponding punishment mechanism for third-party institutions whose pricing deviates significantly from their final market performance in the ChiNext and STAR markets.

CHAPTER 3

Unified National Market and Chinese Modernization

Li Daokui, Zhang Ming, Jia Kang, Wang Wei, Jin Bei, and Zheng Zhigang

A Unified National Market as a Strategic Policy of National Significance

Li Daokui

Constructing a unified national market does not mean returning to the old path of a planned economy. On the contrary, it aims to build a higher-quality market economy and serves as a national strategic policy for achieving the Second Centenary Goal. The key to building a unified national market lies in thoroughly studying and effectively understanding the relationship between government and market economics.

L. Daokui (✉)
Academic Center for Chinese Economic Practice and Thinking, Tsinghua University, Beijing, China

Z. Ming
Institute of Finance and Banking, Chinese Academy of Social Sciences, Beijing, China

National Institution for Finance and Development, Beijing, China

C. Fang et al., *Modernization in a Chinese Style*,
https://doi.org/10.1007/978-981-95-6919-9_3

A Unified National Market: The Foundation for the Rise of Great Powers

Throughout global economic history, all great powers that have successfully risen to prominence have, without exception, established a unified national market. Historical experience shows that the economic takeoff of major economic powers and developed economies has been accompanied by the gradual unification and improvement of their market systems—a process that requires both government support and institutional refinement.

The United States has placed great emphasis on establishing a unified national market since the founding of the People's Republic of China. Many argue that the U.S. Constitution, formulated in 1787 and enacted in 1789, is not so much a political law as an economic one, as one of its core objectives is to ensure the creation and efficient operation of a unified national market. For instance, the Constitution explicitly states that "all duties, imposts, and excises shall be uniform throughout the United States," and "no tax or duty shall be laid on articles exported from any state."

Historically, the U.S. Supreme Court has ruled on numerous landmark cases aimed at securing and strengthening the unified national market. A notable example is the 1824 ruling by John Marshall, the Fourth Chief Justice of the United States, in a commercial dispute between two

J. Kang
Chinese Academy of Fiscal Sciences, Beijing, China

Huaxia New Supply-Side Economics Research Institute, Beijing, China

W. Wei
Market Economy Research Institute, the Development Research Center of the State Council, Beijing, China

J. Bei
Chinese Academy of Social Sciences, Beijing, China

Z. Zhigang
School of Finance, Renmin University of China, Beijing, China

merchants from New York and New Jersey. Both sought exclusive operating rights for ferry services on the Hudson River, which borders the two states. One party claimed that their state had granted them exclusive rights and demanded that the other party cease operations. However, Chief Justice Marshall ruled that no state had the authority to grant exclusive rights to interstate ferry operations, as such services constituted interstate commerce. As a common law country, the United States established an important legal precedent through this court ruling: no state government may interfere with interstate commerce. A similar case involved the city of Baltimore, which unilaterally imposed a tax on wine passing through its port. The U.S. Supreme Court ruled that this action obstructed the formation of a unified national market, as the wine was intended for distribution across the country.

In addition, many believe that the American Civil War, which began in 1861, was also fought to preserve a unified national market. At that time, plantation owners in the South favored free trade, as it allowed them to sell raw materials to Britain and import British industrial products. In contrast, entrepreneurs in the North supported trade protection, arguing that a unified national market should take precedence over free trade. In other words, they believed that Southern agricultural products should be processed by Northern industries and that tariffs should be imposed on British industrial products. The South demanded free trade, while the North called for a unified national market, leading to a stark regional divide. Therefore, the American Civil War can also be interpreted as a struggle between market unification and market fragmentation, with the North ultimately prevailing in the fight to establish a unified national market.

Beyond the United States, the rise of Germany also demonstrated the significance of a unified national market. While the immediate cause of German unification in 1871 was Prussia's victory in the Franco–Prussian War, the unification process had begun decades earlier. As early as 1834, the German states, led by Prussia, had established the Zollverein, or the German Customs Union, to eliminate internal trade barriers, gradually forming a unified national market. This development directly contributed to Germany's industrial revolution in the nineteenth century and played a crucial role in facilitating the transition from economic unification to political unity.

The Importance of a Unified National Market

A unified national market is crucial to the rise of a major economy for three main reasons. First, a unified national market serves as a fundamental pillar for strengthening domestic enterprises. For large economies, establishing a nationwide unified market is even more important than for smaller countries, as their vast domestic markets offer immense potential. Once a unified national market is formed, enterprises in relevant industries can fully leverage economies of scale and continuously increase research and development (R&D) investment. Today, innovation in critical sectors such as biomedicine, semiconductors, 5G, and new energy often requires massive initial investment. Only by relying on a unified national market can enterprises better sustain their R&D efforts.

Second, a unified national market enables domestic enterprises to participate in international competition. Extensive evidence suggests that enterprises achieving scale advantages in the domestic market can compete more effectively with international enterprises. This explains why great powers tend to produce a higher number of globally competitive enterprises. Imagine if the United States had never established a unified national market and instead allowed local protectionism to fragment its economy. In such a scenario, its dominant retail giant, Walmart, would have struggled to achieve the scale necessary to compete effectively. Without first growing strong at home, how could Walmart have expanded globally? Similarly, without a unified national market, it would have been difficult for the United States to foster large, innovative enterprises such as Microsoft and Facebook. In other words, without such a market, both the international competitiveness and global influence of the U.S. economy would have been significantly weakened.

Third, a unified national market is a strategic asset for great powers to lead globalization. A unified national market is not only a key lever for expanding into international markets but also a prerequisite for leading globalization. This principle has been validated by historical experience—whether it was Britain's leadership in globalization during the middle nineteenth century or the U.S. dominance in shaping the global economic order after World War II. The underlying logic is that when a great power possesses a sufficiently large domestic market, it can leverage its advanced technology to drive global economic integration. By proactively opening its market to the world and strategically conceding some domestic market share in traditional industries, it can attract other countries to follow suit.

In doing so, it creates favorable conditions for its high-tech enterprises to dominate international markets. On the whole, great powers benefit more from globalization.

In conclusion, a unified national market is the foundation for great powers to fully harness economies of scale and participate in international competition. This has been the fundamental mechanism behind the United States' role as a leading force in globalization over the years. More importantly, it is an essential condition for nurturing globally competitive enterprises.

China's High-Quality Economic Development Calls for a Well-Established Unified National Market

Since the launch of reform and opening up, China's economy has made remarkable strides. Today, China has built a vast domestic market, with many products leading the world in both production and demand. At the same time, with the widespread application of Internet technology, Chinese products have never flowed as freely and smoothly across the country as they do today. However, as an emerging global power, China has yet to fully harness the potential of its unified national market, as evident in the following challenges.

First of all, local protectionism and market fragmentation still exist. Many products have yet to be fully integrated into the unified national market, and regional protectionism remains widespread, hindering business entry and exit. For example, in the case of the taxi industry, the market is regionally fragmented, with Beijing dominated by BAIC Group, Shanghai by SAIC Motor, and Chongqing by CHANGAN. A truly unified national market would emerge if taxis in Beijing were not restricted to BAIC vehicles but could also widely adopt SAIC or DONGFENG vehicles. Establishing such a market requires dismantling regional barriers to the free flow of products and production factors, promoting mergers and restructuring within the industry, and unleashing the endogenous impetus of China's economic growth.

Second, institutional barriers restricting the free flow of labor still exist, impeding the reconfiguration of economic geography. Throughout global economic history, changes in the geographic distribution of populations have been an inevitable requirement for productivity growth. China's economic transformation over the past 40 years is equivalent to what took 1500 years in some other historical contexts. However, the geographic redistribution of China's population has lagged behind the pace of its economic changes. Although household registration system reforms have gradually eased restrictions on labor mobility, challenges such as transferring and renewing social security benefits continue to impede the formation of a unified national labor market. To address this, China must align with the natural laws of economic and social development, remove institutional barriers, and promote the reconfiguration of its economic geography to unlock long-term drivers of China's economic growth.

Third, restrictions on the free flow of binding development indicators have led to resource mismatches and efficiency losses. As China's economy transitions from high-speed growth to high-quality development, its traditional, extensive economic model requires adjustment. Governments at all levels inevitably face multiple objectives in the process of economic development, such as maintaining capacity, preserving arable land, and reducing emissions. According to market economy principles, these binding indicators should ideally be lifted. But, in reality, every major economy maintains some binding indicators for overarching national consideration, such as overall economic security. The current practice is mainly to pass all kinds of binding indicators from one level of government to another in the form of administrative orders, with lower levels of government facing the pressure of supervision and accountability from higher authorities. Most of these binding requirements are characterized by fragmentation and strict delineation. Yet, as a special type of production factor, restrictive indicators should also leverage market mechanisms—within the framework of national total control—to be effectively allocated among enterprises, thus facilitating the orderly exit of surplus production capacity. However, the current "one-size-fits-all" approach of assigning the national total control targets to localities has resulted in significant resource misallocation and efficiency losses. Take the steel industry as an example. From a macroeconomic perspective, expanding steel production capacity in coastal provinces is more efficient than in inland regions, given their advantages in coastal provinces in transportation, operating costs, and environmental impact. However, because local governments at all levels must comply with strictly enforced production capacity control targets and face rigid inter-provincial capacity replacement restrictions, the scientific distribution of steel production across the country has been constrained, hindering the optimization of the steel product structure. If a unified system for real-time monitoring of steel production capacity, output, and raw material purchases were established, it would be possible to relax restrictions on inter-provincial capacity indicator trading while maintaining overall national capacity control. This would create a production capacity indicator market and potentially form a unified domestic steel market, which would be a key step in optimizing the capacity layout.

Fourth, constructing a unified national market is crucial for China's digital economy, led by Internet platforms, to enhance international competitiveness. Today, the digital economy is booming and has become a battleground in China–U.S. competition. It plays a decisive role in determining whether China can evolve into a world-class economy. The defining characteristic of digital industries is their reliance on economies of scale, which necessitates a unified national market. Key regulatory questions arise: How should these industries be supervised? What behaviors contribute to the disorderly expansion of capital? How should monopolistic behavior be defined? These issues can only be effectively addressed within the framework of a unified national market. Only then can China's digital economy achieve global competitiveness.

Understanding the Government–Market Relationship: A Framework for a Unified National Market

The experiences of the United States and Germany demonstrate that a unified national market does not emerge spontaneously; rather, it must be cultivated and regulated by the government. Thus, the key to establishing a unified national market lies in understanding the relationship between government and market economics. The economics of government and markets is a new branch of economics that studies the role and behavior of the government in a market economy, and it is founded on three basic starting points. First, the government is an important direct participant in a modern market economy. Second, government actions directly influence market performance. Third, an effective mechanism must be established to stimulate the government to foster and regulate market development, ensuring that governmental functions and market forces align in a mutually reinforcing manner.

According to the theory of government and economics, the following considerations are essential when constructing a unified national market.

First, the leading role of enterprises and entrepreneurs must be respected. A unified national market does not signify a return to a planned economy; rather, it represents a more advanced and efficient market economy. Enterprises and entrepreneurs serve as the primary actors in this market, playing a decisive role in determining market efficiency. Only by stimulating and protecting their initiative can a truly unified national market develop with vitality at its core.

Second, the initiative of local governments must be fully mobilized. One of the most valuable lessons for China's economic development from the 40+ years of reform and opening up is that local governments must both support and regulate the market. However, this requires appropriate incentives. A unified national market necessitates that local governments serve and promote regional economic development while ensuring that such efforts do not impede the free flow of factors and products across regions. Achieving this goal calls for deeper tax reforms and adjustments to the official evaluation system. These measures can fully mobilize the enthusiasm of local governments and encourage governments at all levels to improve the local business environment and create favorable conditions for enterprises and entrepreneurs—while adhering to national market regulations within the framework of a unified national market.

Third, establishing uniform national standards through independent regulatory bodies is necessary. A unified national market requires a consistent regulatory framework, which must be formulated by specialized, professional departments with a degree of independence and stability. A useful analogy from global financial governance is that most countries are more successful at controlling inflation and monetary policy than managing fiscal budgets. The number of countries experiencing uncontrolled inflation is far fewer than those facing fiscal deficits. This is largely because central banks tend to operate with greater independence. Similarly, the establishment of a unified national market necessitates independent and professional regulatory departments to develop and enforce standardized rules across the nation.

Fourth, market mechanisms must be fully utilized. The construction of a unified national market should be closely integrated with deepening reforms of key sectors. Market mechanisms should be leveraged to address long-standing challenges faced by administrative departments, such as carbon reduction, excessive capacity, and farmland protection. These issues can be tackled more efficiently by utilizing the mechanisms of a unified national market.

Significance and Potential Impact of Constructing a Unified National Market

Zhang Ming

A unified national market serves as an indispensable pillar in constructing China's new development pattern. The release of the *Opinions ofthe CPC Central Committee and the State Council on Accelerating the Construction of a Unified National Market* signals a deeper and more systematic set of reform measures, which hold great significance for achieving the sustainable and high-quality development of China's economy.

In 2020, the Communist Party of China (CPC) Central Committee and the State Council proposed to foster a new pattern of development that is focused on the domestic economy and features positive interplay between domestic and international economic flows. The backdrop for this new development pattern can be broadly categorized into two aspects. First, from an external perspective, the retreat of globalization, the outbreak of the COVID-19 pandemic, further exacerbating the protracted stagnation of the global economy, and the deterioration of the global trade environment, as marked by the China–U.S. trade dispute, have weakened external demand as a reliable and effective driver of China's economic growth. Second, from an internal perspective, as China's economy continues to expand, particularly with the substantial increase in gross domestic product (GDP), it has become increasingly unfeasible and unsustainable to rely on net exports as the primary engine of growth.

Before the introduction of the dual circulation strategy, China pursued a development strategy characterized by an "international macro-cycle," meaning the country fully integrated into globalization, leveraged its competitive advantages to develop an export-oriented economy, and used opening up as a catalyst for domestic reform. Therefore, fostering a new pattern of development that is focused on the domestic economy and promoting the positive interplay between domestic and international economic flows through the construction of the domestic circulation has become increasingly important. In other words, China is transitioning from a growth model driven by external demand to one in which domestic development serves as the primary engine for internal and external economic engagement.

Fostering a New Domestically Focused Development Pattern

How can a new pattern of development that is focused on the domestic economy be fostered? The author believes that this pattern must be built upon the following three key pillars: consumption expansion and upgrading, industrial structural upgrading and technological innovation, and ensuring the free flow of production factors while building a unified national market.

Since the beginning of reform and opening up, China's economic growth has largely been investment-driven and export-oriented. However, as the economy has evolved—particularly with rising per-capita income and an expanding economic scale—the country's growth engine is shifting from the secondary industry and investment to the tertiary industry and consumption. Therefore, expanding consumption among middle- and low-income groups with upgrading consumption among high-income groups has become particularly important. From the supply side, this necessitates vigorous development of advanced manufacturing and modern service industries to provide consumers with higher-quality products and a greater variety of choices. From the demand side, it requires increasing the disposable income of middle and low-income groups, as they exhibit a higher marginal propensity to consume. This principle is at the core of "common prosperity." Achieving common prosperity, in turn, requires addressing income distribution disparities among regions, between urban and rural areas, and within the residential sector itself.

The COVID-19 outbreak has disrupted global production, supply, and value chains. As a result, global production chains may become shorter and more regionalized. Additionally, the ongoing China–U.S. trade disputes have made it increasingly difficult to rely on the "latecomer advantage" to drive technological progress. As a result, achieving domestic industrial upgrading and technological innovation has become more critical than ever. In this context, efforts to complete, strengthen, and extend supply chains have emerged as a defining theme of the era. Given the increasing regionalization and localization of global production chains, it is essential for China to maintain its leading role in production networks across Asia and countries along the Belt and Road. To promote independent technological innovation, endeavors must be made to enhance intellectual property rights protection, expand opportunities for private enterprises (which contribute approximately 70% of China's technological progress), and reform the educational system by shifting the focus from "engineering thinking" to "innovative thinking."

Whenever China is mentioned, people are impressed by its population of 1.4 billion and its per-capita income surpassing $10,000, which naturally suggests the potential for a vast domestic market. However, China's domestic market remains significantly fragmented, with various restrictions and barriers hindering the cross-regional flow of various factors. This not only limits the free movement and market-oriented pricing of these factors but also obstructs their optimal allocation and the maximization of overall economic welfare. Therefore, to foster a new pattern of development that is focused on the domestic economy, it is imperative to eliminate barriers to factor mobility, break market segmentation, promote the free flow of factors, and construct a unified national market.

It is evident that these three key pillars approach domestic circulation from different angles. Consumption expansion and upgrading focus on demand, industrial upgrading and technological innovation target the supply side, and promoting the free flow of factors and constructing a unified national market addresses the institutional and infrastructural perspective.

Constructing a Unified National Market

On April 9, 2020, the *Opinions of the CPC Central Committee and the State Council on Developing a More Perfect System and Mechanism for the Market-based Allocation of Production Factors* was released. The document emphasizes that improving the market-based allocation of factors is an inherent requirement for building a market system that is unified, open, and ensures orderly competition. It calls for enhancing the efficiency of factor configuration by promoting the autonomous and orderly flow of factors. More importantly, the document proposes to promote the free flow of five key factors of land, labor, capital, technology, and data, while accelerating the market-oriented reform of factor pricing, and optimizing market mechanisms governing their operation. It is worth noticing that this appears to be the first time that a central government document has officially acknowledged data as a vital production factor.

On January 6, 2022, the General Office of the State Council released the *Overall Plan for Comprehensive Pilot Reform ofMarket-based Allocation of Production Factors*, which builds upon and further refines the policy measures outlined in the previous document. First, the plan proposed to conduct pilot reforms on the market-based allocation of production factors in urban agglomerations, metropolitan circles, and central cities where reform demand is urgent, the groundwork is solid, and development potential is high. Second, regarding land factor allocation, the plan calls for exploring a trans-provincial regulatory mechanism for the surplus land use quota under the linkage between urban and rural construction land increase and decrease, optimizing industrial land supply, improving the flexible land grant period system, supporting the implementation of the "standard land" grant for industrial land, and revitalizing idle land through market-based methods. Third, regarding labor factor allocation, the plan supports pilot regions with good conditions in urban agglomerations and metropolitan circles to introduce policies such as mutual recognition of cumulative residence years for household registration (*hukou*) within the same metropolitan area, mutual recognition of residence permits, and pilot projects for registering permanent residence based on habitual residence. Fourth, regarding the allocation of capital factors, the plan proposes selecting regional equity markets that are secure, well-regulated, and have strong risk management capabilities to pilot institutional and business model innovations. Fifth, regarding technology factor allocation, the plan supports colleges, universities, and research institutes in exploring innovative management methods for the commercialization of technological achievements in their professional capacity, and in licensing professional technological achievements to micro-, small-, and medium-sized enterprises. Sixth, regarding data factor allocation, the plan emphasizes improving the mechanism for public data opening and sharing, establishing a sound system for data circulation and transactions, and strengthening data security protections. Seventh, in terms of environmental resource allocation, the plan supports the establishment of a market-based green element trading mechanism, further improving trading mechanisms for carbon credit, pollution rights, as well as energy and water usage rights. Eighth, the plan highlights the need to enhance market-based trading platforms for production factors, continuously integrating and sharing the trading platforms of public resources.

On April 10, 2022, the *Opinions ofthe CPC Central Committee and the State Council on Accelerating the Construction of a Unified National Market* was officially issued. Above all, the document proposes that constructing a unified national market serves as a fundamental pillar and an inherent requirement of China's new development pattern. Next, it underscores the need to accelerate the establishment of a unified national market system and regulatory framework, eliminating local protectionism and market fragmentation and removing bottlenecks that hinder economic circulation, so as to promote the smooth and large-scale flow of goods, production factors, and resources. The goal is to develop a unified national market that is efficient, well-regulated, fair, and fully open, facilitating the transformation of China's market from being large in scale to being strong. These efforts will provide a solid foundation for building a high-standard market system and advancing a high-level socialist market economy. Furthermore, this document outlines the core principles and main objectives for accelerating the construction of a unified national market. The core principles are as follows: First, expand domestic demand to ensure smooth economic circulation. Second, improve institutional frameworks. Third, achieve an optimal balance between an effective market and a proactive government. Fourth, adopt a systematic and well-coordinated approach to ensure steady progress. The document further proposes five key directions for achieving market unification: harmonizing the basic market system and rules, developing a high-standard market infrastructure, integrating factors and resource markets, ensuring the seamless circulation of goods and services, and implementing fair and unified market regulation.

It is evident that the three documents share a common strategic vision, with mutually complementary and coordinated policy measures. For years to come, the Chinese government will continue to follow the direction set forth in these documents, making unremitting efforts to improve the market-based allocation of production factors and build a unified national market.

Promoting the Independent and Well-Ordered Flow of Production Factors

Finally, two important issues must be addressed.

First, one of the deepest-rooted causes of barriers to the flow of production factors and domestic market fragmentation is that the local governments' performance evaluation system places excessive emphasis on GDP growth and public budget revenue. Under such an assessment framework, local governments naturally seek to pool all kinds of production factors within their own jurisdictions and restrict the flow of these factors to other regions. A typical example is the resistance a large enterprise may face when attempting to relocate their headquarters across regions. To facilitate the free flow of production factors and construct a unified national market, it is essential to reform the incentive mechanisms for local governments. This requires a fundamental shift in the performance evaluation system, where less weight is given to GDP growth and public budget revenue, while including indicators such as market-oriented factor pricing and the cross-regional flow of factors.

Second, the free flow of factors will inevitably lead to factor concentration. As China constructs a unified national market, key factors such as land, labor, capital, technology, and data will likely flow at an accelerated pace into specific areas, driving a new round of regional integration. In 2021, the author, along with Wei Wei and Chen Xiao, published the book *Five Growth Poles: Urban Agglomeration and Integration under the Dual-Circulation Pattern*. The book contends that over the next 10–20 years, China's five fastest-growing regions will be the Guangdong–Hong Kong–Macao Greater Bay Area, the Yangtze River Delta, the Beijing–Tianjin–Hebei region, the Central Delta (Zhengzhou, Hefei, and Wuhan), and the Western Delta (Chengdu, Chongqing, and Xi'an). Based on this, China is expected to develop a new domestic "flying geese" model, where the Guangdong–Hong Kong–Macao Greater Bay Area, the Yangtze River Delta, and the Beijing–Tianjin–Hebei serve as the lead geese, the Central Delta and Western Delta act as the body, and other central and western regions form the tail. Together with an international goose queue model (China, Japan, and South Korea take the head; the relatively developed countries in the Association of Southeast Asian Nations (ASEAN) and along the Belt and Road form the body; and the relatively underdeveloped countries in ASEAN and along the Belt and Road make up the tail), this has evolved into the "dual flying geese" model that drives China's future economic growth. In turn, this model will further enhance the improvement of China's new development pattern, fostering mutual reinforcement between domestic and international economic flows.

Grasping the Essence of the Guideline for Constructing a Unified National Market

Jia Kang

Faced with the current intricate domestic and international landscape, the CPC Central Committee and the State Council issued a guiding document on accelerating the construction of a unified national market. This document holds profound significance for improving the socialist market economy system with Chinese characteristics, overcoming challenges in deepening reforms, emancipating productive forces, advancing high-quality development, and implementing the new two-step modernization strategy of the new era. To correctly grasp the essence of building a unified national market, at least five aspects must be emphasized.

Ensuring Equal Protection for All Lawful Property Rights

A unified market can only exist when all lawful property rights are protected on an equal basis. This requires reinforcing the rule of law as an essential cornerstone for long-term stability and governance. With regard to the logical relationship, the central directive on accelerating the construction of a unified national market is closely related to the rule of law in all respects, the long-established fundamental pillar for the establishment of a "high-standard, law-based business environment" in the course of reform and development. In practice, some enterprises and individuals have experienced violations of their property rights, and in certain cases, the principle of equality before the law—a crucial tenet of social fairness and justice—has not been fully upheld. To improve the socialist market economy with Chinese characteristics, China must confront these issues head-on and implement meaningful solutions.

Developing a Unified National Market with Barrier-Free Flow and Low Entry Thresholds for All Production Factors

The central government has already emphasized the free flow of production factors in a unified national market in special documents, which aligns with a fundamental principle of economics: For the market to play a decisive role in resource allocation, the unimpeded flow of production factors must be guaranteed. China has been promoting the supply-side structural reform as a main focus of the country's modernization drive. The fundamental logic behind maximizing the potential and role of various supply-side factors is that the market environment must overcome obstacles to ensure the barrier-free flow of production factors. Of course, technical standards for environmental protection and standardized techno-economic policies are essential and must be legally enforced by government authorities, but this should not serve as an excuse to excessively raise the market entry thresholds. Reform and opening up over the past years have proved that the government's tendency has been to lower barriers to entry and eliminate obstacles. This reflects a fundamental trend in building a unified national market, namely, eliminating unfair and excessive monopolies, with priority given to dismantling administrative monopolies inherited from the old system. Achieving this requires tackling challenges in complementary reforms, the establishment of effective institutional frameworks, and reducing transaction costs, thereby genuinely liberating productive forces under the premise of achieving the free flow of factors, ultimately facilitating the optimal combination and vitality release of supply-side factors.

Promoting High-Level Opening-Up and Integrating the Unified National Market with the Global Market

Under the new development pattern, it is necessary to enhance our ability to navigate uncertainties and maintain strategic initiative, with a stronger emphasis on domestic economic circulation. But this does not mean any relaxation in our commitment to further opening up. The domestic and international economic circulations are mutually reinforcing, creating synergies that drive economic progress. China must further develop and improve the socialist market economy with Chinese characteristics. In this process, enterprises should operate under a "negative list" system, while the government should follow a "positive list" approach. This is also a fundamental principle that has been made clear through the establishment of the Shanghai Free Trade Zone and subsequent rounds of free trade zone development. China must unwaveringly embrace economic globalization and construct a high-standard and law-based business climate through reform and opening up, so as to mobilize all positive global support for China's vision of building a community with a shared future for mankind. The market, featuring a positive interplay between domestic and international economic flows, must be in line with global commercial norms and best practices.

Achieving a Unified National Market through High-Quality Urban-Rural Integration

During several decades of development since the beginning of reform and opening up, China's urbanization rate of the permanent population has reached approximately 65%, while the urbanization rate of the registered population remains at only about 47%. In other words, the majority of China's 1.4 billion people have yet to attain official urban residency. Among them, about 300 million migrant workers and their families who have moved to cities still lack official urban status and do not receive equal access to basic public services. Addressing this issue is essential to ensuring that all members of society share in the benefits of reform and opening up, demonstrating the advancement of the socialist market economy with Chinese characteristics, and promoting common prosperity. In the coming decades, the general tendency of China's social mobility is that approximately 400 million people will gradually move from rural areas to cities, becoming new urban residents. It is necessary to facilitate their transition by making it easier for them to obtain urban residency and access basic public services. This challenge is not only an integral part of building a unified national market but also a tough issue that must be tackled. On the one hand, it reflects the fact that China's true level of urbanization is still insufficient to meet the demand for such services effectively. On the other hand, it highlights the significant potential for further development. With the progressing urbanization and industrialization, along with increasing levels of marketization, internationalization, informatization, and the rule of law, China must develop a unified national market based on urban–rural integration, and usher in a new phase in which urban and rural governance seamlessly aligns with the principles of modern civilization.

Achieving Orderly Competition in a Unified Market Environment with a Consistent Regulatory Framework

The concept of unification in the market environment is reflected in its rules and underlying logic, which ensures equal treatment for all market participants and social members. In essence, this embodies fairness and justice for all market entities and social members alike. We should simply or purely interpret this unified market as being confined to or merely based on so-called quality standards or standardization. The "unification" China now pursues certainly includes improving standardization, but a truly unified market goes beyond this. It requires the comprehensive establishment of a law-based modern governance system, making remarkable progress in fairness and justice. The central government's emphasis on the construction of a unified national market is driven by a strategic objective to maintain economic operations within a reasonable range while focusing on institutional innovation. This, in turn, promotes advancements in management and technological innovation, helping to overcome systemic constraints. By doing so, enterprises are able to unleash their potential and develop long-term operational strategies within a high-standard, law-based business environment. They will have the freedom to experiment and innovate under the "negative list," ultimately leading to the full emancipation of productive forces.

Key Tasks and Measures for Accelerating the Construction of a Unified National Market

Wang Wei

A unified national market is not only a crucial hallmark of a developed market economy but also an institutional foundation for achieving high-quality economic development of a great power. As China enters a new development stage, being the world's largest developing country, accelerating the establishment of a unified national market is a necessary step in building a high-level socialist market economy. It is also a fundamental pillar and intrinsic requirement for shaping a new development pattern and advancing high-quality development. The *Opinions of the CPC Central Committee and the State Council on Accelerating the Construction of a Unified National Market* (hereinafter referred to as the *Opinions*) outline the overall requirements, main objectives, and priority tasks for building a unified national market from a broad and strategic perspective. As an action plan for the 14th Five-Year Plan period and the subsequent period, the construction of a unified national market will drive new progress in the development of a high-level socialist market economy.

Understanding the Connotation and Characteristics of a Unified National Market

A Unified National Market: An Essential Requirement for a Market Economy

A unified national market refers to a set of institutional arrangements that ensure mutual openness, uniform regulations, fair competition, and the smooth circulation of goods and production factors among regional markets within a country (or region). This system is built on the foundations of social division of labor and market economy development. Overall, a well-developed unified national market exhibits four main characteristics.

The first is market openness. All regional markets across the country are interconnected and mutually accessible, without regional restrictions or barriers to market entry and the flow of products and production factors. Additionally, the domestic market is integrated with the global market.

The second is regulatory consistency. A unified set of market operation rules, regulatory frameworks, and legal systems applies within a country (or region), ensuring an open, transparent, fair, and equal market environment for all market entities and the flow of products and factors.

The third is fair competition. Within a unified market, all market entities operate independently, making autonomous business decisions and assuming full responsibility for their profits and losses. They have equal access to production factors and resources and compete on a level playing field.

The fourth is the effective flow of goods and factor allocation. Goods and production factors move freely and are allocated effectively within a country (or region) according to market requirements.

Therefore, in a well-developed unified national market, market barriers are basically eliminated, enterprises can operate independently and compete on an equal footing, consumers enjoy the freedom of choice and autonomous consumption, goods and factors circulate freely and are exchanged on equal terms, and the market mechanism is able to play a decisive role in resource allocation within a country or even on a broader scale. In essence, accelerating the construction of a unified national market is a fundamental and intrinsic requirement for the advancement of a market economy.

A Well-Developed Unified National Market: A Hallmark of an Advanced Market Economy

Globally, the development of a unified national market is a gradual historical progress closely related to the level of market economy development. It is an intrinsic requirement for boosting economic growth, improving the efficiency of market resource allocation, and enhancing overall economic competitiveness. For instance, in the United States, the establishment of a unified national market began in the late eighteenth century during the Industrial Revolution. As industrial production expanded rapidly, the need for large-scale trade across state borders became urgent, necessitating the nationwide circulation of goods. This led to a strong demand for federal oversight of interstate commerce, the elimination of state-imposed tariffs, and the removal of barriers to interstate trade to foster a unified national market. Similarly, in the 1950s, eight European countries initiated the European Coal and Steel Community to facilitate the cross-border trade of coal, steel, and other products and resources. This marked the beginning of Europe's journey toward market unification. On January 1, 1993, the European Community declared the establishment of a unified internal market. The development of the European unified market progressed from a focus on goods trade to a fully integrated system allowing the free flow of goods, people, services, and capital, significantly enhancing Europe's overall competitiveness on the global stage.

Building a Unified National Market: Coordinating Multi-Level Government Relationships

Despite differences in political systems, levels of economic development, historical traditions, and legal frameworks among developed countries (or regions), a key factor in establishing a unified market is the coordination of relationships between governments at different levels, especially the relationship between the central government and local governments (or between national governments in the case of regional unions). In the early years of the United States, the Articles of Confederation granted substantial autonomy and independence to individual states, allowing each state to establish its own tariff policies as well as economic and legal systems, which led to significant trade barriers among states.

To establish a unified national market, the United States leveraged the Interstate Commerce Clause in the federal Constitution, along with federal judicial jurisdiction, to gradually define and delineate the authority of the federal and state governments over trade regulation through numerous legal precedents. This enhanced the federal government's capacity to intervene in economic matters, laying the foundation for dismantling market fragmentation, eliminating local protectionism, ensuring fair competition, and fostering a unified domestic market. Similarly, in the process of fostering the European unified market and establishing the European Union (EU), two key aspects played a decisive role. First, EU member states had to recognize the authority of the EU and its unified policies, delegating the power to formulate unified market rules and standards to the EU's highest governing body, the European Parliament. More importantly, member states had to consciously implement the EU's unified policies and adjust their domestic laws and regulations to ensure the establishment of a cohesive internal market characterized by the free flow of goods and production factors.

A Unified National Market Requires Sound and Consistent Market Rules and Legal Safeguards

Although the United States and the EU follow different legal traditions—the common law system and the civil law system, respectively—the legislation, enforcement, and judiciary of a unified market always operate under the highest level of authority. This ensures the authority of top-level decision making, the establishment of uniform market rules, the protection of a unified market from local government interference, and the elimination of local protectionism. In the United States, the legislative framework for a national unified market is established by Congress. The Interstate Commerce Clause, incorporated into the U.S. Constitution, grants the federal government the power to regulate and oversee interstate trade. Laws such as the *Interstate Commerce Act* and the *Sherman Antitrust Act* provide the federal government with specific enforcement authority to supervise and regulate a unified national market. Additionally, the U.S. Supreme Court holds the power of judicial interpretation and final jurisdiction, and all states must abide by its rulings and judicial interpretation of relevant trade provisions. In the EU, the *Treaty of Rome* and its supplementary protocols, both of constitutional significance, explicitly stipulate the construction of a unified national market. The programmatic document *Compl*etion *of the Internal Market* was ratified either by national parliaments or through direct public votes in member states. The European Commission is responsible for enforcement, while the European Court of Justice holds the final authority on judicial interpretation and final jurisdiction. Under this institutional arrangement, member states must review and amend their national laws to ensure compliance with the *EU Constitution* and the *Compl*etion *of the Internal Market* regulation, preventing any legal conflicts. To date, the EU has enacted 286 pieces of legislation aimed at eliminating non-tariff barriers that hinder the free flow of goods, people, labor, and capital among member states. Of these, 95% have been approved by the European Parliament, with 85% already transposed into national legislation of member states.

A Unified National Market Requires Continuous Improvement in the Governance System and Governance Capacity

In the United States, the Federal Trade Commission (FTC) is the administrative agency responsible for enforcing antitrust laws and maintaining a unified national market. The FTC consists of five members who are appointed by the president and confirmed by the Senate. The FTC not only has the authority to regulate economic management practices by local governments but also holds jurisdiction over interstate and foreign commercial behaviors.

In the EU, the Directorate-General for Internal Market, Industry, Entrepreneurship, and small and medium-sized enterprises (SMEs) within the European Commission is the enforcement body responsible for supervising, evaluating, and promoting member states' development of a unified market. On the one hand, the directorate has established an evaluation index system and a "traffic light" mechanism to assess the development and operation of the unified market across member states. The results of these assessments are made public at regular EU ministerial meetings, clearly ranking each state and identifying shortcomings. This transparency exerts significant pressure on member states that fail to enforce unified market rules, compelling them to make timely corrections. On the other hand, when citizens or enterprises encounter issues that contradict unified market regulations, such as unfair treatment or obstacles in establishing branches in other member states, they can seek assistance from local branches of the European Commission or directly from the directorate. If the issue remains unsolved or the proposed solution is unsatisfactory, they can appeal to the European Court of Justice. This governance system, to a considerable extent, ensures the effective operation of the unified market.

Accelerating the Construction of a Unified National Market Is Both Necessary and Urgent

China's Market Is at a Critical Stage of Transition from Size to Strength

Over the past 40+ years of reform and opening up, China has witnessed the rapid development of a market economy and the continuous deepening of reforms. The country's market development has undergone a series of significant transformations—evolving from nonexistence to existence, from small to large, and from a closed system to an open one. A modern market system encompassing both commodity and factor markets has been primarily established, with notable progress in fostering a unified national market. However, it is crucial to recognize that while China's market is vast, it remains insufficiently strong—this issue continues to be a significant challenge.

On the one hand, China has made significant progress in market development and has ascended to the ranks of major global market economies. China's market size in consumer goods, commodities, securities, credit, insurance, and labor is among the largest in the world. China boasts the world's largest number of market entities and has fostered a dynamic and diversified competitive landscape, where diverse forms of ownership coexist and thrive. By the end of 2021, China had more than 140 million market entities, while the number of state-owned enterprises had fallen to fewer than one million. Non-public economy market entities accounted for more than 90% of the total, contributing over 60% to GDP and more than 80% to employment. In terms of price formation, at the beginning of reform and opening up, 97% of commodities and services were priced by the government. Today, 97% of prices are set by the market, highlighting the increasingly decisive role of market mechanisms in commodity and factor allocation.

On the other hand, the overall strength and competitiveness of China's market remain weak. Market entities are still fragmented and small in scale, with a significant proportion consisting of self-employed individuals and small and micro enterprises. There are still relatively few large-scale market entities capable of operating across regions or internationally, and overall market competitiveness remains insufficient. For instance, although China surpassed the United States in the number of multinational enterprises listed in the Global Fortune 500 in 2021, its leading enterprises still lag behind international counterparts in scale, strength, and operating efficiency. Meanwhile, China's market influence in global markets remains limited. Taking price determination as an example, despite being the world's largest trader, a great manufacturing powerhouse, and the biggest consumer of bulk commodities such as energy, agricultural products, and metals, China still lacks pricing power. The prices of bulk commodities are still primarily determined by markets in the United States and Europe. As China enters a new stage of development, facing the challenges of profound global transformations and the impact of the COVID-19 pandemic, accelerating the establishment of a unified national market has become an urgent necessity. Doing so will facilitate the fostering of a new development pattern, the transformation from high-speed growth to high-quality development, and the creation of new competitive advantages on the international stage. This, in turn, will drive the full transformation of China's market from sheer size to true strength, providing solid support for a high-level socialist market economy.

Accelerating the Construction of a Unified National Market Requires the Elimination of Institutional Barriers and the Deepening of Reforms

Since the 18th CPC National Congress, China has made significant progress in building a unified national market. However, China's market system still faces challenges such as inconsistent regulations and rules, restricted flow of production factors and resources, local protectionism, and market fragmentation. These institutional barriers must be urgently removed, and deeper reforms are also imperative.

First, discrimination in market access still exists. In some regions, there are still explicit or implicit discriminatory practices and additional conditions when providing elements such as land and funding in areas such as infrastructure construction, service sector access, and procurement bidding, to market entities of different ownership structures, business scales, or geographical locations. For instance, enterprises may be required to register as independent legal entities in the local jurisdiction, while restrictions related to years of local tax payments and ownership type are imposed for procurement and bidding.

Second, regulatory rules are inconsistent and opaque. There are significant regional differences in regulatory standards, enforcement criteria, and implementation practices across various sectors, including business qualification, taxation, market access, environmental protection, quality inspection, health, and fire safety. These inconsistencies create uncertainty for enterprises operating across regions and significantly increase institutional costs for businesses.

Third, local preferential policies and subsidies lead to unfair regional competition. Some local governments provide preferential financial, taxation, and land policies targeted at specific enterprises and investors. These non-market factors exacerbate unfair competition and distort enterprises' decision-making. For example, some cities provide excessive subsidies for China–Europe freight trains and air cargo, engaging in competitive subsidy practices. At the same time, they impose restrictive conditions on the use of local infrastructures such as channels and ports, reducing overall efficiency and hindering coordinated regional development.

Fourth, the phenomenon of protecting local markets and enterprises through local regulations and standards is increasingly prevalent. Some regions create local regulations, policies, and standards that form barriers to the free flow of commodities, services, and production factors, significantly disturbing the cross-regional operations of market entities. For example, disputes over local standards for water quality, second-hand cars, and spicy gluten products in recent years reflect this issue.

Fifth, the fair competition review system lacks rigid constraints. Nowadays, China's anti-monopoly law and related laws do not contain direct provisions on the fair competition review system, leading to insufficient awareness and weak enforcement at the local level. Meanwhile, the scope of fair competition reviews remains incomplete. A large number of existing laws, regulations, and policies still require comprehensive review and rectification. The current fair competition review system adopts a model based on self-review supplemented by external supervision, leading to weak constraints on policy-making departments to conduct proactive reviews. Furthermore, stakeholder participation in the evaluation process is inadequate, and competition enforcement agencies face difficulties in effectively intervening.

Sixth, reforms of institutions and mechanisms for assessing political performance are lagging behind, and local protectionism persists. At present, economic growth, investment, and taxation are still important indicators for the performance assessment of local governments, and the pressure on local public service expenditure, especially in large cities, has been increasing. Meanwhile, local governments still exert significant control over resource allocation. The decentralization of approval authority, inconsistent regulatory standards, and variable enforcement have, to some extent, strengthened local governments' intervention in the market.

Seventh, legal constraints on behaviors that undermine market unity are insufficient. There is a lack of detailed implementation rules and judicial interpretations in relevant laws and regulations. The cross-regional judicial and regulatory frameworks require further improvement, as significant discrepancies exist in rules, standards, and enforcement of market regulations across different regions. Furthermore, many national standards related to the safety and fundamental functions of goods and services remain advisory rather than mandatory, weakening their authority and enforceability.

Eighth, the reform of state-owned assets, enterprises, and monopolized industries is lagging behind, which is not conducive to the development of a unified national market. Monopolies in industries of resources, energy, and certain service sectors have yet to be fully broken, and the pace of reforming state-owned assets and enterprises needs to be accelerated. The footprint of the state-owned economy remains overly extensive, with blurred distinctions between government and enterprise, as well as between government and capital. Misalignment, overreach, and neglect in state-owned enterprises management persist, highlighting the urgent need to accelerate reforms in the state-owned asset management system to focus on capital oversight.

Major Tasks and Measures for Accelerating the Fostering of a Unified National Market

In response to the requirements of the new stage of development and the challenges facing China's construction of a unified national market, the *Opinions* adopt a problem-oriented and goal-oriented approach and emphasize both the elimination of outdated barriers and the fostering of new growth while implementing targeted policies based on specific circumstances. Efforts will focus on unifying fundamental market regulations and rules, dismantling local protectionism and market fragmentation, and addressing bottlenecks that hinder economic circulation. By promoting the free flow of goods and factors on a broader scale, China aims to establish a highly efficient, well-regulated, fair, competitive, and fully open unified national market.

Advancing a Unified National Market Through Reform and Innovation

To accelerate the development of a unified national market, it is essential to simultaneously establish new mechanisms while eliminating outdated ones. This requires accelerating reforms and innovations in the unification of basic market regulations and rules, integrating the market factors and resources, enhancing the high-level unification of commodity and service markets, ensuring fair and consistent market supervision, and preventing improper competition and undue market intervention.

In terms of establishing new mechanisms, key reforms focus on the following aspects. The first is to improve the unified system of property rights protection, and establish a unified and standardized law enforcement and judiciary system for cases involving property rights disputes. The second is to implement a unified market access system by strictly enforcing the "one national list" management model, developing a nationwide qualification framework, standardizing evaluation procedures and management methods, and enhancing the effectiveness of mutual recognition and utilization across the country. The third is to maintain a fair and unified competition system by refining the fair competition review system, formulating sector-specific and industry-specific review regulations, improving review procedures, unifying review standards, and improving the efficiency of fair competition assessments. The fourth is to improve the unified social credit system by compiling and issuing a national public credit information directory, formulating an integrated mechanism for sharing public and financial credit information, and developing a comprehensive credit information network covering all credit entities, categories of credit information, and all regions across the country. The fifth is to promote fair and unified market regulation. This involves improving unified market regulation rules, enhancing the stability and predictability of market regulations and policies, and advancing online and offline integrated regulation for new business models such as Internet-based healthcare, online education and training, and online entertainment. Additionally, it is important to strengthen unified market regulation enforcement, promote the construction of comprehensive law enforcement capabilities for maintaining a unified national market, explore legal mechanisms for delegated regulatory oversight in specific industries, and encourage cross-administrative regions to jointly release unified regulation policies, laws, and standards. Finally, there is a need to comprehensively enhance market regulatory capabilities and establish a sound cross-regional networked regulatory coordination mechanism.

In terms of eliminating outdated barriers, the *Opinions* emphasize the need to further regulate improper market competition and government intervention by implementing the following measures: strengthening anti-monopoly efforts with a particular focus on the scrutiny of operators in key sectors such as finance, media, science and technology, and people's livelihood, as well as startups, new business models, and labor-intensive industries; steadily advancing reforms in natural monopoly sectors while enhancing regulatory oversight of network-based monopolies, including power grids and oil and gas pipeline networks; legally investigating and penalizing unfair competition, and cracking down on illicit activities in the black and gray market industries; removing local protectionism and regional trade barriers through a comprehensive review and abolition of preferential policies that discriminate against foreign-invested and non-local enterprises; and removing regulatory obstacles to fair market entry and exit, as well as rectifying unfair procurement and bidding practices that violate the principles of a unified national market, with a clear designation of 12 prohibited practices.

Implementing Tailored Policies to Develop a High-Standard Unified National Market

With continuous economic development and market-oriented reforms, China has made steady progress in improving its diversified and open commodity market system, which features a wide variety of market types. The market size has expanded, and a multi-tiered, diversified factor market system has largely taken shape. However, imbalances remain, particularly with the relatively lagging development of factor markets, which constrains the efficiency of resource allocation under the new development pattern. To address these challenges, a problem-oriented approach must be adopted, with a focus on establishing a unified market for factors and resources. This entails advancing the high-level development of traditional factors such as land, labor, and capital, while actively fostering the orderly and innovation-driven development of emerging markets, including technology, data, energy, and the ecological environment.

First, for land and labor markets, it is imperative to improve the mechanisms for cross-regional trading of linked surplus indicators for the increase or reduction of urban and rural construction land and indicators for replenishing arable land, as well as to improve and optimize policies that tie fiscal transfer payments and urban construction land quotas to the urbanization of migrant agricultural populations.

Second, for capital markets, it is necessary to standardize the registration of movable property and security interests, enhance cooperation and linkage between regional equity markets and national securities market sectors, promote interconnectivity of bond market infrastructure, and improve the supervision system with clearly defined responsibilities, effective coordination, and smooth operation.

Third, for technology and data markets, it is necessary to establish and improve a national technology trading market; promote the interconnectivity between regional technology trading markets; enhance open access and shared use of major R&D infrastructure, instruments, and equipment; and establish fundamental regulatory institutions and standards for data security, rights protection, cross-border data transfer, transaction circulation, open sharing, and security certification.

Fourth, for energy markets, efforts should be made to promote the interconnectivity of oil and gas pipeline networks, ensuring fair and equal access for all market entities, accelerate the development of a unified natural gas measurement and pricing system, explore the creation of a national power trading center, and improve the unified national market for coal trading.

Fifth, for ecological and environmental markets, it is imperative to foster a unified national trading market for carbon emission rights and water rights, facilitate the market-oriented transaction of pollution discharge rights and energy consumption rights, and promote the development of a green product certification and labeling system.

Sixth, for commodity and service markets, it is necessary to accelerate the high-level unification. The focus should be on strengthening product quality systems, establishing a sound system of quality grading, and facilitating cross-industry and cross-regional mutual recognition of certification results; optimizing standards and measurement systems, accelerating the formulation of unified national standards and safety regulations for intelligent recognition systems such as facial recognition, and enhancing the internationalization of standard-essential patents; and comprehensively improving consumer service quality, encouraging market players operating across borders and regions to provide consumers with uniform and convenient after-sales services, and optimizing regulations on the prepaid consumption in the service market.

Making Well-Coordinated Efforts to Create a Favorable Environment for the Development of a Unified National Market

The first task is to accelerate the high-standard connectivity of market infrastructure to ensure the free flow and effective allocation of goods, factors, and resources. To address issues such as poor connectivity of market infrastructure, "last mile" gaps in transportation networks, and the lack of integration among various transaction platforms, efforts should be made to build a modern circulation network, vigorously develop multimodal transportation, and expand the coverage of public resource trading platforms to include all public resources that can be allocated through market mechanisms. These measures will help eliminate bottlenecks in domestic circulation, reduce logistics and transaction costs across society, and improve the efficiency of market operation and resource allocation.

The second task is to create an innovation-friendly environment to provide a new pathway for the construction of a unified national market. It should be noted that the advent of the digital economy, along with the rapid development and widespread adoption of new-generation information technologies such as big data, the Internet of Things, and artificial intelligence, is breaking down market barriers and driving the formation of a network-based market structure, which is of revolutionary significance for building a unified national market. Therefore, on the one hand, efforts should be strengthened to regulate monopolistic behavior and unfair competition in emerging business models such as platform economies. On the other hand, market innovation should be encouraged and supported to give full play to the advantages of platform economies in dismantling regional blockades and market fragmentation, thereby accelerating the building of a unified national market and fostering new competitive advantages in participating in the frontiers of competition in the global market.

The third task is to strengthen overall coordination while encouraging local innovation and regional integration. The development of a unified national market requires both top-level design at the national level and the promotion of local innovation. In regions with a high degree of marketization, regional market integration should be prioritized to pave the way for the nationwide establishment of a unified national market and upgrade China's market from a large market to a strong one. Meanwhile, necessary support and preferential policies should be provided to underdeveloped areas to accelerate their development and integration into the unified national market.

The last task is to enhance guidance, supervision, and assessment mechanisms and to explore innovative policy tools for building a unified national market. Drawing on international experience, a standardized guideline and dynamic evaluation mechanism for fostering a unified national market should be established. Progress reports on the development of a unified national market across regions and departments should be regularly published, along with lists of improper interventions that hinder market unification. Successful experiences and best practices should be actively summarized, replicated, and promoted to accelerate the formation of new effective incentive mechanisms and measures. This will further highlight the advantages of China's super-large-scale unified market and provide a solid foundation for fostering the new development pattern.

Market Entity Behavior in the Unified National Market

Jin Bei

The *Opinions of the CPC Central Committee and the State Council on Accelerating the Construction ofa Unified National Market* (hereinafter referred to as the *Opinions*) emphasize the need to accelerate the construction of a unified national market from an overall and strategic perspective. While China's economic reform has been underway for more than 40 years, yielding remarkable achievements that have drawn global attention, the task of building a unified national market remains challenging and will take time to accomplish. A market space is not a homogeneous "empty box" but rather an ecosystem in which diverse market entities coexist. Likewise, market entities are not uniform "microparticles" but structured organizations that follow specific behavior patterns. Therefore, accelerating the building of a unified national market requires more than just improving transaction mechanisms and facilitating the smooth circulation of goods—that is, optimizing the order of market operations. More importantly, it involves systematically enhancing the quality of market entities and fostering more rational corporate behavior patterns and market orders. At a deeper level, the essence of building a unified national market lies in achieving greater efficiency in the organizational structure and behavioral models of market entities.

Corporate Behavior Patterns and Orders in a Unified National Market

As a hallmark of a major economy, the fundamental trait of a unified national market is the establishment of corporate behavior patterns driven by the motivational logic and value orientation of a modern market economy. The concept of corporate behavior patterns refers to the collective tendencies of corporate behaviors as they operate within the market system. These patterns manifest through specific behavioral motivation and structured sequences of behaviors, which are shaped by the economic nature of enterprises. Meanwhile, they influence the behavioral characteristics and market order of enterprises, exhibiting consistency and continuity in collective enterprise actions. In other words, when the collective enterprise behaviors of enterprises demonstrate certainty, consistency, and continuity, they evolve into identifiable behavioral patterns and structured behavioral orders. These patterns, in turn, shape the overall behavioral order of the market system, rooted in the fundamental nature and ingrained habits of economic entities. Such behavioral patterns and structured sequences of behaviors are not only dictated by economic rationality, but they are also profoundly influenced by the broader social, cultural, and institutional environment.

The concept of the market is an imaginary abstraction that can be understood intuitively but cannot be directly observed. While it can be illustrated through examples, it is difficult to define comprehensively. According to its earliest explanation, a market is simply a place for the exchange of goods. This can be seen in examples such as the free market, the market of agricultural products, small commodity markets, morning markets, and night markets. However, these examples cannot fully encapsulate the meaning of a unified national market. In reality, the essence of a market is not defined by the act of trade nor necessarily by a physical location. A market acts as the space and linkage for economic activities. The true manifestation of market economy activities lies in the existence of its participants. As Adam Smith puts it, when people conceptualize a market economy, they generally assume the existence of the "economic man." This includes both individuals as natural persons and enterprises as economic organizations (also known as firms). In economic discussions, however, the "economic man" is primarily represented by enterprises. Therefore, to study market economics, the first step is to understand the nature of enterprises. Only by grasping the nature of enterprises, their behavioral patterns, and the characteristics of their behavioral orders can we fully comprehend the essence of a unified national market.

Economic theories generally assume that enterprises play a central role in the market and follow distinct behavioral patterns and behavioral orders, namely, enterprises exhibit organizational behaviors. But why is it that "firms," as a form of economic organizations, and their behavioral patterns are solely based on the assumptions of human "self-interest" and instinct to "exchange," along with market mechanisms regulated by price signals? In 1937, American economist Ronald H. Coase addressed this question in his well-known paper *The Nature of the Firm.* He argued that enterprises serve as substitutes for the price mechanism. That is, hierarchical command structures within firms replace the need for market-based price adjustments in certain transactions. Later, Oliver Eaton Williamson expanded on this idea, pointing out that enterprises exist because they help reduce transaction costs. In this view, the substitution of the price mechanism by firms can be viewed as an efficiency choice. As American economist Kenneth J. Arrow put it, the organizational form of enterprises provides a means of achieving the benefits of collective action when the price system fails to function efficiently. To put it simply, market economies operate based on the principles of pursuing transaction efficiency and minimizing transaction costs, choosing between organizational behavior within firms and price regulation mechanisms to determine the most effective system of economic operation. In practice, when the transaction costs of internal business operations are lower than those incurred through the free market and pricing mechanism, enterprises will rely on internal organizational directives.

Following this logic, enterprises function as organizational tools for market operations. This instrumental perspective is consistent with the assumption that behavior in market economies is characterized by instrumental rationality. Enterprises are considered not only as tools for market operations but also as instruments for natural persons seeking profit. The basic logic is as follows: If human nature is inherently self-interested, enterprises—as instruments for profit-making or collective organizational forms—must also aim at maximizing profits. Consequently, enterprises hold an inherent position in the market economy. They must safeguard their own interests, maintain decision-making autonomy, operate freely, and assume responsibility for their own profits or losses. According to this logic, if the relative independence of enterprises is not acknowledged, the very foundation of the market system is called into question.

Nevertheless, if enterprises are regarded as independent entities pursuing their own interests, a fundamental question arises: Who—or what—is an enterprise? An enterprise, as a collective organization, has no self-awareness or the capacity to express its own will regarding benefits and losses. That is, an enterprise does not experience joy from profits or distress from losses. It is merely a virtual interest-bearing entity, while its owners—natural persons—are the real interest-bearing subject, capable of experiencing gains and losses on an emotional level.

Why, then, do business owners invest in and own enterprises? In a well-developed market economy, their primary goal is not to produce goods for personal use, but to generate and accumulate economic benefits as much as possible—what Karl Marx termed "surplus value," ultimately expressed in monetary form or other symbolic assets. Thus, the purpose-means relationship in human productive activity is fundamentally reversed: the original goal of production—creating use value—is reduced to a mere means of generating and gaining economic value, while economic value, or exchange value, ceases to be a means and instead becomes the ultimate objective of production itself. Thus, enterprises seek profit maximization, which is ultimately attributed to capital. Thus, capital capable of appropriating profits becomes the true protagonist of the market, enterprises function merely as instruments of capital, and business owners become capital's agents—or capitalists. In this way, capital accumulation becomes the very essence of productive activity in a market economy. This is precisely what Marx described as the capitalist market economy, which he regarded as a form of alienation, where people become modern slaves ruled by capital. In this logic, it is a society where material wealth rules over people.

Since enterprises serve as tools of capital and are subject to its absolute control, they are not only instruments for capital's self-expansion but also objects of capital in market transactions, commodities to be bought and sold at will. The so-called "independent will" of enterprises is entirely subordinate to capital. Enterprises are not real interest-bearing entities but merely virtual agents of capital, external shells that serve as the outward representation of capital.

Economists widely acknowledge that capital occupies a pivotal position in the modern market economy system. It serves both as the driving force behind economic growth and wealth accumulation and as the dominant power over market entities. From the perspective of economic relations and rationality, particularly in terms of production relations, capital appears to reign supreme. However, capital does not operate in isolation; it is embedded in the broader social system. Within the market system and its operational mechanisms, capital is not allowed to act without constraint. Rather, it is subject to institutional regulations and profoundly shaped by cultural factors. Therefore, the construction of a unified national market inherently involves ensuring that capital plays a more beneficial and effective role within the market mechanism, one that aligns with the principles and rules of a socialist market economy.

In reality, enterprises, especially large-scale ones, are far from being the pure and abstract entities described in theoretical discussions. They are complex organizational structures that function as interest conglomerates rather than singular units of abstract interests. They are composed of multiple groups, including owners, managers, and producers, each with their own distinct interests and behavioral orientations. Decisions are not made by enterprises themselves but are the collective outcomes of their constituent members. Just as Kenneth J. Arrow put it, "In any organization of any size, decisions are made by certain individuals and executed by others." Namely, enterprises do not make decisions; individuals within enterprises do. This makes enterprises function more like small societies or mini-worlds rather than the atomized economic agents assumed in traditional economic theories. To simplify this complexity, enterprises are often regarded as microeconomic entities and treated as black boxes devoid of internal structure in economic studies. This treatment envisions enterprises as atomistic agents, which fails to accurately reflect their true nature.

How, then, should enterprises be understood in the construction of a unified national market? If we follow the micro–macro paradigm of mainstream Western economics, enterprises are assumed to be instrumental microeconomic entities driven solely by economic rationality. Under this logic, granting enterprises maximum laissez-faire autonomy in decision-making and transactions is assumed to lead to the complete homogenization of market entities and singular objectives. This perspective aligns with the logic of market organization espoused by economic fundamentalism, which implies that a unified national market could spontaneously emerge through free and unregulated enterprise behavior. Nevertheless, empirical reality tells a different story: when markets are deregulated, chaos often ensues; when they are overly controlled, stagnation tends to follow. This paradox is precisely the challenge that must be addressed in building a unified national market. Enterprise behaviors are not merely instinctive; they are also well-ordered, expressed within a defined organizational framework.

This reality exposes the limitations of the microeconomic paradigm. The market framework depicted by microeconomic theory is overly simplistic and far removed from economic reality. Therefore, it is necessary to adopt a domain-view paradigm, viewing enterprises as belonging to different domain categories and conducting in-depth research on their domain-specific behavioral characteristics. Enterprises are not merely self-interested subjects guided by economic rationality; they also possess distinct social attributes. In other words, enterprises are not only economic entities driven by instrumental rationality but also social entities whose behavior is influenced by value rationality. Moreover, for enterprises in different domains, economic and social attributes are mutually embedded and interwoven. In reality, there are no purely economically rational enterprises, especially within a socialist market economy, where the social attributes of enterprises play a significant role in shaping their actual behavior. Furthermore, enterprises' behaviors are also deeply embedded in the broader social environment and institutional framework. In any country, enterprise behaviors are never entirely subject to laissez-faire conditions. In a word, building a unified national market is not simply about removing all restrictions and allowing enterprises to operate without oversight. It requires the careful establishment of sound market institutions.

In an ideal unified national market, on the one hand, enterprises should not be subject to unreasonable administrative interventions or hindered by local protectionism. They should be provided with smooth operating conditions and convenient transaction mechanisms. On the other hand, the social attributes of enterprises in different domains must be respected because these attributes reflect their operational intentions, social responsibilities, and broader societal missions. For instance, state-owned enterprises are special entities entrusted with national missions and significant social objectives; their operations are inevitably governed by a distinct set of institutional regulations. Similarly, economic entities with social enterprise characteristics—whether registered as commercial enterprises or social organizations—are inherently oriented toward achieving social goals through economic means. Enterprises in specialized sectors are also necessarily subject to industry-specific regulations and social norms. In certain cases, administrative approval requirements cannot be entirely abolished. Furthermore, localized and sector-specific regulatory frameworks remain essential in some areas, as local governments bear the responsibility of maintaining social order, which may, in turn, influence enterprise operations.

In summary, a unified national market should not be conceptualized as a Newtonian "absolute space" in which homogeneous enterprises make "free choices." Rather, it should be a constructively ordered market that ensures the smooth operation and fair competition of enterprises across diverse domains. A unified national market should foster an inclusive environment for economic development, cultivate a diversified ecosystem in which enterprises of various types can compete and thrive, and lay the social foundation for common prosperity. Building such a unified national market is not only a fundamental pillar and inherent requirement of the new development pattern but also a necessary condition and social requirement for achieving the goal of common prosperity for all.

Fair Competition Among Enterprises ofAll Types in a Unified National Market

Fair competition is not only a fundamental requirement of the organizational system in a unified national market but also the most important behavioral pattern and behavioral orders of enterprises. Enterprises, as a form of economic organization, operate according to specific behavioral patterns that are shaped by both their internal organizational nature and external institutional environment. In this sense, fair competition among enterprises is determined not only by external market rules and government policies but also by the internal behavioral logic embedded within enterprises themselves. The motivations behind enterprise behavior and the choices they make have a decisive impact on the overall state of fair competition in the market.

As previously discussed, a unified national market should not be imagined as the kind of fundamentalist market space depicted by the "micro–macro" paradigm. Instead, it should be understood as a domain-based framework. The vastness of the unified national market is reflected in its universal accessibility, inclusiveness, and non-discrimination. Within the regulatory framework of a socialist market economy, this market accommodates enterprises of various types and scales. All market participants can experience both the vastness of the market space and its inclusiveness toward both strong and weak participants. This is reflected, on the one hand, in the accessibility, non-monopolistic nature, and non-discriminatory character of market competition, and on the other hand, in the non-exclusivity of cooperation for mutual benefits, as well as in the support for weaker and smaller players and the pursuit of mutual prosperity, and on the other hand, in the non-exclusivity of cooperation for mutual benefits, as well as in the support for weaker and smaller players and the pursuit of mutual prosperity. In short, a unified national market is characterized by a more sophisticated system of fair completion and social inclusion. Its institutional framework and regulatory norms are centered on ensuring fair competition and win–win cooperation among diverse market entities.

According to economic theory, competition primarily occurs among homogeneous enterprises. The greater the homogeneity, the fiercer the competition. This is because competition among homogeneous enterprises is substitutive, that is, enterprises can replace one another. In general, enterprises with lower production costs and lower product prices will outperform their competitors. This is the principle of survival of the fittest. In a competitive market composed of completely homogeneous enterprises (with identical technological levels and product quality), if there are no entry barriers or discriminatory regulations, market competition primarily takes the form of price competition. Consequently, the economic profit of all enterprises will tend toward zero. Higher economic profit means higher product prices, meaning that enterprises offering lower prices will inevitably gain the upper hand. Of course, if market competition forces enterprises to cut down prices to the point where they incur negative economic profits, enterprises will not be able to sustain their operations. Even if such competitive conditions arise, they represent a short-lived phenomenon, as the adage goes, "No business can long sustain selling at a loss." Moreover, if a firm deliberately employs abnormally low pricing strategies to drive competitors out of the market, this constitutes predatory dumping, which is prohibited under market competition rules. Thus, competition among homogeneous enterprises represents a state of equilibrium rather than an ideal market condition. To escape this trap, competing enterprises will continuously seek to innovate and alter their production functions, striving to differentiate themselves from their rivals.

Therefore, in reality, business competition primarily takes place among heterogeneous enterprises. In theory, an enterprise's profit arises from differentiation, that is, differences create profit. Only such enterprise operation is economically rational, desirable, and valuable. Thus, the key to understanding fair competition in a unified national market lies in understanding the heterogeneity or differentiation among enterprises, especially the economic heterogeneity across different industries. In business practice, economic differentiation is often prominently reflected in brand strategy.

Theoretically, heterogeneity of enterprises forms the foundation of both the division of labor in production and market segmentation (supply and demand). The division of labor refers to the interdependence and cooperation among actors with different functions. However, the ways and forms of the division of labor vary, and competition is an inevitable consequence. Moreover, competition enhances efficiency in the division of labor, as the survival of the fittest serves as a mechanism for efficiency selection—eliminating inefficient entities contributes to the formation of more efficient groups. The challenge, however, is that enterprise heterogeneity manifests in multiple ways. It may stem from technological or resource-based differences, functional or structural distinctions, or even institutional or policy-related factors. Then, what forms of heterogeneity are benign and beneficial? Which types of heterogeneity fail to meet the efficiency requirements of a market economy and thus hinder fair competition? If heterogeneity of enterprises leads to unfair competition, it will pose barriers to the construction of a unified national market.

In a certain sense, the building of a unified national market is fundamentally about addressing the heterogeneity of enterprises. In theory, heterogeneous enterprises are not necessarily substitutes for competitors; rather, they can form complementary relationships within the division of labor. This complementarity can enhance the efficiency of a unified national market, ensuring the rationality and high quality of the market system. However, in reality, concerns over the fairness of competition among heterogeneous enterprises remain prevalent and even provoke alarm. If the heterogeneity of enterprises solidifies and exacerbates inequalities among enterprises, it may lead to the formation of unjustified market power, which, in turn, hinders the construction of a unified national market. In China's current economic landscape, four particular issues have drawn significant attention.

The Fairness of Competition Between State-Owned and Non-State-Owned Enterprises

The reform of China's economic system began with the restructuring of state-owned enterprises, initially focusing on improving their efficiency, breaking the "iron rice bowl" system, and making enterprises responsible for their own profits or losses. Large state-owned enterprises have primarily pursued a path of scaling up and forming corporate groups. In the process of building a unified national market, it is essential to position state-owned enterprises, possessing significant market power, appropriately within the market structure. The long-term goal of constructing a unified national market is to improve China's market economy system, while the strategic goal is to address global market fragmentation and mitigate risks of industrial chains. Regarding the first goal, state-owned enterprises should adjust their market positioning to prevent excessive market dominance and ensure fair competition with non-state enterprises. However, in relation to the second goal, the advantages of state-owned enterprises in scale and market share may contribute to safeguarding economic security and enhancing the resilience of the supply-side structure. Therefore, the strategic role of state-owned enterprises in building a unified national market is a complex issue that requires careful balancing.

The Fairness of Competition Among Enterprises in Particular Sectors

Within diverse enterprise groups, certain entities operate in domains requiring social responsibility for market entry. In China's economic management and policy system, the business activities of these enterprises are often subject to strict regulation and planning. For instance, due to special policy requirements related to ecological resources and environmental protection, or restrictions imposed by land-use planning, enterprises seeking to operate in these regulated sectors must comply with entry policies and regulations stipulated by national regulatory agencies. In other words, enterprises must undergo an approval and licensing process before being allowed to enter these fields. Thus, this raises a key issue for the development of a unified national market: Is market access competition among enterprises fair? Do such entry regulations create market barriers or lead to discriminatory segmentation? This calls for government departments to enhance the approach of "streamlining administration, delegating power, and improving services," which is essentially a demand to ensure equal treatment for all enterprises applying to enter the market.

The Fairness of Competition in Industries with Natural Monopoly

In certain industries, inherent natural characteristics or economic and technical characteristics may grant early entrants significant scale advantages or first-mover benefits, creating barriers that hinder fair access for other enterprises. Natural monopoly has a degree of rationality, as it reflects the cost advantages of large-scale operations (or even exclusive monopoly). However, it also has potential drawbacks, as it can lead to unequal market entry opportunities, actual market segmentation, and distortions in the price mechanism. These distortions may disrupt the balance of supply and demand within a unified market and result in unfair benefit distribution.

The Fairness of Competition Among Enterprises in Different Regions

One of the most prominent challenges to building a unified national market is local protectionism, which manifests in discriminatory policies against enterprises from different regions and imposes unreasonable restrictions on local market transactions. From the government's perspective, efforts must be accelerated to eliminate and repeal regulations and practices that hinder market unification and fair competition, breaking down fragmented, closed markets and self-contained economic cycles. The ultimate goal is to allow demand to better guide and optimize supply, enable supply to better serve the expansion of demand, and leverage a unified national market to pool resources, drive growth, foster innovation, enhance division of labor, and promote competition. From the enterprise perspective of enterprises, businesses must abide by market rules of fair competition and avoid unfair competition.

Closely related to this issue are the technological conditions and regulatory frameworks governing infrastructure and logistics systems in urban and rural areas, which have a significant impact on the smooth circulation of human, financial, and material resources across the national market. The more developed these infrastructure and logistics systems become, the stronger the unification and accessibility of the national market will be. The effective operation of a unified national market hinges on the free flow of human, financial, and material resources, which depends not only on infrastructure and logistics networks but also on the efficiency of organizational systems and the ability to respond to unexpected economic disruptions.

Therefore, the *Opinions* set forth special requirements for fair competition: maintain a unified and fair competition system. Treat all market entities on an equal basis. Improve the institutional framework and policy implementation mechanisms for fair competition, establish a mechanism for coordinating and ensuring fair competition policies and industrial policies, and optimize and refine the implementation of industrial policies. Strengthen the legal framework for anti-monopoly regulations, accelerate revisions to anti-monopoly laws and unfair competition laws, and improve the review system for fair competition. Develop review rules for key areas and industries, improve the review mechanisms, unify the standards for review, standardize the review procedures, and enhance review efficiency.

Prosocial Behavior Patterns of Economic Entities in a Unified National Market

The prosocial behavior patterns of enterprises represent one of the defining features of a modernized unified national market. Without prosocial corporate behaviors, it is difficult to build a unified national market. The notion of "free enterprise" operating independently of the social environment and social constraints is unrealistic. All enterprises are organizational entities embedded within society, and their behaviors must inherently exhibit social attributes. Prosocial behavior patterns are not only a structured manifestation of corporate values but also a critical factor in enterprise competitiveness in modern society.

When discussing a unified national market, the term "national" inherently includes the social interests of a market economy, and more specifically, national social interests—namely, the interests of the nation-state. The existence of a nation naturally implies the presence of overarching social interests and their manifestations. That is to say, the macro-economy or national economy will become a key concern for economic and social entities. When we speak of the unification of the market, it actually signifies an acknowledgment that the economic system possesses a heterogeneous yet integrated nature, rather than being a completely homogeneous entity. In this sense, the unified national market can be regarded as an ecosystem encompassing diverse social organizations and forms. The social interests of the unified national market must be collectively represented through the coordinated efforts of various economic actors. Moreover, the social responsibilities and objectives (missions) of different economic and social organizations are not only a reflection of their value within society but also an elevation of their instrumental actions to a higher level of significance.

In a modern market economy, all economic and social organizations engage in both economic and social exchanges, and the extent and function of these exchanges vary across different organizational forms, giving rise to the formation of a variety of organizational domains with different natures and characteristics, thereby creating a rich and sustainable economic and social system. All types of social organizations, including enterprises and non-enterprise economic entities, social organizations, and public institutions, have distinct functions, responsibilities, economic and social attributes, and organizational management requirements tailored to the diverse needs of modern economic and social operations. That is to say, the socio-economic system consists of various organizations of all forms, structured as a domain-based distribution. These organizations, akin to the diverse hues of a spectrum, blend together to compose a dazzling natural world.

Therefore, when observing and discussing the unified national market, we should not perceive it as a mechanical economic entity solely driven by economic rationality. Instead, it is an organic economic system with inherent social systematicity. The unified national market is composed of various economic and social subjects, and a fair and competitive order requires enterprises to develop in a prosocial direction.

In a modern market economy, the prosocial orientation of enterprises is a fundamental behavioral trait. Entering the new era, two key trends emerge. On the one hand, the more developed an economy becomes, the broader its social concerns. This shows the progress of society, transitioning from a materially deprived era to one that prioritizes quality of life. On the other hand, the economic and social rule system is undergoing profound transformations in the new era, and the restructuring and contestation of rules will challenge enterprises to adapt. The reason why enterprises must adopt a prosocial development path in this new era is that many economic issues are inherently social issues. As Amartya Sen puts it, the widespread use of a narrow assumption of self-interest has significantly limited the scope of economic predictive research, making it difficult to analyze the broad economic relationships shaped by behavioral diversity. In other words, many major socio-economic issues require collective action by society as a whole to be effectively addressed. Thus, the new era demands that more enterprises follow the path of prosocial development. The whole social environment, including the legal framework and government policies, will increasingly support the prosocial orientation of enterprises. Some major social problems must be resolved through the collective participation of enterprises, making corporate behaviors, in essence, a form of social cooperation.

The prosocial development trend of enterprises profoundly reflects the intrinsic requirements of the unified national market. Corporate behavior is shaped by economic rationality, institutional rules, and the form of civilization—not merely by the pursuit of profit. Enterprises that fail to fully integrate into society will find it difficult to sustainably adapt to the market environment and competition.

A More Open Unified National Market and a More Internationalized Corporate Behavior Model

The ability of corporate behavior patterns to adapt to an open economy directly reflects the internationalization of the unified national market and is a defining trait of enterprises that possess international competitiveness within this market. If corporate behavior patterns lack international adaptability, they will inherently struggle to align with the unified national market because the strategic direction of building a unified national market is not about national isolation, but rather about greater openness, at a higher level and ultimately on a global scale. A closed economy is unlikely to foster a unified national market, and conservative, insular corporate behavior patterns are inherently incompatible with its institutional logic and civilization ethos.

When discussing China's unified national market, two key aspects often come to mind: improving the domestic market system and mechanisms and leveraging China's advantage as a super-large-scale market. While these considerations are crucial, they must not lead to an underestimation of the global market or the critical role of openness in economic development. Market openness, including integration with the global market, has always been a prerequisite for economic development, welfare improvement, and broader social progress. A closed market is not a true market economy. Therefore, the development of a unified national market necessitates dual openness, both domestically and internationally. The advantage of a major economy lies not only in its super-large domestic market but also in its ability to maintain stable economic openness to both domestic and international markets, as well as in its ability to make more balanced strategic choices based on favorable conditions. So, China's unified national market requires that competitive enterprises possess the ability to adapt not only to the domestic market and economic circulation but also to the global market and international economic dynamics.

In fact, enterprises that grow stronger within the unified national market will have greater strength and motivation to expand into the global market. A unified national market can provide favorable conditions from both the supply side and demand side, enabling enterprises to better access international markets. In other words, a unified national market can help nurture the international competitiveness of enterprises. Particularly in the context of China's active promotion of the Belt and Road Initiative, enterprises must be capable of transnational operations under conditions where the institutional rules of the domestic market and the global market differ. Of course, enterprises with different characteristics may choose to focus primarily on either the domestic or international market as part of their business strategy or development direction. However, as a whole, Chinese enterprises operating within a unified national market must possess the necessary qualities and capabilities for transnational operations in both domestic and international markets.

The more robust and well-structured China's unified national market becomes—with a smoother economic cycle and a larger market scale—the more competitive foreign enterprises it will attract. As a result, China's domestic market will become increasingly internationalized, and the connectivity and integration between the domestic and international markets will be further strengthened. Whether in terms of market access regulations or the ability of both Chinese and foreign enterprises to engage in transnational operations, accelerating the development of a unified national market will hasten the pace of Chinese enterprises advancing into the global market. The strategic direction of Chinese enterprises will become increasingly outward-oriented, with most internationally competitive enterprises evolving toward multinational group operations.

In consideration of the reality of global competition, particularly the relationship between China and the United States, the building of a unified national market is closely linked to concerns about national economic security as well as the stability of industrial and supply chains. In this regard, it holds strategic significance for developing a more comprehensive and shock-resistant national economic security framework. In other words, a unified national market must be oriented by internal strength and resilience, but this does not imply isolation or self-containment. Instead, it entails competitiveness, self-improvement, multilateral cooperation, and mutual assistance. Only in this way can risks be spread, confrontation resolved, conflicts eased, and the interests of national economic security more effectively realized. In conclusion, the policy intention behind building a unified national market is by no means aimed at closure, introversion, or isolation; rather, it is about openness, competition, and cooperation.

Are corporate behaviors driven by innate instincts or shaped by structured models? From a philosophical perspective, corporate behavior is both innate and socially determined. Marxism holds that "the essence of man is not an inherent abstraction in each individual, but rather the ensemble of social relations."[1] This principle forms the logical foundation of market system construction. As a form of economic organization, the behavioral patterns of enterprises are contingent upon the structural characteristics of the market, namely, its organizational order. Corporate

[1] Karl Marx. Theses on Feuerbach [M]// The Compilation and Translation Bureau of Works of Marx, Engels, Lenin and Stalin of the CPC Central Committee. Selected Works of Marx and Engels: Volume 1. Beijing: People's Publishing House, 2012.

behavior is not isolated or purely individualistic but collective in nature. Therefore, the formation of a unified national market is essentially an evolution of corporate behavior patterns. Understanding and optimizing corporate behavior patterns and the broader social behavioral order is an inherent requirement for accelerating the construction of a unified national market.

The Internal Logic of China's Unified National Market Construction and Specialized Division of Labor

Zheng Zhigang

After more than 40 years of market-oriented economic transition, it is widely recognized that the market plays a fundamental role in resource allocation across China. Its importance to the national economy and people's livelihoods is self-evident. Why, then, is there still such a strong emphasis on market development today?

The twists and turns of China's economic transition over the past four decades highlight the need for a deeper understanding of the fundamental purpose, internal logic, and external conflicts associated with market construction. Several key questions arise. First, why is the fundamental purpose and internal logic of market construction centered on encouraging and promoting the specialized division of labor? Second, when addressing the internal logic of specialized division of labor in the market, an unavoidable question emerges—how should we logically understand the relationship between Coase's theory of internal division of labor governed by corporate "authority" and the external division of labor facilitated by the market? Third, how can the market be effectively leveraged to promote and achieve the specialized division of labor?

At a time when market development is receiving unprecedented attention, this article aims to offer preliminary reflections on the above questions, with the aim of stimulating academic and public discussion on the internal logic and external conflicts of market construction, thereby effectively advancing China's market-oriented economic transformation process.

Evolution of Market Economy and Specialized Division of Labor

In the traditional theories on the development of productive forces that reveal the emergence of early civilization in human society, an intrinsic and indispensable mechanism is the extensive division of labor within society. In the earliest stages of human society, economic activity was characterized by a natural gender-based farming-weaving division, where communities lived "within earshot yet never interacting." Over time, society transitioned from this natural self-sufficiency toward a more advanced division of labor, with animal husbandry and handicrafts gradually separating from traditional agriculture. This shift marked the rise of early civilizations. Alongside the increasing social division of labor, the fundamental commercial activity of exchange emerged, and with it, the market as the material vehicle of exchange.

Beyond the abstract concept of productivity development, the evolution of human civilization follows two principal threads. The first is the specialized division of labor, driven by the principle of "learning by doing," whereby accumulated production experience leads to efficiency gains. Adam Smith famously illustrated this point in *The Wealth ofNations* through the example of the pin factory.

The other thread is the formation and development of the market economy. The specialized division of labor facilitates socialization, allowing households and enterprises to be linked through the invisible network of the market. A region characterized by a high degree of specialization tends to cultivate a prosperous market, and conversely, a flourishing market further deepens specialization. Areas where family-run workshops cluster with a highly specialized division of labor naturally evolve into cities, driven by geographic advantages and population density. If the term "city" originally denoted a geographic concept—a walled settlement providing protection—the market gradually became the essential space for exchange between households and workshops engaged in the specialized division of labor, ultimately becoming an indispensable part of urban life. In rural areas with a relatively lower degree of specialization, trade took place through temple fairs and periodic marketplaces. In this sense, China's proactive promotion of urbanization in recent years also reflects the internal logic of market development.

These two threads—specialized labor division and market formation—intertwine and mutually reinforce each other, shaping the evolutionary trajectory of human civilization. One path of evolution is the deepening social division of labor across industries. Not only do broad industries fragment into increasingly refined sub-industries—as evidenced by the emergence of the so-called *Six Chen Hang*, or six sub-industries surrounding the brewing industry during the Ming and Qing dynasties—but professional merchants also emerged to facilitate trade and distribution.

The rise of professional merchants reflects an advanced stage of market economy development. During the Ming and Qing dynasties, Shanxi merchants, primarily engaged in trade with Mongolia, capitalized on their geographical advantage connecting Mongolia and inland China. They developed trade in tea and livestock, creating business legends that remain influential today. These merchants exported privately labeled tea from Fujian and the two provinces of Hunan and Hubei to Mongolia and Russia. Then, they acquired cattle, sheep, and horses—plentiful in Mongolia—through credit-based trade with herders and resold them in inland China. This practice was so widespread that during the Ming and Qing dynasties, there was a popular saying, "Where there is a sparrow, there is a Shanxi merchant."

As industries continue to subdivide, they form an extensive social network through market exchanges, with professional merchants serving as key nodes in this invisible network.

The second major evolution path is the specialization within the market itself. One clear marker of this process is the emergence of various professional guilds. The formation of guilds indicates that merchants engaging in similar products or services needed to negotiate and establish transaction rules within their respective market segments. Another important sign of market specialization was the rise of capital markets as a distinct type of factor market. In 1602, the Dutch East India Company emerged as the world's first joint-stock company. Seven years later, in 1609, the world's first stock exchange was established near the Dutch East India Company in Amsterdam, Netherlands, to facilitate the exit of dissatisfied shareholders.

Through equity financing enabled by capital markets, the Dutch East India Company achieved, for the first time in history, unsecured and unguaranteed lending between strangers. It also pioneered the division of labor between professional managers, who handled day-to-day business operations, and external investors, who bore financial risks. Political scientist Nicholas Murray Butler once remarked that the modern joint-stock company that provided the institutional support for the organization of enterprises during the Industrial Revolution was one of the most important inventions in modern human history—to the extent that without it, even the inventions of the steam engine and electric technology would have had far less impact.

In brief, the internal logic of market economy development can be summarized as follows. First, the specialized division of labor facilitated by the market enhances efficiency. Second, market price fluctuations serve as an automatic mechanism to adjust supply and demand. Third, these two effects together lead to more effective resource allocation and what economists refer to as Pareto optimality in market competition. In essence, the market naturally drives the specialized division of labor, which is a fundamental force behind human civilization and social progress.

In regard to the market-based social network of specialized division of labor, a non-negligible factor is the advent of the Internet era in recent years. The Internet has broken through physical boundaries, liberating market transactions from the constraints of time and space. Today, residents in Beijing can easily order and enjoy the creamy-centered dried persimmons from Fuping, Shaanxi Province—once only available in season and at the place of origin. Such convenience was unimaginable in the past when Ming and Qing dynasty merchants conducting trade with Mongolia primarily dealt in non-perishable commodities such as tea bricks and mobile livestock such as horses and sheep, which could withstand long journeys.

Previously, individuals participated in the social division of labor mainly within the boundaries of family or enterprise. However, in the Internet era, these boundaries have been dissolved, allowing individuals to engage in the division of labor via online platforms. For instance, employees may take part-time jobs as online ride-hailing drivers, while homemakers may deliver food alongside cooking for their families.

In conclusion, the history of market economy development is, in itself, an exemplary textbook on the economics of specialized division of labor.

The Role of Authority and Division of Labor: A Reconstruction of Enterprise Theory in Economics

Since the 1970s, a new branch of economics known as the enterprise theory gradually evolved in response to criticisms of the neoclassical theory of the firm, which depicted the "firm" as merely a "black box of profit maximization" or a simple "production function." The core mission of enterprise theory is to explain why enterprises exist and how they are organized and operated. Ronald Coase, often revered as "the father of modern enterprise theory," argued that enterprises substitute the market's "invisible hand" of price mechanisms with authoritative orders to guide resource allocation and reduce transaction costs.

This naturally raises a question: Is resource allocation more efficient when transaction costs are minimized by market price mechanisms, or by authoritative orders and planned coordination suggested by Coase?

To explore this, let us start from Coase's dilemma. Coase, as a leading figure of the Chicago school, faced a fundamental contradiction. On the one hand, he sought to uphold the principles of free markets advocated by neoclassical economics and the Chicago school. On the other hand, he could not ignore the transaction cost savings that result from a division of labor enforced by authority and command.

Coase points out that, beyond the specialized division of labor based on market exchanges and regulated by the "invisible hand" of the price mechanism, enterprises also feature an internal division of labor governed by authoritative orders and planning. His transaction cost theory does not simply reject or favor one model over the other; rather, it stresses that the boundary of an enterprise is determined by a comparative assessment of transaction costs arising from these two modes of production organization and division of labor.

A natural inference from Coase's transaction costs theory is that an internal division of labor under authoritative orders is justified insofar as it reduces transaction costs. However, there is a paradox in reality: Once authority is established, performance appraisal mechanisms dominated by that authority often deviate from efficiency principles. Therefore, we should not assume that enterprises governed by authority will necessarily achieve lower transaction costs. This may explain why no enterprise can maintain eternal prosperity, while the market, in contrast, persists indefinitely. After a period of rapid expansion, enterprises inevitably encounter inefficiencies, such as bureaucratic redundancy and declining productivity under authority-driven appraisal systems—that eventually lead to their decline.

How, then, can we overcome deviations from efficiency principles in authority-driven internal division of labor? Historical experience reveals two paths: either submit to the market's trial—where inefficient enterprises will ultimately confront a day of reckoning, a phenomenon Karl Marx called "the dangerous leap" (a fate as certain as the Christian Final Judgment)—or adhere to market efficiency by embracing specialization and a market-based division of labor. Even under authoritative structures, they should seek to comply with efficiency principles aimed at minimizing transaction costs. In other words, enterprises should replace rigid, authority-based internal division of labor with a more market-based, specialized division of labor.

Some enterprises that succeed in advancing a specialized division of labor consistent with efficiency principles do so by effectively balancing authority, in line with Coase's principle. This balance of authority is reflected in two aspects. First, within the enterprise, governance structures such as the board of directors oversee management, while shareholders exercise oversight over the board through collective voting at shareholders' meetings. In this way, shareholders—though often at an informational disadvantage—bear the consequences of potential misjudgments, which grants them the ultimate authority in corporate governance. Second, beyond the enterprise, specialized legislative and regulatory frameworks are needed to counterbalance the authority exercised by firms. These external mechanisms contribute to the establishment and refinement of modern market institutions in two ways: (1) by facilitating resource allocation that promotes market-driven specialization and division of labor and (2) by checking and balancing authority, both within and outside enterprises, to prevent rigid or disordered internal division of labor, thereby aligning governance structures with the efficiency principle.

It is critical to recognize that authority is not a substitute for specialized division of labor—it is merely a tool intended to enhance efficiency. In fact, this insight presents a significant opportunity for the Chinese government as it pursues the establishment of a unified national market.

So, how might we reconstruct Coase's enterprise theory in light of the economics of specialized division of labor? Perhaps, we can redefine the enterprise as the boundary between the internal division of labor within an enterprise and the external division of labor in the market, with its core objective being to enhance efficiency through specialized division of labor. The rationale behind this approach is that Coase's notion of authority can, to some extent, be understood as the separation of management functions from production and operational functions—a unique form of specialized division of labor within the enterprise. But we emphasize that for a firm to achieve sustained success, its corporate authority must be effectively balanced by shareholders and other corporate governance mechanisms.

How to Achieve Specialized Division of Labor Through the Market?

In recent years, in both domestic and international enterprise practices, there has been a noticeable trend of reinforcing, even eliminating, internal division of labor through authoritative directives. For example, in the pursuit of public interests such as environmental protection, enterprises are often required not only to provide products and services and generate profits but also to actively fulfill social responsibilities, such as making public welfare donations. As a result, enterprises often find themselves operating in a multitasking environment rife with conflicting interests, forcing them to "do this, that, and more."

Moreover, the scope of social responsibilities continues to expand. In recent years, the concept of environmental, social, and governance (ESG) has emerged, comprising environment, social, and governance, emphasizing the role of enterprises in environmental protection and social responsibility. Tracking its theoretical roots, ESG aligns with stakeholder theory, which opposes the primacy of shareholder interests. Stakeholder theory asserts that corporate directors should be accountable not only to shareholders but also to employees, customers, suppliers, communities, and governments. However, the broadening of responsibility and the difficulty in enforcing these obligations pose challenges to the effective implementation of ESG. For a long time, the stakeholder theory has remained a concept rather than a practice. By contrast, shareholders, who are last in line in terms of profit distribution, are able to bear the consequences of their decisions made at the shareholders' meetings, backed by their actual financial investments. Therefore, corporate laws in many countries generally stipulate that directors must uphold fiduciary duties to shareholders, establishing shareholders as the ultimate authority in corporate governance. Directors who fail to fulfill these duties may face collective lawsuits initiated by shareholders.

The current trend toward reinforcing internal division of labor within enterprises or even eliminating division of labor altogether to replace market-based natural division of labor can be analyzed from three perspectives. First, this trend stems from the excessive extension of government intervention, as advocated by the neoclassical synthesis school. Neoclassical economics argues that profit-maximizing enterprises will achieve Pareto optimality under conditions of perfect competition (general equilibrium theory). The government, in this view, should merely act as a "night watchman," intervening only when crises occur. However, in response to market failures caused by externalities, monopolies, or information asymmetry, macroeconomists advocate for short-term government intervention via the "visible hand." In the 1950s and 1960s, the neoclassical synthesis, represented by Paul Samuelson, sought to integrate such intervention within a unified analytical framework. Since macroeconomic operations inevitably require government intervention via the "visible hand," then, following Coase's transaction cost theory, why shouldn't enterprises—which inherently operate under hierarchical authority—also be subject to such intervention? Moreover, wouldn't it be more direct and effective for governments to transmit their macroeconomic regulatory intentions and social governance objectives directly to enterprises, using internal division of labor within enterprises as a means of implementation?

Second, governments responsible for providing public goods may be shifting these responsibilities onto enterprises. One of the fundamental justifications for government involvement in economic life is its ability to levy taxes on citizens and enterprises to finance the provision of public goods, which, due to their non-excludability and non-rivalry, are prone to free-rider problems. By transferring responsibilities for environmental protection and other public goods to enterprises under the guise of corporate social responsibility, governments can effectively reduce or delay their own obligations while deflecting public criticism for failing to fulfill their commitments.

Third, political correctness and public opinion may be driving this trend. Why has the ESG concept gained such widespread popularity in recent years? In my review article, *ESG Concept as Vision and Philosophy*, I pointed out that ESG has been propelled by the combined efforts of capital markets, public opinion, and policymakers in their pursuit of a "greatest common divisor."

The ESG concept is not simply an upgraded version of stakeholder theory in corporate governance. Unlike stakeholder theory, the refined ESG framework no longer places excessive emphasis on the responsibilities of employees, who are theoretically protected by labor laws and trade unions. Nor does it focus on customer interests, as they are safeguarded by contract law. The upgraded ESG concept removes elements of responsibility where rights and obligations are difficult to match, retaining those aspects that are universally relevant and therefore difficult to oppose, such as environmental and social responsibility. This is understandable in the pursuit of common interests. In times of economic stagnation and market downturns, the politically correct and widely accepted ESG provides a convenient theme for capital markets that lack appealing narratives and elements.

A similar example can be observed in international cooperation. When two countries with different systems, cultures, and values seek international cooperation, their options are often limited to universally accepted areas such as environmental protection and public health. This phenomenon is reminiscent of how, in the 1960s, people in economically struggling societies would greet each other with, "Have you eaten?," while in the twenty-first century, people are more likely to start a conversation with, "How's the weather today?"

In light of China's current emphasis on developing a unified national market and reinforcing the market's role in resource allocation, it is crucial to recognize and uphold the logic and efficiency principles underlying the specialized division of labor in market construction. It is also essential to address key challenges and bottlenecks in the development of enterprise market systems. One possible approach is to establish a clearer division of responsibilities based on a specialized division of labor: The government should focus on providing public goods, while enterprises should focus on paying taxes, so as to replace the status quo whereby enterprises simultaneously have to generate profits, pay taxes, protect the environment, and fulfill social responsibilities. As Milton Friedman, a leading figure of the University of Chicago, once pointed out, "The essential role of a business is to generate profits." Of course, all commercial activities of enterprises must operate within the boundaries set by existing laws, including those governing environmental protection.

In fact, to a large extent, by encouraging and promoting specialized division of labor and adhering to principles of efficiency, the construction of a unified national market will naturally progress toward completion.

CHAPTER 4

Innovative Governance and Chinese Modernization

Jiang Xiaojuan, Zhou Li'an, Chen Xiaohong, and Long Haibo

Challenges in Broad-Scoped Digital Governance and Platform Governance

Jiang Xiaojuan

In a broad sense, digital governance encompasses three dimensions: governance empowered by digital technology, governance of digital technology, and governance of the digital society. Each of these dimensions is complex and profound, exceeding conventional understanding and presenting governance challenges from a traditional perspective. Effective governance requires an understanding of the essence of these issues, a

J. Xiaojuan (✉)
Chinese Public Administration Society, Beijing, China

Z. Li'an
Guanghua School of Management, Peking University, Beijing, China

C. Xiaohong
Development Research Center of the State Council, Beijing, China

C. Fang et al., *Modernization in a Chinese Style*,
https://doi.org/10.1007/978-981-95-6919-9_4

renewal of regulatory concepts, and a transformation of governance frameworks and tools.

Governance Empowered by Digital Technology

Generally speaking, digital technology-based governance is understood as leveraging digital tools to enhance government governance capabilities and provide additional governance mechanisms. For example, it includes remotely supervising on-site activities through monitoring equipment and offering better public services to market entities and citizens via online platforms. However, the concept of "governance empowered by digital technology" discussed here extends beyond this conventional understanding. It broadens the discussion to encompass the fundamental issue of defining the boundaries between government and the market.

Elinor Ostrom is the only scholar in the field of public administration to have won the Nobel Prize in Economics. Her most important academic contribution is the concept of polycentric governance. Unlike the binary view presented by some economists—where governance is either market-driven or government-led—modern social governance can involve multiple actors. With well-designed institutional arrangements, citizens, social organizations, markets, and businesses can all participate in governance. Many areas traditionally considered to require government intervention due to externalities can, in fact, be jointly governed through collaborative efforts among all parties within a sound institutional framework.

In the digital age, the scope of polycentric governance can be greatly expanded. Before the advent of digital technology, institutional design solutions were typically limited to specific, localized issues due to the complexity of calculating costs and benefits for different stakeholders. For instance, sewage discharge regulations could only be implemented within a limited geographical area; expanding the scope is nearly impossible to accurately assess the gains and losses of all parties involved.

L. Haibo
Development Research Center of the State Council, Beijing, China

Organization Department at the Center for International Knowledge on Development, Beijing, China

Today, with the vast connectivity and immense computing power offered by digital technology, environmental governance can now operate on a much larger scale. Various forms of pollution emissions and emission reduction efforts can be quantified at a macro level, while at the micro level, responsibilities can be assigned down to individuals, with dynamic tracking of their contributions.

The next question is government control. One of the main reasons for government intervention in the market is its "information superiority," that is, governments have access to statistical data and a comprehensive view of the situation, enabling them to make informed decisions from a macro perspective. In contrast, enterprises and industries may lack such information, and, without government guidance, risk making blind decisions. However, this situation has changed. Government data is collected through hierarchical reporting systems, whereas digital platforms aggregate real-time data directly from a wide range of real-world scenarios. Many industry organizations and even leading businesses now have access to macro-level data, often on par with or even surpassing what governments possess. More importantly, their data tends to be timelier and more accurate.

For instance, several major construction machinery platforms can monitor more than 85% of large engineering machinery and equipment nationwide in real time, tracking their operating hours and usage, thus creating the so-called "excavator index." This index allows for precise assessment of the progress of nationwide investment projects, serving as a key indicator of fixed-asset investment trends. Similarly, truck platforms provide a "logistics heat index," and rental platforms produce a "rental supply-demand multiple index," both of which are now established macroeconomic indicators.

The digital economy holds a significant position in the national economy, yet its operational logic differs from that of the traditional economy. For instance, cyberspace contains vast amounts of reusable, replicable, and reproducible content. While suppliers derive limited profits, consumers gain substantial benefits—but these cannot be reasonably valued or reflected in gross domestic product (GDP) calculations. As a result, the traditional model of government macroeconomic guidance based on information superiority has become a topic worthy of reflection and discussion. While the government's role as a public authority remains irreplaceable, should its macroeconomic regulation, key indicators, and regulatory measures be adjusted and optimized?

Governance of Digital Technology

The governance of digital technology primarily focuses on issues related to data, monopoly, and value orientation, as these areas address the negative impacts of digital technology. Social media platforms are frequently flooded with false information, a challenge that governments worldwide seek to combat. In 2018, the *General Data Protection Regulation* came into effect in Europe, aiming to enhance individuals ' control over their online privacy. Even so, both domestic and international platforms continue to grapple with large volumes of false information, while the amount of personal data held by these platforms continues to grow. This ongoing dynamic reflects the constant struggle between regulators and the entities they seek to oversee.

China's platform enterprises have thrived in one of the most lenient regulatory environments for the past two decades, leading to the accumulation of various problems. Therefore, it is necessary to strengthen governance. However, it is crucial to have a clear understanding of the differences between platform enterprises and traditional large enterprises. "Monopoly" is a frequent term in regulation, but determining whether platform enterprises constitute monopolies remains a complex issue. Monopoly is defined as the ability to exert market control and thereby obtain undue benefits—it is assessed based on both market dominance (status) and anti-competitive behavior (conduct). If a platform enterprise is merely large but does not engage in harmful practices, there should be no issue. Nowadays, platform enterprises are larger than ever before, yet unlike traditional monopolies that harmed consumers through high fees, many modern platforms provide services for free.

Currently, monopoly determinations are often based on two concerns: operators consolidate their position by acquiring competitors, or platforms direct traffic toward their own affiliated businesses, giving them priority access to consumers. Some scholars argue that regulators fail to fully grasp monopoly dynamics in the digital age. However, from my observations, regulators have not acted recklessly by targeting platforms simply because of their size. When imposing penalties, they still adhere to professional standards. Of course, there are many problems worth discussing. For instance, platforms often operate across multiple fields, and consumers tend to switch between platforms, which erases traditional same-sector rivals, yet far from eliminating competition.

Governance of the Digital Society

The concept of a digital society discussed here is not simply about economic or social issues. Rather, it represents an epoch-making social form, on a par with the agricultural society, the industrial society, and the information society. A digital society operates under a new set of rules for market transactions and social interactions, enabled by digital technologies. For example, big data and algorithms can, to some extent, influence the information individuals receive (e.g., smart recommendations) and the resources they can access (e.g., algorithm-driven credit assessments in online banking). Additionally, digital technology can enhance traditional transaction rules. For instance, market reputation has always played a role in facilitating transactions, but in the past, reputations were often localized—allowing fraudsters to deceive people in one region before moving on to another. Today, however, Internet platforms have created a system where dishonesty in one place can lead to restrictions everywhere. This shift has profound implications for maintaining social order.

From a regulatory perspective, platform governance is a key focus in the digital society, but it faces significant challenges:

First, some platforms are too big to regulate effectively. Major platforms integral to consumers ' daily life cannot simply shut down when problems arise; instead, issues must be addressed through corrective measures that do not disrupt ongoing operations.

Second, regulators struggle to keep pace with rapid changes. With millions of merchants, products, and services updating at lightning speed, external supervisory forces cannot match the platforms' dynamism.

Third, complex structures obscure transparency. Large platforms engage in thousands of multi-layered investments and intricate business relationships. Without in-depth investigations, it is difficult to gain a clear and accurate understanding of their operations.

Fourth, innovative models challenge comprehension. Different platforms adopt diverse business patterns, even within the same industry. Similar platforms may also differ greatly. For example, video platforms such as BiliBili, Douyin, Kuaishou, and Xiaohongshu (RedNote) operate under distinct business models and are continuously innovating. It is difficult for external regulators to fully understand and effectively oversee them.

Platform Self-Regulation Is the Foundation

In view of these problems, how should digital platforms be governed? In addition to the government's efforts to strengthen and improve supervision and regulation, platform self-regulation serves as the foundation and must be prioritized. Without this foundation, external regulators would have no effective means to address the complex challenge of platform governance.

For more than 20 years, digital platforms have operated in a relatively lax regulatory environment, with the first decade or so largely devoid of oversight, yet they have experienced rapid growth. Without government oversight of lending credit, how can consumers feel secure in making purchases? Self-regulation is the only viable way for platforms. Although the government has now tightened its oversight, the sheer scale and high-frequency nature of platform transactions far exceed the government's regulatory capacity. Platforms must handle a vast number of disputes and issues each day. Any delay in resolving these can have significant consequences—customer numbers may plummet, and public opinion may escalate. If the public perceives the platform's order as unreliable, it risks shutting down. Therefore, platforms must shoulder the responsibility of coordination and regulation as long as they exist.

Self-regulation is essential for the survival of platforms, such as consumer rights protection, intellectual property protection, dispute resolution, transaction credit maintenance, and upholding appropriate value orientation. Effective self-regulation ultimately relies on technological capabilities. Over 99% of product and content reviews, including screening for infringement, pornography, violence, drug, and gambling, are conducted through intelligence algorithms, with only a small fraction requiring manual verification. In a word, even before and beyond government supervision, the continued orderly operation and growth of Chinese platforms over the years have primarily depended on self-regulation as the main mechanism for maintaining order.

Reflections on Administrative Supervision and Regulation

China's administration supervision and regulation of platforms have been significantly tightened over the past 2–3 years. Looking back at the development history of platforms and evaluating the effectiveness and challenges of regulation in recent years, we believe that in the future, enhancing platform self-regulation should remain the top priority. In other words, the supervision and regulation of internal compliance management within platforms should be prioritized.

First, the government must clearly define the requirements for platform self-regulation, specifying what issues the platforms have to manage by themselves. Platforms, in turn, must demonstrate the effectiveness of their internal compliance management to the government and the public and accept oversight accordingly. Internationally, there are well-established practices for platform compliance, such as compliance management systems for consumer protection, personal data privacy protection, and evaluation standards under the International Organization for Standardization framework. Of course, the government must rigorously supervise and regulate the establishment and operation of platform compliance systems. It is an important governmental responsibility to maintain fair market competition and social stability in the digital age.

Second, the government needs to implement differentiated regulation based on the characteristics of each platform. While there are commonalities in the areas of non-compliance and regulatory focus across different types of platforms, the differences are more pronounced.

Third, regulation should balance the interests of all stakeholders. Consumer preferences vary widely. Some are comfortable with free content with ads, while others prefer to pay for an ad-free experience. Some enjoy personalized recommendations, like receiving book suggestions that precisely match their tastes, and others simply want to surf the platform to discover new content. Overall, the hallmark of platforms is their use of intelligence algorithms. In most cases, if platforms can satisfy consumers' varied preferences and demands in different ways, regulations should avoid being overly rigid, avoiding reacting to extreme incidents with extreme regulatory measures that protect some people's interests while harming others. Platforms should be encouraged to find a balanced approach to meeting the needs of all parties, as long as fundamental regulatory principles are upheld.

Finally, the supervision and regulation of information authenticity and value orientation are a priority for governments around the world, and it is particularly important for China. Platforms are not only commercial entities but also infrastructures for social information dissemination and interaction, necessitating strict regulatory oversight.

Another persistent challenge in regulation is who decides on controversial technology applications. Technologies that have been the subject of repeated discussions and divergent views are often those with outstanding positive and negative impacts; otherwise, they would have been banned outright. Take facial recognition as an example. During the COVID-19 pandemic, its application was widely accepted, but under normal circumstances, its widespread use remains contentious. Opponents cite privacy concerns, while supporters argue its merits. A city administrator once noted that after his city implemented facial recognition, the vast majority of missing children, elderly people, and people with intellectual disabilities could be located within minutes. The core dilemma remains: by what authority is the decision made? There are many similar issues in which opposing viewpoints make it difficult for policymakers to find a balanced solution.

Another challenge is that digital technology is driving profound transformations, making administrative regulation increasingly complex. Regulators must continuously observe, research, and evaluate emerging technologies while considering multiple factors. In areas of digital technology application, China is at the forefront of innovation, often with no prior experience to reference. It is therefore unavoidable that regulators may sometimes struggle to respond swiftly or coordinate effectively. When certain special incidents trigger strong public reactions, the government has no choice but to intervene first, focusing on containing and stabilizing the most serious and prominent aspects of the problem. In conclusion, the whole society must make concerted efforts, along with increased public discourse, to deepen the understanding of the digital society world. Under government leadership, individuals and institutions should both express their perspectives and collaborate to enhance digital governance.

Transformation and Modernization of China's National Governance

Zhou Li'an

Since the founding of the People's Republic of China in 1949, the resilience and vitality of the Chinese governance system have been continuously maintained and developed. This is evident in Mao Zedong's profound reflection and systematic adaptation of the Soviet model in the early days of the New China; the emergence of local decentralization and local industries in the early 1970s; the implementation of fiscal contracting and local competition following reform and opening up; as well as the widespread adoption of responsibility agreements and target accountability mechanisms among governments. With the rapid marketization, modernization, globalization, and the advancement of Internet technology, the traditional Chinese governance model has encountered various challenges and unprecedented pressures. The 3rd Plenary Session of the 18th Communist Party of China (CPC) Central Committee set the goal of modernizing China's system and capacity for governance. At this critical juncture of national governance transformation, it is essential to systematically reflect on the traditional characteristics, internal logic, and the evolutionary path of China's governance system over the past 40-odd years so as to anticipate potential reforms and challenges in the future.

The most significant difference between China's central–local relations and the federal or unitary systems of Western countries lies in their structural nature. China's central–local relationship is a hierarchical power dynamic within a unified authoritative system, whereas the Western model is based on contractual equality with local autonomy as a fundamental principle. This organizational distinction has led to substantial differences in central–local relations and national governance between China and Western countries. Based on this premise, this chapter examines the traditional characteristics, organizational logic, and evolutionary trajectory of China's governance system from two perspectives: the vertical relationship between central and local governments and the horizontal dynamics of local competition. It also reviews the continuity and transformation of traditional governance models since reform and opening up and analyzes the governance changes, challenges, and responses in China over the past two decades.

From the perspective of the vertical central–local relationship, China has long been characterized by an "administrative subcontracting system." This system describes a localized administrative model in which governance responsibilities are delegated across multiple levels. To be specific, the central government delegates a vast majority of administrative and public affairs to provincial governments, which, in turn, further delegate these responsibilities to prefecture-level cities, counties, and townships in a cascading manner. Local governments, as contractors, are responsible for managing all aspects of governance within their jurisdiction while holding comprehensive administrative authority.

From a horizontal perspective—that is, among local governments at the same level—local officials participate in a political tournament for career advancement. This reflects both centralized control over cadre appointments and competitive dynamics among local governments and local officials. In other words, "local contractors" are not only required to complete the tasks assigned by higher authorities but must also outperform their peers in order to win promotion. Successful candidates may then ascend to higher levels of governance, becoming new "contractors" themselves. The central government, through this system of layered delegation and performance-based promotion, grants local officials of all levels considerable decision-making autonomy. Meanwhile, a centralized performance assessment system and personnel management mechanisms create strong incentives for advancement and a strong competitive drive for each local contractor. The interplay between the administrative subcontracting system and the political tournament has fundamentally shaped the distinctive characteristics of China's governance model.

Evolution of Central–Local Relations and China's Governance Over the Past Four Decades

The year 1978 ushered in a new era of reform and opening up in China. With regard to the administrative subcontracting system, the traditional governance model saw a strong resurgence during the 1980s and 1990s, flourishing under the reform era. This model gradually shifted toward systemic reform and transformation as the country entered the twenty-first century, a process that continues to this day. One of the most significant changes in governance since the reform era has been the central role of the political tournament centered on regional economic development. Local officials have engaged in fierce competition over regional economic performance, creating a dynamic where officialdom competition drives market competition among regional businesses. In turn, the market performance of these enterprises influences the career trajectories of local officials within the political arena. This "government + market" dual-tiered model—where both officialdom and market forces drive economic progress—has laid a crucial institutional foundation for the rapid growth of China's economy.

Enhancing the Administrative Subcontracting System in Intergovernmental Relations

In 1979, the central government began implementing the policy of streamlining government and delegating power, which involved transferring certain administrative and economic management authorities from central ministries to local governments.

This process was accompanied by the transfer of many enterprises previously under central control to local ownership and management. This wave of decentralization has been referred to in academic circles as "administrative decentralization." Henceforth, local governments have gradually gained more and more independent decision-making power, such as investment decisions, attracting foreign investment, enterprise management, and foreign trade. The prominent feature of the decentralization reform is its gradualness and partial breakthroughs. There was significant resistance to large-scale decentralization of power all at once by central ministries, so the central government's strategy was to initially tilt toward certain regions. As a result, Shenzhen, Xiamen, Zhuhai, and Shantou were designated as special economic zones. Starting from 1984, the establishment of centrally planned cities, 14 coastal open cities, and the subsequent establishment of the Shanghai Pudong New Area and the Tianjin Binhai New Area all represented the trend of gradually devolving and transferring the power of central departments to local governments. This decentralization further strengthened the role of local governments in the management structure established after the founding of the People's Republic of China. Thus, local governments transformed from passive executors within a planned economy to proactive managers, significantly enhancing their enthusiasm for participating in reform and development.

An important institutional legacy left by the planned economy is that governments at all levels are accustomed to managing through indicators and figures, a practice further reinforced by the improvement of modern national economic accounting statistical methods and technologies. Since China launched reform and opening up, the planned indicators have gradually lost their directive nature and have become an important tool for guiding economic and social work. The general procedure is that the central government sets major economic and social development goals, while local governments respond positively by breaking down and implementing the central government's goals at all levels.

The administrative subcontracting system, aided by modern technologies and management methods, can more effectively carry out task delegation and responsibility assessments. One of the most prominent examples of this is the various forms of government responsibility contracts and target responsibility systems that have been prevalent since the mid-1980s. These contracts cover various aspects of government duties, including economic development, family planning, environmental management, poverty alleviation, and disease prevention. The responsibility in each area is ultimately expressed as quantifiable task indicators, which serve as critical benchmarks for higher-level governments to assess the performance of lower-level governments. Especially in economic development and investment promotion, local governments below the provincial level sign government responsibility contracts, with lower-level governments or department leaders bearing administrative responsibilities for quantitative indicators. Some indicators, such as family planning and safety production, have a "veto power" for rewarding and promoting administrative officials based on their performance.

To promote the work of governments, the leadership responsibility system is quite common. For example, in environmental pollution control, in late 2007, Wuxi city introduced the "River Chief System" for the first time to address the pollution of Taihu Lake, with the responsibility for pollution control assigned to specific individuals. The system was applied in the management of pollution in Dianchi Lake in Kunming city, Yunnan Province, and Donghu Lake in Wuhan city, Hubei Province, and has gradually been promoted across the country. The central government's advocacy for targeted poverty alleviation also adopts a model where responsibility for poverty alleviation is assigned to individuals, progressing from the provincial, municipal, to county and township levels.

The "fiscal revenue-sharing" characteristic of the administrative subcontracting system became particularly prominent after reform and opening up. From the early 1980s to 1993, China's fiscal system operated under a pure fiscal contracting system, in which local governments first submitted the required revenue to the central government and retained the surplus. The tax-sharing system was introduced after 1993, but the central and local governments continued to share tax revenues based on the pre-existing distribution of administrative powers. The administrative affairs subcontracting system remains unchanged, leaving the hierarchical structure of administrative contracting largely unchanged.

A more critical fact is the prevalence of various forms of "fiscal contracting" below the provincial level. Extra-budgetary funds have long accounted for a significant share of local governments' revenues, particularly land transfer revenues, which have historically served to compensate for shortfalls in local budgetary income. In some developed regions, land transfer revenue even exceeds budgeted fiscal revenues. As a result, local governments face enormous pressure to raise funds independently. More importantly, local governments must mobilize their own financial resources to fulfill the tasks and targets assigned by higher authorities. It is a common scenario where "the central government invites, and the local government pays" or "the higher authority orders, and the lower authority pays." Apart from their regular administrative agenda, local governments must navigate a highly uncertain, multitasking environment. To meet newly assigned tasks from higher authorities, local governments have to raise additional funds by diverse approaches as resourceful as the Eight Immortals crossing the sea. The asymmetry between the administrative subcontractors (local governments) and the contract issuers (higher-level governments) necessitates that contractors maintain financial flexibility and budgetary elasticity. This is the fundamental reason for the longstanding duality (the coexistence of on-budget and off-budget components) of China's intergovernmental fiscal system. The rise and development of investment and financing platforms over the past decade and the accumulation of local government debt represent extensions of this fiscal duality, reflecting how local governments have turned to financial instruments to cope with the mismatch between administrative responsibilities and financial resources.

The system in which the performance of local governments is subject to evaluation and acceptance by higher authorities is predominantly result-based, where success is judged solely by outcomes. Following the delegation of administrative tasks layer by layer, the supervisory capacity of higher authorities over lower-level governments is relatively limited and relies primarily on routine inspections, special rectifications, and result assessments as forms of internal control. Particularly in the context of the widespread adoption of target responsibility systems and responsibility contracting systems, various kinds of rankings and last-place elimination mechanisms have become common practice. The core characteristic of these practices is the relative weakening of procedures and rules, with results determining everything.

The hierarchical subcontracting of administrative affairs, characterized by the delegation of tasks and decomposition of performance indicators, is highly dependent on local governments and relevant departments raising their own funds through revenue-sharing mechanisms and budget contracting. Along with result-oriented assessments and supervision, these three aspects together constitute the fundamental characteristics of China's intergovernmental relations and administrative governance for much of the reform and opening up period. Within this framework, local governments enjoy significant discretionary power and informal rights of control. Meanwhile, as China accelerates its market-oriented reforms and deepens its integration into global competition, local governments have become the backbone of regional economic development, openness to the outside world, and institutional reform.

The "Officialdom + Market" Model: Understanding China's Political Tournament for Economic Growth

As the Party shifted its focus toward economic development, especially following Deng Xiaoping's repeated assertion that development is the absolute principle, local Party committees at all levels gradually centered their performance assessments of officials on indicators related to regional economic development, such as GDP growth, financial and tax revenue, and foreign investment attraction. This is commonly referred to as the phenomenon of "GDP supremacy" or "GDP-centric performance evaluation." The emphasis on economic performance in cadre assessments directly led to local officials' competition for promotion centered on regional economic growth, namely, the political tournament driven by economic performance. Given China's multi-tiered governmental structure, these political tournaments are unfolding simultaneously at various levels of local governments (provinces, cities, counties, and townships), with different levels influencing and reinforcing each other. Therefore, China's government system can be understood as a multi-tiered political tournament framework centered on economic development.

The vertical administrative subcontracting system and the horizontal political tournament among officials' supplement and interact with each other. In the era of reform and opening up, the complementary relationship between these two mechanisms has been maximally harnessed and amplified, laying a critical institutional foundation for China's rapid economic growth and smooth institutional transition. The decentralization reforms since reform and opening up have granted local governments at all levels significant administrative and economic resources, such as land leasing, fiscal subsidies, financing, administrative approvals, and infrastructure development. This enabled local governments to become centers and hubs of regional economic and social activities while also serving as rule-makers within their jurisdictions, shaping policy formulation and implementation. The administrative subcontracting system endows local officials with substantial discretionary power. From the perspective of businesses and the general public, this means that officials have the ability to facilitate accomplishments, remain inactive, or even act in ways that hinder progress. However, the political tournament among local officials incentivized them to channel their control over key resources and discretionary power into regional economic development. For instance, they can mobilize all available resources and regulatory tools to create favorable infrastructures and business environments for enterprises within their jurisdictions. This system transformed local officials from potential "grabbing hands" to "helping hands," thereby addressing one of the biggest challenges in China's regional economic development.

The horizontal political tournament based on economic growth not only interacts with the strengthened administrative subcontracting system but also gives rise to a distinctive model of government-market interaction, which I refer to as the "officialdom + market" model. Officialdom refers to competition among officials, where local officials compete for political promotion. Market refers to the competition among enterprises in the economic marketplace. On the one hand, the rules, methods, and intensity of officialdom competition directly determine officials ' incentives for promotion, thereby influencing their enthusiasm for boosting regional economic development, including efforts to formulate industrial policies, invest in infrastructure, improve administrative efficiency, and provide land and financial support, all of which eventually decide the performance of local enterprises in market competition. On the other hand, the aggregate performance achieved by all enterprises within a jurisdiction through market competition contributes to the regional economic performance, as reflected in GDP growth and fiscal revenue, which subsequently affects the success of officials in officialdom competition. Officialdom competition may further intensify market competition among enterprises in different regions. For example, government support in terms of land and financing may encourage enterprises to adopt more aggressive strategies. Conversely, market competition not only shapes the outcomes of officialdom competition but also determines the strategies and approaches officials take in their political contests, such as whether to prioritize state-owned enterprises (SOEs) or foster the growth of private enterprises. The interplay of these two distinct competition processes greatly contributed to the rapid development of China's economy. Of course, regional differences in officialdom competition and market competition have led to diverse models of government–enterprise cooperation and economic development among regions.

In this model, local governments must face market competition, including global competition, and any economic strategies and policies they adopt must ultimately withstand the test of market logic. In this process, a local government can only be a rule-taker rather than a market manipulator in the national and global market. The combination of officialdom and market competition, along with the cross-regional mobility of physical and human capital, forces local officials to treat enterprises and talent favorably, which fundamentally curtails arbitrary, authoritarian, and excessively interventionist government behavior. The outcomes of local enterprises and industries engaging in competition feed back into the system, guiding officials and entrepreneurs within a jurisdiction to collaborate, complement each other's strengths, and seek competitive specialized industries. The "officialdom + market" model has shaped the diversity of regional economic development strategies, industrial policies, and growth pathways while fostering cross-regional learning effects.

Economic transformation and development not only require market entrepreneurs to drive continuous innovation and growth, but also necessitate political entrepreneurs—leaders who dare to pioneer innovations in institutions, policies, and development strategies. The transition from a rigid planned economy to a market-oriented system requires not only the courage to break away from traditional structures and the wisdom to explore reforms but also the ability to confront vested interests and bear political risks. Promoting regional economic development is an especially complex and challenging strategic task for local officials. The economic development of a region depends not only on a pro-business attitude and policies from local governments but also, more importantly, on how local officials leverage resource endowments and institutional conditions to develop competitive industries, attract talent and investments, address market failures, foster institutional and systemic innovation, and provide favorable infrastructure and policy environments, so as to win in the regional economic competition. This requires local officials to possess strategic vision and innovative thinking. In a word, these aspects call for political entrepreneurship among local officials, a quality just as demanding in terms of difficulty, challenge, and creativity as market entrepreneurship. The "officialdom + market" model has precisely facilitated the simultaneous emergence and close integration of both political and market entrepreneurial spirits.

The incentives for officials and the effectiveness of governance present challenges across nations. In developing countries, corruption and inefficient governments are particularly detrimental to economic development. The political tournament among local officials in China has introduced competition within government agencies while also integrating market competition between regions and enterprises to offer a uniquely Chinese solution. The dual-layer competition mechanism of the "officialdom + market" model has served as a driving force behind China's rapid economic growth.

However, the "officialdom + market" model is not a flawless growth mechanism. While it has its strengths, it also has shortcomings and limitations. Although both officialdom competition and market competition are competition mechanisms, they differ in nature. Officialdom competition is inherently closer to a zero-sum game, as there are limited promotion opportunities, with only a few winners being elevated. In contrast, market competition tends to be a positive-sum game. The zero-sum nature of officialdom competition leads to strong incentives to compete but insufficient incentives to cooperate. In its early stages, this conflict manifested as local market protectionism and regional blockades. Over time, it has evolved into difficulties in cross-jurisdictional corporate mergers, acquisitions, and restructurings, slow progress in regional cooperation (such as economic integration and cross-regional environmental governance), and local protectionism in market regulation and the judiciary. All these issues are closely related to the zero-sum nature of the political tournament.

Furthermore, local officials are subject to tenure and age limits in their positions—constraints that do not apply to enterprises in market competition. As a result, short-term behavior among officials is difficult to avoid. Additionally, local officials tend to prioritize the "hard metrics" emphasized in their performance evaluations by superiors—such as GDP growth, fiscal revenue, and foreign investment—while neglecting the "soft metrics" that are crucial to public well-being but receive little attention in the assessment system, such as education, healthcare, and environmental governance. In China, environmental protection, education, healthcare, and quality inspection are all localized services without cross-regional competition. From this perspective, these areas precisely represent the domains where the dual mechanisms of "officialdom competition" and "market competition" have failed, leading to widespread public dissatisfaction. Many of the key challenges China's economic growth model has faced over the past 40-odd years—such as extensive economic growth, environmental pollution, insufficient investments in education, healthcare, and social security, and rising local government debt—can all be analyzed through the lens of the "officialdom + market" model.

Reform, Transformation, and Future Prospects of China's Governance System

Since the mid-1990s, China's traditional administrative subcontracting system has come under growing pressure amid the rapid development of the market economy. As the country has reformed its planned economy system in a market-oriented direction and embraced free trade and globalization, its governance structure has undergone an unprecedented transformation.

With the gradual disintegration of the traditional work-unit system and the weakening of localized administrative ties, the cross-regional mobility of both people and capital has increased significantly. Building a unified, national market requires dismantling various forms of local protectionism and regional discrimination while establishing comprehensive infrastructure and institutional frameworks that transcend geographical constraints. This includes the development of an advanced nationwide transportation and communication network; cross-regionally transferable healthcare, social security, minimum income guarantees, and unemployment benefits; the implementation of unified national market regulatory standards and enforcement mechanisms in areas such as environmental protection, quality control, public health, and workplace safety; and the establishment of a judicial system capable of restraining local protectionism. To achieve these ambitious objectives, two key steps are required: strengthening the state's fiscal extractive capacity and undertaking large-scale reforms of the traditional Chinese governance system, historically structured around localized administrative control.

Since the mid-1990s, both the vertical administrative subcontracting system and the horizontal political tournament model have undergone systematic transformation. A key development has been the shift toward vertical management. Starting with the banking sector and extending to customs, taxation, industry and commerce, land administration, discipline inspection, and the judiciary, numerous departments have transitioned from locally dominated "block management" to vertical oversight by central or provincial authorities. Furthermore, the proliferation of project-based governance—where higher-level authorities allocate special-purpose transfer payments through targeted projects—also reflects this trend. These developments have empowered central ministries and higher-level departments while reducing the discretionary authority of local governments.

In addition, changes in governance are also evident in the evolution of the political tournament. The central government has gradually de-emphasized GDP-centric performance assessment. The past model, which prioritized economic growth above all else, has undergone a series of adjustments. Rather than judging officials based solely on GDP growth, greater emphasis is now placed on evaluating their contributions to environmental protection, improvement of people's livelihoods, technological innovation, and industrial upgrading. At the same time, institutional regulation of governmental power has been strengthened, emphasizing law-based governance. The goal is to ensure that power operates transparently under public scrutiny, with a strong focus on procedural integrity and due process. Even if policy outcomes are favorable, officials may be held accountable if their actions violate laws and regulations.

The modernization of the Chinese governance system faces three key challenges.

First, how to redefine the boundaries between government, market, and society. ensuring both a decisive role for the market and the effectiveness of a proactive government? At present, the Chinese government remains in a dominant role, which monopolizes governance—frequently manifesting as "a never-idle hand." The market and civil society remain highly dependent on government authority and are subject to strict regulation. Further reform requires streamlining administration, delegating power, reforming the administrative approval system, lowering barriers to market entry for non-state enterprises, and fully enabling the market to play a decisive role in resource allocation. These are uncharted waters, and administrative resistance remains strong—but must be overcome. Meantime, economic development will continue to be China's central concern for a long period of time. Local government competition will remain a crucial incentive mechanism. Exploring ways to improve the political tournament model to better align with new development priorities is an important issue worthy of further exploration.

Second, how to delineate the rights and responsibilities between central and local governments, and strike a balance between centralization and decentralization? Thus far, one of China's most successful reform experiences has been decentralization and the promotion of local competition, which spurred regional innovation and development, thereby advancing economic reform and high-speed growth. This valuable experience must be retained. However, using a one-size-fits-all approach to vertical reform in addressing governance issues rooted in the administrative subcontracting system is not always prudent. Excessive centralization risks weakening local government authority, limiting their flexibility, and stifling innovation. It may also lead to increased bureaucracy and inefficiency. Historically, China has cycled between decentralization and centralization, suggesting that adjusting the power balance alone cannot resolve underlying issues. The root cause lies in the top-down decision-making and oversight mechanisms, which create significant information asymmetry. Implementing an effective bottom-up oversight and assessment mechanism, reinforced by the rule of law, can mitigate moral hazards in local governments without requiring extensive centralization of regulatory powers.

Third, how to balance incentives and constraints in the governance of officials? Traditionally, China's governance system has encouraged an entrepreneurial approach, where local officials, under the dual pressure of political tournament and market competition, were willing to take risks and innovate. As long as their initiatives yielded positive results, they were often rewarded, even if some actions violated existing norms. However, as governance becomes increasingly standardized and institutionalized, the decision-making autonomy and operational flexibility of local governments are shrinking. Nowadays, with a growing emphasis on procedural legality, officials now face heightened accountability and a narrower margin for errors. The weakening of GDP-based incentives has further reduced the motivational effect of the political tournament model.

In summary, traditional governance in China was characterized by strong incentives, weak constraints, and outcome-oriented approaches. By contrast, modern governance emphasizes weaker incentives, stronger constraints, and a balance between outcomes and process. In a system characterized by limited government, this may not pose significant problems, as compliance with laws would serve as the primary safeguard against abuse of power. However, China will maintain a strong government for the foreseeable future, and more importantly, local governments still retain considerable influence on regional development. While strong constraints can help prevent abuse of power, they also risk producing inaction, mediocrity, and bureaucratic inertia.

Given these challenges, the next phase of reform in China's governance system should focus on the following areas.

First, reform the political tournament model for local officials by improving performance assessment systems. Promotion criteria should incorporate indicators such as innovation, green development, and environmental protection, thereby broadening the scope beyond mere economic development. Political tournaments and local competition should continue to be used to both incentivize and regulate officials. Considering diverse economic conditions and natural environments across regions, differentiated performance evaluation systems could be piloted. Meantime, long-term impacts of officials' decisions and actions—such as their influence on local government debt and ecological sustainability—should receive greater emphasis, promoting continuity and sustainability in regional development strategies.

Second, complement top-down valuations with bottom-up assessment mechanisms, fostering competition in public service delivery across government departments and regions. This can be achieved by leveraging existing oversight and evaluation mechanisms, such as performance assessments conducted by the National People's Congress and the Chinese People's Political Consultative Conference, which should play a role in influencing officials' promotions, appointments, and dismissals. Additionally, modern mobile Internet technologies can be used to facilitate real-time public and business feedback on government efficiency and responsiveness. Similar to how DiDi (a ride-hailing platform) drivers must accept passenger reviews—where customer reviews and driver reputation determine their ability to take new orders—civil servants and government departments could also be subject to evaluations by their "clients" and "stakeholders." The final evaluation results should be publicly disclosed and used to compile rankings, serving as strong incentives to improve service responsiveness and effectiveness. Public evaluations should focus on services directly related to people's livelihoods, such as education, healthcare, and civil affairs services, while business assessments can emphasize the business environment, efficiency of administrative services, as well as the integrity and self-discipline of civil servants. Cross-regional rankings of the business environment could also be considered.

Third, strike a balance between centralization and decentralization. With the implementation of multiple supervision mechanisms for local governments, the central government can afford to delegate more authority with reduced concerns over information asymmetry and inadequate supervision, thus largely avoiding the typical dilemma of decentralization. More powers—such as taxation and borrowing rights—can be transferred to local governments, while simultaneously restricting local interference in the provision of national public goods. This includes ensuring a unified national market, eliminating protectionism, and preventing regional labor market discrimination. The division of responsibilities between central and local governments should be recalibrated. The central government should assume greater expenditure responsibilities, increase transfer payments, and work toward a better alignment between local fiscal resources and their administrative duties.

The Chinese governance system has the longest continuous tradition in human history. Transitioning to a modern governance model that aligns with modernization principles will be a long and arduous journey. Due to institutional inertia, there is often a tendency for traditional practices to resurface. Therefore, the modernization of governance must be pursued through steady, sustained reform to achieve lasting and meaningful change.

Corporate Innovation Models: Starting With State-Owned Enterprises

Chen Xiaohong

Since the 18th CPC National Congress, General Secretary Xi Jinping has emphasized that innovation is the primary driving force of development. He has repeatedly stressed the importance of firmly establishing a new concept of development and upholding the central role of innovation in China's modernization drive. This vision provides strategic direction and fundamental guidance for building China into a great modern socialist country in all respects and achieving the Second Centenary Goal. The 20th CPC National Congress further underscored that high-quality development is driven by innovation, with SOEs continuing to serve as the backbone of national technological innovation. Below are some perspectives on the innovation in SOEs.

Responsibilities, Contributions, and Challenges of SOE Innovation

First, SOEs have a fundamental responsibility for innovation. This responsibility stems not only from the central government's innovation-driven development strategy but also from the inherent status and role of SOEs in China's economy. Operating primarily in competitive sectors, SOEs can only ensure sustained development through innovation. Moreover, SOEs contribute nearly one-third of China's GDP and act as industry leaders in many sectors. Their innovation efforts are not merely about advancing individual enterprises—they are crucial for driving innovation across entire industrial chains.

Second, SOEs are well-positioned for innovation. Innovation requires knowledge, talent, manufacturing capabilities, market access, and financial capital, all of which SOEs possess. More importantly, years of reform and development have cultivated a cohort of entrepreneurial operators. Unlike startup-type entrepreneurs, who build new businesses from the ground up, operator-type entrepreneurs innovate within the framework of existing enterprises. While this model benefits from a solid foundation, it also faces challenges such as structural constraints and entrenched mindsets, making significant organizational adjustments difficult. Nonetheless, many large enterprises have successfully navigated crises and achieved innovation under this model. International examples include IBM's Louis Gerstner and Microsoft's Satya Nadella, while in China, notable figures include Ning Gaoning (former chairman of Sinochem Holdings), Song Zhiping (former chairman of China National Building Material Group Co., Ltd.), and Wang Dongsheng (former chairman of BOE Technology Group). All of them have made significant contributions to and achieved great successes in corporate innovation.

Third, SOEs have made remarkable achievements in innovation across diverse fields, including aerospace, equipment manufacturing, raw materials, energy, new electronic devices, and advanced materials, as well as in infrastructure construction and services. SOEs have played a leading role in driving innovation.

Fourth, SOEs face substantial challenges in innovation that cannot be overlooked. One major issue is the insufficient intensity and depth of research and development (R&D). Insufficient intensity refers to the low proportion of R&D expenditure relative to sales revenue, while insufficient depth indicates that most R&D expenditures are directed toward development rather than basic or applied research. In 2018, the proportion of basic research in corporate R&D was 0.2% in China, compared to 6.2% in the United States and 7.8% in Japan. Applied research made up 3.8% in China, versus 22.6% in the United States, and 24.1% in Japan. These figures highlight a substantial gap between China and developed nations in corporate R&D structure. Moreover, SOEs need to enhance their innovation systems and capabilities. For instance, in the era of open innovation, how can enterprises maintain openness while retaining control? Amid significant changes in the international environment, how can global cooperation in innovation be effectively integrated with domestic efforts? Other issues include shortcomings in innovation systems and frameworks, as well as in management. Institutional barriers also persist and must be addressed.

In summary, while SOEs have clear responsibilities, favorable conditions, and notable achievements in innovation, they also face challenges requiring further efforts.

Approaches and Models of Innovation

Enhancing SOEs' innovation capabilities requires a clear understanding of innovation approaches and models.

Innovation, as conceptualized by American economist Joseph Alois Schumpeter, refers to the successful commercialization of new businesses or business combinations enabled by technological breakthroughs. Schumpeter was the first to propose a systematic theory that has been widely recognized by the academic community. The theory identifies five types of innovation: new products, new methods, new materials, new markets, and new organizations. New organizations originally referred to business structures, such as Ford's assembly line system, which may differ from today's concept of business models. Nevertheless, if we take a broader understanding of Schumpeter's concept of new organizations, the two can also be regarded as essentially the same thing.

Among these five types, product innovation—especially the introduction of entirely new products—is of particular significance. It allows enterprises to gain a first-mover advantage and potentially secure excess returns or even temporary monopolies.

From the perspective of economic growth, product innovation plays a crucial role. In early growth economics, the Harrod-Domar growth model described key factors influencing economic growth, including capital and labor, but did not include technological progress. As research progressed, it was found that the contribution of technological progress to growth, or the rate of technological progress, could be estimated from this model. But it did not clearly explain how technological progress affected economic growth. After the 1980s, further studies into the mechanisms and processes of technological innovation in economic growth led to modifications of the model, making technological progress an endogenous variable within economic development and being included in the economic growth model. One significant discovery was the mechanism by which product innovation drives economic growth. Product innovation stimulates demand; sustaining such innovation requires investment in R&D and human capital, which, in turn, expands supply. The increase in supply further supports demand, creating an interactive cycle where technological progress in product innovation drives the simultaneous growth of supply and demand, thereby overall economic growth. This is what we now refer to as "innovation-driven development."

New methods and materials are, overall, innovations in intermediate products. Unlike new products that directly target consumers and play a "demand-driven" role at the final stage, their impact is different. However, their importance is equally evident. Historically, China faced many challenges in these areas, such as technological bottlenecks and industrial upgrading pressures, prompting a focus on supply-side reforms and innovations over the years. Currently, equal emphasis must be placed on demand—by integrating supply-side reforms with demand development. However, I believe that demand should not be stimulated through monetary expansion, as advocated by Keynesian economics. Instead, it should be created through innovation, the interactive growth of supply and demand.

There has been extensive discussion around innovation models. In a sense, there is little difference between innovation approaches and innovation models. If one were to identify a distinction, I would say that Schumpeter's concept of innovation approaches is more specific, focusing on concrete elements. In contrast, I understand innovation models as a functional relationship related to innovation—they describe the objectives of innovation, the input–output relationships of relevant resources, and the evolutionary paths involved.

Innovation models vary, including incremental innovation and breakthrough innovation, which differ in terms of the degree and scope of innovation. When both the degree and scope of innovation are significant, there will be qualitative changes, leading to systemic transformations—the disruptive innovation. However, an advanced innovative product introduced to the market may initially struggle to gain market acceptance—due to high prices, deficiencies in key performance indicators that mainstream consumers prioritize, or a lack of supporting resources. Such constraints often prevent these innovations from gaining a foothold in the mainstream market, let alone achieving disruptive innovation. Harvard professor Clayton M. Christensen argued that the key to successful product innovation begins by developing an advanced technology within a specific niche market. As performance improves and cost-effectiveness increases alongside market expansion, the innovation can then enter larger mainstream markets. Christensen's disruptive innovation theory not only explains how innovations succeed but also highlights that rigid organizational mindsets often prevent companies from recognizing innovation opportunities.

Eco-innovation and platform innovation are increasingly recognized as interconnected innovation models. These models emphasize innovation systems, ecosystems, and mechanisms. Platform innovation requires core technological capabilities and resource integration. After the 1990s, the key reason Intel outpaced Japanese companies was its technology platform strategy. Intel independently developed and freely provided an open mainboard, which not only integrated with the company's central processing units but was also compatible with other components. This allowed downstream companies to easily integrate their technologies with Intel's, leading to accelerated growth. Another example of a platform development strategy is the expansion of China's Internet companies. These companies may not have had advanced technology initially, but the Internet's winner-takes-all approach nature enabled leading enterprises to rapidly grow. Once they gained a dominant position, they used technological innovation to further distance themselves from competitors and drive continued growth. Tencent and Alibaba's rapid rise was mainly attributed to Internet-based businesses and ecosystem construction. Google also primarily depends on Internet-based business and, in recent years, has been actively developing artificial intelligence and autonomous driving, as these fields are closely linked to the future of the Internet. The viability of relying solely on Internet advertising for revenue is becoming increasingly uncertain. Amazon and JD.com are Internet-based retail enterprises and new-generation retailers. Despite operating at a loss for several years, they have continued to gain market recognition due to their offline operations and possession of core technological advantages—specifically, Internet technology platforms that other retail enterprises lack. In summary, successful platform innovation must be supported by core technology.

Platform innovation requires both technological strength and market demand. The success of Internet platform companies is largely demand-driven, while companies in other industries—such as Intel—must possess both advanced technological capabilities and the ability to capture and respond to market demand. Huawei's success is rooted in its strong technological foundation, which enables it to deliver high-end, complex products that are directly aligned with consumer needs, thereby generating substantial market demand. Initially, Huawei operated as a system supplier; it has since evolved into a direct product supplier, significantly expanding its growth potential. Additionally, Huawei has established an Integrated Product Development system, which facilitates seamless coordination across technology R&D, production, and market demand. Today, Huawei has emerged as a major innovation platform.

In conclusion, two principles are essential: Entrepreneurs should adopt an open mindset to comprehend innovation approaches and models, avoiding constraints imposed by rigid theories and past experiences. Moreover, they must grasp the essence of innovation and leverage systematic methods and technologies to effectively address market demands.

Original Innovation Models

Original innovation has garnered significant attention over the years. At its core, it refers to the creation of something entirely new from the ground up. But what exactly constitutes an original innovation? Must it always originate from fundamental research, followed by applied R&D, to be considered truly original? In my opinion, from an economic perspective, original innovation refers to innovations that are unique in the market—regardless of their technological origin. Due to the United States' implementation of "technological decoupling," which blatantly contravenes international norms, and in response to gaps in the research capabilities of Chinese enterprises, a prevailing notion has emerged: that only innovations stemming from basic research qualify as original. This perspective is conceptually flawed. It not only contradicts well-established experiences of successful innovation but also misinterprets the Chinese central government's emphasis on fundamental research and original innovation.

In my opinion, Chinese enterprises, which are still in the process of catching up, can learn from and adopt the following three original innovation models.

The first is product innovation driven by technological development based on existing technologies and business models. Successful examples include Apple and Tesla in the United States. These companies were neither the original researchers or inventors of the fundamental technologies in their fields nor were they the first to launch products in their respective markets. However, they excelled at developing and integrating existing technologies, mastering core product technologies, and combining them with innovative business models and technical interactions. This approach ultimately led to their success in producing breakthrough innovations.

The second is original innovation in products via key technological advancement in existing systems, such as the well-known lithium battery. A battery's basic structure consists of a positive electrode, a negative electrode, and a separator. An American professor discovered that using lithium cobalt oxide as a negative electrode material could significantly increase energy density. But it was Japanese enterprises—Sony and Panasonic—that first introduced innovative commercial products. They built upon existing technical principles and structures, leveraging new materials and corresponding design innovations to achieve key technological breakthroughs. By aligning these innovations with the growth of the consumer electronics market, they eventually achieved product innovation.

The third is paradigm-shifting innovation. This model represents a fundamental breakthrough across an entire technological system. A notable example is Japan's development of the blue-light light-emitting diode semiconductors. Japanese companies first succeeded in applying fundamental research and later scaled it into full production. The researchers involved were ultimately awarded the Nobel Prize. The success of this kind of innovation heavily depends on complementary assets, such as specialized knowledge and advanced equipment.

While Chinese enterprises have achieved several notable successes in original innovation, truly ground-breaking and market-transforming innovations remain relatively rare, while incremental improvements closely aligned with the Chinese market are more common. To move further, Chinese entrepreneurs should adopt a broad and open-minded approach to original innovation. They should not only value innovations derived from fundamental research but also explore multiple pathways and experiment with diverse innovation models. At the same time, the government should actively encourage and support these efforts.

Social Capital in the Process of Governance Capacity Modernization

Long Haibo

In the Report of the 20th CPC National Congress, the term "governance" appears 50 times, with the phrase "modernizing China's system and capacity for governance" mentioned four times. The modernization of China's capacity for governance is essentially a process of reform and innovation that evolves in step with the times. It marks the transformation of China's national governance from a pre-modern or non-modernized state toward full modernization.

Currently, the transformation is driven by both internal and external factors. On the one hand, the decline of traditional governance systems has led to a credibility crisis for government institutions. On the other hand, conventional governance models often fail to unleash the vitality of social subjects, highlighting the urgent need for external drivers to spur reform. Among these, social capital—arising from trust-based interactions and cooperation and shared norms within society—plays a crucial role in promoting the modernization of China's capacity for governance. Therefore, enhancing government credibility should be a central focus, and its realization is inseparable from the active participation of social capital. Social capital shapes the effectiveness of governance largely through its impact on government credit, serving as a foundational element in the modernization of China's system and capacity for governance. It is imperative to orderly regulate and guide social capital to build a political-ecological mechanism that supports its positive accumulation.

Governance Significance and Realization of Government Credit

Government credit has been a fundamental value since the inception of the government. It is regarded as one of the primary sources of legitimacy in governance, and the level of government credit directly influences the progress of modern governance modernization. As China's economy enters a new normal, the traditional growth model is becoming unsustainable. Hidden risks and emerging social contradictions pose new challenges to the establishment of a trustworthy government. Without public confidence, comprehensive reforms will struggle to make significant progress, which not only damages the government's image but also undermines the social credit system and may even trigger crises of political legitimacy. In this context, scientific macroeconomic management and effective governance are intrinsic requirements for realizing the benefits of a socialist market economy. Therefore, it is essential to transform government functions, deepen the reform of the administrative system, innovate governance methods, enhance public trust, and improve administrative efficiency. In this new historical phase, the significance of government credit must be fully recognized—it is both a barometer and a driver of governance modernization. The construction of a credit-based government has become a vital pillar in strengthening the government's capacity for governance.

Government Credit as the Foundation for Governance Modernization

The effectiveness of governance often hinges on the extent of social consensus. A country lacking a fundamental consensus cannot achieve effective governance. The core of modernizing China's capacity for governance lies in enhancing the effectiveness of governance practices. As a key factor in governance, the government's policy-making and implementation capabilities directly influence the operational model and effectiveness of all other governance stakeholders. For example, the way in which the government communicates with citizens in the policy-making process plays a crucial role in fostering mutual trust and improving governance efficiency. Since reform and opening up began, the authoritarian governance model replaced the earlier populist disarray, quickly uniting public will and achieving a broad consensus. Through administrative and policy instruments, it has driven rapid economic growth and preserved social stability. In the current phase, strengthening mutual trust between the government and the public and fostering a sense of shared purpose in promoting development have become particularly important.

First, a high level of government credit is conducive to strengthening reform consensus. Currently, the external environment for reform is far more complex than anticipated. The adjustments of structural interests have led to stronger resistance, and contentious public discourse has made consensus-building more difficult. It is important to recognize that forging a consensus on reform at the new stage is more than a continuation of past agreements—it must also respond to new realities and emerging challenges. This cannot be achieved without good government credit. A higher degree of government credit boosts public confidence in government officials, institutions, and policies, which, in turn, strengthens the government's ability to coordinate and communicate effectively. A high level of government credit allows for a better understanding of the demands of other governance actors, maximizes the mobilization of all positive social forces, thereby securing broad trust and strong support from all walks of life.

Second, high-level government credit is conducive to enhancing governance performance. Governance performance is closely related to government legitimacy, organizational capacity, and administrative effectiveness, and it is also influenced by governance structures and institutional frameworks. The key to improving governance performance lies in the government's ability to guide and integrate resources, unleash the potential and vitality of different social actors, maximally improve people's livelihoods, and drive economic growth. However, the most critical factor is strengthening government legitimacy and administrative effectiveness. Studies have shown that trust in government is a core component of government credit, which serves as both a theoretical tool for measuring public recognition and support for governance and a fundamental source of political legitimacy. All government behaviors must be predicated on government credit. A high level of government credit increases interactions between individuals and organizations, reduces the costs of public governance, and significantly improves governance efficiency.

Third, a high level of government credit encourages public participation. A credible government—one that prioritizes the interests of the people and adheres to principles of democracy, the rule of law, efficiency, and integrity—can win widespread trust and strong support from the people. At present, challenges of insufficient public participation and ineffective government responsiveness in governance hinder orderly interactions between the government and society. One crucial way to increase public participation is by improving communication and cooperation between the government and the public. thereby building trust and psychological alignment. Thus, only by establishing a well-functioning, inclusive governance network—anchored in clear development goals, institutional legitimacy, and effective policy implementation—can public participation be effectively guided. This lies at the heart of government credit.

Governance Credit Cannot Be Achieved Without Social Capital

From a driving force perspective, the government is one of the largest sources of social capital. The legitimacy and credit of the government are crucial for the formation and expansion of social capital. Empirical analysis reveals that government credit has a transmissive effect, and the number of transmission pathways is closely related to the stock and structure of regional social capital. Historical experience demonstrates that the more widespread trust is within a community, the more likely it is for positive interaction between the state and society, government and the public, thereby expanding the potential for enhanced government credibility. Overcoming the challenges of modern government credit requires taking trust as the foundation of public-government interactions and seeking new foundations for government trustworthiness through a more complex, open, and dynamic approach. In this way, public trust in the government can be actively cultivated. It is evident that social capital plays a vital role in achieving and enhancing government credit.

On one hand, social capital fosters the foundation of social trust for public recognition. Social capital is grounded in social trust, and economic prosperity depends on the level of trust within a society. The formation of general social trust is based on the participation of members of society through cooperation across different levels and sectors. When government–public communication is smooth, and government decision-making genuinely reflects public interests, the government's social foundation becomes more solid, and public recognition of government authority increases accordingly. Nowadays, China is undergoing a period of comprehensive transformation. The emerging social structure requires the reconstruction of social trust, and the participation of multiple actors in governance needs to be based on social trust. Government credit is the core of social trust. The government should actively promote public participation in decision-making, enhance interaction and communication with citizens, safeguard citizens' rights to express opinions, and provide avenues for public oversight. This can help mitigate the negative effects of "critical citizens" and strengthen social trust in the government.

On the other hand, social capital provides a participation network for strengthening government capacity. Public participation networks help cultivate civic values such as cooperation, solidarity, and democracy. They also increase repeated interactions (or "iterated games"), which facilitate overcoming collective action dilemmas and improving governance performance. Through these networks, the public can better understand shared needs and differences in interests, ultimately fostering consensus through rational dialogue and negotiation. These networks exist not only between the public but also between the government and the people. They are essential—and increasingly urgent—for modernizing the capacity for governance. At present, government dishonesty remains a prominent problem, which, in many cases, stems not from intentional misconduct but from a lack of administrative capacity. This challenge is closely related to the traditional governance model's reliance on a single, rigid participation network and its inefficiencies in providing public goods. To address these shortcomings, social capital must be leveraged to expand and diversify participation networks, making them more flexible and dynamic. By fostering genuine mutual trust among governance subjects and encouraging them to consciously abide by the operational norms of local governance, government capacity can be enhanced through cooperative governance.

The Impact of Social Capital on the Modernization of Governance Capacity

Social capital plays a crucial role in governance, primarily by influencing government credit, which, in turn, affects governance effectiveness. It is essential for the modernization of the national governance system and capacity. It can be said that government governance is inextricably linked to social foundations, and social capital theory may become a research perspective. Key components of social capital—trust, reciprocity, norms, and participation networks—are key to the communication and linkages between the government and the public. The collective strength formed by these elements enhances social cohesion and contributes to diversifying governance actors and sources of authority. A deep understanding of the role of modern social capital requires a clear explanation of the concept of governance capacity modernization. Based on this foundation, we explore the influence of social capital by analyzing both its positive and negative effects.

A Cognitive Examination of Governance Capacity Modernization

National governance, a concept in the field of public administration, has garnered widespread attention among scholars since the year 1992, when the World Bank released its annual development report *Governance and Development*. Since then, terms such as "governance" and "national governance" have been extensively studied and debated by scholars in public administration and political science, becoming focal points in academic research. China's central government has explicitly stated that the overarching goal of comprehensive deepening reforms is to refine and advance the system of socialism with Chinese characteristics while modernizing the national system and capacity for governance. The modernization of the capacity for governance has thus emerged as a new research direction in national governance. It represents an essential requirement for advancing socialist democracy in the new era, and signals a significant shift toward a more scientific approach to governance. The modernization of Chinese governance contains two key aspects: governance system modernization and governance capacity modernization, with particular emphasis on the former. However, a rational governance system alone is insufficient—it must be supported by governance capacity. This discussion will focus specifically on governance capacity.

The modernization of governance capacity is a multifaceted concept with various defining characteristics, which scholars have attempted to classify. In the article *A Review of Research on the Modernization of National Capacityfor Governance*, Liu Jianwei summarizes these classifications into several key theories: The "Three-Feature" theory emphasizes institutionalization, equitization, and orderliness of national governance. The "Four-Feature" theory highlights democratization, legalization, civilization, and scientization of national governance. The "Five-Feature" theory presents two interpretations: one focusing on institutionalization, democratization, legalization, efficiency, and coordination, and another emphasizing diverse governance subjects, interactive governance relationships, composite governance models, and scientific governance methods. The "Comprehensive-Feature" theory underscores the mutual support and balance between the state, market, and social mechanisms; the integration of rule of law and moral governance; and the mutual complementation and coordination between democracy and efficiency. Although these perspectives differ, most studies on governance capacity modernization converge on four fundamental dimensions: institutionalization, democratization, coordination, and efficiency. Some scholars further argue that efforts to modernize China's governance capacity should prioritize four key capabilities: consensus building, institutional development, scientific development, and reform and innovation. Ultimately, governance capacity modernization is reflected in the continuous improvement in institutional implementation.

National governance involves diverse governance actors, various governance tools, and a complex governance mechanism. To enhance the capacity for governance, it is essential to leverage the combined strengths of the government, market and society, utilize a diverse range of governance tools, and mobilize social resources to strengthen public participation and foster a stronger sense of political identity, which, in turn, facilitates the adjustment of social structures and functions, as well as the reconfiguration and regulation of relationships among different social actors. As the central pillar of national governance, government governance plays a crucial role in the national governance system. Transforming national governance first requires the transformation of government governance, that is, shifting from rule by individuals to the rule of law, from an all-encompassing government to a limited government, and from a regulatory-oriented model to a service-oriented model. Therefore, it can be understood that government governance capacity is an important representation of the capacity for national governance. The core features of government governance are inherited from national governance, with institutionalization as the fundamental guarantee and coordination as the basic means, forming a process in which multiple actors participate in governance. From this perspective, the modernization of governance capacity is rooted in government credit, aimed at achieving good governance, and focused on systematic reform in power allocation and operational mechanisms. It prioritizes institutionalization, democracy, coordination, and efficiency, manifesting principally as the framework of "governance structure + institutional arrangement + governance performance."

The Role and Positioning of Modern Social Capital

Social capital refers to the network of interactions and cooperation among social groups and individuals, built on trust and guided by social norms. Essentially, social capital is a form of public good that emerges from social interaction and is primarily manifested through relational networks. Its core elements include trust, social networks, and social norms. At present, social capital is undergoing a transition from its traditional form to a modern one. However, while traditional social capital remains relatively abundant, modern social capital is still in short supply. The modernization of governance capacity increasingly involves harnessing modern social capital, as it emphasizes individual capabilities, the realization of personal value, and the principles of autonomy, equality, mutual trust, and win–win cooperation among social members. Thus, it can be said that the development of modern social capital is conducive to enhancing government credit, improving the traditional governance framework, and fostering greater participation from diverse actors. The functions of modern social capital are manifested in the following aspects.

Improve social mobility. Higher social mobility is a necessary condition for sustaining long-term economic growth and is the only way to safeguard dynamic equality of opportunity, thereby motivating various governance actors to participate actively. From the perspective of trust relationships, the development of modern social capital mainly relies on organizational trust. The effectiveness of government governance is difficult to achieve without the support of organizational trust. Interaction and information exchange among members in modern society must take place within a trust mechanism embedded in abstract systems. Only when a generally shared sense of trust is established can the network of relationships between members of society become more complex, interactions and exchanges of social resources and information become more frequent, and the mobility among social classes be enhanced. Mancur Olson noted that when a society is captured by various interest groups and their interests become increasingly entrenched, development stagnates. Therefore, it is essential to strengthen interactions among social members to build mutual trust, including public trust in the government, so as to improve social mobility between social strata and avoid the formation of a stable social equilibrium characterized by a "refusal to cooperate."

Enhance governance responsiveness. Nowadays, the Internet is a crucial bridge for communication and interaction among people in society, and it also serves as a collection of social actors and their interrelationships. Social capital, carried through relationship networks, can offer multiple channels for the public to articulate their interests, promote positive interaction between the government and the public, and actively create an effective space for the pursuit of "good governance." For government governance, emphasis should be placed on fostering cooperation between the government, the public, and society at large, advocating for well-ordered interaction in pluralistic governance through the sharing of public authority. The broader and denser the relationship network, the more likely the public is to actively participate for the common good and to amplify information of interpersonal trustworthiness. Through public participation networks, the public can better understand shared needs and differing interests, effectively express their views on government decision-making, and thereby help improve the government's responsiveness, expand the foundation for democratic consultation, and lay a solid base of popular opinion for government governance.

Leverage actor diversity. The essence of governance lies in cooperation based on market principles, the public interest, and shared identity. Its management mechanisms do not primarily rely on government authority, but rather on the authority of cooperative networks. The salient feature of modern social capital is precisely the construction of such a network of cooperative relationships, enabling diverse social actors to manage public affairs through cooperation, consultation, and partnerships. The dimensions of power are pluralistic and reciprocal. Such multi-actor participation is one of the core elements of governance and also reflects the "devolution of government power" advocated in good governance. Thus, it can be seen that modern social capital plays a vital role in the modernization of governance capacity. Specifically, trust provides a foundation that encourages different participants to willingly and confidently express their positions; relationship networks offer smooth channels and pathways for the expression of views and demands; and social norms shaped by reciprocity reflect an overall order characterized by mutual trust and close cooperation among participants.

External Effect and Influence of Social Capital

The key issue in government governance is to transform government functions, innovate administrative approaches, and build a service-oriented government based on trust and credibility, thereby creating a favorable environment for diversified governance. Social capital theory helps draw attention to social conditions, economic contexts, and political traditions, with a focus on interpersonal relationships and the public spirit embedded in social structures—such as trust, norms, and participation networks. However, based on cultural traditions and specific historical contexts, social capital can also lead to a "refusal to cooperate." Informal relationships, such as traditional customs and unspoken rules, may negatively affect government governance and the allocation of social resources. Therefore, social capital is a double-edged sword—if it is harnessed properly, it can fully unleash institutional dividends; if misused, it may trap governance efforts in stagnation.

From the perspective of positive externalities, social capital creates fertile social ground for effective government governance, boosts economic prosperity, and supports the healthy functioning of democratic politics. It serves as an important foundation for the innovation of governance models and the enhancement of governance performance. This can be described as "positive social capital," which is typically associated with horizontal and open organizational structures, community culture, and civil culture, as well as autonomous civic associations. The result is the formation of a broadly shared sense of trust. Carles Boix identifies five micro-level mechanisms through which social capital promotes government governance: networks that encourage active civic engagement strengthen bureaucratic accountability and expand channels for interest articulation; stronger trust in others' compliance with government rules reduces enforcement costs; social capital fosters a civic virtue that seeks to cultivate a concern for public affairs; trust and cooperation among bureaucrats reduce the cost of supervision from superiors to subordinates, thereby improving bureaucratic efficiency; and social capital facilitates compromise among elites and helps bridge divides between different social groups.

From the perspective of negative externalities, as a form of informal institutional arrangement, social capital is an expedient substitute when formal institutions are deficient. While it can support the modernization of government governance, it may also hinder improvements in governance performance if not guided and regulated by formal institutions. China's traditional social norms and ethics are rooted in kinship or pseudo-kinship ties, with social capital primarily embedded in family-centered clan relationships and friendships. Under such conditions, the externalities of social capital can tighten the bonds within these small, family-centered groups, thereby exacerbating the closed nature of such group structures. In modern society, although various external ethical concepts have impacted traditional Chinese ethics, the small group relational model has persisted. However, the basis for maintaining these relationships has gradually shifted from "kinship" to "interest." Under the influence of utilitarianism, the once clearly defined rights-and-obligations structure within these small groups has become increasingly loose, giving rise to a pervasive "circle culture" that defies social morality but nonetheless infiltrates all areas of society. Corruption networks also emerge from this environment.

Benign Accumulation of Social Capital: A Key to Improving Government Governance

From the perspective of social capital theory, many negative social phenomena in China today are closely related to the officialdom-centric governance mechanism, which not only erodes the social capital of public life but also accumulates into negative social capital, amplifying its adverse effects over time. Once a vicious cycle forms among relationships, norms, and trust, social capital deteriorates and seriously undermines the healthy development of the political ecosystem.[1] Thus, how to regulate and guide social capital, and how to construct a political ecological mechanism for its benign accumulation, has become a crucial issue for modernizing the government's capacity for governance. This requires a nuanced understanding of the complexities of political ecosystems at various levels, further integration of social capital, and active cultivation of modern social capital to foster a healthy political environment. Efforts to accumulate and consolidate benign social capital should focus on three main aspects: reconstruction of social norms, reshaping of the relationship network, and rebuilding of trust-based relationships.

Reconstructing Social Norms: Rational Guidance of Informal Regulations

Generally speaking, social norms are categorized into formal and informal types. Formal norms refer to laws, regulations, and administrative rules that possess legal authority; informal social norms are the unwritten yet widely accepted standards of behavior in everyday life, such as moral codes, customs, and traditions. Formal and informal social norms are closely related. Typically, formal social norms embody elements of informal norms and have an actual mandatory binding force on citizens. Informal social norms, however, have a broader scope than formal norms. Although they do not have the coercive backing of the state apparatus, they exert significant and even decisive influence on people's ideas and behaviors through mechanisms such as public opinion pressure and social penetration. When

[1] Shi Hexing, New Challenges in China–Europe Public Governance and Administrative Reform, Beijing: National Academy of Governance Press, 2015.

formal and informal social norms align in purpose, informal norms can facilitate the implementation of formal norms. However, when they are in conflict, informal norms may hinder the effectiveness of formal norms.

A well-ordered public life relies on the consistency of formal and informal norms, as this consistency helps generate both rational and legitimate authority and fosters impersonal compliance with rules. However, negative forms of social capital—such as the officialdom-centric governance mechanism and personal authority—along with the informal norms they rely on, can distort relationships between rights and obligations, formal and informal norms, as well as legal principles and ethical values. This, in turn, undermines social trust and reciprocity. The root cause lies in the lack of a modern democratic and rule-of-law culture. Reconstructing social norms does not mean rejecting all informal practices such as traditions or kinship ties. Rather, it entails rationally guiding those aspects that contradict the spirit of the rule of law or hinder effective governance, while recognizing and incorporating factors into the rational and formal system.

Changing the personalized authority–submission relationship means breaking the traditional rules of dependent interpersonal interactions. Regardless of one's relational status in public life, all actors must adhere to the principles of the rule of law and public ethics, and the "circle culture" and "unspoken rules" must not be allowed to substitute for legal institutions. Without a stable institutional structure and predictable behavioral expectations, it is difficult to build a law-based society and government. Hence, the government must strengthen institutional development, adhere to law-based administration, and reduce the role of personal relationships in the allocation of public resources. In doing so, social capital can become a supplement to the legal system and a lubricant for the healthy functioning of society. Only by doing so can lay a solid institutional foundation for the benign accumulation of social capital, gradually transforming positive informal norms into formal regulations while working to reform outdated and counterproductive informal practices.

Reshaping Relationship Networks: Responding Effectively to Different Types of Social Networks

To achieve the benign accumulation of social capital, it is essential to reshape relationship networks and strengthen citizens' political engagement and awareness of participation. As the nodes of social networks, the various actors who participate in public life and collective action on their own are interconnected through a contractual spirit, forming a comprehensive structure of social interactions. These networks are characterized by equality, autonomy, and contract-based collaboration, and they typically facilitate cooperation in the public sphere and enable effective resource allocation. How to create public spaces that allow for equal participation and how to orderly promote the autonomous development of social organizations is the key to reshaping the network of relationships in the process of modernizing the capacity for governance. Open and fluid social networks help foster communication and cooperation across diverse social groups, laying the foundation for mutual trust and ultimately improving the effectiveness of social governance. In contrast, fragmented "small circles" within social networks can lead to negative outcomes. Therefore, it is crucial to clearly distinguish between strong-tie and weak-tie relationship networks and to rapidly establish a sound institutional framework and response mechanism for "co-governance by officials and citizens." This will enable broader, lawful, and orderly public participation in the management of public affairs.

It should be noted that social networks based on traditional ties such as kinship, regional region, or former workplace affiliations typically fall under the category of strong-tie networks. Individual social capital accumulated through these ties can play a positive role in promoting regional economic development and improving government governance. Empirical observations show that when senior local officials are transferred to new regions, they often leverage the social capital built in their previous posts to channel various resources toward their new posts, particularly in areas such as industrial investment, corporate financing, and talent recruitment. This constitutes an inherent advantage unattainable through formal institutional arrangements. As long as such exchanges avoid illegal transfer of interests, favoritism, or other corrupt practices, the personal social capital of officials can be effectively and productively utilized. However, strong-tie networks—while beneficial in terms of internal coordination and trust—also tend to be closed and segmented, and can easily become breeding grounds for unspoken rules and nepotism. Furthermore, these networks often hinder the participation of diverse actors due to rigid group norms and internal contracts, with a few key nodes dominating the operation of these networks.

By contrast, weak-tie networks create links among groups and organizations, where the frequency and intimacy of interactions between different actors are lower. Social networks are essentially weak-tie networks, which embody rational social exchange. In fact, most everyday interactions occur within weak-tie networks. On the one hand, it is important to build open and inclusive social networks centered on weak ties, responding to the interests and demands of various social groups and organizations, and expanding the network's scope. On the other hand, it is equally necessary to guard against the corrupt tendencies that can arise within strong-tie networks. Strong ties must not be allowed to override legal norms in pursuit of private gains for insiders. Instead, members of strong-tie networks should be guided toward engaging in investment and cooperation through legal and transparent means.

Building Trust: Continuous Improvement of the Social Credit System

Trust depends on the reliability of the social environment, the capacity of social structures to facilitate information flow, and the presence of norms tied to incentives and sanctions. Elements of social capital, including a certain degree of trust, are indispensable for local governance, which can foster rational and positive public participation, thereby nurturing engaged actors in the governance process. In the context of public affairs, trust and cooperation among citizens are essential, directly affecting the effectiveness of government governance. Only by strengthening communication and mutual trust with the public can government officials truly understand the needs and expectations of the people. In this regard, trust serves as both the core and foundation of social capital, and the construction of a social credit system should begin with the government. However, the widespread occurrence of government dishonesty poses the greatest challenge to building a robust credit system. On the one hand, social credit development relies heavily on the power of the government. On the other hand, in many cases, the government itself is the primary underminer of public trust. While a single instance of government untrustworthiness may not completely collapse the social credit system, it can still inflict serious damage on the system.

Rebuilding trust must go beyond slogans—it requires concrete institutional mechanisms for action. Only by properly guiding informal norms and effectively responding to the needs of different types of social networks can the government earn public trust through social interactions. First and foremost, government functions must be swiftly redefined, clarifying power lists, responsibility lists, and negative lists, increasing transparency in government affairs, and ensuring that administrative power operates within the framework of the rule of law. Second, based on information disclosure, the enthusiasm of the public to participate in public deliberation and policy-making should be actively encouraged. A well-functioning response mechanism should be established through broad-based social networks, enabling citizens to play a substantial role in governance. Finally, the government must uphold the principles of public administration, fully respect the legal rights and interests of citizens, and continuously improve the sense of responsibility and public service competence of administrative personnel—ultimately working to maximize the public benefit in the exercise of public authority.

In conclusion, a credit government is the basic form of government development in modern society and the baseline of administrative values. Only a government that consistently places the interests of the people first and upholds democracy, the rule of law, efficiency, and integrity can be trusted by the public, remaining vibrant, incorruptible, and pragmatic in its governance.

CHAPTER 5

Common Prosperity and Chinese Modernization

Cai Fang, Liu Shangxi, and Zhu Keli

Three Pathways to Achieving Common Prosperity

Cai Fang

Achieving common prosperity for all is a basic requirement of Chinese-style socialist modernization. There are many paths toward common prosperity, but in light of the current challenges China faces, the process can be accelerated through the following three approaches.

C. Fang (✉)
China Top Think Tanks at the Chinese Academy of Social Sciences,
Beijing, China

L. Shangxi
Chinese Academy of Fiscal Sciences, Beijing, China

Z. Keli
China Institute of New Economy, Beijing, China

C. Fang et al., *Modernization in a Chinese Style*,
https://doi.org/10.1007/978-981-95-6919-9_5

Making the Pie Bigger and Ensuring a Fair Share for All

To make the pie bigger and ensure everyone gets a fair share, the following three points must be addressed.

First of all, maintain economic growth within a reasonable range.

The 5th Plenary Session of the 19th CPC Central Committee set the long-range objectives of basically realizing socialist modernization by 2035, including raising gross domestic product (GDP) per capita to the level of moderately developed countries. To achieve this goal, development is the key and foundation for solving all problems.

According to projections of China's potential growth capacity, the country must maintain an average annual growth rate of 14.7–14.9% over the next 15 years in order to accomplish the above-mentioned goal. Based on current development trends and the potential of production factors (capital and human capital) and productivity growth, China's GDP per capita is expected to reach $13,000–$14,000 by the end of the 14th Five-Year Plan, allowing it to enter the ranks of high-income countries. By 2035, GDP per capita will approach $23,000, drawing very close to yet falling just short of the level of moderately developed countries.

If necessary, reforms are implemented to raise the potential growth rate, China's GDP per capita could reach $14,000 by 2025 and nearly $23,000 by 2035—equivalent to Portugal's current level. This would allow China to join the ranks of moderately developed countries. This is the goal China must achieve and the foundation for advancing toward common prosperity.

Second, ensure that income growth and economic growth progress in step.

Historically, the growth of GDP and income growth often diverged. However, since the 18th CPC National Congress, China has seen a strong synchronization between GDP growth and the growth of disposable personal income. This means that increases in GDP per capita have translated into rising incomes for residents, enabling them to share in the fruits of development.

Looking ahead, efforts shall be made to further adjust the national income structure to increase residents' income and labor remuneration. Meanwhile, the income distribution system must be reformed to narrow income gaps.

Third, efforts must be made to strengthen both primary distribution and secondary distribution.

Since the 18th CPC National Congress, income inequality—as measured by the Gini coefficient—has declined, but stabilized again after a few years. The Gini coefficient reflects the distribution of wealth in a country or region: the lower the number, the more equitable distribution among members of society, and vice versa. A Gini coefficient of 0.4 is generally considered the warning threshold for income disparity.

At present, China's Gini coefficient hovers around 0.46, indicating that the country's income distribution remains imbalanced. In fact, primary distribution alone has its limitations and is unlikely to reduce the Gini coefficient below 0.4. From the experience of the Organisation for Economic Co-operation and Development (OECD) countries, the Gini coefficient after primary distribution is generally above 0.4, and in some cases even exceeds 0.5. The reason their final distribution Gini coefficient falls below 0.4—and in some cases even below 0.3—is due to secondary distribution achieved through taxation and transfer payments.

Therefore, in order to improve the structure of income distribution to a reasonable level, secondary distribution is essential. As China enters a new stage of socialist modernization, secondary distribution must play an increasingly important role. The experience of many developed countries shows that while economic growth, technological advances, and globalization can make the pie bigger, they do not naturally lead to a fair division of that pie. Hence, secondary distribution is a necessary measure.

Accelerating and Expanding Social Mobility

The 19th CPC National Congress made it clear that China must promote social mobility. Historically, mobility has mainly been horizontal, such as migrant workers moving from agricultural work to non-agricultural sectors, and from living in rural areas to small towns, medium-sized cities, large cities, and coastal areas. However, within this horizontal mobility, there is also vertical mobility, such as improvements in personal income, identity, social status, and job positions. This has been made possible by two factors: first, the rapid educational expansion, particularly through universal 9-year compulsory education and higher education enrollment growth, allowing more people to enter the education system; and second, the rapid economic growth, which has greatly increased the size of the "pie.".

Currently, China has entered a period of medium-to-high growth or moderate growth, and labor mobility has significantly slowed. At this stage, more attention should be given to upward mobility. Without concrete measures, social mobility can easily become a zero-sum game, much like people trying to squeeze onto a crowded bus—when one gets on, another must get off. This social phenomenon is likely to occur and can lead to social conflicts. The central government has identified accelerating social mobility as the key to expanding the middle-income group.

If residents' income is divided into five groups, from a macro perspective, each group's income must rise. If this cannot be ensured, China will not be able to expand the middle-income group. From a micro perspective, the income of each family should continue to increase. This was a key feature in the past, but in the future, it may become a zero-sum game, where some families' income growth may slow down relative to others. From an intermediate perspective, many families can transition from low-income or lower-income groups to higher income groups. These groups are crucial for social mobility and for expanding the middle-income group.

Therefore, we propose a "national income multiplication plan" to expand the size of the middle-income group, which mainly involves the following three groups.

Target Group 1: Low-Income Rural Population in the Post-Poverty-Alleviation Era

Since the 18th CPC National Congress, nearly 100 million rural residents have been lifted out of absolute poverty. However, they still belong to the low-income group. The relative poverty standard in OECD countries is 50% of the median income of the population. In 2019, the median income of China's rural residents was RMB 14,389, meaning the poverty threshold under this standard would be RMB 7195. This figure rose slightly in 2020.

Assuming that 30% of rural households meet this standard, the population involved would reach at least 153 million—a significant number. If this group can be nurtured into the middle-income group, it would represent another remarkable achievement in the pursuit of common prosperity.

Target Group 2: Urbanizing Migrant Workers

In 2020, the average monthly wage of migrant workers was RMB 4549—equivalent to the lower threshold of the middle-income group. Although most migrant workers can technically be classified into the middle-income range, they still face an "invisible wall"—inadequate social security and limited access to basic public services. Therefore, only by becoming urban residents can migrant workers be truly considered part of the middle-income group; otherwise, their status remains unstable. For instance, in 2020, due to the COVID-19 pandemic, the number of migrant workers working away from home and living in urban areas decreased by 3%.

In 2020, China had 285.6 million migrant workers, including 169.59 million working outside their hometowns. If these workers can be transformed into members of the middle-income group, it would be of enormous significance—enough to realize the middle-income group's expansion under the multiplication plan.

Target Group 3: Enabling the Elderly to Live a Middle-Income Life
China's 7th National Population Census shows that the elderly population and the degree of population aging are more serious than previously expected. Currently, the number of people aged 65 years and over has reached 190 million, while those aged 60 years and above have reached 260 million. This demographic represents a substantial reserve for the middle-income group. Enabling the elderly to achieve a middle-income standard of living is a basic requirement for ensuring adequate elderly care. Meanwhile, it is an essential requirement of common prosperity and a prerequisite for expanding the middle-income group and maintaining sufficient consumer demand to support sustained economic growth in China.

Equal Access to Nationwide Social Welfare

Michael E. Porter, in *The Competitive Advantage of Nations*, explains that economic growth progresses through four stages: the first stage is factor-driven growth, relying on resources and labor; the second is investment-driven growth, involving large-scale capital inputs; the third is innovation-driven growth, which depends on advances in technology and productivity; and the fourth is wealth-driven growth. Porter argued that economic growth is upward during the first three stages, but in the wealth-driven stage, economic growth tends to slow down and may even stagnate unexpectedly.

China's economic development has already passed through the factor- and investment-driven stages. What is needed now is to closely integrate innovation-driven and wealth-driven growth.

For a long time, particularly since 2012, China's economic growth rate has been constrained by supply-side factors and its potential growth capacity. However, with the population approaching zero growth, demand-side constraints are becoming increasingly evident. This means that China is now facing dual constraints. According to Porter's framework, the country must integrate the approaches of both the innovation-driven and wealth-driven stages, and work to simultaneously boost supply and demand. It is not only necessary to maintain a reasonable growth rate but also to learn how to leverage accumulated wealth to sustain long-term development.

At this development stage, modernization in China cannot avoid the task of building a welfare system with Chinese characteristics. If GDP per capita reaches between $10,000 and $25,000, and government expenditure on social welfare rises from 26 to 36%, this 10-percentage-point increase would be enough to lay the foundation for a basic welfare system.

From now until 2035, China will be in the third and fourth stages of development. It is therefore essential to establish a robust welfare system. Moreover, building a social security system ensures that people's basic needs are met and provides a policy safety net that supports creative destruction. Without macro-level support, the focus would remain on protecting jobs, production capacity, businesses, and industries at the micro level—resulting in a failure to eliminate outdated and inefficient enterprises.

A welfare system is an inevitable path a country must take once its comprehensive national strength reaches a certain level. With distinctive Chinese characteristics, our approach manifests as seven "guarantees" covering the entire life cycle: children have access to early childhood care, youth receive compulsory education, workers obtain fair employment, the ill have access to medical services, the elderly receive elderly care, families secure decent housing, and vulnerable groups gain social assistance.

Therefore, at this stage, China must focus not only on the supply side to maintain potential growth capacity but also on the demand side through the lens of common prosperity, in order to raise consumption capacity and thereby boost the potential growth rate.

Promoting Common Prosperity Through Holistic Integration into Human Modernization

Liu Shangxi

Achieving common prosperity is an essential requirement of China's socialist system. At a Ceremony Marking the Centenary of the CPC, General Secretary Xi Jinping delivered an important speech, stressing that on the journey ahead, China will make more notable and substantive progress toward achieving well-rounded human development and common prosperity for all. The Report to the 20th CPC National Congress placed even greater importance on achieving common prosperity for all, identifying it as one of the five defining features and essential requirements of Chinese modernization.

Sharing the fruits of development and promoting common prosperity is not only an economic issue but also a political one. Poverty is not socialism, nor is socio- economic polarization. This means that building socialism must begin with unleashing and developing productive forces to achieve prosperity, while at the same time avoiding polarization in the process. It is an integral part of upholding and developing socialism with Chinese characteristics. As a major developing country, China's GDP per capita has only just surpassed $10,000, and it cannot yet be considered a wealthy nation by global standards. Meanwhile, China ranks relatively high in terms of the Gini coefficient, indicating a significant income gap. Preventing the further widening of the wealth gap is a pressing and long-term challenge. Promoting common prosperity does not mean egalitarianism or measuring progress by equal wealth distribution. Rather, it means advancing human modernization, with a focus on narrowing capability gaps among different social groups. Only by centering the efforts on people can China unlock the pathway to common prosperity.

Promoting Common Prosperity and People-Centered Modernization

Common prosperity is a longstanding challenge in the development of human civilization. To date, no country has offered a perfect solution to this issue.

From an economic perspective, common prosperity refers to the production and distribution of material wealth, including property and income. From the perspective of social development, however, its essence lies in human development. If the focus remains solely on the production and distribution of material wealth without addressing the development of people—of all people—then common prosperity becomes merely a goal of distribution policy, with only short-term significance. Historical experience from developed countries shows that relying solely on adjustments in distribution policy cannot reverse the fundamental trend of widening wealth gaps.

One should not assume that the mere optimization of material production and distribution in a given period will spontaneously lead to human development or the development of all people. This is a form of deterministic or linear thinking. Material living conditions only provide the foundation for human development; they are not equivalent to it. Human development is reflected in people's subjectivity, creativity, and civility. Improvements in material and cultural living standards do not automatically lead to a rise in personal quality and capability.

People are at the core of modernization. The intrinsic value pursuit of socialism is to provide equal opportunities for individuals to achieve personal development. Equality in material living conditions is merely a means or a path to this end. Therefore, the essence of common prosperity lies in the common development of all people—not in the equal distribution of material wealth. History has shown that equal distribution of wealth does not lead to the common development of all and may even result in stagnation. The outcomes of past "social experiments" have made this clear, and they are closely linked to prevailing social and historical conditions.

In times of material scarcity, the pursuit of production growth and the satisfaction of basic survival needs—such as adequate food and clothing—could be regarded as promoting human development. However, as per capita income rises, the production and distribution of material wealth increasingly diverge from the needs of human development. In other words, material development often outpaces human development, let alone the all-round development of all humanity. In the process of achieving Chinese modernization, the greatest systemic risk lies in the alienation of people amid material development—that is, people becoming dominated by material wealth, rather than being its masters.

Promoting common prosperity and people-centered modernization are two sides of the same coin. This is a long-term vision and objective. It cannot be assessed solely by relying on the Gini coefficient as an indicator of whether substantial progress has been made toward common prosperity.

Integration of Equity and Efficiency Under the People-Centered Logic

Throughout world history, the basic logic for promoting common prosperity has long been trapped in the conflict between equity and efficiency. In times of polarization, the equalization of wealth and poverty was once the fundamental approach to achieving common prosperity. From peasant uprisings to labor movements, the focus has always been on distribution. The distribution of production outcomes and conditions reflected the depth, breadth, and intensity of social revolution. These have all been part of humanity's exploration in the pursuit of common prosperity throughout the course of civilization.

The path of socialism with Chinese characteristics is a path to modernization guided by Marxism and rooted in China's actual national conditions. China must shift toward a people-oriented logic, which aligns closely with the CPC's people-first development philosophy and fits well with the current strategic transition toward high-quality development and innovation-driven growth. The essence of people- oriented logic lies in highlighting human subjectivity, creativity, and civility. It aims to foster a new, upward-spiraling logic of social development (human development—material development—human development) to replace the material-centered development model (material development—human development—material development), thereby transforming human development from a means and factor into both the starting point and the ultimate goal.

Ensuring Basic Capabilities for All

Shifting toward a people-oriented logic of social development means embedding economic issues within the broader context of society. The economy is the material foundation of society, but it is only one part and is subject to the overall condition of society.

The development of the individual—and the all-round development of all people—can only be fully understood within the context of society as a whole. Viewed purely through the lens of economics, only part of the picture is visible. From the perspective of society as a whole, the production and distribution of material wealth merely provide a necessary condition for human development and the all-round development of all people—but not a sufficient one.

The sufficient condition for common prosperity is that society, through collective efforts, ensures that all people have access to basic capabilities. Income cannot substitute for capability. A reduction in income disparities does not automatically lead to a narrowing of capability gaps. While the availability of consumption is related to income, its accessibility is not necessarily tied to income.

Consumption is the process through which people are produced and reproduced; it is the process of human development, human capital accumulation, and capability enhancement. It is also the process that provides the purposes and creates the conditions for economic activities. Consumption includes both private and public forms, which should work together to meet everyone's basic consumption needs— ensuring access to essential nutrition, education, healthcare, and housing—so that each person can attain basic capabilities.

The universal enhancement of people's basic capabilities lays the foundation for equality in starting points and opportunities, while also creating a broad social foundation for innovation and entrepreneurship. This, in turn, fuels sustainable development, inherently harmonizing efficiency with equity. To promote common prosperity and escape the longstanding dilemma between efficiency and equity, as well as between "making the pie" and "dividing the pie." Only by shifting focus from material outcomes to human development, and from asset-income metrics to consumption-based welfare benchmarks, can we authentically transition from a material-centered to a people-centered logic.

Key Challenges in Advancing Common Prosperity

Based on China's current reality, human development is constrained not only by the economy—namely, issues pertaining to property and income—but also by the segmented structure of social governance.

Although China has entered a stage of comprehensively deepening reform, the reform progress remains uneven. This fundamentally constrains China's further development and the realization of common prosperity, as reflected in the following three forms of "duality."

The first is ownership duality. The dual structure of ownership by the whole people and collective ownership is a legacy of history. As the economic foundation, it fundamentally restricts the deepening of reforms in both the economic and social systems. Although public expenditure and investment are no longer confined to this dual ownership structure, the land and housing markets remain dualistic. People maintain dual social identity—farmers not only hold a rural household registration (*hukou*) but also possess membership in collective economic organizations. The urban–rural governance system is rooted in this dual ownership system. Reforms targeting the property rights systems, including rural land, homesteads, farmer housing, and forests, are all attempts to break through the constraints imposed by ownership duality.

The second is economic duality. This refers to the relationship between the backward, traditional agricultural sector and the modern, advanced industrial sector. A dual economic structure is common among developing countries and can gradually be resolved through marketization and industrialization. However, in China, this dual economic structure is based not only on the level of productive forces but also on the structure of production relations.

The third is social duality. This refers to the dual structure of social identity and basic rights that stems from ownership duality. In the process of marketization, this dual social structure has become a source of inequality in starting points and opportunities. It has also contributed to disparities in social distribution among different groups, which, in turn, has evolved into a root cause of group-based capability gaps. This structure further reinforces the intergenerational transmission of family poverty.

These three forms of "duality" fundamentally constrain China's pursuit of the goal of common prosperity.

Promote Common Prosperity Through Reform

Advancing common prosperity is both a goal of upholding and developing the socialist system with Chinese characteristics and a key indicator of advancing along the Chinese path. However, this endeavor allows for neither undue haste nor complacency. We must not be hasty, because common prosperity depends first on the process of development—both material development and human development—which cannot be achieved overnight. We must not wait, because realizing the interplay between domestic and international economic flows, expanding domestic demand, constructing a new pattern of development, and achieving innovation-driven growth all hinge on incremental progress toward common prosperity.

Narrowing group-based disparities in consumption is currently the top priority in reform. How to bring private and public consumption into synergy, how to simultaneously expand short-term domestic demand and enhance human capabilities, and how to reshape social expectations—these are all critically important. In particular, it is essential to cultivate favorable expectations regarding distribution outcomes related to capabilities, innovation, entrepreneurship, and employment. Expectations of secondary distribution should be downplayed, while expectations of primary distribution—where everyone participates and contributes—should be strengthened.

To advance reforms based on the goal of equal human development, it is necessary to focus on addressing the above three forms of "duality" and improve top-level design by integrating reforms in the economic, social, and other spheres. Only by generating synergies can the overall design process identify priorities and distinguish between what is urgent and what is less so. Fragmented, compartmentalized reforms tend to operate in isolation, making it difficult to achieve coordinated reform and systemic integration.

Constructing the Common Prosperity Demonstration Zones Through a "One Body, Two Wings" Framework

Zhu Keli

Deng Xiaoping once said, "Allow some regions and some people to get rich first, and guide them in bringing along others toward common prosperity."[1] As a modern interpretation of the traditional ideal of *Datong* (Great Harmony), common prosperity is neither a political slogan nor a social utopia. It represents the original aspiration and fundamental mission of China's reform and opening up. As China's total economic output has surpassed RMB 100 trillion and its GDP per capita exceeds $10,000—with eastern regions expected to be the first to achieve modernization—exploring the pathways to common prosperity has become an inevitable trend. Given the reality of unbalanced and inadequate development, it is necessary to designate some regions to take the lead and serve as examples in this pursuit.[2] As a long-term strategy following the eradication of abso-

[1] Deng Xiaoping. There is no Fundamental Contradiction Between Socialism and a Market Economy (October 23, 1985) [M]// Deng Xiaoping. Selected Works of Deng Xiaoping: Volume 3. Beijing: People's Publishing House, 1993.

[2] Opinions of the Central Committee of the CPC and the State Council on Supporting Zhejiang Province in Building a High-quality Development and Common Prosperity Demonstration Zone (Chin. ed.) [OL], [2021-06-10]. http://www.gov.cn/zhengce/2021-06/10/content_5616833.htm.

lute poverty, realizing common prosperity will certainly require more time and effort. So, where should the efforts be focused on in building such demonstration zones?

Why Zhejiang?

From central authorities to local communities, it is widely acknowledged that in recent years, the development of each region has its own characteristics and highlights. Identifying the region best positioned to blaze a trail toward common prosperity requires careful consideration. In terms of total economic output, Guangdong ranks first because, with a GDP exceeding RMB 11 trillion in 2020, earning it the nickname "Yue Boss." Jiangsu follows closely behind, with its GDP also surpassing RMB 10 trillion and is known as "Mighty Su." Shandong is third with more than RMB 7.3 trillion, while Zhejiang ranks fourth at nearly RMB 6.5 trillion. In terms of GDP per capita, the top five are Beijing, Shanghai, Jiangsu, Fujian, and Zhejiang—with Zhejiang coming last on the list. Regarding per capita disposable income, Shanghai ranked first in 2020 at RMB 72,000, followed by Beijing at RMB 69,000, and Zhejiang at RMB 52,000, placing third.

Admittedly, Zhejiang may not be the "single-item champion" in any of these dimensions. However, this does not prevent it from being an "all-around champion" in exploring the path to common prosperity. The key criterion for such an endeavor is the degree of balanced development. Different comparative perspectives can yield different conclusions. For example, there are significant economic disparities among cities within the same province. In Jiangsu, the GDP of Suzhou (the highest) is 6.2 times that of Suqian (the lowest). The ratio is 11.2 between Hangzhou and Zhoushan in Zhejiang, and a striking 29 between Shenzhen and Yunfu in Guangdong. From this perspective, Jiangsu exhibits a relatively higher degree of balanced development.

However, city-level economic comparisons alone are insufficient. It is also crucial to examine residents' income levels and overall affluence. Take per capita disposable income, for example, Zhejiang province ranks first among all provinces (excluding centrally administered municipalities), for both urban and rural areas. Moreover, the urban–rural income ratio in Zhejiang is below 2, making it one of the lowest in the country. In addition, Zhejiang merchants are active across the country, with many accumulating substantial wealth that may not be captured in local statistics—a true case of "wealth being widely distributed among the people." In short, Zhejiang stands out as a province with one of the smallest urban–rural income gaps, the narrowest regional development disparities, and one of the highest overall levels of economic development in the country. Its strength and confidence in building a demonstration zone for common prosperity may appear debatable at first glance, but are, in fact, beyond question.

To support the construction of a high-quality demonstration zone for common prosperity, does Zhejiang have the necessary development experience? Are there phased and quantifiable targets in place? Based on its development trajectory, Zhejiang—a region historically defined by 70% mountains, 10% water, and 20% farmland—has achieved decades of rapid progress while consistently narrowing wealth disparities, urban–rural gaps, and regional imbalances. Balanced and integrated urban–rural development and regional coordination have long been its formula for success. Looking ahead, the pursuit of high-quality common prosperity will still rely on further balanced development. As for phased quantifiable indicators to evaluate a region's progress toward common prosperity, the following are critical: GDP per capita, per capita disposable income, the maximum-to-minimum ratio of per capita GDP and disposable income, the urban and rural income ratio, and the proportion of households reaching targeted annual disposable income thresholds.

To fully carry out the *Implementation Plan for the High-quality Development and Construction ofthe Common Prosperity Demonstration Zone in Zhejiang (2021–2025)*, Zhejiang aims to lay a solid material foundation for common prosperity. By 2025, the province seeks to reach a GDP per capita of RMB 130,000 and a per capita disposable income of RMB 75,000. Although this level of GDP per capita would still lag behind Beijing and Shanghai, it would meet the international standard for moderately developed economies, marking a significant step toward overcoming the "middle-income trap." Moreover, Zhejiang has set goals to reduce its maximum-to-minimum regional ratios for GDP per capita, per capita disposable income, and urban–rural income to be within 2.1, 1.55, and 1.9, respectively. These three targets align with Zhejiang's key focus areas for building the demonstration zone: narrowing regional, urban–rural, and income disparities. For instance, the urban–rural income ratio in Zhejiang was 1.96 in 2020—well below the national level of 2.56. Striving to bring it below 1.9 demonstrates a bold and ambitious approach. In addition, Zhejiang plans to expand its middle-income population. By 2025, the proportion of households with an annual disposable income between RMB 100,000 and 500,000 is expected to reach 80%, while those earning between RMB 200,000 and 600,000 are expected to reach 45%. These two targets reflect Zhejiang's efforts to implement an action plan for expanding the middle-income group and to establish an "olive-shaped" social structure in which the middle-income group is the majority.

According to World Bank standards, middle-income households earn between RMB 25,000 and 250,000 annually—a tenfold range. Economist Liu Shijin offers a more targeted definition: "a three-person household with an annual income between RMB 100,000 and 500,000." In typical olive-shaped societies, the middle-income group usually comprises over 60% of the population. Zhejiang's 2025 targets clearly exceed these thresholds. These indicators emphasize balanced development and directly reflect the principles of "coordination" and "sharing" among China's five new visions of development. Fully promoting coordinated development and accelerating inclusive growth are essential. Reaching these goals depends on reform—and, above all, on people. How to inspire greater motivation to pursue common prosperity? How to remove the barriers to achieving it? The answer lies in implementing and deepening reforms centered on sharing.

Promoting Common Prosperity Through High-Quality Development

Returning from vision to reality—whether in Zhejiang or across the country—differences in people's perceptions and understandings of common prosperity will persist, despite a growing social consensus on this vital issue of our time. For example, some may still express doubt or confusion about whether the current conditions are favorable for advancing the common prosperity agenda.

At a press conference held by the CPC Central Committee following the close of the 6th Plenary Session of the 19th CPC Central Committee, a journalist posed a representative question: "China has officially placed common prosperity on the agenda, but given the current slowdown in economic growth, will this pose a challenge to achieving common prosperity? How can China realize common prosperity amid mounting economic pressure?" In response, Han Wenxiu, Deputy Director in charge of routine work of the Office of the Central Financial and Economic Affairs Commission, provided a clear and authoritative answer.[3]

Han opened his remarks with a resolute statement: "Promote common prosperity through high-quality development." He needs to strike a balance between development and distribution, asserting "To promote common prosperity, solving the problem of development comes first. While distribution matters, China cannot rely solely on distribution to achieve common prosperity." He noted that although China's GDP per capita has surpassed $10,000, it remains below the threshold for high-income countries. Even if the country's total income were evenly distributed, it would still fall short of true common prosperity. Therefore, Han underscored that "There is no shortcut to common prosperity—it is not magic. It can only be achieved through the hard work and perseverance of over 1.4 billion Chinese people." He then outlined three key pathways to promoting common prosperity: achieving high-quality development, improving the income distribution system, and encouraging enterprises to fulfill their social responsibilities.

First, advancing common prosperity requires high-quality development. Han emphasized that China remains the world's largest developing country and must continue to rely on development to resolve its problems. In the new era, development must be guided by the new development philosophy in a complete, accurate, and comprehensive manner to ensure high-quality development. It is essential to enhance the balance, coordination, and inclusiveness of development, continuously narrow gaps between urban and rural areas and among regions, and lay a solid foundation for common prosperity at the source. A people-centered development approach must be upheld to ensure equal opportunities, rules, and rights for all to participate in development—enabling the people to jointly create wealth and share in the fruits of growth. Fundamentally, the process of high-quality development is also one of addressing the principal contradiction of unbalanced and inadequate development, one of increasing the proportion of the middle-income group to optimize income distribution, as well as one of advancing all-round human development and moving toward common prosperity. Han particularly noted that since 2020, China has taken the lead in economic recovery amid the COVID-19

[3] Han Wenxiu: Common Prosperity Admits no Shortcuts—It Must Be Achieved Through Hard Work and Perseverance (Chin. ed.) [OL].[2021-11-12]. http://www.scio.gov.cn/xwfbh/xwbfbh/wqfbh/44687/47390/zy47394/documen t/1716243/1716243.htm

pandemic, achieved its poverty eradication goals as scheduled, and built a moderately prosperous society in all respects—demonstrating the strong resilience of the Chinese economy. "Economic fluctuations are short-term, while common prosperity is a long-term objective. With a sound economic foundation, immense domestic demand potential, and vast development space, China is fully capable of achieving sustained and healthy economic growth and building a solid and material foundation for advancing common prosperity." This directly addressed the first part of the journalist's question regarding economic growth.

Second, advancing common prosperity requires the establishment of an income distribution system that is both efficient and equitable. Han pointed out that primary distribution plays a fundamental role in shaping the overall distribution structure. China must uphold the principle of distribution according to work as the mainstay while allowing multiple forms of distribution to coexist. It should encourage and support people in becoming prosperous through honest work, innovation, and entrepreneurship. Primary distribution must balance efficiency and fairness by regulating the distribution order and keeping income disparities after primary distribution within a reasonable range. Secondary distribution must enhance its role in narrowing income gaps through reforms such as improving the tax system, increasing the share of direct taxation, and enhancing tax administration to better fulfill income-adjustment functions. Meanwhile, the social security system and transfer payment systems must be improved, with greater support directed toward low-income groups and underdeveloped regions to ensure a robust safety net. The goal is to shrink the two ends and expand the middle of the olive-shaped income distribution structure. Secondary distribution must also balance efficiency and fairness, both promoting fairness and safeguarding productivity to avoid lopsided outcomes. All in all, a coordinated and complementary institutional framework must be established that integrates primary, secondary, and tertiary distribution so as to ensure that both divide the economic pie fairly and continue enlarging it.

Third, advancing common prosperity requires enterprises to "manage their own affairs well." In Han's view, entrepreneurs have many ways to contribute to common prosperity. At a basic level, this means operating lawfully and with integrity, paying taxes in accordance with the law, fulfilling their social responsibilities, treating employees and customers fairly, and safeguarding the rights and interests of workers and consumers. Running a successful business and creating social wealth are both responsibilities and effective means through which enterprises can support the common prosperity agenda. Meanwhile, the country encourages and supports businesses and entrepreneurs—particularly those with the will and capacity—to actively participate in public welfare and charitable initiatives. These efforts can serve as a form of tertiary distribution. Han expressed optimism that as more businesses grow stronger and more individuals become prosperous, along with the refinement of incentive mechanisms, China's charitable sector will experience robust development. However, he also cautioned that charitable giving must remain voluntary. Practices such as "robbing the rich to aid the poor" or coercing donations—whether through pressure or policy—distort the original intention of common prosperity and will ultimately prove counterproductive. Following the press conference, many experts commented that "Han's response hit the nail on the head." It addressed widespread public concerns and helped dispel misunderstandings about the concept of common prosperity.[4]

Common Prosperity: Understanding Its Meaning, Drivers, and Strategies

This is not the first time Chinese authorities have addressed public concerns surrounding the issue of common prosperity. At a press conference organized by the Publicity Department of the CPC Central Committee, a widely discussed exchange took place. A journalist raised the following question: "China has achieved a moderately prosperous society in all respects and is now advancing toward the Second Centenary Goal of building China into a great modern socialist country. In this context, what challenges lie ahead in narrowing the wealth gap and achieving common prosperity, and how will they be addressed?" In response, Han unequivocally emphasized that common prosperity must be realized through the joint efforts of all members of society—it is not about "robbing the rich to

[4] Feng Qiaobin. Advancing Common Prosperity Requires Balancing the Relationship between Development and Distribution (Chin. ed.) [OL], [2021-11-13]. https://www.bjnews.com.cn/detail/163679211014220.html.

help the poor." His answer addressed three core dimensions: what common prosperity is, what drives it, and how it can be achieved.[5]

First, what is common prosperity? Han began by noting that China has already built a moderately prosperous society in all respects. Building on this foundation, the current focus must be on both enlarging the economic pie and ensuring it is distributed more fairly. China should vigorously pursue high-quality development to increase incomes across both urban and rural areas, narrow income disparities, and firmly prevent polarization. Common prosperity, Han explained, is prosperity for all the people, not just limited to a small group. It encompasses enrichment in both material and spiritual life, not merely an increase in material wealth at the expense of cultural or moral well-being. He also clarified that common prosperity does not mean absolute equality or uniform affluence for everyone—it acknowledges that certain gaps will remain (Table 5.1).

Second, what drives common prosperity? Han underlined that the fundamental pathway to achieving common prosperity lies in collective effort. People should be encouraged to attain prosperity through hard work and innovation. China supports those who achieve wealth through diligence, entrepreneurship, and legitimate business activities. While allowing some to prosper first, greater emphasis is placed on ensuring they help others follow suit. China does not believe in "robbing the rich to aid the poor." Instead, it is essential to safeguard and improve people's well-being through development, fostering more inclusive and equitable conditions for people to improve their education and enhance their capacities for self-development. Efforts will be made to ensure clear and open channels for upward mobility, granting more people the opportunity to become better-off. Solid progress is needed in providing equal access to basic public services. Efforts should be made to operate within realistic means, avoiding welfare dependency that discourages initiative—there must be no room for idleness, reliance on handouts, or passive expectation of aid. It is crucial to establish basic institutional arrangements enabling the coordination and complementarity among primary, secondary, and tertiary distribution. Greater efforts will be made to adjust income distribution through taxation, social security, and transfer payments. These measures aim to expand

[5] Live Transcript of the Press Conference on the Document: *The CPC: Its Mission and Contributions* (Chin. ed.) [OL], [2021-08-26], http://www.xinhuanet.com/politics/ddwxzb/wzsl.htm.

Table 5.1 What common prosperity is and is not[a]

Common prosperity is	*Common prosperity is not*
The underlying template and upgrade of Chinese modernization	A replication of Western high-welfare policies
Prosperity based on high-quality development	"Wearing new shoes but walking the old road"
A phased process toward shared prosperity	Simultaneous and uniform prosperity for all
Achieved through the effort and participation of all	"Lying flat" or "free riding"
Prosperity for all	Prosperity limited to a small group
Prosperity pioneers lifting others	"Robbing the rich to help the poor" and "Down with the landlords, share out the land"
Relative affluence built on general prosperity	Absolute equality or averaging out rewards
Enrichment of both "wallets" and "minds"	A purely materialistic pursuit of wealth
The result of individuals fulfilling their own duties	Prosperity achieved by "Forced donation"
A long-distance race requiring patience and endurance	A sprint seeking immediate results

[a]What Common Prosperity Is and Is Not (Chin. ed.) [N/OL]. Zhejiang Daily, [2021-11-05], http://zjrb.zjol.com.cn/html/2021-11/05/content_3488642.htm

the middle-income group and form an olive-shaped distribution structure—broad in the middle and narrow at both ends. Tertiary distribution is voluntary, not compulsory. National tax policies should provide appropriate incentives to encourage charitable donations as a supplementary means of improving income distribution.

Third, China must fully recognize the long-term, complex, and challenging nature of achieving common prosperity. As Han pointed out, China is building a modern socialist country in all respects, moving from moderate prosperity toward common prosperity, and from a middle-income country to a high-income country. Achieving common prosperity is a dynamic and forward-moving process; it cannot be accomplished overnight, nor can all regions progress at the same pace. Therefore, he stressed the importance of seeking progress while ensuring stability, advancing step by step, and persevering over time. "We must tackle one issue after another, year after year, to promote well-rounded human development and ensure that substantial progress is made in enabling all people to share in prosperity."

Understanding the Key Points of Common Prosperity

Promoting common prosperity requires unwavering strategic resolve. From top-level design to expert interpretation, there is a broad consensus that a solid economic foundation is essential. This is a key reason why Zhejiang, an economic powerhouse, was designated as a demonstration zone.

Since Deng Xiaoping explicitly proposed the goal of common prosperity in 1984, China's total social output has grown from RMB 0.9 trillion in 1985 to RMB 101.6 trillion in 2020—a 112-fold increase over more than 30 years. According to the National Bureau of Statistics, China's GDP per capita exceeded $10,000 in both 2019 and 2020. The actual growth of national per capita disposable income in 2020 increased by 100.8% compared to 2010. In addition, significant breakthroughs have been achieved in the "three critical battles"—preventing and resolving potential risk, conducting targeted poverty reduction, and controlling pollution. These accomplishments form a solid foundation and provide the confidence needed to advance common prosperity on the new journey.

As a long-term and arduous endeavor, common prosperity is a road fraught with challenges. It must confront various real-world problems, such as unbalanced and inadequate development across regions, between urban and rural areas, among industries, and among residents. These are the "tigers on the road" that must be overcome to advance toward common prosperity.

In terms of inadequate development, as a developing middle-income country, China must sustain relatively high economic growth in order to join the ranks of high-income countries. According to the International Monetary Fund, China ranked 63rd among 194 countries and economies in terms of GDP per capita in 2020. The United Nations Development Program's Human Development Index ranked China 85th among 189 countries and economies. These figures indicate significant room for China's high-quality development.

As for unbalanced development, the challenges are even more formidable. Estimates from relevant departments and scholars suggest that China's Gini coefficient—a measure of income inequality—may exceed 0.5, well above the commonly accepted warning threshold of 0.4. Moreover, the proportion of the middle-income group remains relatively low. In 2018, about 30% of the national population—roughly 400 million people—belonged to the middle-income group, but their distribution was severely unbalanced: less than 10% of rural residents were part of this group, while more than 90% of the rural population fell into the low-income bracket.

The key to addressing unbalanced and inadequate development lies in high-quality development, which is both a prerequisite for and a necessary path toward achieving common prosperity. Under the guidance of high-quality development, what are the core features or standards of common prosperity? "Common prosperity is prosperity for all. It entails both the material and spiritual well-being of the populace. It is not the wealth of a few, nor uniform egalitarianism, but the promotion of common wealth in phases." This is the standard defined at the 10th Meeting of the Central Financial and Economic Affairs Commission. According to relevant reports, the key to correctly understanding common prosperity lies in the concepts of "The Three Multiplicities" and "The Two Pillars" .

"The Three Multiplicities": First is multiplicity of reach—common prosperity is for the many, not a few. Second is multiplicity of dimensions—it encompasses both material and spiritual enrichment. Third is multiplicity of phasing—it must be achieved through phased and gradual progress, not through enforced uniformity.

"The Two Pillars": Achieving common prosperity is like making a pie—first making it bigger, then sharing it fairly. Making the pie bigger depends on high-quality development. This requires innovation and education as key drivers, continual exploration of new methods, and expanded opportunities for more people to become better-off. Sharing the pie fairly requires sound institutional arrangements to ensure that those who get rich first help those who follow.

Moreover, the 10th meeting of the Central Financial and Economic Affairs Commission laid out key tasks for promoting common prosperity. These include advancing high-quality development, enhancing both equity and efficiency, and establishing basic institutional arrangements to coordinate primary, secondary, and tertiary distribution. Policies must be strengthened to regulate income distribution through taxation, social security, and transfer payments with greater vigor and precision. The goal is to expand the middle-income group, raise the income of low-income earners, reasonably adjust excessive incomes, and eliminate illicit income—ultimately shaping an olive-shaped income distribution structure that is broad in the middle and narrow at both ends. This calls for a delicate balance between efficiency and equity, more balanced income distribution, and stronger, more targeted basic safety nets. The aim is not only fairer distribution but also adequate protection—ensuring that no one is left behind. In this way, common prosperity can be promoted step by step and stage by stage.

Constructing the Impetus System of Common Prosperity

To steadfastly promote common prosperity, it is necessary to build an impetus system based on the framework of "One Body with Two Wings" (Table 5.2). The "One Body" refers to balanced development, which serves as the core of common prosperity, while the "Two Wings" refer to digital development and green development, which are the two driving forces for its continued advancement.

Returning to Zhejiang's pilot exploration, among the key goals for building the common prosperity demonstration zone by 2025, in addition to several core indicators focused on balanced development, there are three particularly important indicators: first, the value added by the digital economy is to account for 60% of Zhejiang's GRP; second, the average life expectancy is to exceed 80 years, with the physical fitness pass rate surpassing 94.5%; third, the household waste classification coverage rate is to reach 100%, and the protection rate of key biological species is to reach 95%. The first set of indicators reflects digital development (digital economy), while the latter two highlight green development (public health and ecology). Together with balanced development, they form the "One

Table 5.2 Construct the "One Body, Two Wings" impetus system for common prosperity

Role	*Impetus*	*Available ways and strategic priorities*
One Body	Balanced development	Advancing integrated urban–rural development Doubling the middle-income group Cultivating an olive-shaped social structure
Two Wings	Digital development	Tech leadership with innovation propulsion Digitally empowered industries Optimizing the business environment Upgrading industries
	Green development	Achieving carbon peaking and neutrality Eco-priority development models Green growth transition Healthy living standards Trinity integration of ecology-production-lifestyle

Body, Two Wings" impetus system for common prosperity, where balanced development is the core (the body), and digital and green development are the driving forces (the wings). Furthermore, both digital development and green development ultimately serve the goal of balanced development.

Digital development underscores the "innovation" pillar among the five new visions for development. Currently, Zhejiang is spearheading systemic and institutional reforms through digital transformation, driving changes across all sectors. It is working to foster optimal environments for business, investment, entrepreneurship, and government–business relations. Advancing digital industrialization and the digital transformation of industries is an effective way to increase the share of the digital economy in GDP and to narrow the digital divide between urban and rural areas as well as between regions. To reduce urban–rural and regional disparities, Zhejiang has increased an upgraded version of the "Mountain-Sea Collaboration" initiative and is promoting "Cross-Mountain Integration" to support the accelerated development of 26 underdeveloped countries. Focusing on innovation-driven cooperation between developed and underdeveloped regions, Zhejiang is exploring effective mechanisms for the transfer of resources—such as technology, talent, and information—from developed areas to those that are catching up.

Green development reflects the "green" pillar among the five new visions for development. Zhejiang was the first in China to propose the idea that "lucid waters and lush mountains are invaluable assets." While promoting economic development, the province also prioritizes public health and the sustainable integration of living, production, and ecology. It refuses to sacrifice the environment for growth, or vice versa. For instance, rural areas such as Anji, Deqing, and Yuhang, which once relied on selling mineral resources, have shifted toward selling culture and tourism, leading to prosperity, beautiful environments, and sound ecosystems. In this process, innovative ecological protection mechanisms are crucial. While promoting the equalization of public services between urban and rural areas, greater attention must be paid to diversification and differentiation, especially in ecological compensation across regions. For instance, fiscal transfer payments for ecological protection should be increased for areas where development is restricted or prohibited. Standards for watershed-wide ecological compensation should be raised, and mechanisms should be improved to link ecological protection outcomes to the allocation of transfer payment funds.

Serving as a pioneer for the nation and taking the lead in realizing common prosperity is the primary intention behind building the demonstration zone. Consolidating the foundation for common prosperity requires exploring the establishment of a comprehensive system covering goals, implementation, policy, and evaluation—one in which those who become prosperous first help those following behind, thereby jointly advancing toward common prosperity. Zhejiang is working to develop replicable and scalable institutional and policy mechanisms for common prosperity. Two core principles lie at the heart of this effort: first, dynamically managing the relationships between the government and market, and between equity and efficiency; second, advancing balanced development, digital development, and green development. No matter how promising or complex the road ahead may be, only by continually making the pie bigger can we ensure its fair distribution. This is the only viable path to achieving common prosperity—and the right posture for setting an example.

Focusing on the principal contradiction of unbalanced and inadequate development, China must make solid progress toward common prosperity. The main direction should be narrowing the urban–rural and regional development gaps and income disparities. Reforming and improving the income distribution system, achieving all-round human development, and meeting the multi-dimensional needs of the people have become essential challenges under the new pattern of development.

CHAPTER 6

Conclusion: Transcendent Achievements of Chinese Modernization

Huang Qunhui

General Secretary Xi Jinping pointed out, "As we have upheld and developed socialism with Chinese characteristics and driven coordinated progress in material, political, cultural-ethical, social, and ecological terms, we have pioneered a new and uniquely Chinese path to modernization, and created a new model for human advancement."[1] Chinese modernization is well-suited to China's national conditionsIt reflects the laws of socialist construction and human development, represents a fundamental surpassing of Western modernization theories, and embodies profoundly historical, theoretical, and practical logic.

[1] Xi Jinping. Speech at a Ceremony Marking the Centenary of the CPC (Chin. ed.) [OL], [2021-07-01]. http://www.gov.cn/xinwen/2021-07/01/content_5621847.htm

H. Qunhui (✉)
School of Economics, Chinese Academy of Social Sciences, Beijing, China

C. Fang et al., *Modernization in a Chinese Style*,
https://doi.org/10.1007/978-981-95-6919-9_6

What Is New About the Chinese Path to Modernization

As a new path, Chinese modernization holds significant theoretical and practical value for the advancement of human society.

Adhering to a People-Centered Development Philosophy and Discarding the Old Western Modernization Path

Chinese modernization follows the general laws of modernization theory, which promote the development of productive forces through industrialization, marketization, and economic globalization. However, it differs fundamentally from the basic logic underlying Western modernization.

Chinese modernization rejects the Western logic in which the development of productive forces is subordinated solely to capital. It repudiates the capital-centered model of modernization characterized by polarization, materialistic excess, and foreign expansion and plunder. In doing so, it not only transcends Western modernization theories but also enriches and advances Marxist development theory. This path adheres to a people-centered development philosophy, placing the improvement of people's well-being, the comprehensive development of individuals, and steady progress toward common prosperity at the beginning and end of economic development. The goal is to make solid progress in achieving common prosperity and continuously enhancing the people's sense of fulfillment, happiness, and security. Chinese modernization promotes coordinated progress across the economic, political, cultural, social, and ecological domains. It drives new forms of industrialization, informatization, urbanization, and agricultural modernization simultaneously. Through this approach, it fosters a well-coordinated and systematic model of modern civilization, emphasizing balance across material, political, cultural, ethical, social, and ecological aspects. By focusing on meeting the people's growing needs for a better life while tackling the problems of unbalanced, uncoordinated, and unsustainable development, Chinese modernization aims to transform the quality, efficiency, and drivers of economic growth. It strives for high-quality development characterized by innovation as the primary driving force, coordination as an endogenous feature, green development as a prevailing norm, openness as the only path forward, and sharing as the fundamental goal. These theoretical innovations and breakthroughs in modernization in the new era are guiding China's transformation from a latecomer in modernization to a key driver of global modernization.

Exploring Modernization Driving Mechanisms and Strategies Based on National Realities: Insights from Chinese Modernization for Developing Countries

A key reason for the success of Chinese modernization lies in its commitment to charting an independent path and formulating modernization driving mechanisms and strategies tailored to China's specific national conditions.

In terms of modernization driving mechanisms, the Communist Party of China (CPC) has creatively integrated the socialist system and a market economy, establishing a socialist market economy that not only enhances the efficiency of resource allocation through market mechanisms but also leverages the institutional strengths of socialism to mobilize national efforts for major undertakings. This ensures the decisive role of the market in resource allocation while enabling the government to effectively fulfill its functions. It fully harnesses the role of capital in promoting productive forces while curbing its unchecked expansion, thereby achieving a more effective integration of a dynamic market and a capable government. This system unleashes the full potential of labor, knowledge, technology, management, and capital and promotes the unfettered flow of all sources of social wealth. As a result, it has profoundly liberated and developed the country's productive forces.

From a strategic standpoint, since the founding of the People's Republic of China, the CPC has consistently based its modernization agenda on national realities and development stages, implementing its goals through successive Five-Year Plans. Entering the new era, the Party Central Committee with Comrade Xi Jinping at its core has set out a two-step strategic plan for fully building China into a great modern socialist country: to basically realize socialist modernization from 2020 to 2035, and to build China into a prosperous, strong, democratic, culturally advanced, harmonious, and beautiful modern socialist country from 2035 to the middle of this century (the 21st century). In addition, the Committee put forward a number of landmark major strategies in the recommendations for the 13th and 14th Five-Year Plans, and introduced major measures that are forward-looking, overarching, foundational, and problem-oriented. General Secretary Xi Jinping's important discourses on entering a new stage of development, implementing the new development philosophy, fostering a new pattern of development, and pursuing high-quality development provide a roadmap for overcoming developmental bottlenecks, strengthening endogenous drivers, building durable advantages, and accelerating the path to modernization. A modernization strategy suited to China's national conditions has guided the country toward a development path that is higher in quality, greater in efficiency, more equitable, stronger in sustainability, and more secure.

The success of Chinese modernization demonstrates to the world that a latecomer country—even without the initial conditions enjoyed by early industrialized nations—can still achieve leapfrog development. As long as it remains committed to its modernization goals and independently explores a path grounded in its own national conditions, it can chart a successful course toward modernization.

Advocating Exchanges and Mutual Learning Among Civilizations: Breaking Free from the Constraints of the Western "Clash of Civilizations" Narrative

Western modernization followed a linear progression from agricultural to industrial and then to information civilization. This trajectory fostered a binary opposition between tradition and modernity, with a tendency to prioritize and replace the traditional with the modern. Many Western scholars and political figures have asserted that diverse civilizations are inherently incompatible and destined to clash. In the history of Western modernization, some Western powers, leveraging their early advantages in industrialization, imposed colonization, oppression, and enslavement upon nations that remained in pre-industrial stages of development. Even today, some Western scholars and politicians continue to equate Western civilization and modern civilization and seek to reshape other civilizations in its image, thereby exacerbating global cultural tensions and impeding the flourishing of diverse human civilizations.

Chinese modernization advocates transcending civilization estrangement through exchanges, overcoming cultural conflict through mutual learning, and moving beyond notions of civilizational superiority through peaceful coexistence. It aims to explore and promote a new, inclusive form of human civilization. The CPC upholds the integration of the basic tenets of Marxism with China's specific national conditions and its fine traditional culture. This has revitalized the profound spiritual heritage of Chinese civilization and unlocked the enduring vitality of a culture developed over thousands of years. China advances a vision of civilization grounded in equality, mutual learning, dialogue, and inclusiveness. It respects the diversity of civilizations and promotes intercultural exchanges, dialogue, peaceful coexistence, and harmonious interactions among civilizations. It strives to make mutual learning among civilizations a bridge of friendship between peoples, a driver of social progress, and a bond for safeguarding peace. Chinese modernization challenges the Western narrative of inevitable civilizational conflict and offers a vision of global cultural flourishing through mutual respect, shared growth, and harmonious coexistence.

Staying on the Path of Peaceful Development: Safeguarding World Peace and Promoting Common Development

General Secretary Xi Jinping has emphasized that Chinese modernization pursues a path of peaceful development. Unlike Western countries that have long adhered to the jungle-law principle of "might-makes-right" and a confrontational, zero-sum mindset, peaceful development defines the Chinese approach to modernization. In contrast, China has always upheld its solemn commitment never to seek hegemony, engage in expansionism, or carve out spheres of influence. Instead, it is firmly committed to building a human community with a shared future. While striving for its own development, China also actively contributes to world peace and global development.

The world today is undergoing profound changes unseen in a century—transformations that are not limited to isolated events or specific regions but signal a sweeping shift in the global era. These changes have been further accelerated by the COVID-19 pandemic, plunging the world into a new phase of turbulence and uncertainty. People across nations are voicing stronger aspirations for peace and development, louder calls for fairness and justice, and firmer resolve for cooperation and mutual benefit. Against this backdrop, China's path of peaceful development has taken on even greater global relevance in the broader context of modernization. In response to the mounting challenges of the contemporary world, China has proactively advocated for the building of a human community with a shared future. It has promoted the high-quality development of the Belt and Road Initiative and launched the Global Development Initiative and Global Security Initiative. These initiatives offer thoughtful responses to the pressing questions of our time and the broader trajectory of humanity. and pointed to a constructive direction for the advancement of human civilization and global modernization. Through these contributions, China not only shares its wisdom and solutions but also lends its strength to the building of a world marked by lasting peace, universal security, common prosperity, openness and inclusiveness, and ecological harmony.

Deepening the Understanding of Economic Laws in the Modernization Process

As China enters a new development stage and embarks on the new journey of fully building a modern socialist country in all respects, it becomes increasingly important to recognize that the world today is undergoing profound changes unseen in a century. In particular, the COVID-19 pandemic and the Ukraine crisis have led to increasing risks and challenges, making China's economic development environment more complex, severe, and uncertain. China now faces considerable pressures on both long-term development and short-term economic growth. At the Central Economic Work Conference in 2021, it was pointed out that China's economic development was confronting "triple pressures" of shrinking demand, supply shocks, and weakening expectations. In this context, it is imperative to deepen the understanding of the economic laws governing modernization, accurately identify the fundamental trends in economic modernization, and carry out sound analysis of the evolving economic landscape. By doing so, China can enhance confidence, formulate more targeted economic strategies and effective policy measures, and guide high-quality development in alignment with economic laws.

Deepening the Understanding of Fundamental Economic Laws by Grasping the Distinctive Features of the Formation of the Chinese Modernization

Since the founding of the People's Republic of China, the Chinese path to modernization has undergone three distinct phases. The first phase was the period of socialist revolution and construction, during which China established the basic system of socialism and pursued the Four Modernizations—industry, agriculture, national defense, and science and technology. This period saw the establishment of an independent and relatively complete industrial system and national economic system, laying the essential groundwork for the Chinese path to modernization. The second phase was marked by reform and opening up, as well as the launch of socialist modernization. During this time, China established a vigorous socialist market economy and charted a course for new-type industrialization. The living standards of the Chinese people experienced a historic transformation, progressing from subsistence to moderate prosperity and, ultimately, to comprehensive well-being, and the Chinese path to modernization began to take shape. The third phase is the new era of socialism with Chinese characteristics. A moderately prosperous society in all respects has been achieved, and China has entered a new stage of development. The country is now closer than ever before to the goal of national rejuvenation and more confident and capable of realizing it. The Chinese path to modernization has gained increasingly robust theoretical and institutional frameworks, fortified by more solid material foundations, while witnessing growing global reach and influence.

A central takeaway from the evolution of the Chinese path to modernization is the decisive role of the leadership of the CPC. Historical experience—in terms of both economic development and economic thought—demonstrates that, for late-developing countries, a proactive, strong, and effective central leadership is essential for economic catch-up. Throughout the process of exploring socialist modernization, China has navigated a complex and ever-changing environment. Under the strong leadership of the CPC, the country has developed and continuously refined its short- and middle-term goals of fully building a modern socialist country. The CPC has led the people in unlocking potential, seizing opportunities, and ensuring that China has achieved the twin miracles of rapid economic growth and long-term social stability. Moreover, this leadership has enabled China to blaze a new trail for modernization and foster a new model of human advancement.

Historical experience also affirms that adhering to the centralized and unified leadership of the CPC Central Committee is a fundamental principle for achieving economic modernization in China. The more severe and unprecedented challenges China faces in economic work, the more vital it is to strengthen the confidence and deepen the understanding of this fundamental principle. Aligning the country's overall thinking and actions with the major decisions and strategic plans of the CPC Central on economic work is essential. Furthermore, it is crucial to continue improving the institutional mechanisms that enable Party leadership in economic affairs and fully leverage the Party's role in top-level design, overall planning, strategic coordination, comprehensive advancement, and the supervision and implementation of major economic initiatives.

Deepening the Understanding of the Law of High-Quality Development by Grasping the Characteristics of the Modernization Stage

Economic laws are objective in nature and independent of human will. However, this does not imply that such laws are universally applicable across all countries, regions, or stages of economic development. In particular, economic work must be grounded in the realities of each economic development stage and each country's unique context. As China has entered a new development stage, it is essential to actively explore the economic laws that are specific to this phase.

Since socialism with Chinese characteristics entered a new era, the principal contradiction in Chinese society has evolved into one between unbalanced and inadequate development and the people's ever-growing needs for a better life. China's economy has shifted from a phase of rapid growth to one centered on high-quality development. The main task of economic work has thus become the promotion of high-quality development, which requires a deeper and more accurate understanding of its underlying laws. High-quality development is guided by the new development philosophy—innovation, coordination, green, openness, and sharing—with an emphasis on addressing unbalanced and inadequate development. Therefore, in this new stage of development, it is essential to actively explore the laws governing innovation-driven, coordinated, green, open, and shared development and apply them to specific areas of economic work. These five components together constitute the law of high-quality development. Each dimension contains rich theoretical implications and may correspond to specific branches of economics. For example, the law of innovation-driven development corresponds to innovation economics or the economics of technology. Taken as a whole, however, the law of high-quality development forms an interconnected and systematic framework that is people-centered and aimed at resolving the problem of unbalanced and inadequate development. It must be understood from a holistic perspective. Within this framework, the law of shared development reflects the purpose of socialist production and emphasizes social equality and justice. The other four laws—innovation, coordination, green development, and openness—are more closely related to the modes of production. The law of innovation-driven development addresses the challenge of insufficient development momentum. The law of coordinated development aims to resolve issues of regional and structural imbalance. The law of green development seeks harmony between humanity and nature. The law of open development emphasizes strengthening the internal–external linkages in development.

Given the systematic nature of the law of high-quality development, its practical application requires not only a clear understanding of the individual requirements of each of its five components but also an integrated approach that emphasizes coordination and grasps the intrinsic linkages between them. In the face of persistent imbalances and mounting economic pressures, it is critical to uphold a systems-oriented mindset, remain problem-oriented, address principal contradictions, and ensure synergy among various policies. In particular, in response to the "threefold pressure" of shrinking demand, supply shocks, and weakening expectations, it is important to coordinate counter-cyclical and cross-cyclical policies and ensure alignment between supply-side structural reforms and demand-side management strategies. All government departments and local authorities must resolutely uphold the centralized and unified leadership of the CPC Central Committee when formulating and implementing economic policies. They should fully consider the synergistic effects of various policy tools and adopt well-coordinated policy packages to prevent policy misalignment or the fallacy of composition.

Deepening the Understanding of Economic Operation Laws by Improving the Socialist Market Economy

General Secretary Xi Jinping has profoundly noted that developing a market economy under socialist conditions is a great innovation by the CPC. A key reason behind China's remarkable economic success lies in its ability to harness the strengths of both the market economy and the socialist system. Over the years, China's economic development has achieved extraordinary accomplishments that have garnered global attention, greatly advancing the cause of socialist modernization and fully demonstrating the vitality of the socialist market economy. Advancing Chinese modernization requires continued commitment to improving and developing the socialist market economy system.

At the heart of this process is the organic integration of the strengths of the market economy with the institutional advantages of socialism. This requires a deeper understanding of the laws governing economic operations and socialist development, with the aim of identifying the economic laws applicable under the conditions of a socialist market economy. It is necessary to give full play to the role of economic laws intrinsic to the market system—such as the law of value, the law of economic cycles, and the law of monetary circulation—in promoting the development of productive forces, while ensuring that such development aligns with socialist goals. In practice, economic regulation must strike a balance between an "effective market" and a "proactive government". The "effective market" refers to respecting market laws and allowing the market to play a decisive role in resource allocation, while the "proactive government" emphasizes the government's role in overall planning and coordination. These two must be organically integrated within the unified framework of the socialist market economy.

After years of exploration, China has made remarkable progress in building mature and well-defined institutions across various domains. However, as the process of socialist modernization continues to deepen, and the world undergoes profound changes unseen in a century, new problems and challenges continue to emerge. These developments call for further exploration of the laws governing economic operations and growth under a socialist market economy, with particular attention to the laws related to capital and the realization of common prosperity.

Regarding the law of capital, it is essential, on the one hand, to deepen the understanding of capital's multifaceted nature. In a socialist market economy, capital plays a key role in aggregating and allocating production factors and is a vital driver of social productivity. Meanwhile, capital inherently seeks profit, and without appropriate regulation and constraints, it may give rise to significant risks to both economic and social development. Thus, a historical, developmental, and dialectical approach must be taken to fully understand the types of capital and their roles in society. Only by fully grasping its multiple attributes can we identify the laws governing its behavior—enabling us to maximize its productive potential while effectively curbing its negative effects. This ensures that capital operates in alignment with socialist objectives and contributes to the realization of common prosperity. On the other hand, it is also critical to understand the diversity of capital forms. China today is home to various types of capital, including state-owned capital, collective capital, private capital, foreign capital, and mixed-ownership capital. A nuanced understanding of the characteristics of each form of capital—and the ability to manage their interactions appropriately—is essential for promoting their sound and regulated development and for advancing the overall development of the socialist market economy.

As for the law governing the achievement of common prosperity, it is important to first recognize the staged and historical nature of this goal. Common prosperity is a fundamental requirement of socialism and a defining feature of Chinese-style modernization. It cannot be achieved overnight, nor can it be realized uniformly across all regions or social groups. Rather, it is a long-term historical process that must unfold in stages. Initially, efforts must focus on expanding and strengthening the economy—making the pie bigger—followed by establishing sound institutional arrangements to ensure its equitable distribution. It is essential to fully understand the intrinsic connection between common prosperity and high-quality development. The two are mutually reinforcing: common prosperity is both a goal and a requirement of high-quality development, while high-quality development is the primary pathway and means to achieving common prosperity. Realizing this goal requires firm adherence to the new development philosophy—centered on innovation, coordination, green development, openness, and sharing—and the continuous promotion of common prosperity through sustained high-quality development.

The manufacturer's authorised representative in the EU is Springer Nature Customer Service Centre GmbH, Europaplatz 3, 69115 Heidelberg, Germany. If you have any concerns regarding our products, please contact ProductSafety@springernature.com

Printed and bound by CPI Group (UK) Ltd, Croydon, CR0 4YY

21/09/2026

02220011-0009